OUTPATIENT BEHAVIOR THERAPY

OUTPATIENT BEHAVIOR THERAPY
A CLINICAL GUIDE

Edited by

MICHEL HERSEN, Ph.D.

*Professor of Psychiatry and
Psychology
Western Psychiatric Institute
and Clinic
University of Pittsburgh School
of Medicine
Pittsburgh, Pennsylvania*

GRUNE & STRATTON
A Subsidiary of Harcourt Brace Jovanovich, Publishers
New York   London   Paris
San Diego   San Francisco   São Paulo
Sydney   Tokyo   Toronto

Library of Congress Cataloging in Publication Data

Main entry under title:

Outpatient behavior therapy.

Bibliography: p.
Includes index.
1. Behavior therapy. 2. Psychotherapy. 3. Child
psychotherapy. I. Hersen, Michel.
[DNLM: 1. Ambulatory care. 2. Behavior therapy.
3. Mental disorders—Therapy.   WM 425 094]
RC489.B4088   1983   616.89′142   83-12620
ISBN 0-8089-1575-4

Grune & Stratton, Inc.
111 Fifth Avenue
New York, New York 10003

Distributed in the United Kingdom by
Grune & Stratton, Inc. (London) Ltd.
24/28 Oval Road, London NW 1

Library of Congress Catalog Number 83-12620
International Standard Book Number 0-8089-1575-4
Printed in the United States of America

To my parents, Leon and Betty

Contents

Preface

The idea for this book germinated for several years while I was at the Western Psychiatric Institute and Clinic at the University of Pittsburgh School of Medicine. Its need became apparent to me during the course of giving lectures on behavior therapy to psychiatry residents and staff, supervising the clinical work of psychology interns, and teaching practicum to graduate students in clinical psychology. Although there is hardly a scarcity of books on behavior therapy (my colleagues and I are guilty of contributing a few), most of them focus on the research issues underlying behavioral assessment and treatment. I have found very few texts that have a practical "how-to-do-it" flavor for the treatment of the wide variety of patients (adults and children) we tend to see as practicing behavior therapists. For students especially, the day-to-day "nitty-gritty" of the behavior therapist's work still is something of a mystery. Thus, in this book I have endeavored to give these students the "feel for what it is really like" in the clinical world.

The volume is divided into three parts: general issues, problems in adulthood, and problems in childhood. In Part I general issues and problems in behavior therapy are discussed in addition to the mechanics of the office practice of outpatient behavior therapy. In Parts II and III the contributors have focused on detailing how and what to do with adult and child outpatients. The chapters in these sections involve a brief description of the disorder, an outline telling the clinician how to do a proper clinical assessment, a design of the typical treatment strategy, a case description including therapist and patient dialogue, and discussion of certain problems that often fail to be mentioned in print. I believe that the contributors have been most forthright in presenting to us how they function within the confines of their consulting rooms.

Many individuals have participated in this particular project. Let me first thank the contributors for their time and energy, but especially for their willingness to be specific. Next, I wish to thank my editors at Grune & Stratton, for their patience and continued encouragement. Finally, but hardly least of all, my gratitude is extended to Mary Newell for typing the manuscript and to Susan Capozzoli, Paula Piper, and Jan Twomey for preparing the subject index.

Michel Hersen, Ph.D.

Contributing Authors

JUDITH V. BECKER, PH.D.
Department of Psychiatry, College of Physicians and Surgeons, Columbia University; Research Scientist, New York State Psychiatric Institute, New York, New York.

GARY R. BIRCHLER, PH.D.
Department of Psychiatry, School of Medicine, University of California, San Diego; Director, Family Mental Health Program, Veterans Administration Medical Center, San Diego, California.

PAUL M. G. EMMELKAMP, PH.D.
Department of Clinical Psychology, Academic Hospital, Groningen, The Netherlands.

ANK EMMELKAMP-BENNER,
Institute of Medical Psychotherapy, Groningen, The Netherlands.

STEVEN T. FISHMAN, PH.D.
Institute for Behavior Therapy, New York, New York.

WILLIAM J. FREMOUW, PH.D.
Department of Psychology, West Virginia University, Morgantown, West Virginia.

STANFORD W. GRANBERRY, M.A.
Department of Psychology, Louisiana State University, Baton Rouge, Louisiana.

ALAN M. GROSS, PH.D.
Department of Psychology, Emory University, Atlanta, Georgia.

FRANCIS C. HARRIS, PH.D.
Western Psychiatric Institute and Clinic, School of Medicine, University of Pittsburgh, Pittsburgh, Pennsylvania.

MICHEL HERSEN, PH.D.
Western Psychiatric Institute and Clinic, School of Medicine, University of Pittsburgh, Pittsburgh, Pennsylvania.

NICHOLAS E. HEYNEMAN, M.A.
Department of Psychology, West Virginia University, Morgantown, West Virginia.

L. K. GEORGE HSU, M.D.
Western Psychiatric Institute and Clinic, School of Medicine, University of Pittsburgh, Pittsburgh, Pennsylvania.

MARY MARGARET KERR, ED.D.
Western Psychiatric Institute and Clinic, School of Medicine, University of Pittsburgh, Pittsburgh, Pennsylvania.

ELISE E. LABBE, M.A.
Department of Psychology, Louisiana State University, Baton Rouge, Louisiana.

DAVID M. LAWSON, PH.D.
Department of Psychiatry, Shaughnessy Hospital; Clinical Assistant Professor, Department of Psychology, University of British Columbia, Vancouver, British Columbia.

PETER M. LEWINSOHN, PH.D.
Department of Psychology, University of Oregon, Eugene, Oregon.

BARRY S. LUBETKIN, PH.D.
Institute for Behavior Therapy, New York, New York.

THOMAS H. OLLENDICK, PH.D.
Department of Psychology, Virginia Polytechnic Institute and State University, Blacksburg, Virginia.

MARJORIE A. PELCOVITS, M.A.
Department of Psychiatry, The Children's Hospital Medical Center; Harvard Medical School, Boston, Massachusetts.

CAROLYN F. PHELPS, B.S.
University of Pittsburgh, Pittsburgh, Pennsylvania.

DENNIS C. RUSSO, PH.D.
Behavioral Medicine Program, Assistant Professor of Psychology, Department of Psychiatry, The Children's Hospital Medical Center; Harvard Medical School, Boston, Massachusetts.

BERNARD V. SILVER, PH.D.
Department of Psychiatry, The Children's Hospital Medical Center; Harvard Medical School, Boston, Massachusetts.

LINDA J. SKINNER, PH.D.
Department of Psychology, University of Hartford, West Hartford, Connecticut; Lecturer in Psychiatry, College of Physicians and Surgeons, Columbia University, New York, New York.

PHILLIP A. STRAIN, PH.D.
Western Psychiatric Institute and Clinic, School of Medicine, University of Pittsburgh, Pittsburgh, Pennsylvania.

LINDA TERI, PH.D.
Department of Psychology, University of Oregon, Eugene, Oregon.

DAVID WASSERMAN, M.A.
   Department of Psychology, University of Oregon, Eugene, Oregon.
DONALD A. WILLIAMSON, PH.D.
   Louisiana State University, Baton Rouge, Louisiana.

OUTPATIENT BEHAVIOR THERAPY

Part I

GENERAL ISSUES

Perspectives on the Practice of Outpatient Behavior Therapy

Michel Hersen

As WE NOW APPROACH the Orwellian year of 1984, there can be no doubt that behavior therapy, as a psychotherapeutic approach, is very well entrenched. This is particularly so when one considers the outpatient practice of behavior therapy. Despite some of the more dire predictions of the fate of behavior therapy (Freeman, 1968; Weitzman, 1967), this has not materialized. Behavior therapy neither has eclipsed as a passing fad nor has it stultified the freedom of choice of the individual patient or client. The Orwellian nightmare and the unethical control, as portrayed in "A Clockwork Orange," was more a product of the imagination of the eager lay press than any reality of actual clinical practice. Indeed, practitioners of the art simply are unable to exert this kind of control over their patients and families. Moreover, there never was any such intent on the part of the individual clinicians.

As an approach to therapeutics, behavior therapy has had a most varied and interesting history. Although some of the foundations of this movement can be traced to ancient times (Kazdin, 1978), the real impetus took place in the late 1950s and early 1960s. The two landmark publications of that era are Joseph Wolpe's (1958) *Psychotherapy by reciprocal inhibition* and Hans J. Eysenck's (1960a) *Behaviour therapy and the neuroses*. Both of these publications heralded the new and presented the first real challenges to the then psychoanalytic establishment. Eysenck's (1960b) statement, "Get rid of the symptom and you have eliminated the neurosis" (p.9) bordered on "heresy." Such a notion was totally alien to the psychoanalytic clinicians. And, of course, numerous controversies over the respective merits of the two approaches appeared in press (Breger & McGaugh, 1965; Eysenck, 1970; Freeman, 1963; Weitzman, 1967). Fortunately for the field, the acrimonious debates that earlier plagued the field have totally dissipated. In my opinion conclusions reached in a task force organized by the American Psychiatric Association helped to defuse much of the controversy: "The work of the Task Force has reaffirmed our belief that behavior therapy and behavioral principles employed in the analysis of clinical phenomena have reached a stage of development where they now unquestionably have much to offer informed clinicians in the services of modern clinical and social psychiatry" (Task Force Report 5, 1973, p. 64). This was bolstered by a similar report emanating from the National Institute of Mental Health, also acknowledging the contribution of behavior therapy for a variety of problem areas (Stolz, Wienckowski, & Brown, 1975). Indeed, official recognition proved to be of considerable help to the behavioral cause.

In the early 1960s behavior therapists engaged in frequent and strident "breast-beating," extolling the virtues of their strategies in exaggerated fashion. This, of course, does not take place today. But it is understandable why it occurred two decades ago. Elsewhere I have argued that, given the hostile climate in which behaviorists found themselves:

> Were it not for the ultra-assertive voices of yesterday, we would not be here today. However, the exaggerated claims of success, the ease and simplicity with which behavioral therapies were allegedly applied, and the myopia concerning the contribution of other disciplines to mental health still plague us at this time. Now that behavior therapists have begun to attack the entire vast canvas of human suffering, it is crystal clear that the problems we deal with are considerably more complex than we originally believed. The notion that through a rapid behavioral analysis problems could easily be concretized and then rapidly therapized has proven illusory. To the contrary, our day-to-day clinical and empirical discoveries tell us that complex problems do indeed require complex solutions.*

During the earlier part of the movement one would hear such notions as (1) a therapist was a "verbal reinforcement machine," (2) the relationship between therapist and patient was not critical to behav-

---

* From Hersen, M. Complex problems require complex solutions. *Behavior Therapy*, 1981, 12, 18. With permission.

ioral change, (3) there was no such thing as patient resistance, (4) symptom substitution never occurred after application of behavior therapy, (5) treatment for most phobias could be successfully accomplished in 12–15 sessions, (6) token economy was an effective treatment regime for schizophrenia, (7) attention to the patient's self-report and cognitions was not an important element of the treatment, and (8) there was little or no role of pharmacotherapy in the overall behavioral treatment of the patient.

Perhaps my presentation, too, is a bit on the exaggerated side. If one looks carefully at what behavior therapists said and wrote in the earlier days (Eysenck, 1960b), however, much of what I alluded to above is apparent. Fortunately, however, most behavior therapists dealing with outpatient populations today have taken a much less naive stance (Hersen, 1979; Hersen & Bellack, 1978) and have been willing to assume a more open posture to the empirical currents outside of behavior therapy (Bellack, Hersen, & Kazdin, 1982).

Indeed, treatments, by necessity, are lengthier, more comprehensive in scope, and considerably more sophisticated as to the elements necessary for ensuring maintenance of gains. For example, in the case of sexual deviation, one simply does not administer an aversive strategy to deal with inappropriate sexuality. (This might have been so in the earlier days when behavioral procedures were applied in isolation.) On the contrary, a sexual deviate today would receive a multicomponent assessment and treatment. The patient's physical condition first would be assessed; heterosexual anxiety (if any) would be evaluated and treated; misinformation about adult heterosexuality would be corrected; social skills involved in dating and heterosexuality would be taught; inappropriate cognitions and fantasies would be assessed and treated; and strategies (perhaps self-control) would be taught to the patient in order to counter inappropriate sexual impulses. Moreover, treatment would continue at a reduced rate during a maintenance phase; and periodic boosters could be provided if required during a prolonged follow-up period. (I might add that for those individuals who are married, attention to the marital relationship would be mandatory, particularly with respect to sexual functioning within that relationship.)

The aforementioned is vastly different from the more simplistic and rapid behavioral therapizing that typified the early 1960s. Greater attention to detail and the nuances of the specific case are becoming standard in today's practice of clinical behavior therapy. Where necessary, furthermore, behavioral approaches are combined with pharmacotherapy (Alford & Williams, 1981; Hersen, 1981; Hersen & Breuning, in preparation). This, then, represents a combination of the two most empirically based treatments that are extant in our field.

As I already have noted, the relatively brief history of behavior therapy has been fraught with dissension, controversy, and exciting change. This history has been described in several brief and more extended accounts over the years by a number of authors (Hersen, Eisler, & Miller, 1975; Kazdin, 1978; Krasner, 1971). Rather than repeating these historical accounts here in this introductory chapter, I trust that the reader will indulge me if I take the liberty of presenting some personal glimpses of the field since the early 1960s. In so doing, I will focus primarily on my experiences as a graduate student, outpatient therapist (in private practice and in a number of hospital settings), consultant, writer and reviewer of articles and books, journal editor, and teacher of others.

PERSONAL GLIMPSES

In presenting the reader with my unique experiences in behavior therapy, I should note that for those of us receiving graduate training in the late 1950s to early 1960s, little in the way of formal course work on the topic was available. This was particularly so with respect to the graduate classes I attended. Indeed, most of the "earlier" behavior therapists were self-taught, self-motivated, and generally disenchanted with application of the more traditional techniques then in vogue. Joseph Cautela refers to this switch from traditional—"dynamic" to empirical—"behavioral" as the "conversion." For some of us, this happened gradually over time (the present author is included in this category); for others, the change was more abrupt and dramatic. A perusal of the individual's curriculum vitae usually tells the story and documents the dates of demarcation. One sometimes sees Rorschach publications in one year and analyses of operant phenomena in the next.

My own formal training in behavior therapy was almost nonexistent. As part of Dr. Matthew Chappell's course on learning theory at the Master's level at Hofstra University, I was expected to read Hull's (1943) *Principles of Behavior* and Eysenck's (1960a) *Behaviour Therapy and the Neuroses*. In 1963 I first attended the State University of New York at Buffalo, working toward my doctorate. In the two years I spent there, the *only* exposure I had to behavior therapy consisted of two lectures by Dr. James Geer on the strategy of systematic desensitization. (Parenthetically, let me point out that attendance at these lectures was on a strictly voluntary basis.) Surprisingly, however, other earlier graduates of this program include Richard M. Eisler, Sandra Harris, Peter Lang, and Robert Weiss, each of whom, of course, today is a leader in the field of behavior therapy.

After I completed my doctoral dissertation in Buffalo in 1965, for personal reasons I moved to New Haven and began a year of combined intership and postdoctoral work at the West Haven Veterans Administration Hospital (VA), an affiliate of Yale Medical School. Psychology was, and still is, under the direction of Dr. Jacob Levine, a good friend. Psychiatry then was under the direction of Dr. Louis B. Fierman, who espoused a psychotherapeutic approach best described by me as quasiexistential or experiential (Fierman, 1965). both departments as the VA were strongly influenced by Fierman's edited book, which contained several essays by Hellmuth Kaiser, a lay psychotherapist who had practiced in Hartford, Connecticut.

When confronted with the task of treating difficult clinic patients at this facility, my supervisors would encourage me to "communicate better" with them. When I asked them what specific technique or strategy to use, they said, "it was not necessary." Communication definitely was the password here. I must say that I did learn a great deal about the various communication patterns of my patients, that I enjoyed good therapeutic relationships with them, but that the absence of sound behavioral change techniques unfortunately resulted in no change in their psychiatric status.

Frustrated with my therapeutic efforts à la Ficrman, I continued to pursue my research in the area of verbal conditioning (Hersen, 1966, 1967a, 1967b, 1968b, 1970a, 1970b). But at this time I was unable to combine my empirical interests in research with what went on in the psychotherapy setting. Indeed, I did very traditional assessments [Rorschach, Thematic Apperception Test (TAT), Minnesota Multiphasic Personality Inventory (MMPI)], and described myself as a "dynamic" therapist; however, I did begin to take note of the more empirical currents in psychotherapy that were running through the clinical journals *(Journal of Abnormal Psychology and Journal of Consulting Psychology)* that I read in the mid-1960s. Directly and indirectly, these articles began to influence my thinking about the psychotherapeutic process, although my full "conversion" did not take place until 1970, when I joined Dr. Stewart Agras and Dr. David Barlow at the University of Mississippi Medical Center.

Fairfield, Connecticut

In 1966 I joined a psychiatrist, Dr. Charles Zigun, in the full-time outpatient practice of psychotherapy. I will not regale the reader with the vicissitudes of this kind of professional life and with the strain of seeing seven to nine patients a day some five days a week. But I must say that this three-year experience surely was an "eye-opener" with regard to the problems and limitations of our psychotherapeutic techniques, including the behavioral (Hersen, 1979). I also found the experience to be highly instructive in that I was able to see an extremely wide range of diagnostic conditions, including rather severe psychotics who were controlled pharmacologically and initially seen for daily outpatient visits until psychotic symptoms began to remit.

Not only did I accept patients for individual treatment, but frequently I saw other family members in order to obtain a more comprehensive picture of the complex interactions taking place in the system. Especially in cases of school phobia, I began to spend much more time in dealing with the parents than with the child (who usually was the identified patient). I quickly discovered that operant retraining programs worked remarkably well with such parents of school-phobic children (Hersen, 1968a, 1970e, 1971a). This was especially so when children as well were taught anxiety-reduction techniques to enable them to confront the feared situation (i.e., school). In addition to these two components of the treatment for school phobia, however, it was clear to me that one had to deal effectively with a mother's feelings of loneliness, often due to the absent nature of father. Indeed, I found that mothers of school-phobic children, certainly at one level, derived some gratification from the child being at home with her during the long day. This of course, sounds very much like a psychoanalytic concept. But in my opinion, good clinical practice does not necessarily exclude notions that may not totally fit in with the theoretical paradigm within which the therapist generally is operating. Clinical considerations obviously should supersede theoretical allegiance.

During the four-year course of my "conversion," I still used a more traditional approach to outpatient therapy, applying behavioral strategies within the context of the psychotherapy (e.g., Hersen, 1970c, 1970d). In retrospect, however, it is the behavioral strategies that brought about the greatest symptomatic improvement in my patients. But also, I should underscore, the therapeutic relationship I developed with the majority of the patients was the primary fulcrum enabling me to persuade them to carry out the details of our more laborious behavioral techniques. [My current observation of younger colleagues and students today is that they begin to apply behavioral strategies before a sufficiently bonding therapeutic alliance has been established and well before a complete assessment of all problems has been completed (Hersen & Bellack, 1981). The Western option of "shooting first and asking questions later" is not applicable here.]

Despite my best attempts to generate the most favorable therapeutic alliance with patients, I found a substantial number who simply did not carry out the behavioral homework assignments that I required of them. In an article well over a decade ago I referred to this phenomenon as resistance to direction in behavior therapy (Herson, 1971b). I first attempted to publish these clinical observations in one of the American Psychological Association journals but incurred serious rebuff from the reviewers. They apparently felt that the concept was alien to behavior therapy and that I had erected a "straw-man" (caveat emptor). Nonetheless, this was, and still is, a very real phenomenon experienced by behavior therapists, irrespective of the religiousity of their views or the persuasiveness of their personalities. Indeed, in a review in *Progress in Behavior Modification;* Vol. 13, Worthington and Martin (1982) have considered in detail issues related to performance of homework assignments in behavior therapy. In still another chapter for *Progress in Behavior Modification*, Collins and Stark (in preparation) have outlined the problems in persuading patients and clients to comply with the task requirements of behavioral interventions. Obviously, these concerns are still very much with us and represent stumbling blocks to successful treatment.

From my perspective, there are a good many reasons why our patients fail to carry out their behavioral homework assignments. The *first*, of course, is inadequate patient preparation on the part of the therapist. This is more likely to occur with the beginner who is applying behavioral strategies. Frequently, the patient will be asked to do "homework" without an adequate rationale having been provided or will be asked to engage in behaviors that may be too difficult at that point in the therapy. In the former case a better "selling job" is required from the therapist. The importance and integral nature of the extratherapy activity must be underscored to the patient—that is, the therapist must be very persuasive about this issue. Indeed, continuation in treatment could be made contingent on such cooperation. In the latter case a more graduated approach to extratherapy activity should lead to more consistent patient compliance.

A *second* major reason for poor patient compliance concerns the nature of the patient's expectations about therapy in general. Given how the media have popularized the process of psychotherapy, most patients enter treatment with a passive stance. They tend to expect the therapist to "do something to them" but seldom are prepared for the *active participation* that is integral to behavior therapy. Here again, it behooves the behavioral therapist to clarify the patient's role in therapy at the outset of treatment. I think that it is critical that therapists really believe themselves in the importance of the religious adherence to a behavioral regimen. If this is so, "half the battle is won," and clear communication between therapist and patient has been established. Naturally, if there is excellent rapport between the therapist and patient, the patient is more likely to fulfill homework obligations in an effort to please. This is a primary reason why the therapeutic relationship in behavior therapy is of such paramount importance.

A *third* reason for resistance is related to the long-standing nature of our patients' complaints. Generally, by the time we see any given patient, that patient's presenting symptomatology has been very well established. Although painful and aggravating in many instances, these long-term habits imply some sort of consistency (even "comfort") in the patient's life. Removal of symptoms even might alter the delicate balance of interpersonal relationships in that particular environment. Moreover, in some instances (e.g., agoraphobia) the symptomatic behavior itself seems to manipulate and control significant others at home. In these cases, therefore, it should not be surprising that symptomatic removal is difficult and that often the patient will be most resistant to carrying out the requisite assignments to ensure gains. Here, it may be quite useful to intervene directly in the family system, as well as centering attention on the identified patient.

Newtown, Connecticut

In 1969, I finally tired of full-time private practice and moved on to a new position as Psychology Internship Director at Fairfield Hills Hospital in Newtown, Connecticut (a state hospital facility). During the 1½ years that I stayed there, the staff was embroiled in patients' rights political problems, with one superintendent of the facility resigning under pressure. Albeit fascinating, being engulfed in this political crisis (willy-nilly) proved to be emotionally and physically draining. Nonetheless, I furthered my gradual "conversion" to being a "purer" behavioral therapist. Fortunately for me, Dr. D. A. Begelman, a first-rate theoretical behaviorist, was Chief of Psychology at Fairfield Hills. He was most facilitating of my continuing research interests in verbal conditioning (Hersen, 1970b; Hersen & Greaves, 1971; Hersen & Sudik, 1971a, 1971b) and the personality patterns of nightmare sufferers (Hersen, 1971c, 1972). More importantly, we teamed up in writing two theoretically oriented papers related to the assessment and treatment of phobia (Begelman & Hersen, 1971, 1973). In spite of these strong behavioral leanings, my psychotherapeutic practice still was quite eclectic. Behavioral strategies were applied in the *context* of traditional therapy as opposed to their being the central focus. Furthermore, my research still was remote from the behavioral issues needing evaluation in the psychotherapeutic arena. But I was a bit closer than a colleague I encountered some years later, who precisely studied licking behavior in rats while administering Rorschach tests to his clinical patients.

Jackson, Mississippi

In 1970 I left Fairfield Hills Hospital and assumed my duties as Chief of Psychology at the VA Medical Center in Jackson, Mississippi and Associate Professor of Psychiatry at the University of Mississippi Medical Center. Being 30 years old, I felt the need to be director of a program at this stage of my career. When I was interviewed earlier that year by Dr. David Barlow, he, and later Dr. Stewart Agras, both thought that I would serve as a useful "bridge" between the "hard-line" behavior therapists at the university hospital and the more dynamically oriented psychiatrists at the VA. I had talked to them about my notions of carrying out behavioral techniques within the context of traditional psychotherapy (Hersen, 1970c, 1970d). Consistent with our ability to predict human behavior, however, things turned out quite differently from what had been anticipated. Apparently, the setting and collegiality of the Department of Psychiatry was the stimulus required for the completion of my "conversion." Given the fact that others, such as Drs. Edward Blanchard, Leonard Epstein, Peter Miller, Tom Sajwaj, Robert Scott, Larry Doke, Gene Abel, and Richard Eisler were colleagues in the program, the stage was set.

For the first time in my career, I was able to combine my research interests with what went on in the psychotherapeutic context. In the early 1970s in Mississippi my colleagues and I conducted a fair number of experimental analyses of psychotherapeutic approaches for a variety of behavioral disorders. Using single-case experimental designs, we evaluated the efficacy of (1) visual feedback in spasmodic torticollis (Bernhardt, Hersen, & Barlow, 1972), (2) token reinforcement for young psychiatric patients (Hersen, Eisler, Smith, & Agras, 1972), (3) electrical aversive conditioning in alcoholism (Miller & Hersen, 1972), (4) modification of caloric intake in anorexia nervosa (Elkin, Hersen, Eisler, & Williams, 1972), (5) token economy on neurotic depression (Hersen, Eisler, Alford, & Agras, 1973), (6) music feedback as a treatment for tension headache (Epstein, Hersen, & Hemphill, 1974), (7) covert sensitization for controlling incestuous behavior (Harbert, Barlow, Hersen, & Austin, 1974), (8) assertion training on marital interaction (Eisler, Miller, Hersen, & Alford, 1974), (9) contingent reinforcement of lowered blood alcoholic levels in an outpatient chronic alcoholic (Miller, Hersen, Eisler, & Watts, 1974), and (10) social reinforcement in the case of conversion reaction (Kallman, Hersen, & O'Toole, 1975).

Many of these experimental analyses were conducted in collaboration with our psychology interns, who consistently "kept us on our toes." Not only did we discover the efficacy (or lack thereof) of our behavioral strategies, but because of the rather unusual nature of some of the disorders we encountered (e.g., hysterical spasmodic torticollis), in many instances we had to be "quick on our feet" in order to develop appropriate behavioral assessment strategems. Some of these certainly are not sophisticated given more recent thinking about behavioral assessment (Hersen & Bellack, 1981). Indeed, they even may appear comical to some. But they did provide us with the basis for ascertaining therapeutic efficacy, directing our attention to the problems in the field.

In 1972 Dr. David Barlow and I first collaborated to write a paper explicating the importance of the single-case strategies as a viable research approach for studying psychotherapeutic phenomena. We directed our attention to psychiatric colleagues—hence publication of the paper in the *Archives of General Psychiatry* (Barlow & Hersen, 1973). In 1973 I suggested to Dave that we elaborate on this paper, concretizing all our thoughts about the role of the single-case strategy, individually and in relation to other research approaches (e.g., the group comparison design). In 1973 and 1974 we thus worked on our graduate text, *Single-Case Experimental Designs: Strategies for Studying Behavior Change,* which eventually was published two years later (Hersen & Barlow, 1976). In retrospect, I might note that the research and writing for this text definitely helped me master the intricacies of these numerous designs. I must confess that when I first began to tackle this task my knowledge of the single-case strategy was woefully limited. Since then I have found that the editing and writing of undergraduate- and graduate-level texts certainly will enable one to master a portion of a given area of the field. If one is not an expert at the beginning of the project, the cognitive dissonance subsequently experienced impels one to fill in the gaps. Signing of the book contract is tantamount to a declaration of expertise; writing it, however, often convinces the author of his initial misjudgment!

I have already mentioned that a very fine psychology internship training program was developed at the University of Mississippi Medical Center. Of course, interaction with interns and other graduate-level students always has the reciprocal function of sharpening one's own diagnostic and therapeutic skills. This seems to be an inevitable function of engaging in a pedagogical activity concerned with patients, but it also gave us the opportunity to observe the deficiencies of training in our students and younger colleagues. I found this to hold true for both the assessment of in- and outpatients. The major problem from my perspective is the incomplete behavioral analysis (Hersen, 1981; Wolpe, 1977). What I am referring to here is the tendency to seize the first (or most apparent) "juicy" behavior that obviously can be measured and operationalized, without considering that behavior within the context of the entire case. This, unfortunately, could lead to failures in treatment and even tragic consequences.

Consider the case of the patient who complained of chest pains with no apparent physical etiology and who was treated behaviorally with anxiety-reduction techniques and biofeedback. Progress was very modest at best, and during the course of the treatment this patient made a suicide attempt. The intern in this case, and the supervisor as well, neglected to probe sufficiently to unmask the chest pain (the presenting symptom) as indicative of a more chronic depressive disorder. In another case with less dire consequences, a patient presenting with fear of riding in elevators was treated with an in vivo variant of systematic desensitization. (Again, the presenting symptom was seized by the student as the behavioral target for modification.) Little progress was noted in the "phobia," however, and this case was presented at the weekly "grand rounds." It seemed fairly clear that an incomplete behavioral analysis had been accomplished. The patient, from the description of her life circumstances, seemed depressed to me. I suggested to this student that she evaluate and treat for depression and ignore the phobic element. With this change of therapeutic focus, not only did the depression lift, but phobic symptoms disappeared completely without therapeutic attention specifically directed to them. Phobic symptomatology was of a secondary nature here.

Clinical observations based on our own work, and as a result of our supervisory interactions with psychology interns, led Dr. Edward Blanchard and me to write a theoretical paper entitled "Behavioral treatment of hysterical neurosis: Symptom substitution and symptom return reconsidered" (Blanchard & Hersen, 1976). Among other issues, the importance of a comprehensive behavioral assessment and treatment was underscored, especially so in hysterical neurosis. Indeed, psychoanalysts have been most critical of us behaviorists with regard to the *mere treatment of symptoms*. They claim that without attacking the underlying cause of the conflict, symptom substitution and return are inevitable. Of course, behavior therapists counter these arguments by illustrating the clear success of the symptomatic treatment of phobic disorders.

In our reexamination of the data, it became apparent to us that we were arguing on two different channels. Analysts were deriving their conclusions, for the most part, on the basis of their experience with cases of hysterical neurosis. We had derived our conclusions primarily on the basis of the treatment of phobia. In contrasting the *two distinct* disorders, it is apparent that phobic behavior is maintained by anxiety reduction, with the neurotic behavior engaged in to reduce subjective distress and discomfort. Hysterical neurosis, on the other hand:

> is maintained through a process known as "secondary gain." The latter term means that the conditions supporting neurotic behavior are the external social reinforcers that the patient receives contingent upon evidencing his particular symptoms. This set of conditions predominates in hysterical neurosis, particularly the conversion reactions. In these disorders, neurotic symptoms functionally serve as a means for attaining external social reinforcement. In contrast to the neurotic patients in the first group, patients categorized as hysterical neurotics *do not* experience great subjective discomfort or distress.*

We thus argued that our analysis had

> some interesting implications, particularly for the phenomena of symptom substitution and symptom return. Removal of symptoms through one of several behavioral approaches . . . in our first type of neurotic (the phobic is the prototype) should lead to definite positive benefits. The patient is then freed to engage in a greater variety of behaviors, and his subjective discomfort is reduced or eliminated. In such patients one would *not* expect to find symptom substitution or return following behavioral treatment. Such absence of symptom substitution and return has been documented in the voluminous literature on the behavioral treatment of phobia and similar disorders. . . . For patients suffering from a hysterical neurosis, the opposite results would be predicted. Removal of the symptom *without* making changes in the patient's environment and *without* teaching him new ways to obtain reinforcement, would have mainly negative effects in terms of the loss of external reinforcement. Thus, one would expect the patient either: (1) to adopt new symptoms in order to regain the external reinforcement he had been receiving for displaying his symptomatic behavior; or (2) to relapse and begin to show the same or similar symptoms once he leaves the treatment situation, again in order to regain external reinforcers.

With our "hysterical neurotic," therefore, a three-pronged behavioral treatment regime appeared warranted in order to prevent symptom substitution and symptom return. First, extinction procedures were to be implemented to decrease and/or eliminate the patient's hysteri-

---

*From Blanchard, E. B., & Hersen, M. Behavioral treatment of hysterical neuroses: Symptom substitution and symptom return reconsidered. *Psychiatry*, 1976, *39*, 118–129. With permission.

cal presentation (i.e., symptoms). Frequently this would be accomplished while the patient was hospitalized. Second, the patient's immediate and more extended environment required programming to reinforce positive initiatives while simultaneously ignoring symptomatic presentations. This would be tackled first while the patient was hospitalized and later when returned to the home setting. Third, and most important, the patient had to be taught a more effective way of obtaining gratification from the environment (i.e., possibly social skills training). Without this latter feature of training, there could be no permanence of gains obtained through the first two strategies. Indeed, our clinical experience (and those of others) has borne out our theoretical notions (Blanchard & Hersen, 1976). The longer-lasting improvements are noted when assessment is comprehensive and treatment is multilevel.

Pittsburgh, Pennsylvania

In 1974, despite great fondness for my colleagues and the program in Mississippi, I decided that it was time for me to return to the northeast. I assumed my duties as Professor of Psychiatry at Western Psychiatric Institute and Clinic, the main teaching hospital for the Department of Psychiatry at the University of Pittsburgh School of Medicine. The Chairman, Dr. Thomas Detre, had left Yale Medical School the year before to reorganize and stimulate the Psychiatry Department in Pittsburgh toward more empirical directions. Although biological in orientation, Dr. Detre has seen fit to hire a fairly substantial number of behaviorists (Drs. Leonard Epstein, Alan Kazdin, Mary Margaret Kerr, Johnny Matson, Matig Mavissakalian, Larry Michelson, Samuel Turner, Phillip Strain, etc).

From 1974 to 1982 I collaborated chiefly with Dr. Alan Bellack, whose main assignment was in psychology, but who also held an appointment in psychiatry. During this period we founded two journals *(Behavior Modification;* and *Clinical Psychology Review)*, wrote and edited several books on behavioral assessment and treatment (e.g., Bellack & Hersen, 1977, 1979; Hersen & Bellack, 1976, 1978, 1981), collaborated with Alan Kazdin on the *International Handbook of Behavior Modification and Therapy* (Bellack, Hersen, & Kazdin, 1982), studied assessment and treatment issues in social skills training (e.g., Bellack, Hersen, & Turner, 1976, 1978), and have evaluated the effects of behavioral and pharmacological interventions in unipolar depressed woman (Bellack, Hersen, & Himmelhoch, 1981, in press; Hersen & Bellack, 1982).

Our studies involving the comparative and additive effects of behavioral and pharmacological treatments especially were stimulated by the presence of our pharmacologically oriented colleagues in Pittsburgh. Indeed, we have found that this strategy of group comparison research has proved most illuminating. At least in our own work with female outpatient unipolar depressives, we have been able to document that a behavioral approach (social skills training) is as effective as amitriptyline (a tricyclic antidepressant) in bringing about changes in both the biological symptomatology of depression and the social behavior of our patients (Hersen, Bellack, Himmelhoch, & Thase, 1982) Indeed, one of our residents, Dr. Michael Thase, has reexamined our data and has shown that the skills approach even is effective with the endogenous patients, whose symptomatology previously was considered to be modified only through biological means. On a more sobering note, however, our behavioral treatment *was not* vastly superior to a traditional short-term nonbehavioral psychotherapy in effecting change.

My clinical and research experiences over the last nine years in Pittsburgh have convinced me that applications of behavioral strategies is less clear-cut and more complex than previously thought. As I indicated in a talk in New York a few years ago:

> I think we all are beginning to recognize that life for the behavioral assesser and therapist is a bit more complicated today than it was a decade or two ago. I would suspect that, in the future, such complexity will increase as we broaden our perspectives and become more willing to tackle all facts of the existing problems with which we deal. For the outsider first peering in, the apparent simplicity of the behavioral therapies will be misleading. But as the examination proceeds beyond its superficial stage, the intracacies of the assessment strategies, the countless details of the resulting treatments, and the interrelatedness of assessment and therapy will be elucidated.*

It is toward this end that I undertook to edit this volume on the outpatient applications of behavior therapy. Because of my initial skepticism of behavior therapy and as a result of my general caution about the workings of all psychotherapeutic strategies, I felt it imperative that contributors carefully detail what and how they do in their respective areas of expertise. In some instances the reader will thus find descriptions of failure or only partial success rather than the detailing of glowing triumph. This, of course, is very much consistent with my thinking that considerably more is to be learned from the gaps in our strategies rather than in their routine application.

---

*From Hersen, M. Complex problems require complex solutions. *Behavior Therapy*, 1981, *12*, 26. With permission.

SUMMARY

In this chapter I have endeavored to give the reader some of my personal glimpses of the field of behavior therapy. Rather than rehashing the history of behavior therapy, I have considered some of the developments and problems in behavior therapy from the vantage point of traditionalists, who over time "converted" to behaviorism but who undoubtedly still maintain a vestige of their original training. There are obvious advantages of having one's training initially and directly in behavioral assessment and treatment; however, I have outlined some of the clinical limitations of our current trainees that do require remediation.

I also have articulated particular concerns with respect to (1) the importance of the therapeutic relationship in behavior therapy, (2) the prevalence of patient resistance to extratherapeutic tasks, (3) the problems associated with an inadequate behavioral analysis, (4) the contribution of biological psychiatry to behavior therapy, (5) the issues of symptom substitution and symptom return, and (6) the relevance of multifaceted treatment in the behavior therapy of the 1980s. The complex nature of both the assessment and treatment process has been highlighted throughout.

REFERENCES

Alford, G. S., & Williams, J. G. The role and uses of psychopharmacological agents in behavior therapy. In M. Hersen, R. M. Eisler, & P. M. Miller (Eds.), *Progress in behavior modification*, Vol. 10. New York: Academic Press, 1980.

Barlow, D. M., & Hersen, M. Single case experimental designs: Uses in applied clinical research. *Archives of General Psychiatry*, 1973, *34*, 516–520.

Begelman, D. A. & Hersen, M. Critique of Obler and Terwillinger's "Systematic desensitization with neurologically impaired children with phobic disorders," *Journal of Consulting and Clinical Psychology*, 1971, *37*, 10–13.

Bellack, A. S., & Hersen, M. *Behavior modification: An introductory textbook*. New York: Oxford University Press, 1977.

Bellack, A. S., & Hersen, M. (Eds.). *Research and practice in social skills training*. New York: Plenum Press, 1979.

Bellack, A. S., Hersen, M., & Himmelhoch, J. M. A comparison of solicited and non-solicited female unipolar depressives for treatment outcome reaearch. *Journal of Consulting and Clinical Psychology*, 1981, *49*, 611–613.

Bellack, A. S., Hersen, M., & Himmelhoch, J. M. A comparison of social skills training, pharmocotherapy, and psychotherapy for depression. *Behaviour Research and Therapy*, in press.

Bellack, A. S., Hersen, M., & Kazdin, A. E. (Eds.). *International handbook of behavior modification and therapy*. New York, Plenum Press, 1982.

Bellack, A. S., Hersen, M., & Turner, S. M. Comments on the utility of suggestive versus definitive data: A reply to Curran. *Behavior Therapy*, 1978, *9*, 469–470.

Bellack, A. S., Hersen, M., & Turner, S. M. Generalization effects of social skills training in chronic schizophrenics: An experimental analysis. *Behaviour Research and Therapy*, 1976, *14*, 391–398.

Bernhardt, A. M., Hersen, M., & Barlow, D. H. Measurement and modification of spasmodic torticollis: An experimental analysis. *Behavior Therapy*, 1972, *3*, 294–297.

Blanchard, E. B., & Hersen, M. Behavioral treatment of hysterical neuroses: Symptom substitution and symptom return reconsidered. *Psychiatry*, 1976, *39*, 118–128.

Breger, L., & McGaugh, J. L. Critique and reformulation of "learning theory" approaches to psychotherapy and neurosis. *Psychological Bulletin*, 1965, *63*, 338–358.

Collins, F. L., & Stark, L. Compliance to behavioral treatment. In M. Hersen, R. M. Eisler, & P. M. Miller (Eds.), *Progress in behavior modification*. New York: Academic Press, in preparation.

Eisler, R. M., Miller, P. M., Hersen, M., & Alford, H. Effects of assertive training on marital interaction. *Archives of General Psychiatry*, 1974, *30*, 643–649.

Elkin, T. E., Hersen, M., Eisler, R. M., & Williams, J. G. Modifications of caloric intake in anorexia nervosa: An experimental analysis. *Psychological Reports*, 1972, *32*, 75–78.

Epstein, L. H., Hersen, M., & Hemphill, D. P. Music feedback as treatment for tension headache: An experimental case study. *Journal of Behavior Therapy and Experimental Psychiatry*, 1974, *5*, 59–63.

Eysenck, H. J. Behavior therapy and its critics. *Journal of Behavior Therapy and Experimental Psychiatry*, 1970, *1*, 5–15.

Eysenck, H. J. *Behavior therapy and the neuroses: Readings in modern methods of treatment derived from learning theory*. New York: Pergamon Press, 1960. (a)

Eysenck, H. J. Learning theory and behaviour therapy. In H. J. Eysenck (Ed.), *Behaviour therapy and the neuroses*, New York: Pergamon Press, 1960. (b)

Fierman, L. B. (Ed.), *Effective psychotherapy: The contribution of Hellmuth Kaiser*. New York: Free Press, 1965.

Freeman, T. A psychoanalytic critique of behavior therapy. *British Journal of Medical Psychology*, 1968, *41*, 53–60.

Harbert, T. L. Barlow, D. H., Hersen, M., & Austin, J. B. Measurement and modification of incestuous behavior. *Psychological Reports*, 1974, *34*, 79–86.

Hersen, M. Generalization of positive and negative response biases. *Journal of Experimental Psychology*, 1966, *72*, 832–840.

Hersen, M. Experimentally induced response biases as a function of positive and negative wording. *Journal of Experimental Psychology*, 1967, *74*, 558–590. (a)

Hersen, M. Repeated inquiry during training in a verbal conditioning paradigm. *Journal of General Psychology*, 1967, *76*, 108–111. (b)

Hersen, M. Treatment of a compulsive phobic disorder via a total behavior therapy program: A case study. *Psychotherapy: Theory, Research, and Practice*, 1968, *5*, 220–225. (a)

Hersen, M. Awareness in verbal operant conditioning: Some comments. *Journal of General Psychology*, 1968, *78*, 287–296. (b)

Hersen, M. Experimental induction of generalized response biases: A confirmatory note, *Journal of General Psychology*, 1970, *82*, 95–98. (a)

Hersen, M. Controlling verbal behavior via classical and operant conditioning. *Journal of General Psychology*, 1970, *83*, 2–22. (b)

Hersen, M. The complimentary use of behavior therapy and psychotherapy: Some comments. *Psychological Record*, 1970, *20*, 395–402. (c)

Hersen, M. The use of behavior modification techniques within a traditional psychotherapeutic context. *American Journal of Psychotherapy*, 1970, *25*, 308–313. (d)

Hersen, M. Behavior modification approach to a school-phobia case. *Journal of Clinical Psychology*, 1970, *26*, 128–132. (e)

Hersen, M. The behavioral treatment of school phobia: Current techniques. *Journal of Nervous and Mental Disease*, 1974, *153*, 99–107. (a)

Hersen, M. Resistance to direction in behavior therapy: Some comments. *Journal of Genetic Psychology*, 1971, *118*, 128–132. (b)

Hersen, M. Personality characteristics of nightmare sufferers. *Journal of Nervous and Mental Disease*, 1974, *153*, 27–31. (c)

Hersen, M. Nightmare behavior: A review. *Psychological Bulletin*, 1972, *78*, 37–48.

Hersen, M. Limitations and problems in the clinical application of behavioral techniques in psychiatric settings. *Behavior Therapy*, 1979, *10*, 64–80.

Hersen, M. Complex problems require complex solutions. *Behavior Therapy*, 1981, *12*, 15–29.

Hersen, M., & Barlow, D. H. *Single-case experimental designs: Strategies for studying behavior change.* New York: Pergamon Press, 1976.

Hersen, M., & Bellack, A. S. (Eds.). *Behavioral assessment: A practical handbook.* New York: Pergamon Press, 1976.

Hersen, M., & Bellack, A. S. (Eds.). *Behavior therapy in the psychiatric setting.* Baltimore: Williams & Wilkins, 1978.

Hersen, M., & Bellack, A. S. (Eds.), *Behavioral assessment: A practical handbook (2nd ed.).* New York: Pergamon Press, 1981.

Hersen, M., & Bellack, A. S. Perspectives in the behavioral treatment of depression. *Behavior Modification*, 1982, *6*, 95–106.

Hersen, M. Bellack, A. S., Himmelhoch, J. M., & Thase, M. E. Effects of social skills training, amitriptyline, and psychotherapy in unipolar depressed women. Unpublished manuscript, 1982.

Hersen, M., Bellack, A. S., & Turner, S. M. Assessment of assertiveness in female psychiatric patients: Motor and autonomic measures. *Journal of Behavior Therapy and Experimental Psychiatry*, 1978, *9*, 11–16.

Hersen, M., & Breuning, S. (Eds.). *Pharmacological and behavioral treatment: An integrative approach,* New York: Wiley, in preparation.

Hersen, M., Eisler, R. m., Alford, G. S., & Agras, W. S. Effects of token economy on neurotic depression: An experimental analysis. *Behavior Therapy*, 1973, *4*, 392–297.

Hersen, M., Eisler, R. M., & Miller, P. M. Historical perspectives in behavior modification: Introductory comments. In M. Hersen, R. M. Eisler, & P. M. Miller (Eds.). *Progress in behavior modification, Vol. 1.* New York: Academic Press, 1975.

Hersen, M., Eisler, R. M., Smith, B. S., & Agras, W. S. A token reinforcement word for young psychiatric patients. *American Journal of Psychiatry*, 1972, *129*, 228–233.

Hersen, M., & Greaves, S. Rorschach productivity as related to verbal reinforcement. *Journal of Personality Assessment*, 1971, *35*, 436–441.

Hersen, M., & Sudik, E. Verbal conditioning as related to awareness, paranoia and suspiciousness. *Journal of Clinical Psychology*, 1971, *27*, 43–47. (a)

Hersen, M., & Sudik, E. Verbal conditioning as related to awareness and grade point average. *Journal of Clinical Psychology*, 1971, *27*, 266–269. (b)

Hull, C. L. *Principles of behavior: An introduction to behavior theory.* New York: Appleton-Century, 1943.

Kallman, M. W., Hersen, M., & O'Toole, D. H. The use of social reinforcement in a case of conversion reaction. *Behavior Therapy*, 1975, *6*, 411–413.

Kazdin, A. E. *History of behavior modification: Experimental foundations of contemporary research.* Baltimore: University Park Press, 1978.

Krasner, L. Behavior therapy. *Annual Review of Psychology*, 1971, *22*, 483–532.

Miller, P. M., & Hersen, M. Quantitative changes in alcohol consumption as a function of electrical aversive conditioning. *Journal of Clinical Psychology*, 1972, *28*, 580–593.

Miller, P. M., Hersen, M., Eisler, R. M., & Watts, J. G. Contingent reinforcement of lowered blood/alcoholic levels in an outpatient chronic alcoholic. *Behaviour Research and Therapy*, 1974, *12*, 261–263.

Stolz, S. B., Wienckowski, L. A., & Brown, B. S. Behavior modification: A perspective on critical issues. *American Psychologist*, 1975, *30*, 1027–1048.

Task Force Report 5. *Behavior therapy in psychiatry*. Washington, D.C.: American Psychiatric Association, 1973.

Weitzman, B. Behavior therapy and psychotherapy. *Psychological Review*, 1967, *74*, 300–317.

Wolpe, J. Inadequate behavior analysis: The achilles heel of outcome research in behavior therapy. *Journal of Behavior Therapy and Experimental Psychiatry*, 1977, *3*, 1–3.

Wolpe, J. *Psychotherapy by reciprocal inhibition*. Stanford, Calif.: Stanford University Press, 1958.

Worthington, E. C., & Martin, G. A. Behavioral homework. In M. Hersen, R. M. Eisler, & P. M. Miller (Eds.), *Progress in behavior modification;* Vol. 13. New York: Academic Press, 1982.

2

Office Practice of Behavior Therapy

Steven T. Fishman
Barry S. Lubetkin

BEHAVIOR THERAPY has enjoyed considerable attention in the professional literature since its formal beginnings in the mid-1950s. Since that time it has emerged as a viable psychotherapeutic system and as an alternative to the more traditional, evocative psychotherapies. The most prominent characteristic distinguishing behavior therapy from other forms of psychotherapy, (and considered its strongest asset), is that most of the specific treatment procedures utilized in clinical practice have been spawned in the laboratory under tightly controlled conditions. The fact that behavior therapy is an empirically based psychotherapy, however, has exposed it to a host of criticism from its rivals. Unfortunately, impressions about behavior therapy have not been customarily formed by observing the behavior therapist in practice, but rather are gleaned from reports of empirical work that appear in the professional journals. Drawing inferences about clinical practice from laboratory investigations is analogous to watching the "bare-bone" construction of an edifice and referring to the consequate structure as cold and unimaginative without viewing the finished product complete with interior design and decoration. Even within the ranks of behavior therapy, it is a recognized fact that there is a "generalization gap" between the laboratory studies and what actually ensues in clinical practice (Fishman, 1981).

As long time practitioners of behavior therapy engaged in full-time office practice, we hope to shed light on some of the finer nuances of clinical practice and in so doing lay to rest notions about behavior therapy as being simplistic, dehumanizing, and limited in its application. This chapter is divided into two parts. In "Part One" we briefly overview the many transformations in the field of behavior therapy that have had a direct bearing on the office practice of behavior therapy. Then extensive attention is devoted to the more subtle issues in the actual practice of clinical behavior therapy. Drawing on our own experience over 10 years of clinical practice, in "Part Two" we present a manual written in a discursive style, addressing an often overlooked subject for the aspiring clinician: the "how-to's" of practice development.

PART ONE: TRANSFORMATIONS IN THE FIELD OF BEHAVIOR THERAPY

Since its inception, the field of behavior therapy has undergone a number of changes that have had a direct bearing on the way in which it is practiced in the office setting. As it turns out, most of these developments have helped to provide the "on-line" practitioner with a more efficient, durable system of psychotherapy. Some of these changes are summarized in the following four paragraphs.

On the theoretical level, there has been a fundamental shift in the field from a neobehavioristic stimulus–response S–R mediational model grounded in orthodox learning theory [i.e., what Lazarus (1971) refers to as the "one problem, one antidote model"] to a more comprehensive multiform model (Lazarus, 1971, 1977), which, for the most part, has found a theoretical home in social learning theory (Bandura & Waters, 1963). The former model, which prevailed in the early stages of the development of behavior therapy, conceptualized all maladaptive behavior, including private events, strictly in learning terms, whereas the latter paved the way for the inclusion of cognitive explanations for behavior, both prosocial and unadaptive, into the system. As a consequence of this reformulation, the therapies of such prominent cognitive theoreticians as Beck, Ellis, Mahoney, and Meichenbaum have over time become an integral part of clinical practice. Present-day office practice of behavior therapy is best characterized by what Mahoney has termed "cognitive-behavioral" therapy, which focuses on the cognitive styles, affectual states, and manifest behavior for the spectrum of psychological problems.

Most behavior therapists originally were called on by their more "insight-oriented" colleagues to function in an adjunctive "technician" capacity, helping to alleviate troublesome symptoms, so that the "real work" of therapy could then proceed. Consequently, most treatment was geared toward symptom removal for limited, circumscribed problems. The most prevalent of these were the gamut of phobias. As behavior therapy has reached a new level of theoretical and procedural sophistication, it has gained wider acceptance in both the professional and public sectors as a *primary* intervention procedure, and it is currently sought out for the spectrum of emotional and behavioral problems. Some "traditionalists," however, have tenaciously clung to their earlier views about behavior therapy as being applicable to limited or specific disorders.

Comparative studies between behavior therapy and evocative approaches, as reviewed by Kazdin and Wilson (1978), have revealed that behavior therapy appears to have greater *cost effectiveness* (i.e., results can be achieved in a shorter period of time, and to have *broader applicability* in terms of problems addressed and the variety of populations treated. Behavior therapy does demonstrate clear superiority in certain problem areas such as childhood disorders, neurotic depression, addictive disorders, and in the management of the institutionalized patient. Interestingly enough, the one area to which behavior therapy is most closely identified, that of anxiety-related disorders, did not prove to be more efficacious than the evocative psychotherapies, even though results are achieved in a shorter time period. Data accumulated over the past 10 years on our own patient population have yielded findings that are consistent with those cited above, with the exception that anxiety-related disorders (e.g., fears, phobias, obsessive-compulsive reactions, sexual dysfunctions, and especially those problems falling in the interpersonal-social sphere) were indeed the most frequently presented problems and were also the problem areas most responsive to treatment.

As patients' problems have become less circumscribed and multi-faceted (this distinction may be more apparent than real—the change may be due to the way problems are currently assessed) over the decade of our practice, our own emphasis has shifted from a problem-centered, technique-oriented approach to strategies that provide our patients with more general coping capabilities (Goldfried & Merbaum, 1973). Our goals for therapy are to provide the patient with skills for exercising greater control over their presenting problems and further, to provide them with the means for both assessing and remediating problems that may arise in their future functioning. This shift in emphasis in our own treatment planning is reflected in the fact that our mean number of sessions from intake to termination has increased from approximately 22 sessions, 10 years ago, to about 50 sessions per patient currently. By way of summary, this change in the actual number of contact hours per patient can be attributed to a number of or combination of factors alluded to above: (1) the field, has been modified in general, which has led practitioners to being sought out for and addressing more global problems; (2) with increased procedural sophistication in methods of assessment, practitioners are now focusing on more aspects of patients' problems and not targeting only the manifest problem: and (3) practitioners are functioning in a much more holistic way in the application of the various cognitive-behavioral approaches in a "coping skills" paradigm (Goldfried, 1980).

Process Variables in
Clinical Behavior Therapy

Even through the "nontechnical" or the unspecified aspects of clinical treatment have long been the focal point and, in fact, constitute the principal thrust of treatment in the evocative psychotherapies, behavior therapists have only recently begun to divert their attention from the development and refinement of their techniques to these process variables. It has become evident from our own clinical experience that it is the management of these "nontechnical" variables in the treatment process that often spells the difference between successful and unsuccessful treatment outcomes (Fishman & Lubetkin, 1980). These more subtle factors, which can exert a marked influence the efficacy of treatment, include such "undefinables" as relationship factors, problem conceptualization, orientation to treatment, issues of compliance and resistance, the "consolidation" of treatment outcomes, and termination from treatment. It is to these process variables to which we now turn our attention.

Relationship Factors

Certain individuals are more suited for the practice of psychotherapy than others, and there are certain personal qualities in therapists that serve to secure a therapeutic alliance, such as the well-documented triumverate of genuineness, understanding, and warmth, as well as the ability to create a nonpejorative climate. These qualities are important factors affecting outcome of psychotherapy, regardless of the discipline one embraces; certainly, behavior therapy is not an exception. In our clinical experience, only a small percentage of each therapy hour is utilized administering the specific behavior therapy techniques. The greater portion of each hour is spent providing understanding to clients, lending support and encouragement for their intentioned therapeutic steps, and helping them to generate alternatives to the way they may interpret life situation(s).

Although the relationship between therapist and client is not the "sine qua non" of treatment in behavior therapy as it is in psychodynamic therapy, it is our opinion and that of others (Wilson & Evans, 1976) that it plays a central role in the eventual outcome of a behavior therapy treatment program. There are a number of factors that underscore the importance of relationship factors in behavior therapy. First, generally, behavior therapy is a *directive* psychotherapeutic approach and presupposes both the cooperation and the active participation of the client in the therapy process. Without the establishment of a constructive therapeutic relationship, it is doubtful whether the client will carry out the between-session home practice that is necessary for behavior therapy to be maximally efficacious. If the therapist is uncertain, vague, or unassertive in his or her approach to the client, there is a high probability that treatment will also suffer. Second, a high percentage of patients' presenting problems fall in the interpersonal-social sphere. Role-playing and behavioral rehearsal which involve the therapist and the client "playing out" a number of the situations in which the client is experiencing difficulties comprise a significant part of treatment. By means of this process, the therapist can supply constructive and corrective feedback to the client about the verbal and nonverbal behavior that seems to be interfering with his or her optimal functioning. The socially reticent client, unless the therapeutic relationship is sound, will be reluctant to participate in the role-playing process and, in all likelihood, will be unresponsive to the therapist's feedback. It is hoped that a client will acquire the more socially appropriate behavior of the therapist through the process of modeling. Thus vicarious learning is more likely to occur when the therapist represents a viable reinforcer in the individual's life (Bandura & Walters, 1963). Third, as indicated earlier, many of the methods and techniques in behavior therapy involve skill acquisition, which requires a continuity of between-session practice on the part of the client. Additionally, in keeping with the "canon of gradualness," the client is typically asked to progress by approximations; such progress is predicated on the assumption that the behavior therapist can keep the client sufficiently motivated to continue with his or her independent practice. It is further hoped that reinforcement on the part of the therapist for the "smallest of gains" has real value for the client. Finally, frequently used techniques, participant modeling and "in vivo" desensitization, require the therapist to accompany the client into their fear-producing situations and to model "nonfearful" behavior. In such instances the therapist must provide a sense of support and encouragement and, more importantly, impart a sense of security to the client. Unless such relationship factors are operative, it is highly doubtful that behavior therapy would have much value in the treatment of a clinical population.

Problem Conceptualization

Another significant factor that has a direct bearing on the efficacy of behavior therapy is the behavioral "diagnosis." The art of behavior therapy becomes apparent when therapists utilize their knowledge to formulate a treatment program based on their conceptualization. Problem conception and subsequent treatment planning are not as straightforward as some therapists would like to believe. A multitude of factors must be taken into consideration during the assessment period: factors that ultimately affect treatment planning and eventual outcomes. From our perspective, the goals of behavioral assessment are multifold: (1) to cull out the parameters of the manifest problem, that is, the overt and covert or mediational determinants; (2) to identify trouble spots or dysfunctional thinking and behavior in all spheres of clients' functioning (e.g., familial, social, sexual, academic, and vocational) from an historical perspective to their current functioning; (3) to determine how each of the clients' problems is differentially weighted and interrelated, particularly with regard to the manifest problem; (4) to assess for the more subtle factors such as "secondary gain" and other such maintenance factors, which are discussed below; and (5) to prioritize treatment focus. These elements, along with keeping a watchful eye on the so-called unspecified variables, then become building blocks for the conceptual framework from which treatment planning follows. It is rather inefficient for a therapist merely to "potshot" areas of treatment focus rather than devoting the necessary time to formulating a viable plan based on the conceptualization (or conceptual framework) of the clients' problems.

Priority Setting

Most clients who seek psychotherapy present with multifaceted rather than circumscribed problems. Several factors must be considered when formulating the treatment focus within such multiple problems. The *urgency* of the various aspects of clients' overall symptom should be given the greatest priority. If some aspects of their symptomatology are potentially life-threatening (to themselves or to others) or have legal ramifications, they obviously demand immediate attention. In a number of cases (sexual deviants, suicidal, child abusers, etc.) that we have seen, it would have been therapeutically more judicious to focus on other than the dominant problem, but the urgency of the problem precluded such a course. Consideration must be given to clients' *expectations* for treatment. They may be at odds with therapists as to which areas should be focused on in treatment. Behavior therapists must then use their "clinical common sense" to determine whether to run the risk of alienating the client and incurring resistance by insisting that the focus be on one area, or whether to focus on a less therapeutically desirable area until such time as a relationship of trust can be established. Therapists must give attention to the "core" area or problem that, when ameliorated, will generalize to other problematic areas. This core area is what we refer to as the "behavioral dynamics" of the problem. Specifically, by "behavioral dynamics" we mean the underlying processes such as feelings of worthlessness, inadequacy, dependency, inferiority, and so on, which, once identified, are then concretized and translated into behavioral terms. For example, feelings of worthlessness and inadequacy can be tranlated to nonassertiveness in specific situation interpersonal-social anxiety and/or fears of negative evaluation. We do not wish to confuse the word "dynamics" in the sense of an *ongoing process* that intrudes on the client's functioning.

Underlying Determinants

There also are other, more subtle, factors to be determined during the assessment period, lest behavior therapists finds themselves led "down the proverbial garden path" and having to battle resistance on the part of clients. Many practicing behavior therapists are too wedded to the "prima facie" problems that clients bring to therapy. We have observed from our own clinical experience that "under material" may often be directly responsible for maintaining the manifest behavior. This phenomenon is especially true when clients are deriving a "secondary gain" from their overt problems. In a sense, the manifest problem serves as a cover for a more severe problem; consequently, it is being maintained by the principle of negative reinforcement. The examples of the "secondary gain" phenomenon are boundless. For instance, successful business and professional people may present with a circumscribed phobia but with further probing reveal that they feel like "imposters" in their chosen occupations. They feel that they have somehow slipped by with their incompetence unnoticed. Obviously underlying their circumscribed phobias are rather profound feelings of insecurity for which they have compensated by achieving success in their chosen fields. The phobia seems to surface whenever the thin veneer of confidence is threatened.

Another area that is rarely discussed in the literature is the extent to which clients are involved in their problems and the degree and extent to which these problems have become the center of their lifestyles and everyday functioning. For instance, with grossly overweight clients, once significant weight losses occur, there is a greater onus to begin functioning independently and confidently in the interpersonal-social sphere, which previously they had a ready excuse for avoiding. At the least, family and friends expect these clients to begin to blossom socially. Consequently, unless considerable attention is given to clients' social functioning, there is a good chance that when they meet their first awkward or uncomfortable social challenge, they will once again escape into their old and familiar self-defeating patterns. Another necessary part of the assessment process is the attempt to understand the context or the physical environment that gave rise to a client's particular problem complex. On occasion, once a particular problem such as alcoholism or drug abuse is ameliorated, the individual's physical environment or context must be altered or daily routines altered in order to maintain treatment gains. Sometimes the assistance of a significant other is solicited to help facilitate the transfer of treatment effects into the individual's home environment. Such programs have been established for obsessive and compulsive clients; another such program exists for agoraphobics (Mathews, Teasdale, Munby, Johnston, & Shaw, 1977).

The point of raising these various considerations in problem conceptualization is to emphasize that in the clinical setting the process of treatment formulation is a highly complex and intricate process. If improperly managed, this limits the efficacy of behavior therapy and leads either to the patient evincing the classical signs of resistance (late or missed appointments, failing to complete or inadequately completing homework assignments, generally uncooperative or argumentative, etc.) or to patient-initiated premature termination.

Behavior Therapy Treatment

"Setting the Stage"

Before actually embarking on a treatment program, practicing behavior therapists spend considerable time "setting the stage" for treatment proper. In this preparatory phase of the therapeutic sequence, therapists devote attention to a number of areas that help to provide clients with a better understanding of what can be expected in the change process and a better understanding of the actual treatment strategies. This process, in turn, leads to greater client cooperation and motivation.

There are a number of areas that exemplify this process. First, clients are alerted to the inevitable "peaks and valleys" that are apt to be encoutered in the course of treatment. With such preparation, if a setback should occur, there is less likelihood that treatment will be disrupted as is often the case when clients are ill prepared for unexpected setbacks. Second, clients are introduced to the "canon of gradualness," which underlies the workings of many of the behavior therapy techniques and is fundamental to the change process. Grasping of this principle helps the client to progress steadily, building on his or her successes without imposing self-defeating demands that invariable stall their potential progress. Third, as suggested by Goldfried and Davison (1976), this phase is also a time during which "advance organizers" are implanted, which serve to "fix" client expectations and guide their participation. Finally, techniques are described to clients and the rationale for each is offered to encourage them to carry out technique-related prescriptions. It also is made clear, often through treatment planning charts, how these techniques generally fit into the overall picture, and additionally, what one should expect at the time of termination.

Behavior Therapy Strategies

As noted in an earlier section of this chapter, the multiform behavior therapist approaches client problems in a comprehensive fashion, emphasizing holistic treatment programs rather than concentrating exclusively on manifest problem behaviors. Multiform behavior therapy is geared toward getting clients to reevaluate themselves in regard to their new potential for actual functioning. This results from either (1) cognitively restructuring clients' perspectives on themselves, others, and the world about them, (2) teaching them specific strategies for coping more effectively with problematic situations, or (3) focusing on their emotional responses in such problematic areas. Of course, the acutal treatment focus may be disproportionately weighted with regard to one or another of the dimensions of functioning, but this is generally determined only after considerable time is spent in conceptualizing clients' global functioning. This perspective is consonant with Bandura's (1977) "self-efficacy" theory, which states that individuals change as a consequence of *experiencing* themselves functioning more effectively. In doing so they are more willing to endure the discomforts of problematic situations long enough to function more effectively, or at least with less discomfort. The key to change, interestingly enough, remains the same as it has done so from the nascent stages of behavior therapy, i.e., that people change only after experiencing some improvement in their overt performance.

Compliance and Resistance

Behavior therapy, perhaps more than any other psychotherapy, relies heavily on the active participation of the clients in the change process. As we have indicated, improvement ultimately has to occur on the behavioral level of client functioning. Consequently, if clients resist to carrying through with prescribed between-session assignments, the therapy process will be severely hampered. For clients may begin resisting behavioral interventions for a number of reasons, some of which were mentioned in other sections of the chapter. The most salient reasons are that behavior therapy may not have met client expectations about psychotherapy, especially the participatory aspect and that the therapist–client relationship may breed client resistance, particularly in clients who are uncomfortable with or distrustful of their therapists. In fact, some clients may have sexual or erotic feelings for their therapists. The former situation usually eventuates in a premature termination, whereas the latter typically triggers anger in the client. Resistance then takes the form of overcompliance, wherein a client appears to be working hard at therapy but is merely "window-dressing." Alternatively, assessment or therapist evaluation may be incorrect, so the client, aware of the fact that the therapist has "missed the boat" in his or her assessment, will not carry out what he or she perceives to be inconsequential homework. In the same vein, the client may be deriving a secondary gain from the manifest problem and is not about to have it tampered with or run the risk of uncovering a more debilitating problem. Also, the client may be afraid of change or functioning on "uncharted grounds," especially when he or she feels ill prepared to do so. Finally, as far as homework assignments are concerned, for some of the above reasons such assignments may be irrelevant, too difficult, or threatening at that point in therapy or may be too time-consuming, not understood, or even sabotaged by a well-meaning family member.

Even though space does not permit us to delve into the issue in depth, the primary prescription for therapists when clients begin to exhibit the classical signs of resistance (missed appointments, tardiness at sessions, incomplete assignments, hostility, etc) is to go back to the "drawing board" to assess and probe all areas of client functioning more closely. Interested readers are directed to two excellent chapters on the subject by Goldfried and another by Lazarus and Fay in a recent book by Wachtel (1982).

Consolidation Period

In the final stages of treatment, when clients report and exhibit observable signs of progress over a reasonable period of time, they then are shifted into the "consolidation phase" of the psychoterapeutic sequence. This phase must occur if transfer and ultimate maintenance of gains is to be incorporated into client functioning. Typically, the clients will begin coming into each session accouncing their successes that they had enjoyed that particular week. It becomes evident that they are employing to their benefit, the specific techniques, cognitive and behavioral, rather consistently and spontaneously. Until that point in therapy, the treatment process is under the active direction of the behavior therapist. During this phase, clients are allowed to plateau with only minimal interventions being imposed on them. In essence, they are allowed a period of time to consolidate their treatment gains. It is a time during which behavior therapists become more passive in treatment planning and problem resolution. Clients begin to apply their accumulated therapeutic experiences, as well as the principles garnered from therapy to their daily functioning. Problems of the week are no longer discussed, played out, and so on in detail, but are discussed in a more general way such as: "What happened? How did you handle it? What did you learn from the experience? Have you ever encountered something like that before?" Therapists look for clear evidence that clients have not only learned new skills, but have integrated "principles of coping" and self-control, which then may be utilized across a variety of situations in the future. In addition to clients assuming greater responsibility for planning and strategy, the consolidation period also is a time during which formal treatment sessions can be spaced and therapist influence faded until formal termination is in effect.

There are several other reasons that underscore the importance of this intermediate phase between treatment and termination in the therapeutic sequence: (1) it allows for the continued practice of the newly acquired coping skills with sights set on building habit strength with each until their usage is truly automatic and spontaneous; (2) it allows clients to internalize and "own" their successes, for the positive feelings of accomplishment can never catch up to clients' behavioral accomplishments if the demands to do more are ever present; and (3) it affords clients the opportunity to incorporate their new cognitive and behavioral and affectual responses into their lifestyles. This, of course, serves to minimize the possible fears of a radically altered lifestyle.

Termination

Assuming that the consolidation period has led to continued but independent progress and that the gains enjoyed up to that point have been maintained, termination is considered and discussed with the client. Needless to say, this time is always difficult for both clients and therapists. Several points should be stressed to the client regarding termination. Even though the word "termination" implies finality, it is important that the client need not be made to feel that termination is permanent or that such an agreement ends any future professional contacts with the therapists. The model of the general practitioner from medicine is used, and where new "psychological wounds" develop, it is appropriate to return to treatment. Moreover, it is important that clients be made to realize that there will never be a time when they are totally free of life's problems or any emotional discomforts. Hopefully, at the time of termination, their current problems are well within manageable limits, as they have cultivated a number of varied strategies to cope more effectively with the problems focused on in the course of their behavior therapy. Ultimately, if problems that were raised at the time of discussion about termination are new material for the therapist and were only lightly touched on during the course of the assessment and treatment phases and determined not to be of central importance, one can only assume that the client is feeling the pains of separation and, most likely, requires some further reassurance.

Mechanisms for Follow-Up Treatment

As indicated above, it may be harmful to close the door behind a client on termination. At the same time, it is crucial that therapists impress their clients with the fact that they have the response capabilities for functioning effectively and non-self-defeatingly outside the regularly scheduled treatment sessions. All future progress should be refinements of their gains. It is imperative that the clients attribute their improvement to themselves rather than to their therapists, so that treatment gains will stand the test of time.

When therapy ends, any one of a number of mechanisms can be implemented to ensure the transfer and maintenance of progress. It is always good practice for a client's spouse, parents, or mate to be asked to participate in one or two sessions at the time of termination. This is recommended so that the significant others can be apprised of the changes the client has realized and the effects these changes may have on the family constellation or the relationship. In addition, it should be clearly specified how these significant others can change to accommodate the client's changes. Finally, it is important to clearly specify the conditions of termination, so that they will not be misinterpreted. If such significant others have been active in the ongoing treatment program, they then can be equally active in the termination phase. Briefly, for instance, a spouse can recognize the early warning signs of a client's depression, such as loss of appetite or less concern for physical appearance or clothes coordination. With this information the spouse can help the client to resolve the sources of depression or can urge the client to telephone the therapist before the depression becomes too incapacitating. Clients can be instructed to telephone their therapists on a specified date after termination to apprise them of their level of functioning. Often, brief trouble-schooting or a bit of encouragement can forestall a major slippage. Frequently, this takes the form of reminding the clients of self-control or self-management prescriptions that they have been neglecting to follow. Throughout its development, behavior therapy practitioners have had clients return intermittently for brief reinstatement of treatment techniques implemented in the course of formal therapy. It was thought that such booster sessions would inoculate clients against relapse and ensure the durability of treatment gains. Recently, the efficacy of booster sessions has been called into question by Kazdin and Wilson (1978) on the grounds that they are conceptually inaccurate. Specifically, in the past, booster sessions were arbitrarily scheduled by therapists, usually inconsistent with the needs and functioning level of clients. For this reason, their purpose is not best served. The control for scheduling of booster sessions should lie with the clients and should be done so when they begin to experience some signs of slippage or a slackening of control over their previously maladaptive patterns. Therapists must make every effort to assist clients in identifying, processing, and reacting to early warning signs of slippage. In this way, clients can be taught to use therapy follow-up or booster sessions judiciously and most beneficially. Another practice with which several therapists have had good success, particularly in helping to sustain therapy gains, is with yearly "check-ups" for good therapeutic maintenance. Just as the phrase implies, clients once terminated continue to return on at least a once-a-year basis, merely to discuss with their therapists current functioning and objectives and particularly the means through which they are coping with their particular problems. The various problem areas dealt with in their previous therapy are reviewed as well as the specific coping mechanisms they had acquired at the time. Therapist notes from the assessment phase are sometimes shared with clients to underscore gains made. Practice sessions for the techniques assessed at the time as either being devalued, not actively used, or apparently losing their potency are encouraged. Another method for sustaining progress was suggested by Keefe, Kopel, and Gordon (1978) and Kazdin and Wilson (1978) and termed by the present authors as "fail-safe" planning. Specifically, in the penultimate session clients are asked to anticipate what could interfere with their current functioning over the next several years. Indeed, clients are asked to imagine such occurrences. They are then asked to write down in columnar fashion each anticipated problem and in the columns beside it to remediate that particular problem on the cognitive, affectual, and behavioral levels. This exercise, of course, gives clients the practice of applying their newly learned coping skills to a range of potentially problematic situations. After writing up their complete "fail-safe" plan, they puts it away for safe-keeping, just in case.

PART TWO: A GUIDE FOR ESTABLISHING AND MAINTAINING A BEHAVIOR THERAPY OFFICE PRACTICE

Until only recently, there were few guidelines for behaviorally oriented mental health practitioners to assist in the development and/or maintenance of a viable office practice. The plain truth is that, for most clinicians, conventional graduate training does not offer the necessary curriculum or provide exposure to instructors that serve as role models or the successful practitioner. In reality, most behaviorally oriented instructors were themselves trained primarily as academic researchers and not as clinical practitioners; few maintain active involvement in clinical practice. Couple this with the fact that many behavior therapists still encounter a degree of resistance from both the community and their fellow professionals because of the ever-present misconceptions about "modification techniques"; thus the business of setting up an office practice can be problematic. In light of some of these stumbling blocks, special and frequently innovative strategies are necessary to aid the aspiring behavior therapist to establish such an office practice.

Specialization

The importance of specialization in developing a successful practice cannot be overstated. This is expecially true with respect to the practice of behavior therapy where referrals are frequently made for the alleviation of some highly specific problems. These may be for anorexia nervosa, shyness, agoraphobia, sexual dysfunctions, social or modified drinking, or other problems, or for the utilization of a highly specific treatment approach such as hypnotherapy, biofeedback, and aversive conditioning. The behavioral clinician is particularly identified with a problem area or a treatment method; the smaller and more segmented the pool of potential client referrals, the greater the probability that this "specialist" will be the recipient of the lion's share of those referrals. In actuality, referrals to behavior therapists are most often made on the basis of a perception that a particular colleague "has more of an expertise in treating a specific problem area than anyone else that I can think of."

In a recent edition of a popular psychotherapy newsletter, five steps were outlined for crystallizing one's thinking about creating a speciality:

1. *Develop clear objectives.* Begin by asking yourself "How do I really want to practice? Shall I (as many behaviorists do) expand my dissertation population into a specialization? The key here is to think practically about how your training and interests can help to define a specialty direction.

2. *Decide what you do not want.* The experience of observing a certain population of patients for doctoral or graduate research for a circumscribed period of time may be very different from the experience of devoting the majority of your professional practice time for the next 40 years to this same population.

3. *Shift to match your own changing interests.* Freudenberg (1981) and others in their work in preventing professional "burnout" emphasize the importance of "tuning in" to the personal changes occurring within you in terms of shifting needs and values and modifying your practice accordingly.

4. *Narrow specialization isn't necessary.* In fact, limiting the parameters of your practice too much may turn off old referral sources for more general cases. Obviously, it is counterproductive to reinforce in your colleagues' minds the old stereotype of the behavior therapist who operates with such a narrow focus on client complaints that they miss the "big picture" and perform only a part of therapy. Remember that you must work to turn your specialization into referrals. Obviously, the best source of referrals are the colleagues, students, and friends who may know of your work and who have identified you as possessing that "unique" quality (specialty, fee, advanced training, desirable office location) that they feel is just right for that referral. Do not be shy about letting your colleagues know that you are looking to fill client hours.

5. *Do not expect an easy transition.* Developing a specialty takes time and work. In addition to continuing education commitments, which help you keep abreast of the latest developments in your area, you must consider strategies to market your skills and increase your professional visibility. These may include sending out

announcements emphasizing your specialty, developing a network of referral sources by offering your skills to other established professionals in the community, delivering community presentations, developing media exposure, working with self-help groups, and advertising. We now examine each of these strategies.

Announcements

These should always note the practitioner's particular specialty, such as biofeedback and sex-therapy, as well as any particular special conveniences that the practitioner offers, including weekend hours, late evening hours, or medicare acceptance. Enclose reprints of articles that you have written and that are related to your area of specialization. Enterprising behavior therapists have followed up their announcements with a letter a week or two later. This communication reintroduces them and their services, rates, availability of hours and at the same time requests colleagues to call for further information. A rather clever modification of this approach is to ask a select number of the individuals to whom you have sent announcements if they would be willing to serve as professional advisors for your practice. This would mean asking them if you could *refer your patients to them* when their particular specialties would be required. This strategy would be particularly useful in developing professional relationships and a referral network with specialists such as dentists, family doctors, attorneys, psychopharmacologists, speech therapists, and ministers.

It is strongly encouraged that you make it a habit to acknowledge every referral from your colleagues with a thank you note and a brief report of the consultation; including a description of possible future interventions. The form of the report is outlined in Table 2-1. Of course, such reports must protect the confidential relationship with your client.

Community Presentations

Since the opportunity to give presentations to colleagues generally occurs at national and regional meetings, where increased exposure will not necessarily increase numbers of referrals, it is more pragmatic to focus your attention on community and "lay" groups in your immediate geographical location. Obviously, such presentations should be given in your area of specialization. It is helpful for each presentation to have a "catchy" title. For example, you are much more likely to attract an audience and impress the committee that chooses speakers if your talk is entitled "How to be More Forceful" or "How to Cope with a Boss you Hate" rather than an "Introduction to Assertiveness

Table 2-1 Consultation and Future Goals Report

Findings from my consultation
  Overt behavioral problems (e.g., specific assertion defeats)
  Covert (thought and image) problems (e.g., overgeneralized thinking)
  Other problems (e.g., depressed affect)
Client's stated goals and expectation of therapy
Behavior therapist's decision concerning goal priorities
Recommended interventions with approximate time periods
Special instructions to referring colleagues if they are also maintaining professional relationships with their clients (e.g., encourage clients to attempt relaxation exercises despite the fact that you will continue to write prescriptions to tranquilizers)
Dates of future follow-up notes to be expected by referring colleagues

Training." Similarly, a talk entitled "Help! My Kids Are Driving Me Crazy" is more likely to attract attention than "New Methods for Modifying Children's Behavior." In any community there are numerous churches, singles' groups, PTAs, and groups that need to fill their speaker's calendar. It is important to contact the speaker's bureaus well in advance of the time the calendars are filled. Parent–teacher associations frequently request speakers for the calendar year starting after the summer, sometime in early spring. In such talks, real-life examples should be used so that the audience can identify with the particular problem and concerns that they may have. Emphasis should be placed on the importance of *prevention* of emotional problems as well as discussing the *management* of problems once they occur. Many of the people in your audience will be reluctant to seek out therapy. If, however, they can be convinced that they do not have to have a severe mental aberration to consult a therapist, but merely a desire to increase the enjoyment of their lives by ridding themselves of emotional blocks, their fears will be diminished.

Obviously, it is unethical and unprofessional to actively solicit new clients into your practice when giving a community presentation. Potential clients in your audience must first be impressed by what you have to say and then *make up their own minds* about whether to seek out your professional assistance.

The Use of Media in Practice Development

In our experience, appearances on radio and television (either local or national network presentations) have by and large proved to be ineffectual in furthering our practice. We have found the same to hold true for national magazine coverage. For example, after we have been interviewed numerous times by national magazines, aside from a few letters from readers, these articles did little more than fill a scrapbook.

There is, however, one form of media coverage that has proved to be consistently effective in generating interest in our practice (i.e., local newspaper coverage). Such coverage can be in the form of interviews with you as an interesting professional personality in the community or of quotations from you about important psychological issues, or perhaps articles about your particular area of interest (e.g., contemporary sex therapy, biofeedback for headaches, therapy for shyness). Since opinion polls generally conclude that the public views reports in newspapers as the most reliable source of news, it is not surprising that articles will generate many inquiries from the public. As behavior therapists, we are fortunate to be at the forefront of many of the new developments in the field of psychology that often prove to be of real interest to the general public. Science and feature editors of local newspapers are always interested in covering new developments in behavioral psychology. If you are providing some innovative service in your community, it is likely that science editors of local newspapers will "get wind of it" and will call you and ask for an interview. If you wish to expedite the process a bit, you can write a brief synopsis in the form of a "press release" of either the research you have been doing or the treatment programs you have been developing and providing at your office. Then submit it to your local newspaper editor. Be careful to include the appropriate disclaimers with any "press release." (For example, while Dr. Smith is optimistic about the future promise of his work with autistic children, he points out that more critically controlled experiments must be carried out successfully before the therapy can be unequivocally considered an acceptable treatment for the disorder). As behavior therapists and as ethical mental health professionals, we are obligated to support empirical investigations of innovative therapy intervention whenever possible.

Another ethical approach to increasing public visibility is to offer weekly or monthly workshops free of charge to members of the community. Workshops—such as "coping with divorce," "responsive parenting," "problems of everyday living," and so on—correspond to a variety of needs from the community. Most local newspapers would be enthusiastic to not only announce this ongoing workshop series in their schedule of events column, but also to dispatch a reporter to interview participants as well as yourself for a feature-length article in an upcoming issue of the newspaper. Some particularly enterprising mental health practitioners have taken it one step further and hired professional public relations people to ensure placement of articles about them in local newspapers and other media. This approach, however, is best saved for more comprehensive facilities, such as larger clinics and mental health centers, that can afford both the inflated fees that public relations people charge and can also provide sufficiently varied programs to warrant repetitive exposure in local newspapers.

One final note about newspaper coverage is warranted. There are a number of behavior-oriented psychologists around the country who have quite wisely begun to write their own column for their regional newspaper. Usually this is done on a weekly or monthly basis, and, unlike the typical "Dear Abby" column, these behavioral practitioners communicate to their readers the latest developments from the *science of psychology*. These columns focus on mental health interventions, prevention issues, particular emotional and behavioral syndromes, the application of behavioral procedures to community-wide problems, and other issues. Such columns obviously provide a service in communicating information that probably would not be available in capsule form anywhere else. Apparently this idea has proved so effective in helping to enhance one's professional practice that at least one firm has begun to market prewritten columns to which profesionals can add their by-lines (for a fee). Obviously, we frown on these ghost-written columns because they are often written by nonprofessionals and are replete with inaccuracies. Finally, as one wag so aptly put it, mental health professionals are likely never to go out of business because when they run out of patients they will spend their time training each other! In fact, providing continuing education in your specialty to your fellow colleagues can enhance your visability and your practice. Most of us frequently refer to other colleagues who have skills and expertise in areas we do not possess. It is good practice to contact your local psychological and professional societies, local colleges and universities, and local groups of practitioners and volunteer your services in their particular continuing education programs.

Affiliation with Self-Help Groups

As a consequence of soaring medical and therapy costs and the generally poor economic climate, large numbers of potential therapy consumers are turning to self-help programs in order to receive the support and guidance they require. Since most such groups provide rather pat formulas for emotional growth and could not possibly respond to individual idiosyncratic needs (an example is the estimated 50% of Alcoholics Anonymous members who may be suffering from depressive illness and cannot achieve sustained sobriety until the depression is appropriately treated), many of their members eventually seek out professional help. It is thus sensible for their clinicians to work with self-help groups in order to increase their exposure with these potential patients. To find out more about this subject, contact the National Clearing House for Self-Help Groups in New York City.

Advertising

Since the late 1970s, we have seen a tremendous change in the policy and attitudes toward advertising from both the professional and private sectors. This began with a series of antitrust rulings from the Federal Trade Commission that permitted lawyers to advertise their services in a variety of ways. We have since witnessed many professionals breaking from traditional conservative announcement of their services. Radio and television commercials, newspaper advertisements, and the like are not uncommon for attorneys and various specialties of physicians and other professionals. In our experience, it appears that the most successful professional advertising is both repetitive and dignified. Once you have segmented "the market" to which you wish to direct your advertising, you need to repeat your announcement of services rather than switching from one medium to another. The various mental health professions have issued clear guidelines concerning advertising, and they should be followed as closely as possible. This not only protects you from unprofessional conduct charges; it also represents your profession in the best possible light. Also, many people are "turned off" to professionals who advertise and are particularly turned off by professional people who advertise in a nonprofessional manner. It has been our experience that the most effective advertising medium for our services consistently has been the yellow pages of the telephone directory. Dignified and conservative display advertisements, announcing your services in specific fashion increase your visibility over simple listings.

A Word About the Mechanics of Practice Management

It is not our intention in this chapter to review all the "nuts and bolts" involved in the mechanics of practice management such as setting fees, managing insurance claims, handling malpractice insurance and potential litigations, fee splitting, tax credits, selling a practice, collections, and so on. But suffice it to say that these are all detailed issues that require meticulous thought and attention if one is to maintain a viable practice.

REFERENCES

Bandura, A. Self-efficacy: Toward a unifying theory of behavioral change. *Psychological Review*, 1977, *84*, 191–215.

Bandura, A., & Walters, R. H. *Social learning and personality development.* New York: Holt, Rienhart, & Winston, 1963.

Fishman, S. T. Narrowing the generalization gap in clinical research. *Behavioral Assessment*, 1981, *3*, 243–248.

Fishman, S. T., & Lubetkin, B. S. Generalization and maintenance of individual behaviora therapy programs. In P. Karoly & J. Steffen (Eds.), *Improving the long term effects of psychotherapy: Contemporary perspectives*. New York: Gardner Press, 1980.

Freudenberg, H. J. *Burnout: How to beat the high cost of success*. New York: Bantam, 1981.

Goldfried, M. R. Some views on effective principles of psychotherapy. *Cognitive Therapy and Research*, 1980, *4*, 271–306.

Goldfried, M. R., & Davison, G. C. *Clinical behavior therapy*. New York: Holt, Rinehart, & Winston, 1976.

Goldfried, M. R., & Merbaum, M. (Eds.). *Behavior change through self-control*. New York: Holt, Rienhart, & Winston, 1973.

Kazdin, A. E. & Wilson, G. T. *Evaluation of behavior therapy*. Cambridge, Mass.: Ballinger, 1978.

Keefe, F., Kopel, S., & Gordon, S. B. *Behavioral assessment*. New York: Springer, 1978.

Lazarus, A. A. *Behavior therapy and beyond*. New York: McGraw-Hill, 1971.

Lazarus, A. A. *Multimodal behavior therapy*. New York: Springer, 1977.

Mathews, A. M., Teasdale, J., Munby, M., Johnston, D., & Shaw, P. A home-based treatment program for agoraphobia. *Behavior Therapy*, 1977, *8*, 915–924.

Wachtel, P. L. (Ed.). *Resistance: Psychodynamic and behavioral approaches*. New York: Plenum, 1982.

Wilson, G. T. & Evans, I. M. Adult behavior therapy and the therapist–client relationship. In C. M. Franks & G. T. Wilson (Eds.), *Annual review of behavior therapy: Theory and practice*, Vol. 4. New York: Brunner/Mazel, 1976.

Part II

PROBLEMS IN ADULTHOOD

3

Anxiety-Based Disorders

Paul M. G. Emmelkamp
Ank Emmelkamp-Benner

FOUR GROUPS OF anxiety disorders can be distinguished, as shown in Table 3-1.

CLASSIFICATION

Phobic Disorders

Phobias can be defined as special types of fear that are out of proportion to the reality of the situation, can neither be explained nor reasoned away, are largely beyond voluntary control, and lead to avoidance of the feared situation (Marks, 1969). In the adult population agoraphobia is the most common *clinical* phobia, although other fears are much more frequent in the general population. Relatively few individuals with simple or specific phobias come for treatment. Examples of simple phobias are claustrophobia (fear of enclosed spaces), acrophobia (fear of heights), and animal phobias. The bulk of the remaining clinical phobias consists of social phobias (or social anxiety) and illness phobias. It should be noted that in *DSM-III* illness phobias are diagnosed as a somatoform disorder rather than as an anxiety disorder.

The term *agoraphobia* refers to a syndrome in which the most characteristic feature is attacks of anxiety or panic in a variety of public

Table 3-1   Classification of Anxiety Disorders

Phobic disorders
  Agoraphobia with panic attacks
  Agoraphobia without panic attacks
  Social phobia
  Simple phobia
Anxiety states
  Panic disorder
  Generalized anxiety disorder
Obsessive-compulsive disorder
Posttraumatic stress disorder

places, such as streets, crowds, stores, buses, and so on that cause "fear of fear" and lead to an avoidance of these situations. Agoraphobics become anxious when walking, shopping, traveling by bus, or visiting cinemas and churches. Most agoraphobics feel less anxiety when accompanied by a trusted person (partner), but they usually remain anxious, although to a lesser degree. The few agoraphobics who succeed in visiting churches, cinemas, and parties will choose a chair near the exit. A number of agoraphobics experience panic attacks in other than the specific situation (e.g., at home).

Examples of *illness phobias* are fears of heart disease and fears of cancer. Patients are extremely sensitive to sensations in their bodies (e.g., palpitations, dizziness) and frequently visit their general practitioner for a check-up. Avoidance behavior consists of avoiding hospital areas, cemetries, and people who might be ill. Furthermore, these parients often avoid reading about diseases, obituaries, and watching television programs that might include scenes involving blood, illness, injury, or death. They also may ask continuously for reassurance (e.g., from general practitioners, or family members), may check regularly to see if their heart is beating, or may read medical books compulsively.

Social anxiety consists of disabling fears in social situations, which cause patients to avoid such situations as much as possible. A number of these patients experience fears in any social situation, but in others fears are limited to specific situations. For example, some patients fear that their hands will tremble when writing or holding a cup in front of others. Others may be afraid of blushing or of eating in public places. Avoidance behavior often is subtle. Patients who are afraid of blushing often wear scarves and turtle-neck sweaters, use a lot of makeup, and are inclined to sit in dark places. Some people wear their hair long, and some men may grow beards so that their faces can hardly be seen. When patients go out, they often wear sunglasses and feel that they must have something in their hands such as a bag.

When confronted with the phobic situation, phobic patients become anxious or may even panic. Patients will attempt to *escape* from this situation, which eventually leads to anxiety reduction that has powerful reinforcing effects. Future confrontations with these situations will be *avoided* as a result of anticipatory anxiety. If avoidance becomes impossible, patients tend to make themselves anxious, often weeks ahead. This anticipatory anxiety may sometimes be felt more intensively than the anxiety that occurs when the patient is confronted with the actual phobic situation. The scheme shown in Figure 3-1 illustrates this point.

The behavioral procedures may focus on either the anxiety component (e.g., systematic desensitization, anxiety management) or escape and avoidance components (exposure in vivo procedures); the latter procedures are the most effective.

Anxiety States and Stress Disorder

Anxiety states are divided into two categories: panic disorder and generalized anxiety disorder. *Panic disorders* are characterized by recurrent panic attacks for which patients have no explanation themselves and that occur outside typically phobic situations. Common symptoms are dyspnea, palpitations, chest pain, dizziness, sweating, faintness, and fear of dying or "going crazy." The essential feature of *generalized anxiety* disorder is generalized, persistent anxiety. With *posttraumatic stress disorders* the anxiety develops as a result of an extreme traumatic event, such as rape, military combat, or automobile accident. Commonly, the individuals have nightmares during which the traumatic event is reexperienced.

It should be noted that anxiety and the somatic concomitants of anxiety are also common in hyperventilation and mitral valve prolapse (MVP) syndrome. Hyperventilation is due to an increased rate of respiration, deepened respiration, or both. The main controversy over the etiology of the hyperventilation syndrome is whether such hyperventilation is a response to anxiety or a bad breathing habit with secondary production of anxiety. In the latter case breathing exercises are useful as a treatment strategy.

The MVP syndrome is a cardiological disease with symptoms sim-

Figure 3-1 Schematic illustration of development of escape and avoidance.

ilar to those of anxiety states. It has been suggested that the palpitations and dyspnea associated with MVP can lead to panic attacks, thus further aggravating the symptoms and so creating a vicious circle.

With anxiety states, a medical check-up is recommended. Apart from hyperventilation and MVP, other organic conditions that may be associated with the anxiety symptoms are angina pectoris, cardiac arrhythmias, hyperthyroidism, hypoglycemia, and some neurological disorders. Furthermore, excessive use of caffeine and withdrawal from some medications (e.g., benzodiazepines) may produce anxiety symptoms.

There is considerable overlap between social anxiety, agoraphobia, illness phobia, and anxiety states. Rather than consider them as distinct diagnostic categories, anxiety disorders are better viewed as lying in a number of different continua. The actual clinical diagnosis depends on the predominant features in a particular patient. The overlapping diagnostic groups are graphically depicted in Figure 3-2.

Figure 3-2   Relationship between agroaphobia, illness phobia, social anxiety and anxiety states. (From Emmelkamp, P. M. G. Phobic and obsessive-compulsive disorders: *Theory, research and practice.* New York: Plenum Press, 1982. With permission.)

Obsessive-Compulsive Disorder

Obsessive thoughts (obsessions) and compulsions (rituals) may be distinguished. Obsessions are recurring thoughts—often anxiety-inducing but not necessarily—that recur despite active attempts to ward them off. Obsessions may involve sexual themes, thoughts of causing physical harm to self or others, or obsessional fears of contamination. Obsessions are often—but not always—accompanied by urges and rituals. *Rituals* or *compulsions* are repetitive actions, which usually serve to reduce anxiety and discomfort. The most common compulsive behaviors involve "cleaning" and "checking."

About 80 percent of obsessional patients have obsessions as well as compulsions. A minority suffers from obsessions only. Pure rituals without accompanying obsessive thoughts are rare. Usually, obsessions precede the rituals, but sometimes the obsessive thoughts follow the performance of rituals, especially with obsessional doubting.

Cleaning compulsions usually are associated with contamination fears. Patients fear that they may become contaminated and therefore clean their house, themselves, and their children. Whenever such patients touch anything that might be contaminated (e.g., door knobs, money, other people, food), they wash their hands and arms, often for many minutes, or take a bath. With some patients, thoughts by themselves may provoke washing and cleaning rituals. Checking rituals may involve checking whether doors and windows are closed and whether the gas is turned off. Whenever they leave their house, such people often return numerous times to see if everything is allright. Checking may also occur in other situations, such as driving back to see if no accident has happened, going back to the office to see if no one is locked up in a cupboard, and so on. Both washing and checking rituals lead to avoidance of situations that are likely to provoke these rituals.

The rituals (e.g., checking, washing, cleaning, repetition) have discomfort and anxiety-reducing effects. There is now considerable evidence that urges to perform rituals are provoked by exposure to distressing situations (e.g., washing after contamination with dirt) and that the performance of the rituals leads to relief of anxiety and discomfort (Rachman & Hodgson, 1980). A number of studies have shown that prolonged exposure to distressing stimuli plus prevention of the performance of compulsive behavior (response prevention) is effective in dealing with the obsessive-compulsive behaviour [reviewed by Emmelkamp (1982)].

It is important for treatment planning to establish the exact nature of the content of the obsessions. Obsessive thoughts can be either anxiety-inducing or anxiety-reducing. When obsessions are *anxiety-*

inducing they may be accompanied by rituals to reduce anxiety. With anxiety-inducing obsessions treatment should focus on exposure to the distressing thoughts and/or stimuli with response prevention of the rituals. Obsessional patients often engage in "neutralizing" thoughts (*anxiety-reducing* obsessions) in order to undo the possible harmful effects of their obsessions. For example, one of our obsessional patients thought: "I may kill you," which was always followed by neutralizing thoughts such as: "I do not mean it" and "I will kill myself" or just "myself . . . myself . . . myself . . . myself." The thinking of the neutralizing thoughts led to temporary relief of anxiety provoked by the aggressive thought. The neutralizing thoughts presumably serve the same function as the checking or washing rituals of obsessive-compulsives i.e., to produce anxiety reduction. Treatment here should thus involve exposure to the distressing thoughts with response prevention focused on the neutralizing thoughts.

ASSESSMENT

Before beginning treatment, it is necessary to attain a thorough assessment of the problems. Assessment is something different from establishing what diagnostic labels patients are to be given. Although patients may have the same diagnosis, this usually says little about the treatment the patient ought to have. A functional behavioral analysis is very important for treatment planning. When drawing up a functional analysis, it is worthwile to make a distinction between a macroanalysis and a microanalysis (Emmelkamp, 1982a). In practice, the two stages of behavior analysis are interwoven.

Macroanalysis Versus Microanalysis

Macroanalysis is the mapping out of the different problems a patient has and the establishing of possible connections between these problems. For example, a patient suffers from panic attacks and in addition has relationship problems with his wife. It is necessary to establish whether the relationship problem has anything to do with the panic attacks or whether it is a matter of the two problems functioning independently. If there is a connection between the relationship problems and the panic, the next step would be to find out exactly what this connection is. There are several possibilities. When the relationship problems lead to anxiety, it makes sense to focus the treatment on the relationship. With some patients, however, the connection is just the opposite: here the anxiety problems cause the relationship problems. It makes little sense, therefore, to focus the treatment on the relationship problems; a treatment focused directly on the anxiety will be more meaningful. Some other relationships between anxiety disorders and marital conflict and the therapeutic implications have been dealt with elsewhere (Emmelkamp, 1982a). Perhaps an example may illustrate the process of macroanalysis.

CASE STUDY 1

Janet is a 28-year-old married woman with the following problems: (1) Agoraphobia—she is completely housebound and is afraid of going one step in the street alone; (2) sexual anxiety—she avoids sex with her husband as much as possible and is afraid of looking at her own body even when dressed; (3) social anxiety and subassertiveness; (4) marital distress; and (5) psychosomatic complaints (e.g., headaches). Further questioning concerning the developmental history reveals the following information: the patient has suffered from social anxiety for as long as she can remember. The first panic attack occurred in a social situation in which she felt watched and that led to her agoraphobia. Because of her agoraphobia, she could now avoid all kinds of social situations (e.g., visiting her parents-in-law, who were constantly criticizing her). Her anxiety concerning sexuality appeared to be independent of the other problems. Her sexual anxiety was rooted in the fact that her elder sister was a prostitute, so that everything that was related to sex or sexuality was negatively loaded from an early age. During sexual contact she felt like a prostitute. The psychosomatic complaints appeared to be used as a means to avoid having sex with her husband. If she said she had a headache, her husband no longer insisted. She did not dare to say directly that she did not feel like having sex. The lack of social contacts and the lack of practically any sexual contact both led to considerable friction in her marriage. The relationship between the problem areas can be depicted as shown in Figure 3-3.

On the basis of this analysis, it was decided first to treat the social anxiety by means of assertiveness training and exposure in vivo for social and agoraphobic situations. After that, sexual anxiety was treated by a gradual exposure in vivo program, in which her husband's participation was required. At the end of the treatment program, social anxiety, sexual anxiety, and agoraphobic complaints seemed to have

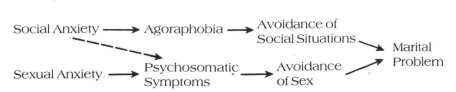

Figure 3-3 Hypothesized relationship between problem areas.

disappeared almost completely. Interestingly, the psychosomatic complaints and the relationship problems "spontaneously" improved, thus suggesting that the proposed functional analysis was indeed correct.

While macroanalysis deals with the relationship between the various problem areas, microanalysis deals with the behavioral analysis within one problem area only. The therapist examines the situations in which the patient becomes afraid, how the patient behaves (e.g., escape), and the consequences of this behavior (e.g., anxiety reduction). The part played by the environment is also included (e.g., reinforcement of the avoidance behavior). In addition, it is important to determine what the patient *feels* in such situations (e.g., palpitations, stomach ache) and *thinks* (e.g., "everybody must think me a fool").

The interviews with the therapist form an important means of gathering information about the functioning of the complaints. The following possibilities exist for gathering additional information: (1) self-monitoring (behavioral diary), (2) questionnaires, and (3) behavioral assessment.

Self-Monitoring

As soon as the therapist, in consultation with the client, has determined one or more target behaviors, it makes sense to have the patient keep a structured diary to find out under what conditions this behavior occurs. It is important for the patient to fill out the diary regularly throughout the day so that there will be no need to recall events. Inspection of the diary may reveal significant associations between problem behavior and particular events. It is recommended to design recording forms that are tailor-made to the individual needs of the patient and that contain specific questions particularly relevant to this patient.

Monitoring of the situations in which anxiety occurs is especially important with patients with anxiety states. After inspection of the diary, apparently "uncontrollable" anxiety attacks very often turn out to be related to specific events, as the following example illustrates:

Therapist: I see in your diary that you had a panic attack last Sunday when you were visiting your parents.

Client: Yes, we were just having a discussion and all of a sudden I became anxious.

T: Can you tell me exactly how it happened?

C: Well, we were having a discussion about taking the law into one's own hands. My father said that the people should take the law into their own hands in connection with that little girl's murder. Well, I think that it's not allowed, you should never do such a thing.

T: That's what you said?

C: No, I got angry . . . and then I felt strange . . . anxious . . . I didn't say anything.

T: Why not?

C: Because . . . I'm afraid something will happen then.

T: What could happen?

C: Well, my father could get angry and have a heart attack.

T: That's what bothering you and that's why you don't say anything. . . . Does the fact that you are afraid that he might die without you being able to make it up with him also have something to do with it?

C: Yes, exactly, that's what I'm so terribly afraid of . . . that he might die when I'm quarrelling with him and that I will never again be able to make it up with him . . . that's why I keep my mouth shut in these situations.

An important advantage of self-monitoring is that patients themselves begin to see connections they have not seen before. For example, in the case mentioned above, it became clear to the patient that the "spontaneous" panic attacks were related to the restrained aggression. Another patient felt compelled to break dishes during panic attacks. In this case self-monitoring made the patient herself notice that this only happened when somebody else was present and that she was then in need of attention. This led her to redefine her "spontaneous" anxiety.

It makes sense to have patients rate their level of anxiety (e.g., on a scale of 0 to 10). Such a barometer gives more precise information with regard to the relative degree of difficulty of certain situations than the monitoring of the occurrence of anxiety. An additional advantage of such an anxiety barometer is that patients learn to distinguish their feelings. This is especially important for patients who are inclined to evaluate themselves negatively "I am *always* anxious" and for patients with generalized anxiety states. It goes without saying that other feelings (e.g., depression) and thoughts (e.g., obsessions) can also be monitored.

Many patients find it difficult to fill in a diary. Patients suffering from fear of failure often experience the keeping of behavioral diary as an assignment at which they might fail. Other patients are afraid that by having to monitor their behavior, feelings, and thoughts, they might be confronted with aspects of themselves that they find quite painful. A clear explanation of just what is expected of the patient and the filling in of some examples together with the therapist in the consulting room may help to prevent this.

Questionnaires

There are several fear questionnaires that may provide useful information for treatment planning. In clinical practice, *general* fear questionnaires are particularly useful, since this type of questionnaire provides information on a wide range of specific phobic situations. The Fear Survey Schedule (FSS-III) (Wolpe & Lang, 1964) lists 76 items of fears that are common in phobic patients. An advantage of this inventory is its subdivision in several categories: (1) social anxiety; (2) agoraphobia; (3) fears related to bodily injury, death, and illness; (4) sexual aggression; and (5) small-animal phobias. The psychometric properties of this scale are satisfactory (Arrindell, Emmelkamp, & van de Ende, in preparation).

Another general inventory is the fear questionnaire (Marks & Mathews, 1979). This form includes the commonest 15 phobias and 5 associated anxiety-depression symptoms found in clinical practice. The phobia score is composed of (1) agoraphobia, (2) social fears, and (3) blood and injury fears. Reliability and concurrent validity of this questionnaire are satisfactory (Arrindell et al., in preparation).

In addition to the general fear questionaires, a number dealing with *specific* fears have been constructed (e.g., questionnaires dealing specifically with fear of snakes, spiders, and mutilation and test-anxiety questionnaires), but most of these are of little clinical use. Useful questionnaires, which provide information on social anxiety are the Social Avoidance and Distress Scale (SAD) and the Fear of Negative Evaluation Scale (FNE), both developed by Watson and Friend (1969).

Few inventories exist to assess obsessive-compulsive complaints. The Leyton Obsessional Inventory [(LOI) (Cooper, 1970)] consists of 69 questions, each printed on a separate card that the patient puts into either the "Yes" or "No" slots of an answer box. The LOI gives four scores: (1) symptoms, (2) obsessive trait, (3) interference, and (4) resistance. The interference score reflects the disability caused by the symptoms, and the resistance score reflects the severity rather than the extent of the symptoms.

The Maudsley Obsessive-Compulsive Inventory [(MOCI) (Rachman & Hodgson, 1980)] consists of 30 items that differentiate between obsessional and nonobsessional patients. The questionnaire provides five scores: (1) total obsessional score, (2) checking, (3) washing, (4) slowness-repetition, and (5) doubting-conscientious. An advantage of the MOCI over the LOI is its easy administration.

Behavioral Assessment

The behavioral tests typically used in research studies are of little value in clinical practice. There is increasing evidence that these behavioral test are far from valid. Performance on standardized behavioral tests may be very different from actual behavior in everyday situations. Behavioral observation can provide important information, however. It thus makes sense to have a patient with an extensive hand-washing ritual demonstrate how he or she washes. Rehearsal in role play of certain situations that evoked anxiety can also reveal important information. One patient suffered from harming obsessions every time he had had a quarrel. Repeated questionning about the course of these quarrels yielded little information. The course the quarrel takes becomes clearer when it is rehearsed in role-playing. One of the patient's colleagues criticizes him. The patient becomes furious but does not say anything, and when the tension becomes unbearable he finally goes to the manager and says: "If he doesn't shut up, I'll skewer him on a pitchfork." Such diagnostic role-playing gives important information about the stimuli that gave rise to the patient's obsessions.

Another example is about a patient who is afraid of conflicts and quarrels but claims never to avoid quarrels. Rehearsal of some conflict situations in role play shows that the patient indeed does not avoid conflicts. When criticizing, the patient become obviously tense. It also appears that he take back every expression of criticism on his part immediately, which leads to anxiety reduction.

In summary, whereas standardized behavioral tests are of little avail, behavioral observation, either in vivo or in role playing, may add to the information gathered in the interview.

Treatment Goals and Evaluation

After the initial assessment stage in which the problems are formulated, a goal for the treatment must be established. This goal can be either simple or more complex. An example of a simple goal with an agoraphobic patient is the reduction of the anxiety in buses, in the street, and other public places. A more complex goal for the treatment is "becoming independent." Even when a simple goal is chosen, it is necessary to formulate precisely what the desired final result is to be (shopping alone in the neighborhood versus going abroad alone for a holiday). Often, a relatively simple goal is chosen at first; when this is achieved, a new goal may be formulated.

Of course, the patient and the therapist may have a different idea about what a desired goal should be. For example, Cathleen, a 23-year-old woman, had as a goal for her treatment the reduction of her "phobic anxieties." Examples of these anxieties consisted of becoming anxious when sailing in a storm and feeling tense when sleeping in a tent among the bears in the woods in Canada. She took part in these activities but felt tense, which was very annoying to her boyfriend. After a functional analysis, the problem was redefined by the therapist as an assertiveness problem in her relationship. She did not really like these activities, but she was afraid to tell this to her boyfriend.

When having reached an agreement, it can be established how the effect of the treatment is to be evaluated. Questionnaires and specific rating scales can be of use to this evaluation. Thus the patient can judge a number of situations on rating scales for anxiety and avoidance (Watson & Marks, 1971) before, during, and after treatment. General anxiety level, panic attacks, and obsessions can be monitored daily during the treatment. Psychophysiological assessment is of little use. The psychophysiological recording is very time-consuming and costly without actually contributing to treatment decisions or treatment evaluations.

TREATMENT

As has become clear from the preceding paragraph, there is no standard method for treating anxiety disorders, but the choice of method depends on the functional analysis. In the remainder of this chapter, only those treatments are discussed that are aimed directly at changing the anxiety. During the last 20 years a great number of procedures have been developed that aim at reducing anxiety, such as systematic desensitization, flooding, exposure in vivo, covert reinforcement, (covert) modeling, and anxiety management procedures. It is impossible, however, to deal with all of these within the scope of this chapter. For a critical review, the reader is referred to (Emmelkamp, 1982a).

The element that most of these treatments have in common is exposure to distressing stimuli. Exposure can be carried out in two ways: (1) in imagination, in which patients must imagine themselves to be in a certain situation or (2) in vivo, in which patient is really exposed to the situation. Exposure in vivo is usually more effective than exposure in imagination. Other important variables in exposure treatments are the degree of anxiety and the duration of exposure trials. Exposure can be either self-controlled, (as in systematic desensitization in which the patient himself decides when to begin on a more difficult item,) or controlled by the therapist, such as in flooding or prolonged exposure in vivo. Sometimes additional components are added to the exposure. In systematic desensitization, relaxation is added to exposure for distressing stimuli. There is no evidence, though, that relaxation is essential to a successful treatment. Modeling, the showing of approach behavior by the therapist or someone else in anxious situations, also appears to add little to the effect of exposure itself.

The most successful exposure programs are those carried out in vivo, during a longer uninterrupted period of time (prolonged), and in which escape and avoidance of the phobic situation is prevented (Emmelkamp, 1982a). A number of complaints remain in which it is difficult or impossible to realize exposure in vivo, and here imaginary methods may be of help (e.g., obsessions).

Exposure in Vivo

Prolonged exposure in vivo can be illustrated most easily by means of a description of its application in the case of patients with simple phobias.

Simple Phobias

CASE STUDY 2

Renata is a 34-year-old woman with a moderate fear of heights. She becomes afraid on staircases, flyovers, bridges, and such stimuli. She is afraid of falling over and thus avoids such situations. It was explained to the patient that because of her avoidance, she would not be able to notice that her anxiety would decrease when she stayed in those situations long enough. An open fire escape was used as a practice situation.

The patient was told to climb the stairs by herself as far as possible. "If you really cannot go on, you can stop for a while until you have mustered enough courage to go on climbing. But do not forget to look down from each floor." The patient also was asked to indicate how anxious she felt every three minutes on a scale of 0 (= relaxed) to 8 (= panic). Figure 3-4 shows the subjective anxiety course. The patient at first climbed up to the third platform and then became afraid to go on; after about six minutes her anxiety had decreased to

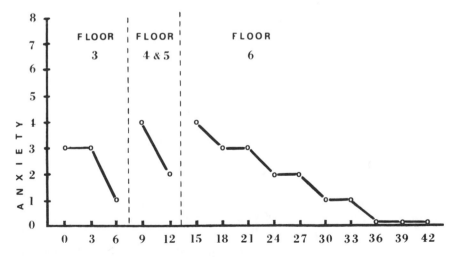

Figure 3-4   Subjective anxiety during exposure in vivo in the treatment of fear of heights.

a reasonable extent, she was not afraid of looking down, and went on climbing until she reached the fourth platform at which the anxiety again increased. When anxiety had again decreased, she continued to climb to the fifth platform. After a few minutes she ventured to climb to the highest platform, which again led to an increase of anxiety. In about 20 minutes anxiety had decreased to zero. The total exposure time was 45 minutes.

It is important for exposure to occur to those cues that evoke anxiety. For example, in the case of fear of heights, a closed staircase within a building is far easier than an open staircase outside. When somebody (e.g., the therapist) accompanies the patient, it is usually easier than when the patient has to go alone. Many patients who suffer from fear of heights tend to press themselves against the building and do not look down or hold on to the banisters firmly with both hands. These are all subtle forms of avoidance behavior to be tackled in an exposure program if treatment is to be successful.

A maximum anxiety experience is not necessary for a successful treatment. It is usually better to let patients themselves indicate how much anxiety they find bearable. Force on the part of therapists only leads to unnecessary panic on the part of patients or even to a drop out of treatment. If a patient continues avoiding, some insistence from the therapist is, of course, required. If during an exposure session a patient has a panic attack, it is essential for the patient to remain in that situation until anxiety has decreased *there*. By proceeding to an easier situation, the anxiety and avoidance behavior are reinforced by negative reinforcement (anxiety reduction) that occurs because the patient leaves the difficult situation.

It is not necessary—and is often impossible—for the anxiety to be completely reduced before the patient goes to a new situation. If the patient feels that anxiety has decreased to a reasonable extent, another situation can be introduced.

Agoraphobia

With agoraphobics two major variants of exposure in vivo can be distinguished: (1) self-controlled exposure in vivo and (2) prolonged exposure in vivo. With *self-controlled exposure in vivo*, patients must confront the feared situation (e.g., walking on the street) until they feel tense. Then they are allowed to return. Although patients are allowed to avoid the phobic situation, they have to practice again and again until the 90-minute session is over. The instructions that patients receive are depicted in Table 3-2.

With *prolonged exposure in vivo*, patients are asked to walk outside until anxiety declines. They thus are not allowed to return when feeling anxious but must stay there until they feel better. Other situa-

Table 3-2 Instructions for the Self-Observation Procedure

When you are troubled by fear, the best treatment is to practice in those situations, in which the fear occurs. When you practice *systematically* and *persistently*, you will experience a decrease of your fear. For those people who are fearful of going into the street alone, the treatment procedure is as follows:

1. Each treatment session takes 90 minutes of your time. It is very important that you stick to these times. It is necessary to choose these times when you have nothing else to do and when you are at home alone. During treatment hours you are therefore not allowed to receive any guests.

2. You will have to practice 90 minutes *in one stretch*. So you *cannot* practice 30 minutes in the morning and then do the rest in the afternoon: in that case it is very likely your fear will increase rather than decrease. When you are tired of walking, you may, of course, rest for a few minutes.

3. You go into the street alone, and we start walking until you feel uncomfortable or tense. Then you return to your home immediately. (Taking dogs and bicycles with you is not permitted.)

4. Note the time that you are out on the street. Take a special notebook in which you write down this period of time.

5. After this you go outside again. Again you walk until you become tense or anxious. Then you return to your home immediately, and as before you write down the time that you have spent out on the street.

6. You continue practicing until 90 minutes have passed by.

7. Copy down the times you have scored during the last three practice sessions on a special form. Put the form in an envelope and send it to us that same day. We then check how you are coming along. Postage is free.

8. It is very important writing down the times you have scored. This way you can see for yourself how much you progress. Research has shown that people who write down their times improve more than people who do not.

9. You are supposed to try to enlarge the distance you walk away from your house. Therefore, you are not allowed to walk in circles. You are not allowed to do any shopping or any talking to friends and acquaintances. Your therapist will make an agreement with you on which route to take.

10. *Progress will not always continue at the same pace.* You should not let yourself be discouraged by this fact. Some people might notice an initial fast progress and later on a deterioration. Usually this is only a temporary problem. You might feel better on one day than the other. Still, you have to continue to practice.

From Emmelkamp, P. M. G. In vivo treatment of agoraphobia. In D. Chambless & A. Goldstein (Eds.), *Agoraphobia: Multiple perspectives on theory and treatment.* New York: Wiley, 1982, p. 53. With permission.

tions that are included in the treatment sessions are shopping in department stores and supermarkets and riding in buses.

It is important to determine the exact stimulus that produces fear in a patient. Although most agoraphobics are afraid of crowds, other situations that are feared differ from patient to patient. One patient is afraid of quiet alleys outside the town center, another of walking past water, and another of unfamiliar places. Most patients are afraid to be in places where they cannot take a bus or taxi to flee home in case of an "emergency."

The therapist is less and less frequently present during exposure in vivo periods. The reason for less involvement of the therapist during actual practice is to make the in vivo practice more difficult for the patients. Knowing that a therapist is nearby prevents actual exposure to distressing situations (i.e., being alone) for a substantial number of agoraphobics.

The treatment of agoraphobia by exposure in vivo procedures is illustrated in case study 6.

Social Anxiety

Socially anxious patients are often unsystematically exposed to those daily life situations that they fear, but this does not lead to improvement. A systematic and prolonged exposure in real-life situations is difficult to arrange.

Group treatment offers an excellent opportunity for socially anxious patients to confront their feared situations in the group. For example, patients who are afraid of blushing have to sit in front of others while wearing an open blouse until anxiety dissipates. Others who fear that their hands may tremble have to write on the blackboard and serve tea to the group. Or to give another example, patients who fear that they might stutter (but in fact rarely do) have to give a speech in front of the group.

Actual expore in vivo in "town" often forms part of the treatment of socially anxious patients. Patient and therapist go to shops, restaurants, and other public places where the patient must perform a number of difficult tasks. Examples of exposure tasks in the treatment of a socially anxious agoraphobic are discussed in Case Study 6.

Usually, anxiety does not dissipate during one task because of its short duration; therefore, patients must practice various tasks of the same sort and of the same subjective anxiety level without any break until they feel better.

Exposure in vivo procedures with agoraphobia and simple phobias are generally effective; however, the effects of exposure in vivo on social anxiety is less clear. Often, other procedures must be included in the treatment of social anxiety. For example, when social anxiety is due to social skill deficits, treatment should involve social skills training. Alternatively, when social anxiety is the result of irrational beliefs, cognitive procedures may be included.

Obsessive-Compulsive Disorder

The application of exposure in vivo in the case of compulsions is described with the help of an illustration.

CASE STUDY 3

Ronald is a 38-year-old man who describes his complaints as a lack of confidence, which means that he must check all kinds of things, like checking to see whether he has turned nuts tight (he is a mechanic), whether doors are closed, whether the gas is turned off, whether packets he has thrown away are really empty, and whether he has remembered the right time for an appointment. When he cannot check these things, he becomes very tense. His uncertainty decreases by checking a number of times (10 times) or by asking his wife for reassurance: "Has the gas been turned off?" "Do I have to go to the dentist at half past nine tomorrow?" His wife takes an increasing amount of responsibility in order not to be bothered any longer. She makes his appointments, locks up everything at night, repairs plug sockets, and accompanies him everywhere to reassure him and avoid his checking.

Because of these compulsions, the patient was forced to give up his job and now lives socially isolated and does not do anything at home. From the functional analysis, it appears that there are more problems (e.g., social anxiety), but here only the treatment of the compulsions by exposure in vivo and response prevention is discussed.

Before the actual treatment begins, the *treatment rationale* is explained to Ronald. In a number of situations Ronald experiences anxiety and becomes uncertain ("Did I do it right?"). To get rid of this anxiety he checks to see whether he has done it right, remembered it right, and so on. As a result of such checking, the anxiety and/or uncertainty is reduced temporarily. Because of the anxiety reduction, checking is maintained. By means of checking he does not resolve his uncertainty. On the contrary, in the long run he will need to check even more, and even more minutely to reduce his anxiety to some degree. Ronald has to learn by exposing himself to situations that provoke anxiety and uncertainty (e.g., closing doors, throwing away packets, tightening screws) without checking (response prevention) that in the long run his anxiety and uncertainty will decrease and with it the urges to perform rituals.

Subsequently, a detailed inventory is drawn up of situations that provoke anxiety and lead to checking. This is a continuous process. During treatment, other situations, which at first were "too normal" or "too embarrassing" to be mentioned, can be added to the list. All listed situations are written down on note-cards and scored by Ronald by means of an anxiety bar (range 0–100). Subsequently, a hierarchy is constructed, ranging from easy to difficult assignments. During treatment it may happen that situations appear to be more or less anxiety-provoking than when scored at first. Changes can be made in the hierarchy. Table 3-3 presents a number of assignments from the hierarchy used in Ronald's case. The total hierarchy consisted of about 50 items.

Exposure and response prevention sessions will take two hours and will take place at Ronald's house twice a week, in the presence of the therapist. During those two-hour sessions Ronald carries out the assignments that are written down on the note cards one by one, going from easy to difficult without performing his checking rituals. The therapist takes care that Ronald remains in a situation until anxiety has decreased. Afterward, Ronald is told to carry out the assignments practised henceforth without checking. This is particularly

Table 3-3 Examples of Hierarchy Items Used in the
Treatment of Checking Compulsions

Item	Anxiety
1. Connect the waterhose to the tap, turn tight in one time, do not ask if it's tight, and do not check.	10
2. Take last cigarette from packet and throw packet away immediately, without checking to see if it is really empty.	10
3. Walk *closely* past the gas cooker, but do not look to see if it is turned off, and do not ask spouse to check.	15
4. Throw away old newspapers; check once, and no more.	20
5. Open envelope, take the letter out of the envelope, throw away envelope immediately, and do not check to see if it is really empty.	20
6. Drive car into garage, switch off the headlights in one go, get out, and do not look at lights anymore; lock garage door in one go, do not check, and leave immediately.	20
7. Fill in a check, do not check further, and mail it.	25
8. Turn off hot-water tap, do not turn it off tightly, do not check, and do not ask spouse to check.	30
9. Change a bulb, turning it until tight; do not check, and do not ask spouse to check.	30
10. Lock up car by pushing down the locks on the inside; close the door, check only once, and walk away.	30
11. Make an appointment with the therapist; do not check, and do not ask spouse to check—write down in memo book yourself.	40
12. Get money from bank, count it only when the clerk hands it over to you, then put it in your wallet, put the wallet in trouser pocket, and do not check of it is still there, on the way home.	40
13. Mend leather washer, turn it tight once, and do not check but leave at once.	40
14. Lock front door; do not check to see if it is locked, and do not ask spouse to check.	50
15. Fix plug socket to wall at home, turn it tight once, do not check, and do not ask spouse to check.	60
16. Close children's bedroom window, do not check, and do not ask wife to check.	60
17. Light the gas cooker and turn it off; do not look at it anymore, but leave at once, and do not ask wife to check.	60
18. Change tire, turn nuts tight following the instructions; do not check anymore, and do not ask somebody else to check.	80
19. Repair gas heater: unscrew, repair, screw tight in one go; but *not too tight*; do not check, and do not ask spouse to check.	90
20. Change tire of therapist's car, and do not check.	100

important because Ronald's urge to check is less strong when the therapist is present than when he must do it by himself. "When the therapist is present, I am not responsible."

Ronald's wife is involved in the treatment. She is present when the rationale is explained. She is told not to check the heirarchy items practiced any more and no longer to reassure her husband.

In many situations Ronald does not know what "normal" behavior is. In such cases he is instructed by his wife or the therapist.

It is important to take care that the exposure exercises do not become substitutes for checking and have an antitherapeutic effect. It is wrong, therefore, to repeat an exercise such as "closing the garage door once without checking" several times in one and the same session. In carrying out the exercise for the second time the patient, in fact, checks to see whether he or she has done it right the first time. It is, of course, possible to give such task as a homework assignment or to practice it once again during another therapy session.

Homework assignments are discussed at the end of each session. In the case of Ronald, for instance, these consist of a repetition of a number of assignments that Ronald has practiced together with the therapist during a therapy session. Furthermore, he is given assignments that could not be easily practiced in the presense of the therapist (e.g., closing the door once without checking just before going to bed). Before each exposure session, homework is discussed; situations that still presented problems are practiced during that session once again. In the case of Ronald, the total hierarchy, which consisted of 50 assignments, was successfully finished in eight sessions.

It often is possible to give the entire treatment in the form of homework assignments. In that case it is important that patients fully understand the rationale, are given *exact* assignments, practice their assignments at fixed times (for two uninterrupted hours), and frequently (after one or two practice sessions) discuss their homework with their therapists and are given new assignments.

Compulsions are often accompanied by obsessions. In a number of cases the obsessions disappear "spontaneously" as a result of exposure in vivo and response prevention. In other cases obsessions must be attended to separately, such as by means of prolonged exposure in imagination.

Exposure in Imagination

In a number of cases exposure in vivo is not possible or practicable and—if an exposure program is chosen—exposure must be in imagination.

CASE STUDY 4

Suzanne is a 27-year-old female suffering from fear of dying. She is subject to obsessions in which she sees herself dying. This happens several times a day. Cue selection also plays an essential part here before beginning the actual exposure. Part of the cue selection is given below.

Therapist: Can you describe what is going on with you at that moment?

Client: Well, I begin to get hot in my head and so I think I have a tumor.

T: What happens next?

C: Well, I become anxious and say "Oh, God, I feel odd" and than I see that it has all ended.

T: What do you see exactly?

C: Well, for example, that I'm running to my neighbor—she's a nurse—to call a doctor and then all of a sudden . . . I'm gone.

T: And then?

C: Well, I'm dead and the neighbor phones David (her husband) and he tells my parents and then they say: "So sudden, she was so young."

T: You see all that before you?

C: Yes, it is just like in a film.

T: And then what happens?

C: I don't know.

T: Try to concentrate; go ahead and close your eyes. Imagine you're dying . . .

C: (she closes her eyes)

T: Tell me what you see.

C: Well . . . I'm dying, and . . . the funeral . . . and then they see my house isn't tidy.

T: Who sees this?

C: Martha and Iris (sisters-in-law).

T: Keep your eyes closed. How does it continue?

C: Well, later on they tell the family, they say: "That Suzanne sure had a mess in her cupboards."

Further questioning yielded the following information: the patient is afraid of illnesses that lead to a sudden death (e.g., cerebral hemorrhage, tumor, heart attack). Because of this she also has body sensations (e.g., hot head, stifling, shortness of breath, a burning pain in chest and arms). Death is always sudden (no long illnesses), and she is terrified of her housekeeping being criticized after her death. She visualized the funeral vividly.

It is important to include all these cues in the scenes to be used during prolonged exposure in imagination. Following is a scene used during the treatment:

> Imagine you're at home, the weather is fine, but you don't feel well. You have a headache and you think: "I'd better take an aspirin to make it go away." You lie down in bed but it doesn't pass. It is a very strange feeling, a different kind of headache. You get up . . . you feel dizzy, warm in your

head and then you think—if this only turns out allright—you feel yet stranger, can no longer tell where you are . . . you have to go to the neighbor . . . you think you're having a seizure . . . she has to phone the doctor . . . you ring the neighbor's bell—she opens the door: "What's the matter with you" she asks. But you can no longer say anything—you fall down, just like that . . . and then you feel that you are going to die . . . then it is over . . . you're dead . . . on the neighbor's step. David dashes home . . . your parents as well. They do not understand: "How is this possible, she is only 27?" Your mother is crying, your father is trying to console her—you can never speak to them again, never go out with them—you are dead. Then there's the funeral—you are lying in your coffin . . . at the front of the church. . . . Everybody is there . . . the whole family . . . your friends . . . and then the reverend says that is is so incomprehensible that a such a young woman is snatched away in the prime of her life, and the people cry—then they go to the grave-yard . . . you are lying in your coffin in the grave . . . slowly the coffin is lowered—your mother is crying—David is crying—and then for the last time they wish you goodbye—then they leave . . . they leave you behind in the graveyard.

After the funeral Iris and Martha go to your house to prepare dinner for the family. Iris opens the kitchen cupboards and says to Martha: "What a mess, just look at that, she had little to do and still the place is a mess." They tell the family what mess the place is in. . . . Iris wipes her fingers across the windowsill, sees all the dog's hairs on the floor, and shows the others . . . that you could be so untidy.

It is important to correspond to patients' factual thought in these scenes and not to exaggerate. The best way to present the scenes is in a matter-of-face tone. Dramatization usually leads to ridicule and offers an opportunity for cognitive avoidance: "This is not real—this is not how it happens in real life." The recording of these scenes is not advised, because such a method of presenting a situation generally has little effect.

The therapist is constantly on the look out for outward signs of anxiety to discover whether certain items especially evoke anxiety. Such an item can then be offered repeatedly until it no longer evokes anxiety. With exposure in imagination, too, it is handy to score patients' subjective anxiety levels after each scene. Care must be taken, however, that no breaks are introduced in the actual exposure. Such breaks obstruct habituation. For the same reason, it is not sensible to ask for further information during an exposure session. This should be done before or after the exposure session. Duration of exposure sessions depends on whether anxiety has diminished; therefore, there are no general rules to be given. After 1½ hours, however, it becomes impossible for most people to continue concentrating on scenes. It is advisable not to introduce new material or variations at the end of an exposure

Table 3-4 Homework: Imaginal Exposure Sessions

Location of Exposure	Procedure
In Therapist's Office	1. Therapist guides patient
	2. Patient aloud—therapist present
	3. Patient subvocal—therapist present
	4. Patient alone—therapist absent for prolonged periods
At Home	5. Partner present
	6. One hour before partner arrives
	7. Partner absent the whole day

session. Chances are that little time will remain for reducing the anxiety. Such a mistake was made with Suzanne during the second exposure session. The anxiety had decreased to a reasonable extent when after 45 minutes the therapist changed the presentation of scenes in such a way that the client had to describe the scenes herself. As a result of this variation, the anxiety level increased again, and unfortunately there was not enough time left to reduce the anxiety. This caused the client to suffer some days of anxiety and the therapist to feel guilty about it.

Variation of scenes is necessary to prevent patients from habituating to the text instead of to the situation. When patients have difficulty in identifying themselves with their roles, it helps to have the patient describe the scenes aloud. The therapist should pay attention to subtle avoidance behavior. In the example mentioned above (Suzanne) the patient kept referring to *it* when in fact she was referring to herself or the coffin. The therapist must correct this, such as by asking "Who is lying in the coffin?" After some time—if exposure sessions have been successful—the patient may be given exposure for homework. The patient must make time, once a day for at least one hour, to go through the scenes until anxiety has decreased. If the patient cannot do this (too threatening) alone at home, it may help to use successive approximation to achieve this. An example of such a program is given in Table 3-4.

Anxiety Management

This heading covers a number of techniques that should enable a patient to control the anxiety. Import elements of anxiety management are *relaxation* and *self-statements*.

Coping Relaxation

Coping relaxation procedures emphasize acquisition and application of relaxation as an anxiety management skill. Patients are trained to recognize the physiological cues of tension and to apply relaxation whenever tension is perceived. An element that these relaxation procedures have in common is that patients learn active coping skills that they can apply in a variety of anxiety-arousing situations in daily life. When avoidance is involved, application of relaxation in real-life situations may promote exposure in vivo. Furthermore, relaxation as a coping skill may also be useful to patients with generalized anxiety and panic attacks (Jannoun, Oppenheimer, & Gelder, 1982).

Self-Statements. With *self-instructional training* (Meichenbaum, 1975), patients are instructed to substitute positive coping self-statements for the anxiety engendering self-statements. In *systematic rational restructuring*, patients are instructed to modify their internal sentences. A heirarchy of increasingly more anxiety arousing situations is constructed. Patients have to imagine these situations and reevaluate their anxiety-producing self-statements rationally. Successful coping determines progression to the next item of the heirarchy.

CASE STUDY 5

Shirley is a young woman with recurrent panic attacks in social-evaluative situations. As a first step, Shirley was taught relaxation to cope with the anxiety in the real life situations, but this was not very successful. Although she was quite able to relax in the consulting room and at home, she was unable to do so in social-evaluative situations. To deal with her anxiety in these situations, a hierarchy was constructed. Each item of the hierarchy is followed by the coping self-statements that Shirley used to handle her anxiety. Shirley imagined each item presented by the therapist and attempted to control her anxiety by means of the productive self-statements. The hierarchy (consisting of 12 items) was successfully finished in four sessions. Part of the hierarchy and the coping self-statements are presented in Table 3-5.

The content of coping self-statements should be productive in reducing the anxiety level. Although it is preferable to use "rational" alternatives, this is not required. If "rational" self-statements fail to reduce anxiety whereas less rational self-statements are quite productive in the management of anxiety, the latter are to be preferred. It should be noted that anxiety management is not similar to rational emotive therapy, where the emphasis is on *insight* into the irrational beliefs presumed to underlie the problem. Anxiety management is more "eclectic" in that the therapist chooses in a cafeterialike manner coping stratigies that help this particular patient.

When patients are able to control their anxiety in imagination by means of coping self-statements, they are assigned to look for similar situations in real life and to control their anxiety by such self-statements.

Table 3-5   Examples of Items from Hierarchy of Social
Situations and Coping Self-Statements

1. You are at a meeting and do not have to contribute to the discussion:
    O.K., you feel the anxiety, but what on earth can happen, this can't go wrong.
    You can cope with the anxiety: mind your muscles, breathe calmly. You see,
    you're quite able to follow the meeting.

2. You are at a meeting and want to ask a question:
    You will be able to ask a question if only you breathe calmly; try to relax. And
    pay attention to what the others say. It's more important that they understand
    the question than how you formulate it.

3. You visit a couple of friends and want to tell a story:
    Think only about the beginning, don't try to think about the whole story. Once
    begun, the rest will come by itself. There is no reason to panic because you
    feel anxious; try to breathe calmly.

4. A colleague has his birthday. You and 15 colleagues are sitting in a circle. Atten-
    tion is focused on you in a rather devisive way:
    It's no disaster if you blush. You don't depend on how you come across. Oh,
    then you feel that tension and there you are blushing—so what if they notice.
    It just shows you're not such a tough person. Blush! And stare back at them.
    The tension will lessen.

5. At recorder lessons you have to play something:
    Try to play in a relaxed way. It doesn't have to be perfect. Concentrate on the
    music and try to relax.

6. When visiting some friends, you have to read something out loud:
    You can do it, just pay attention to the sentence that follows. Concentrate on
    the contents. You can cope with the tension. Pay attention to your breathing:
    very calmly, breathe out deeply and relax.

With anxiety management procedures, patients must not forcefully try to avoid anxiety. When it comes to relaxation, it is important for a patient not to nourish unreal hopes of its effect in actual situations. Even if patients are able to relax in the therapist's office and at home, it does not immediately follow that they are able to attain the same degree of relaxation in anxiety-provoking situations. Too high expectations may lead to failure and may result in dropping out of treatment.

It is important to note that the effects of anxiety management procedures with clinical patients are limited. In a recent review on the effects of anxiety management procedures on phobic and obsessive-compulsive patients (Emmelkamp, 1982a), it was concluded that these procedures were generally less effective than exposure in vivo. Ramm, Marks, Yüksel, and Stern (1981) found some effects of self-instructional training on anxious patients, but these authors noted that training patients to emit negative (i.e., anxiety inducing) self-statements had almost similar effects.

In summary, anxiety-management procedures must not be applied to phobic patients without due consideration. When it is difficult to

Table 3-6   Anxiety and Avoidance Scales (0–8)

Situations	Anxiety	Avoidance
Walking in the street, alone	4	7
Visiting a department store, alone	4	8
Traveling by train, alone	4	5
Attending a cinema, alone	3	4
Waiting (in shops) alone	4	6

realize exposure in vivo, however, they may be of some use. Further-more, anxiety management procedures may have some effect on pa-tients with panic attacks and generalized anxiety. It should be stressed that, however, especially with this latter category of patient a func-tional analysis might reveal that other approaches are indicated.

COURSE OF THERAPEUTIC INTERVENTION

CASY STUDY 6

John is a 20-year-old male nurse with both agoraphobic and social anxiety complaints. For a year now he has been afraid to do all kinds of things alone, such as walking in the street, traveling by bus or train, shopping and waiting, and so on. He lives with a couple of friends who have to accompany him everywhere. When he visits someone and becomes anxious, his friends have to take him home. Sometimes he is able to go out by bike. John has been suf-fering from social anxiety for a long time. He is afraid of talking in groups, and in talks à deux he often "closes up." In therapy sessions he does not tell very much of his own accord, either. It is difficult for him to assert himself, and he cannot bear criticism. John formulated his *treatment goal* as follows: "I want to be able to manage things on my own, to go everywhere alone, to go out shopping on my own."

Clinical Assessment

To get a more accurate idea of the degree of anxiety and avoidance in ago-raphobic situations, John scored five different situations on rating scales (Watson & Marks, 1971) that range from 0 to 8. The scoring is reported in Table 3-6. To assess the level and extent of the social anxiety, John was re-quested to fill in the Social Anxiety Scale (Willems et al., 1973), which ranges from 0 to 92. John's score was 79, which is quite high. The mean score for agoraphobics on this scale is 55. The following items are examples of situa-tions that aroused maximum anxiety: to feel beeing looked at, seem ridiculous, tell something, talk with superiors, make mistakes, pay in shops, be criticized unfavorably, and show affection toward someone.

John was asked to keep a behavioral diary; recording information such as in which situations did he become anxious, which situations did he avoid, and when did he close up. At first John failed to do it. In a discussion with the therapist, it appeared that John did not dare write down anything for fear of carrying if out in the wrong way, which he thought would disappoint his therapist. The next time John succeeded in taking down brief notes. In discussing the behavioral diary, both the therapist and John got a deeper insight into how the problems functioned.

Therapist: Did you experience any difficult situations last week? . . . What did you write down?

John: Well, on Monday while cycling I had such a strange feeling, so unreal. . . . I had to convince myself all the time that nothing would happen. . . .

T: Let's see if we can get this somewhat clearer. . . . Where did you go?

J: Home . . . I had finished work.

T: Can you tell me about that, how did it go?

J: It was O.K., except for a boring meeting in which there was a lot of twaddle, which irritated me.

T: You were bored with all the twaddle. Did you say anything about it?

J: Yes, I proposed talking about something else, but they kept talking twaddle.

T: So, you tried to change the topic, but they ignored you?

J: No . . . someone said: "Yes, in a while."

T: Hmm . . . and you?

J: I didn't say anything anymore.

T: It annoyed you that they didn't do what you proposed . . . you felt they didn't take you seriously?

J: Yes, I didn't even wait for them but cycled home alone.

T: And then you felt unreal?

J: Yes . . . I was angry . . . felt shut out . . . maybe that had to do with why I felt so strange.

Functional Analysis and Treatment Planning

The information gathered in five interviews, a questionnaire, and a behavioral diary was used to draw up a functional analysis. John's agoraphobic complaints developed a year ago after a "spontaneous" panic attack in the street. John felt stifled, became dizzy, and felt papitations. He thought he would die and ran home. After this incident he became more and more afraid (anticipatory anxiety) of going out in the street, shops, and train alone, and avoided these situations as much as possible.

It is hypothesized that John's social anxiety, which had existed for quite some time, led to a hyperventilation attack (feeling stifled, dizziness, palpitations) in the street. The development of the complaint can be described schematically as shown in Figure 3-5.

Social Anxiety ———→ Hyperventilation ———→ Escape ———→ Anxiety Reduction

Thoughts of Street, Shops, Etc. ➔ Anticipatory Anxiety ➔ Avoidance ➔ Anxiety Reduction

Figure 3-5   Hypothesized development of the agoraphobia.

The social anxiety appeared to be caused by a lack of social skills and negative cognitions. In discussing the diary situations, John recognized that anxiety in social situations often led to anxiety in agoraphobic situations, especially that the social aspects of agoraphobic situations provoked anxiety: "In trains you have to make conversation." "At the check out counter everybody is looking at you." The social anxiety and agoraphobia were on the one hand maintained by anxiety reduction resulting from avoidance of social and agoraphobic situations, and on the other hand because John's friends accompanied him when he had to go somewhere.

Although the social anxiety appeared to play an important part in the agoraphobic complaints, it was decided first to break through the avoidance behavior in agoraphobic situations by means of exposure in vivo. Because of the avoidance of these situations, a treatment of the social anxiety was less practicable at this moment. Moreover, John felt most handicapped by the fact that he could not go anywhere alone and wanted to solve that first. It was agreed that the social anxiety would be dealt with at a later stage by means of exposure in vivo and social skills training.

Exposure in Vivo for Agoraphobic Complaints

When agoraphobic situations with respect to anxiety and avoidance were scored, John recorded a relatively low anxiety score. This led to the assumption that the therapist's most important task was to break through John's avoidance behavior, after which his anxiety in vivo would present little problem. This argued for an exposure treatment in which the therapist's role would be minimal: (i.e., self-controlled exposure in vivo).

Self-Controlled Exposure

It was agreed on to practice three times a week in 1½-hour sessions. The exercise consisted of walking in the street alone, without a bike or other aids. John was told to go out into the street and walk in a straight line from his house (or the therapist's office), along a fixed route. Before he became anxious he had to turn round and walk back the same route. At home (or at the therapist's office) he would record the time he had been out in the street. Immediately after that he was to go out again for a next attempt along the same route. He would have to repeat this procedure for 1½ hours. The first two sessions were practiced, starting from the therapist's office (therapist present) to familiarize John with the procedure. He practiced in subsequent sessions starting from his own house, without the therapist being present. The exact routes and practice time for these homework sessions had been settled during therapy sessions. After two homework sessions the practice results were discussed with the therapist. Table 3-7 gives a survey of the course of the self-controlled exposure.

In the first exposure session a quiet route was chosen to make it easier for John. Many people in the street might very well lead to greater social anxiety. In this session John did not experience any anxiety; however, he reported having "sleepwalked" the whole route (derealization). This derealization probably had the function of avoiding anxiety. During the second session John did not get so far into the street. It is likely that absence of such a "sleepwalking" feeling made the situation more real and hence more difficult. Besides, the bustle in the street made it more difficult to walk. The next three homework sessions went marvelously. John walked calmly through the streets as far as he pleased. He was so satisfied with his improvement that he succeeded in traveling by train by himself. His success in walking through the street gave him self-confidence. And this generalized to his traveling by train.

John then wanted to tackle "walking in the street" and "traveling" himself without the therapist's help. His assignment for the next period was to walk to some place everyday (e.g., to his work, to friends, to the therapist's office, or to shops).

Prolonged Exposure in Vivo.

The other important situations that John had to deal with were to buy something in a shop, a department store, or in a supermarket by himself, to stand in line and pay at the checkout counter, and to visit bars. The nature of these situations made a self-controlled exposure procedure difficult. When one waits at the checkout counter, it is difficult to turn back before becoming anxious and then have to go through the same situation again. That was the reason for choosing a prolonged exposure in vivo procedure.

During the exposure in vivo sessions of 1½ hours, John first practiced together with the therapist. Later the therapist gradually withdrew. After each session John's homework assignment was to carry out an identical prolonged exposure in vivo without the therapist being present. The therapist was present during two sessions; five sessions were done as homework.

Prolonged exposure in vivo sessions were as follows: at first a time was chosen when the shops were quiet. John and the therapist went into the first supermarket together. John bought an article, walked to the checkout counter, and paid. The therapist stood close to the counter clearly in view (then quickly off to the second supermarket, where John again bought an article and paid at the checkout counter). The therapist was now standing further away. When tne next article was bought, the therapist waited outside. Afterward, John passed the checkout counter a few times before going outside to look for the therapist.

The same procedure was practiced in bars. First the therapist and John went inside together, after which the therapist quickly left, while John left only when the anxiety had decreased. Although John had dreaded this session (anticipatory anxiety), he found it much easier than he expected. He did not

Table 3-7 Course of Self-Controlled Exposure

	Session	Place	Route	Trials	Length (minutes)	Reason for Return	Remarks
Therapist present	Session 1	Therapist's office	Quiet route; broad, open streets	1	45	Thought time was up	Unpleasant walk as if sleepwalking (derealization)
				2	35	Thought time was up	
	Session 2	Therapist's office	Busy route through town center	1	15	Prevention of anxiety	Walking is more anxious; less feeling of sleepwalking
				2	35	Prevention of anxiety	
				3	30	Time was up	
	Homework Session 1	John's home	Busy route through town center	1	55	Prevention of anxiety	Little anxiety
				2	35	Time was up	Little anxiety
Therapist absent	Homework Session 2	John's home	Busy route through town center	1	80	Time was up	Excellent; walked calmly
	Homework Session 3	John's home	Busy route through town center	1	85	Time was up	Excellent; walked calmly

become really anxious. He was given the assignment to spend one session doing shopping along the same lines for homework. It was agreed to do this at a quiet time. In the next session *busy* stores and bars were visited. John had to stand in line longer this time. He was now able to do so by himself without the therapist's assistance. This session, too, proceeded without too much anxiety. A program for four homework sessions was drawn up along the same lines.

In order to see how far the first goal of the treatment had been realized, John again scored the five situations for anxiety and avoidance (Table 3-8). Both the anxiety and avoidance had decreased, John's selfconfidence had increased. He noticed that although he still dreaded some situations, in reality he no longer became anxious. He could go wherever he pleased, and whenever he was anxious, he remained in the situation until his anxiety decreased. Then it was decided to tackle the social anxiety next.

Prolonged Exposure for Social Anxiety

The main reason for John's anxiety when dealing with people in stores, restaurants, and the street was that he was afraid of being considered foolish. That is why he avoided these situations and was afraid of saying much. In addition, he lacked a number of social skills in such situations.

To deal with his social anxiety, prolonged exposure in vivo was used. If necessary, behavioral instructions were given by the therapist or the behavior was modeled in vivo. Sessions lasted for at 1½ hours so that there would be enough time to reduce the anxiety. The following items were practiced during these sessions:

1. Walking through busy streets and asking passers-by what time it is, the way to the station, or for a light
2. Asking precedence at the checkout counter in a supermarket with the exact money
3. Forgetting the money and asking whether the articles could be put aside and collected later without having to wait in line
4. Asking for information on articles without buying them
5. Returning or exchanging an article
6. Trying on many clothes without buying any
7. Asking for information at a travel agency

The therapist was always present at the beginning of these exercises and gave John instructions on the way. When John did not know how to deal with a situation, the therapist showed him. The therapist supplied feedback on John's verbal and nonverbal behavior. John repeated the same exercise until it was performed to satisfaction and his anxiety had decreased. Only then did another exercise follow. The therapist withdrew more and more every time. Two exposure sessions were performed in this way. Furthermore, an exercise program for a homework session was made every week. In the homework sessions, difficult situations were repeated, and when they no longer evoked anxiety, new situations were added. Some examples of homework situations

Table 3-8 Anxiety and Avoidance Scales

Situations	First Rating		Second Rating		Final Rating	
	Anxiety	Avoidance	Anxiety	Avoidance	Anxiety	Avoidance
Walking in the street, alone	4	7	1	3	1	0
Visiting a department store, alone	4	8	2	4	1	1
Traveling by train, alone	4	5	3	3	0	0
Attending a cinema, alone	3	4	1	1	1	0
Waiting (in shops), alone	4	6	3	3	1	1

that John practiced alone in 1½-hour sessions include: ordering an article and canceling it, making an appointment and canceling it, asking for information by phone, saying hello clearly to all the persons in a group, calling for the waiter aloud in a bar, going through a door first, and so on.

Social Skills

The last phase of the treatment (sessions 13–25) was spent on training social skills. Although most of the avoidance behavior in social situations had been overcome, social skill deficits had not yet been dealt with systematically and thus still led to distress in interpersonal situations. Furthermore, it was felt to be necessary to deal with these social skills directly so as to prevent a relapse in the future.

Difficult situations were practiced by means of behavior rehearsal in the therapist's office. The usual sequence was as follows: (1) role-playing a situation from the diary, the aim of which was to assess John's skill deficits in that particular situation; (2) feedback on John's behavior and suggestions on how to change it; (3) modeling by the therapist of socially skillful behavior in that situation; (4) behavior rehearsal by John; and (5) feedback of the therapist and, if necessary, repetition of modeling and behavior rehearsal until John and the therapist were satisfied with his behavior. Examples of topics dealt with in the course of these sessions are to criticize and be criticized, to compliment and to be complimented, to deliver a speech, to invite friends, to enter into a conversation, and to develop listening and conversation skills.

In passing, some attention was paid to the irrational cognitions that John had (e.g., "everybody must like me"), but these were not dealt with systematically. Most of these irrational beliefs changed spontaneously as a result of the social skills and exposure in real life.

After session 25 it was decided to increase the spacing of sessions to prepare John to proceed independently from the therapist. At intervals of 2–12 weeks, another three sessions followed. At the end of the treatment the anxiety and avoidance scales were filled in (see Table 3-8). Both anxiety and avoidance had decreased considerably. John could manage on his own, and he reported an increased feeling of self-confidence in social situations.

SPECIAL PROBLEMS

Hyperventilation

Hyperventilation is often a concomitant of anxiety. During exposure patients may hyperventilate, but this usually diminishes as anxiety reduces. In a number of cases (especially with panic disorders and illness phobias), however, treatment should deal with the hyperventilation more directly. First, it is important that patients who hyperventilate are informed about the hyperventilation syndrome and the somatic manifestations. In a number of cases, just being informed about the nature of the symptoms is sufficient to let the patients relabel the somatic symptoms and the anxiety as hyperventilation. With other patients, it may be useful to provoke hyperventilation a number of times in the office to show them more directly the relationship between hyperventilation and their symptoms. Symptoms usually appear within a few minutes of provoked hyperventilation, although often to a lesser degree than when the patients are at home. With some patients we use an exposure program in order to habituate to the hyperventilation. After they can "successfully" hyperventilate in the therapist's office without the therapist being present, they are instructed to hyperventilate at home, first with a trusted person present, and then alone. Furthermore it is important that patients be taught how to control hyperventilation. Although breathing for a few minutes in a small plastic bag is a useful "emergency" measure, relaxation and breathing exercises may be necessary for long-term improvement.

Partners

Partners of patients may interfere with the treatment process, especially with some agoraphobics. In the course of treatment, some partners are resistant to change on the part of the patient. Often the patient's partner feels that he or she becomes less important to the patient when the patient becomes more independent as a result of treatment. When this occurs attempts must be made to involve the partner in the treatment.

Failures

When treatment fails, an analysis of assessment and treatment variables is warranted. Assuming that the treatment procedure has been applied according to the rules, there are at least two possibilities: (1) this technique does not work with this patient. In this case another procedure can be applied; and (2) the functional analysis was not correct. In fact, the functional analysis is a *hypothetical* construction of the patient's problem(s), and the treatment can be conceived of as an experiment to test this hypothesis. It may appear that the problem is more complex than initially appraised. For example, phobic behavior may yield additional reinforcers to the patient (such as receiving attention; not having to take job responsibilities, etc.) that were initially overlooked. A reanalysis of the problem may result in another treatment program. For a more detailed discussion of factors associated with treatment failures, the reader is referred to Foa and Emmelkamp (1983).

Drop-Out

Dropping out of treatment is another problem that may occur. Steps to minimize drop-out include a proper clinical assessment and a full explanation of the treatment rationale and the treatment requirements (including the anxiety to be experienced). Especially with prolonged exposure, patients have to be informed in advance that stopping the treatment halfway may even aggravate rather than improve the problem. In some cases it might be useful to provide a written contract that specifies what is expected from the patient and the therapist. Finally, the patient should receive information to get realistic expectations about which kind of improvements can be expected within which length of time.

Depression

Often, patients are depressed when applying for treatment of their anxiety disorder. When the depression results from the anxiety problems, treatment of the anxiety may proceed without taking special measures to deal with the depression. Then depressed mood will improve as a result of the treatment of the anxiety disorder, if successful. In other cases, depressed mood stems from other sources (e.g., marital difficulties, negative self-evaluation) that must be dealt with separately. Only in very few cases do we advise taking antidepressant medication. Again, a proper functional analysis must be made in order to decide on the appropriate treatment strategy.

Therapeutic Relationship

The therapist's attitude should be warm yet firm. Especially during the initial states of treatment, therapists should provide a climate in which patients feel trusted and have the opportunity to speak freely of problems that bother them. When a decision has been made on a specific treatment program, the therapists should be firm in holding on to this program. Discussion of other problems—how important these may be to the patient—is discouraged during exposure sessions. If discussion of these problems cannot be postponed, one can have a brief interview at the end of the exposure session. During an exposure program, the therapist should not only be interested in the achievements of patients, but give due attention to the feelings of the patients. There is some evidence that such achievement-oriented therapists come across as insensitive, which may lead to treatment failure (Emmelkamp & Van de Hout, 1983).

SUMMARY

In this chapter the clinical application of behavioral treatment procedures for anxiety disorders was described. The importance of a functional behavioral analysis was stressed, an issue that is neglected in the research literature on anxiety disorders. The treatment techniques have been illustrated by case descriptions. Most attention was devoted to exposure in vivo techniques, since these have been shown to be the most effective. Other procedures such as imaginal exposure and anxiety management techniques were also described, but it has to be noted that the clinical effects of the latter procedures are less well understood. In a lengthy case description the treatment of a socially anxious agoraphobic has been described. Treatment involved exposure in vivo to agoraphobic and social situations and social skills training.

Finally, some problems were discussed, including hyperventilation, marital complication, failures, drop-outs, depression, and the therapist's attitude.

REFERENCES

Arrindell, W., Emmelkamp, P. M. G., & van de Ende, J. A psychometric evaluation of fear questionnaires (Manuscript in preparation).

Cooper, J. The Leyton Obsessional Inventory. *Psychological Medicine*, 1970, *1*, 48–64.

Emmelkamp, P. M. G. *Phobic and obsessive-compulsive disorders: Theory, research and practice.* New York: Plenum Press, 1982. (a)

Emmelkamp, P. M. G. In vivo treatment of agoraphobia. In D. Chambless & A. Goldstein (Eds.), *Agoraphobia: Multiple perspectives on theory and treatment.* New York: Wiley, 1982. (b)

Emmelkamp, P. M. G. & van de Hout, A. Failure in treating agoraphobia. In E. B. Foa & P. M. G. Emmelkamp (Eds.), *Failures in behavior therapy.* New York: Wiley, 1983.

Foa, E. B., & Emmelkamp, P. M. G. *Failures in behavior therapy.* New York: Wiley, 1983.

Joannoun, L., Oppenheimer, C., & Gelder, M. A self-help treatment program for anxiety state patients. *Behavior Therapy*, 1982, *13*, 103–111.

Meichenbaum, D. H. Self instructional methods. In F. H. Kanfer & A. P. Goldstein (Eds.), *Helping people change.* New York: Pergamon, 1975.

Marks, I. M. *Fears and phobias.* New York: Academic Press, 1969.

Marks, I. M., & Mathews, A. M. Brief standard self-rating for phobic patients. *Behavior Research and Therapy*, 1979, *17*, 263–267.

Rachman, S. J., & Hodgson, R. J. *Obsessions and compulsions.* Englewood Cliffs, N.J.: Prentic Hall, 1980.

Ramm, E., Marks, I. M., Yüksel, S., & Stern, R. S. Anxiety management training for anxiety states: Positive compared with negative self-statements. *British Journal of Psychiatry*, 1981, *140*, 367–373.

Watson, D., & Friend, R. Measurement of social-evaluative anxiety. *Journal of Consulting and Clinical Psychology*, 1969, *33*, 448–457.

Watson, J. P., & Marks, I. M. Relevant and irrelevant fear in flooding—crossover study of phobic patients. *Behavior Therapy*, 1971, *2*, 275–293.

Willems, L. F. M., Tuender-de Hann, H. A., & Defares, P. B. Een schaal om sociale angst te meten. *Nederlands Tijdschrift voor de Psychologie*, 1973, *28*, 415–422.

Wolpe, J. & Lang, P. J. A fear survey schedule for use in behavior therapy. *Behavior Research and Therapy*, 1964, *2*, 27–30.

4

Depression

Peter M. Lewinsohn, Linda Terri, and David Wasserman

DEPRESSION, by itself or in combination with other problems, is a very common mental disorder. Consequently, depressed clients constitute a large proportion of any clinician's case load. A particularly debilitating disorder, depression affects (and is, in turn, affected by) the daily functioning of the individual: impairing work performance, damaging social interaction, hampering family relationships, and undermining the individual's feeling of self-worth.

The *Diagnostic and Statistical Manual* of the American Psychiatric Association **DSM-III;** 1980) distinguishes among three subtypes of pure (unipolar) depression: chronic (dysthymic), episodic (major), and atypical; and three subtypes of mixed (bipolar) depression: bipolar, cyclothymic, and atypical bipolar.*

---

*The distinction between the "bipolar" disorders (bipolar, cyclothymic, atypical bipolar) and "unipolar" disorders (major, dysthymic and atypical depression) is a crucial one (Perris, 1982). There is ample evidence that a biochemical imbalance accounts for the emotional lability of individuals with bipolar disorders. Furthermore, the concordance rates for the bipolar disorders are considerably higher than for the unipolar disorders. Thus a much higher probability of genetic predisposition is indicated. The treatment of choice of bipolar disorders is lithium. Although the specific action of this drug is still unknown, research indicates that individuals with a history of mania or hypomania respond quite favorably to lithium. Psychotherapy without proper pharmacotherapy is contraindicated. In this chapter we deal only with the treatment of unipolar depression.

The primary symptom of unipolar depressive disorder is dysphoric mood. The presence of dysphoric mood, however, is not sufficient to merit a *diagnosis* of depression. A specific pattern of other sypmtoms must be present with sufficient intensity and duration for the patient to meet the *DSM-III* criteria (which are shown in Table 4-1) for major, dysthymic, or atypical depression. Depression, as a clinical syndrome, therefore, is a multifaceted pattern of symptoms and complaints with individual patients differing in the degree to which they manifest specific components of the depression syndrome.

Although most prevalent in women and in young adults, depression is a problem for people of all ages and socioeconomic strata. In its most severe form, depression can lead to such intense feelings of hopelessness and despair that suicide becomes a serious consideration. In fact, previous feelings of depression are reported by a majority of those attempting or successfully completing suicide (Beck, 1967).

In spite of its clinical importance, the systematic investigation of the treatment of depression within a behavioral framework is less than 25 years old. The last decade, however, has witnessed a virtual explosion of interest and several major reviews have been published (e.g., Blaney, 1977; Lewinsohn, Teri, & Hoberman, in press; Rehm & Kornblith, 1979; Rush & Beck, 1978). The first behaviorally oriented single-case studies began to appear in the literature during the 1960s (e.g., Burgess, 1969; Lazarus, 1968; Lewinsohn & Atwood, 1969; Stuart, 1967). Since then, numerous well-designed treatment outcome studies with large samples have been reported (e.g., Bellack & Hersen, 1978; Fuchs & Rehm, 1977; Rush, Beck, Kovacs, & Hollon, 1977; Zeiss, Lewinsohn, & Muñoz, 1979).

Treatments derived from "behavioral" positions have been aimed at the improvement of social skills (e.g., Hersen, Bellack, & Himmelhoch, 1980; Sanchez, Lewinsohn, & Larson, 1980; Teri & Leitenberg, 1979), increasing pleasant activities and time management skills (Lewinsohn, 1976), and general problem solving skills (McLean, 1976). Treatments derived from "cognitive" positions have been aimed at depressive thought processes (e.g., Beck, Rush, Shaw, & Emery, 1979; Fuchs & Rehm, 1977).

Stimulated by the increasing evidence that a variety of short-term behavioral and cognitive therapies are effective in ameliorating unipolar depression, this prolific activity has resulted in an increased acceptance of such approaches among clinicians. These encouraging results, however, also present a challenge to the practitioner to sift through and choose from among these promising therapeutic approaches.

In the present chapter we assume that an ideal treatment approach

Table 4-1 Diagnostic Criteria for Pure and
Mixed Depressions

Pure depressions

Episodic/major depressive disorder
Symptoms
Dysphoria
At least *four* of the following: appetite change; sleep difficulties; psychomotor agitation or retardation; loss of pleasure or interest; loss of energy/fatigue; feelings of worthlessness, self-reproach or guilt; concentration difficulties; recurrent thoughts of death or suicide
Duration: every day for at least two weeks
Exclusion criteria: mood-incongruent delusions or hallucinations; bizarre behavior; schizophrenia, schizophreniform disorder; paranoid disorder; organic mental disorder

Chronic/minor depression
Symptoms
Depressed mood
At least *three* of the following: sleep difficulties; low energy level or chronic tiredness; feelings of inadequacy; loss of self-esteem or self-deprecation; decreased effectiveness or productivity; decreased attention or concentration; social withdrawal; loss of interest or enjoyment; irritability or excessive anger; anhedonia; pessimism; tearfulness or crying; recurrent thoughts of death or suicide
Duration: most or all of the time during the past two years
Exclusion criteria: psychotic features

Atypical
Symptoms: same as major or dysthymic depression
Duration: variable
Exclusion criteria: adjustment disorder

Mixed depressions

Bipolar disorder—depressed/mixed
Symptoms
Same as major depressive disorder
Mania
Elevated, expansive, or irritable mood
At least three of the following: increased activity; talkative; flight of ideas or racing thoughts; inflated self-esteem; decreased need for sleep; distractibility; excessive activity without awareness of negative consequences
Duration: most of the time during at least one week
Exclusion criteria: same as major depressive disorder

Cyclothymic
Symptoms
Depressive periods with
Depressed mood
At least three of the following: sleep difficulties; low energy or chronic fatigue; feelings of inadequacy; decreased effectiveness or productivity; decreased concentration; social withdrawal; loss of interest of pleasure in sex; restricted activities or guilt over past activities; feeling slowed down; less talkative than usual; pessimism; tearfulness or crying

(continued)

Table 4-1 (continued)

> *Hyponamic periods* with
> Elevated, expansive or irritable mood
> At least three of the following: decreased need for sleep; more energy than usual; increased productivity; unusually creative thinking; extreme gregariousness; hypersexuality; excessive activity without awareness of negative consequences; physical restlessness; more talkative than usual; over-optimistic; inappropriate laughing, joking, or punning
> *Duration:* two years; depressive and hypomanic periods may be separated by intervals of normal mood, may be intermixed or may be alternate
> *Exclusion criteria:* psychotic features; attributable to other mental disorders
> Atypical
> *Symptoms:* same as bipolar disorder (depressed/mixed) or cyclothymic disorder
> *Duration:* variable
> *Exclusion criteria:* attributable to other mental disorders

Adapted from *Diagnostic and Statistical Manual (DSM-III)* of the American Psychiatric Association, 1980.

to unipolar depression: (1) includes training in specific skills that are useful to depressed individuals in the management of their daily lives; (2) combines the specific components or techniques that have been shown to be successful and useful to depressed individuals; and (3) organizes these techniques in such a way that their implementation in clinical practice is facilitated. The Coping with Depression Course approach presented in this chapter was designed to include interventions that address the specific target behaviors that have been shown to be problematic for depressed individuals. The approach is called a "Coping with Depression Course" because it teaches people techniques and strategies to cope with the problems that are assumed to be related to their depression. It is a highly structured, time-limited, skill training program that makes use of a text entitled *Control your depression* (Lewinsohn, Muñoz, Youngren, & Zeiss, 1978), a participant workbook (Brown & Lewinsohn, 1979) and an instructor's manual (Lewinsohn, Antonuccio, Steinmetz, & Teri, 1982). The course was developed at the University of Oregon Depression Research Unit and has been evaluated there since 1979 with over 300 depressed persons. Research findings on the course have been reported elsewhere (Antonuccio, Lewinsohn, & Steinmetz, 1982; Brown & Lewinsohn, 1979; Teri & Lewinsohn, 1982).

The general rationale for the Coping with Depression Course is derived from social-learning theory (Bandura, 1977). The social-learning approach (1) focuses on the amount of maladaptive interactions between persons and environments and (2) sees these interactions as governed by the same laws of *learning and development* that influence

normal behavior. Problems or disorders are considered *learned* phenomena that influence, and are influenced by, person–environment
interactions. Alteration of these *learned maladaptive* interactions will
enable new adaptive interactions to be learned. Disorders that are
learned can thus be remedied by *new learning*.

ASSESSMENT

The goals of assessment of depressed patients are threefold (Lewinsohn & Lee, 1981): assessment should (1) lead to correct and early
differential diagnosis, (2) result in the formulation of a *functional diagnosis* and the *indentification of targets for intervention*, and (3)
facilitate evaluation by providing ongoing information regarding treatment effectiveness. Periodic assessment of changes in depression level
and in functionally related problem behaviors will enable therapists
to evaluate the effectiveness of their treatment plans.

Differential Diagnosis

The clinician must determine whether depression is *the*, or at least
a, problem for the individual. Other mental disorders, especially the
bipolar disorders, should be ruled out. If a history of manic or hypo-
manic episodes is revealed, lithium therapy should be considered. In
addition, it must be ascertained whether an existing medical disorder,
or medications prescribed for a medical disorder, might be responsible for the depression. It is now well established that depressive
symptoms can be induced by a variety of physical conditions and
pharmacological agents. Especially with elderly patients, a physical
examination and a good medical history are necessary in order to rule
out depression secondary to a medical condition.

The most intensive and detailed method for arriving at a diagnosis
of depression is afforded by a structured clinical interview in conjunction with a reliable diagnostic system. The Schedule for Affective Disorders and Schizophrenia [(SADS) (Endicott & Spitzer, 1978)], used
with either the Research Diagnostic Criteria [(RDC) (Spitzer, Endicott,
& Robins, 1978)] or *DSM-III* provides an effective method. The SADS
is a two-hour structured interview that systematically assesses a wide
variety of symptoms to facilitate diagnostic classification. It covers a
range of psychiatric disorders, with primary emphasis on unipolar
depressive, bipolar, schizophrenic, and schizoaffective disorders. The
SADS is organized to focus on differential diagnosis; the progression
of items and probes allows the examiner to sequentially rule in, or
rule out, specific diagnoses. The RDC and *DSM-III* are elaborate clas-

sification systems that have been designed for research and clinical use, respectively. The highly reliable RDC describes 10 nonmutually exclusive subtypes of depression (although at this time the subtypes have not been shown to have implications for treatment). Although clinicians are not likely to use the complete SADS or RDC for everyday assessment purposes, the instruments can alert the clinician to probes that are important in evaluating depressed patients.

A less sophisticated but also less time-consuming method to assess the presence and severity of depressive symptoms involves ratings of specific symptoms or symptom clusters by the clinician. Several well-known rating scales are available, including the Feelings and Concerns Checklist (Grinker et al., 1961), the Hamilton Rating Scale for Depression (Hamilton, 1960; 1967) and the Raskin Depression Scales (Raskin, Schulterbrandt, Reatig, Cook, & Odle, 1974). All these scales reliably discriminate depressed from nondepressed individuals. Within depressed populations, they differentiate clients with varying degrees of symptom severity. Because depressed persons manifest symptoms in different combinations and with different intensities, each client will have a unique pattern of scores. Rating scales typically cover six general categories of complaints: dysphoria, reduced rate of behavior, social-interactional problems, guilt, feelings of material burden, and somatic symptoms.

Client self-report depression scales are useful as screening devices for determining whether depression is likely to be present, and if so, to what degree. If individuals obtain low scores on these scales, it is unlikely that they are depressed (Lewinsohn & Teri, 1982). High scores may indicate depression, but because of the sensitivity of the scales to transient dysphoric mood and to discomfort caused by medical illness, an in-depth interview is necessary to establish a differential diagnosis. Four widely used depression self-rating scales are the depression scale from the Minnesota Multiphasic Personality Inventory [(MMPI-D Scales) (Hathaway & McKinley, 1967)], the Zung Self-Rating Depression Scale [(SDS) (Zung, 1965)], the Beck Depression Inventory [(BDI) (Beck, Ward, Mendelson, Mock, & Erbaugh, 1961)], and the Center for Epidemiological Studies Depression Scale [(CES-D) (Radloff, 1977)]. These scales correlate significantly with each other and correlate substantially with interview ratings. The 60-item MMPI-D scale is the best known of the self-report measures for depression. The briefer Zung scale contains 20 statements, which patients rate according to how frequently they apply to them. The BDI consists of 21 items, each defining a symptom category (e.g., sadness, social withdrawal, and weight loss) rated for severity. Used in many research studies, the BDI was originally designed for assessing depressed inpatients (Beck, 1967). The

CES-D lists 20 symptoms that patients rate according to their frequency and severity. The CES-D was developed for use with community samples, and extensive normative data are available (Radloff, 1977).

Functional Diagnosis

The purpose of functional diagnosis is to identify specific aspects of person–environment interactions that are problematic for patients and presumed to be related to their depression. Together, functional diagnosis and identification of target behaviors lay the groundwork for the treatment plan. The question concerns what kind of therapeutic assistance, and how much assistance, is necessary in order to produce improvement.

The four areas of person–environment interactions most important to examine for discovering functional relationships between depressed mood and problem behaviors are (1) social-relationship problems, (2) depressive cognitions, (3) low rate of engagement in pleasant activities, and (4) high rate of occurrence of unpleasant events. Assessment instruments for identifying difficulties in each category are available and constitute important components of the assessment armamentarium for depression.

Depressed individuals, as a group, tend to have many interpersonal difficulties (Youngren & Lewinsohn, 1980). Depressed clients often state that relationships with family, friends, and co-workers have become troublesome. Social interaction may be a source of anxiety, and therefore such interactions are avoided. The Interpersonal Events Schedule (Youngren, Zeiss, & Lewinsohn, 1975) is a 160-item self-report inventory that assesses the frequency of, and subjective comfort in, interpersonal activities, as well as cognitions about those activities. There also are numerous self-report scales for specific aspects of social interaction. For example, the Assertion Inventory (Gambrill & Richey, 1975) and the Wolpe-Lazarus Assertiveness Questionnaire (Wolpe & Lazarus, 1966) focus on assertion, a common problem for depressed clients (Sanchez et al., 1980; Teri & Leitenberg, 1979).

Observations of overt behavior can be used for baselining and later for monitoring progress in specific target areas. The behaviors may be relatively common verbal and nonverbal deficits, such as low speech rate and infrequent smiling, or verbal and nonverbal excesses, such as frequent crying and complaining. Although some behaviors can be tracked in session, others are better assessed in the client's usual environments: at home, work, or school. Either the client, or (with the client's permission) significant others can be provided with a checklist for behavioral monitoring.

The role of problematic cognitions in depression has been noted by theorists such as Beck (1967), Ellis and Harper (1961), and Rehm (1976). Depressive cognitions can be categorized into (1) negative expectancies, (2) cognitive distortions, (3) irrational beliefs, (4) negative thoughts, and (5) faulty attributions of causality. Again, a variety of assessment devices exists, most of which are brief self-report inventories: the Hopelessness Scale (Beck, 1974), the Cognitive Events Schedule (Muñoz & Lewinsohn, 1976), and the Dysfunctional Attitudes Scale (Weissman & Beck, 1978).

Engagement in pleasant activities is markedly reduced in depressed individuals (Lewinsohn, 1976). Furthermore, there is a significant association between daily participation in such activities and daily mood (Grosscup & Lewinsohn, 1980). The major instrument for assessing engagement in pleasant activities is the Pleasant Events Schedule [(PES) (MacPhillamy & Lewinsohn, 1971; 1982)], a self-report inventory that asks the client to provide both frequency and enjoyment ratings for 320 activities. A client's response to the PES enables the clinician to pinpoint areas in which rate of activity or enjoyment is low. The PES has recently been published in its entirety (MacPhillamy & Lewinsohn, 1982). Teri and Lewinsohn (1982) have described a modified version for use with elderly clients.

A high rate of aversive events is also related to depression (Paykel, Myers, Dienelt, Klerman, Lindenthal, & Pepper, 1969). Research has thus far demonstrated that (1) depression is often preceded by aversive events (particularly "social exits" such as death of a spouse, divorce, and separation); (2) depressed persons are especially sensitive to aversive events, and (3) the rate of unpleasant events covaries with depressed mood. One instrument for assessing aversive events is the Unpleasant Events Schedule [(UES) (Lewinsohn & Talkington, 1979)], which, like the PES, is a 320-item self-report inventory. Clients indicate both the occurrence and impact of negative events in the past month. The UES aids the clinician in determining which life areas are the major sources of distress for the client, both objectively (in terms of frequency) and subjectively (in terms of rated aversiveness). As with the PES, a modified version for elderly individuals has been developed (Teri & Lewinsohn, 1982).

Assessment of Suicide Risk

When assessing the presence of depression, it is particularly important to evaluate the risk of suicide (Farberow, 1981). Clients should be asked if they have reached the point where life doesn't seem worth living any more. If the client's response is affirmative, it is important to determine whether he or she experiences only vague, occasional thoughts about suicide or has more concrete plans. Predictions about the probability of suicidal behavior can be made on the basis of relatively simple information (Burglass & Horton, 1974; Lettieri, 1974). Suicide is more likely if the client (1) is currently single or recently divorced; (2) has no close friends or relatives in the immediate vicinity and lives alone; (3) has problems involving the use of alcohol; (4) has been arrested and charged with a crime (excluding traffic violations) such as drunkenness, disorderly conduct, drug abuse, or a sexual offense; (5) has had previous psychiatric treatment; and (6) has omnipresent suicidal feelings and previous suicidal behavior with a high degree of lethality.

Evaluation

Any of the assessment procedures described above can play a central role in treatment evaluation—during therapy, at termination, and at follow-up. Clients' depression level and the behaviors functionally related to their depression should be periodically evaluated.

If daily monitoring of depressed mood is desired, two scales may be useful: the Depression Adjective Checklist [(DACL) (Lubin)] or a visual analogue scale (Lewinsohn et al., 1978). The DACL requires clients to endorse adjectives that describe how they are feeling. Alternate versions of the DACL exist to facilitate repeated testing, and the instrument has been shown to possess excellent psychometric properties. A simpler yet untested method for assessing depressed affect is to use a visual analogue scale, a 10-point scale that covers a continuum from "best mood" to "worst mood." Clients make one rating per day, indicating their "mood" for that day.

Clients can also monitor thoughts, behaviors, or external events considered functionally related to their depression by writing them down on an individually designed tracking sheet. If the clinician's original functional diagnosis was accurate, the events selected for monitoring should covary with daily mood ratings. If covariance is not found, a reformulation of the functional diagnosis would be indicated.

At termination, measures previously administered at intake can be given again. A structured interview, symptom ratings by the clinician, self-report depression scales, and behavioral observations by the client or another person would all yield important information. Follow-up appointments, from one month to one year after termination, are ideal for determining whether treatment gains are being maintained. When appointments are not feasible, information from clients can be obtained on the telephone or by a brief self-report questionnaire.

TREATMENT

During the past 10 years there have been major therapeutic developments in the outpatient treatment of depressed individuals, and an impressive number of rationally derived and empirically tested interventions have been described.

The most influential approaches may be divided into those that emphasize "behavioral" and those that emphasize "cognitive" interventions. Cognitive approaches, such as those advanced by Beck (1967) and Rehm (1966), attribute a causal role to cognitions in the etiology of depression. Depression is seen as created and maintained by a host of negative thoughts about oneself and one's life. The goal of therapy is to change these cognitions in a more positive and constructive direction.

Behavioral approaches are more concerned with behavior–environment interactions. Depression is seen as resulting from two few person–environment interactions with positive outcomes and too many with negative outcomes. Although the cognitive and behavioral conceptualizations differ in where they place the locus of causation, it is important to recognize similarities. Both assume that the depressed person has *learned* maladaptive reaction patterns that can be *unlearned*. Symptoms are seen as important in their own right rather than as manifestations of underlying conflicts. Treatments, therefore, are aimed at the modification of relatively specific behaviors and cognitions rather than at a general reorganization of the person's personality. All cognitive–behavioral treatments are structured and time-limited.

For a number of these treatments, complete treatment manuals are available; thus the utilization of these approaches should not pose major problems for the experienced clinician. The major approaches to the treatment of depression are summarized in the following sections.

Decreased Unpleasant Events and Increased Pleasant Activities

This approach (Lewinsohn & Grosscup, 1978) aims to change the quality and the quantity of the depressed person's interactions with the environment. The PES and UES, described above, are used to pinpoint specific person–environment interactions related to the client's depression. An Activity Schedule (Lewinsohn, 1976) is then constructed for clients to monitor the occurrence of their most pleasant and unpleasant activities and their mood. The covariation of certain pleasant and unpleasant events and mood is used to pinpont specific person–environment interactions influencing the client's dysphoria. Treatment provides assistance to clients in decreasing the frequency and subjective aversiveness of unpleasant events in their lives and then concentrates on increasing the frequency and subjective pleasantness of events. A wide range of cognitive-behavioral interventions such as assertion, relaxation training, daily planning, time management, and cognitive procedures are employed. A more detailed description, case illustrations, pre- and posttreatment, and follow-up data for depressed clients treated with this approach are presented elsewhere (Lewinsohn et al., 1982).

Cognitive Therapy

Beck's theory of depression (Beck et al., 1979) assigns the primary causal role for the occurrence of depression to automatic negative cognitions. Such distorted or unrealistic cognitions are assumed to produce misinterpretations of experiences leading to the affective reactions and to the other behaviors associated with depression. Cognitive therapy aims to help clients identify the assumptions and schemas that are supporting recurrent patterns of stereotypical negative thinking and to delineate specific stylistic errors in thinking. Detailed treatment protocols are presented in Rush and Beck (1978) and in Beck et al. (1979).

Interpersonal Therapy

The interpersonal disturbance theory of depression postulated by McLean (1976) considers depressed persons' interactions with their social environments to be crucial for the development and for the reversal of depression. Mclean considers depression to result when individuals lose the ability to control their interpersonal environment and when ineffective coping techniques are utilized, to remedy situational life problems. Interpersonal therapy attempts to maximize patient competence in specific coping skills that incorporate behavioral and cognitive techniques: communication training, behavioral productivity, social interactions, assertiveness, decision making and problem solving, and cognitive self-control. Perhaps the most distinctive component of interpersonal therapy involves communication training between patients and their spouses, or significant others. The inclusion of the relevant social network member is considered important in the promotion of social interaction and in maintaining treatment effects. This treatment is described in greater detail by McLean and Hakstian (1979).

Self-Control Therapy

Rehm's (1979) self-control theory of depression emphasizes the importance of self-administered reinforcement and punishment. According to this formulation, depressed individuals selectively attend to negative aspects of their experience, set very high standards for themselves, self-reinforce infrequently, and self-punish frequently. A treatment based on the self-control theory has been described by Fuchs and Rehm (1977). Treatment sessions are devoted to each of the three self-control processes (self-monitoring, self-evaluating, and self-reinforcing skills).

Assertion and Social Skill Training

Assertion training has also been used with depressed individuals. Wolpe & Lazarus (1966), Lazarus (1968), and Seitz (1971) reported case studies in which training depressed persons to behave assertively was related to significant decreases in the level of depression. Teri and Leitenberg (1979) and Sanchez et al. (1980) found assertion training effective in alleviating depression and increasing assertion in two samples of depressed outpatients. Clients receiving assertion training improved more than clients in traditional therapy conditions and maintained these gains at follow-up.

A broader social-skills training program has also achieved promising results (Bellack & Hersen, 1978; Hersen et al., 1980; Wells, Hersen, Bellack, & Himmelhoch, 1979). Although assertion may be one of the social skills targeted, this program is more broadly social-skills-oriented. The format of the program is to identify four specific social skill "problem areas" and then proceed to train in each area through modeling, role-playing, and reinforced practice. Training in social perception, self-evaluation, and self-reinforcement is also conducted.

Coping with Depression Course

The above-mentioned treatments employ overlapping behavioral and cognitive intervention strategies, including training in assertion, relaxation, self-control, decision making, problem solving, communication, time management, and increasing pleasant activities. Each strategy, either alone or in combination, has been shown to be effective in ameliorating depression.

The Coping with Depression Course presented in this chapter was designed to incorporate the specific strategies shown to be effective in ameliorating depression and thereby to address those target behaviors problematic for depressed persons.

This course is based on a social-learning theory of depression. Depression is viewed as multifaceted disorder maintained by (1) a low rate of positive and high rate of negative reinforcement, (2) the individual's negative cognitions, and (3) the individual's own inability to alter those cognitions and behaviors. The depressed person is thus viewed as experiencing an array of *affective, behavioral,* and *cognitive* problems. The goal of treatment is to provide a multifaceted approach to the problems the depressed person is experiencing.

The Coping with Depression Course is offered within a psychoeducational framework. Treatment is conducted in the context of an eight-week course specifically designed to help depressed persons learn to manage depression. The basic goal of the course is to teach new skills. While surfacing in different ways, a major difference between the educational format and the therapeutic approach is in terms of mutual expectations and responsibilities. The therapist is a teacher. The patient or client is a student. The therapy session is a class. The teacher heads a class in which students are enrolled to learn skills to cope with their depression. The student is considered to be a responsible adult capable of learning. The teacher provides structure in terms of lectures, activities, and homework to facilitate that learning. Consistent with the social learning model, no one is "sick" or "crazy," and students can (and do) learn *skills* to change their depression.

Although lectures are indispensable to the format of the course, discussion among the group members, focusing on problem solving, is strongly encouraged. Students learn much by sharing their successes and failures on the assignments. Also, they are often able to suggest to each other novel and workable solutions.

Before the Coping with Depression Course begins, the instructor meets individually with each student to explain the philosophy of the course and to outline the responsibilities of instructors and students. Students are introduced to the social learning model of depression. Each class session is divided into three parts: (1) a review of the homework for the previous unit, (2) lecture and discussion on a new topic, and (3) presentation of homework relevant to the new topic. At the initial group session, rationale, responsibilities, and expectations are reiterated. The social learning view of depression is discussed. At the next meeting, self-change methods are taught and students begin formulating their first self-change plan. Two sessions each are then spent on relaxation training, increasing pleasant activities, constructive thinking, and improvement of social skills. The final two sessions are devoted to maintenance of gains and the development of a life plan for preventing depression in the future.

Thus far, four studies have been completed on the Coping with Depression course. (Antonuccio, Lewinsohn, & Steinmetz, 1982; Brown & Lewinsohn, 1979; Steinmetz, Lewinsohn, & Antonuccio, 1981; Teri & Lewinsohn, 1982). Its effectiveness has been supported by significant changes obtained on self-report and interviewer report of depression from pre- to postassessment and from pre- and postassessment to follow-up intervals of one, three, and six months. Improvements have been obtained when the Coping with Depression Course has been conducted in a group, on a one-to-one "tutoring" situation, and over the telephone.

A textbook entitled *Control Your Depression* (Lewinsohn, Muñoz, Youngren, & Zeiss, 1980), an instructor's manual (Lewinsohn, Steinmetz, Antonuccio, & Teri, 1982), and a student workbook (Brown & Lewinsohn, in press) are available. The instructor's manual and the student workbook have a syllabus providing a complete description of the material to be covered and all the homework assignments necessary for completion of the course.

CASE STUDY

Intake

Liz Foster, 27 years old, learned about the Coping with Depression Course through an advertisement in the newspaper. She arrived for the intake interview wearing jeans and a worn plaid work shirt. Her voice was soft and unexpressive, and her movements were lethargic. Liz reported that for the past two months she had been feeling sad and tense. She also had felt discouraged and helpless, was eating poorly, had headaches, and was sleeping too much.

Liz had frequent suicidal thoughts. "I feel nothing matters," she said. Upon filling out the BDI, next to the item that reads "I have thoughts of harming myself, but I would not carry them out," she penciled in, in tiny letters, the words "Would I?"

During the past eight years, Liz had often experienced problems similar to the ones she reported now. Her first bout with depression had taken place about the time she entered college. Since then she had had only brief periods of "normal" mood. Her physical health, however, had always been good, and a recent medical examination revealed no abnormalities. As Liz currently met *DSM-III* criteria and had met criteria several times in the past, she was given a diagnosis of "major depression, recurrent." Her score on the BDI was 29.

Functionally, Liz's depression seemed to be maintained by two factors: infrequent engagement in pleasant activities and considerable social isolation. Liz was spending almost all of her time now at home—reading, watching television, or sometimes "just sitting." A college graduate in fine arts, Liz had held several short-term jobs. Eleven months ago, however, she had been laid off and had been unemployed since then. To keep busy, Liz had begun some renovations on her home, but she quit when she realized that her boyfriend took no interest in her projects. She had no confidence that she could complete them without his help.

Aside from her boyfriend, Liz had almost no social contacts. Her older brother lived in the next town, but she rarely saw him. Her two best friends had just moved away. Friends she had made at work rarely called her or visited, nor did Liz seek them out. "Not many close people" were left.

At the end of the intake interview, Liz received a brief introduction to the Coping with Depression Course. She quickly decided to enroll. The breadth of topics was appealing to her, and she was eager to join in a structured activity with other individuals. In preparation for the first meeting, Liz was asked to fill out the PES and begin making daily ratings of her mood.

Treatment

Liz was assigned to a class composed of nine women. The group members were diverse. Liz, at 27 years of age, was the youngest member; the oldest was 58. Several of the women were college graduates, but others had no education beyond high school. The women quickly coalesced into a highly supportive, solution-oriented group. Throughout the course, attendance and homework compliance continued at a high level.

The course was led by two instructors, one male and one female, both advanced level clinical graduate students trained to conduct Coping with Depression Courses.

Session 1: Depression and Social Learning

The instructors explained the structure of the course, offered guidelines for student participation, and gave an overview of the social learning approach to depression. Interaction between group members was facilitated by a "get acquainted" exercise in which the students conversed in pairs about their interests and hobbies and then introduced their partners to the entire group. The exercise went well, creating a lively atmosphere.

Of all the group members, Liz was the most reticent. She gave a fine introduction of her partner but said nothing else during the session. When the other women spoke to her, she smiled but looked down at the table. Even during the coffee break, while the other women socialized, Liz kept to herself.

At the close of the session, the instructors introduced the idea of self-change methods. For homework, students were given the task of designing their own plans to modify a problem behavior.

Session 2: Self-Change Methods

The students received a more detailed explanation of self-change strategies. They became acquainted with the basic skills of (1) pinpointing the behavior to be changed, (2) baselining, (3) identifying antecedents, (4) discovering consequences, (5) setting goals, and (6) choosing reinforcers. The self-change plans the students had designed were in various stages of completion. During much of the session, therefore, the group members provided each other with suggestions for improving their plans. The most frequently chosen target behavior was overeating; five of the nine women had concerns about weight. Liz had decided to create a plan for increasing her pleasant activities, which she briefly described. Liz's participation during the second session was slightly greater than in the first meeting, but she was still the group's quietest member. The instructors and other students persisted in trying to draw Liz out, but with minimal success.

For homework, students were instructed to monitor their daily tension level and to note the times at which they were most and least relaxed.

Session 3: Relaxation and Depression—Learning to Relax

Before beginning the new topic for session 3, the instructors answered questions about students' individual self-change plans. Many of the participants had had difficulty choosing reinforcers. They could remember what *used* to be reinforcing to them before they became depressed, but few things appealed to them now. Liz was especially vocal about the problem. "I don't feel like doing anything," she compalined. The instructors acknowledged that, initially, rewards would be hard to select. They encouraged the students to try the activities and material things that had once been desirable to them, and to see whether those reinforcers still worked.

After a break, the instructors introduced the new topic: relaxation. A rationale for relaxation training was presented, and Jacobsen's deep muscle procedure was explained. A relaxation exercise was then conducted.

When the exercise was over, Liz spontaneously expressed optimism that relaxation would be useful to her. This was her first unsolicited positive contribution to the group. Liz's monitoring of relaxation indicated that relaxation practice might indeed be helpful. Her average daily tension rating on an 11-point scale ["Most relaxed you have ever been" (10) to "Most tense you have ever been" (0)] was a 5. Even at her most relaxed times, her ratings were still near the middle of the scale.

For homework, students were asked to practice relaxation, to continue monitoring their tension level, and to identify the specific situations in which they felt most tense.

Session 4: Relaxation in Everyday Situations

The students discussed their relaxation practice and then discussed the day-to-day hassles they found most stressful. To encourage student participation, especially in brainstorming a list of stressful situations, the instructors decided to curtail the lecture portion of the session.

Liz had practiced relaxation for 15 minutes each day. She rewarded herself by listening to her favorite recordings, and she was pleased that her reinforcement plan had worked. She explained the system to the group and then helped the other students handle the difficulties they had with practicing. Liz also pinpointed nine situations in which she became especially tense, including brooding alone at home, conflicts with her boyfriend, and waking up in the middle of the night.

Liz's involvement and enthusiasm in the session were remarkable. She was much more talkative than before and worked quite productively in a small-group problem-solving exercise. The other women were receptive to her contributions and congratulated her on her ideas.

In preparation for session 5, the students were given the assignment of applying the relaxation techniques they had learned to specific problem situations.

Session 5: Pleasant Activities and Depression

In attempting to practice relaxation during stressful times, Liz had had an interesting experience. Although brooding alone at home was at the top of her problem list, she reported that she had suddenly ceased brooding as soon as she started to self-monitor. Also, although other events on her list had occurred several times, her perception of them as problematic had begun to change. She had written down high tension ratings for some of the situations, but she said she no longer regarded them as particularly troublesome. Apparently, her new awareness of specific problem situations, together with her daily relaxation practice, gave Liz a heightened sense of control over her tension level. The lecture for session 5 was on pleasant activities and their relationship to mood. After the lecture, students received the results from their Pleasant Events Schedules. Liz and the other students were given information about how they compared with their age peers in terms of frequency, enjoyability, and amount of pleasure experienced over the past month. They also received individually tailored lists of 100 pleasant activities. Liz's PES scores were markedly low. Her frequency score was one standard deviation below the mean for women her age; her enjoyability and experienced pleasure scores were both two standard deviations below the mean. From this, it was evident that Liz could benefit from a program to increase pleasant events. Along with the other students, she began monitoring her pleasant activities and graphing her daily totals with her mood ratings. The students also began thinking about a plan to increase their activities.

Session 6: Formulating a Pleasant Activities Plan

The students brought in their graphs of pleasant activities and mood and the activity plans they had devised. Most of the women, including Liz, noticed a strong relationship between activities and mood. Some found a relationship between mood and certain types of activity, such as positive social interactions and competence-related activities. During small-group discussions, the students helped one another solidify their plans and made sure that their goals for increasing activities were realistic. Liz found that her average number of pleasant activities per day was about eight. She decided that a reasonable increase would be to between 15 and 20 per day, and she drew up a plan to help herself meet that goal. The plan was to add 25 cents to her bank for every activity over 13 and then, once she had "earned" $8, to buy a record album.

For homework, the students were to implement their plans for increasing pleasant activities and read the section in their text on controlling thoughts.

Session 7: Thinking and Depression—Two Approaches to Constructive Thinking

The session began with students reporting on their progress in increasing pleasant activities. Liz had been quite successful with her plan: her average number of activities rose from 8 to 20. Her mood also improved. During baseline, Liz's average daily mood score was 6.0, just to the positive side of neutral. The week of intervention, it climbed to 7.4. Liz was happy about the change but did not see her role in creating it. "It just happened. It wasn't anything I did," she said. The group however, was skeptical that such a large shift could happen by chance and encouraged Liz to take credit for the increase. Liz remained doubtful.

After all the students had reported on their plans, a new topic was introduced: controlling thoughts. Students had been asked to record negative and positive thoughts and choose a cognitive control technique discussed in the text, such as thought stopping, time projection, or the ABC method of constructive thinking (Kranzler, 1974). Liz had recorded an average of seven negative thoughts per day (e.g., "Life isn't worth living") and six positive (I'll find a good job"). The major assignment for the next session was to implement a cognitive modification plan. Liz decided to alter her thinking with a simple reinforcement-punishment strategy—charging herself a nickel for every negative thought and paying herself for every positive one.

Session 8: Formulating a Plan for Constructive Thinking

The instructors reviewed the various thought-control techniques from the last session. Then, in small groups, the students discussed their progress with the cognitive approaches they had chosen. By following her plan for decreasing negative and increasing positive thoughts, Liz had reduced her daily average of negative thoughts from 7 to 2; she had increased her daily average of positive thoughts from 6 to 11.

Session 8 seemed to mark a major shift for Liz. Not only had her thinking become more constructive, but she had resumed remodeling her house, a project that she had abandoned because of her boyfriend's lack of interest. During the session she was more alert, more assertive, and more helpful and reinforcing to the other students. She looked healthy. When someone remarked on the changes, Liz said, "I'm not depressed any more." She added that she felt much more in control of her tension level, activities, and thoughts and consequently more in control of her mood.

For homework, students were assigned the chapter in the text on assertion and asked to make a list of situations in which they had difficulty being assertive.

Session 9: Social Skills—The Ability to be Assertive

By Session 9, Liz appeared to be benefiting greatly from the course. She announced that she was no longer having negative thoughts, and her success apparently spurred her on to make many contributions to the session. For homework, the students brought in a list of problematic interpersonal situations they wanted to handle better. Liz quickly volunteered to read hers; some of the items were asking a favor from her boyfriend, dealing with aggressive salespeople, and initiating conversations with strangers. Several of the women had found if difficult to pinpoint situations for themselves, and Liz helped them think of appropriate situations.

The session consisted much more of class discussion than lecture. The students themselves came up with much of the material on assertion. They generated a long list of situations, which was put on the blackboard, and then brainstormed suggestions for appropriate assertive behavior. For the next meeting, the students were asked to come up with ways of increasing their number of social interactions.

Session 10: Using Your Social Skills

The instructors answered questions on assertion, and a few members related instances in which they were able to behave more assertively with family members and coworkers. There was a brief discussion about positive assertion, and members discussed being able to accept compliments and to ask friends to join them in activities. Then the group turned to discussing methods of maintaining an adequate level of social participation. For homework, each student was to generate a list of social activities to increase and a list of interferences with social participation that he or she wanted to decrease. Liz was unable to complete the social skills homework assignment, but she had accomplished a major feat. She now had a job. After being unemployed for one year, Liz was understandably excited. The job was in her chosen field; she was now a teacher in an art studio. The students were proud of her, and Liz, although somewhat apprehensive about meeting many new people, said she thought she could handle her anxiety by relaxing and monitoring her thoughts, as she had learned to do in the group.

Session 11: Maintaining Your Gains

The material covered in class thus far was reviewed. The students showed a good understanding of various topics, with a few women even deciding they could now teach the course themselves!

A major goal of the session was to have students identify the skills that had been most important to them and then produce an emergency plan for applying them during any major life events they might be anticipating. Liz said that the most important thing she had learned was to maintain a high level of pleasant activities. She had noticed, over 27 days, a strong positive relationship between her activities and her mood (see Figure 4-1). (The calculated correlation was quite high, 0.77.) Liz believed that, since she was now working, it would be simple to maintain a high level of activity. But she also realized that she had to keep monitoring her pleasant activities to ensure that they stayed above a critical level.

Session 12: Developing a Life Plan

In preparation for the final meeting, each group member prepared a written life plan composed of a "role sketch," a "philosophy of life" statement, and an "emergency plan." Students varied greatly in their willingness to pres-

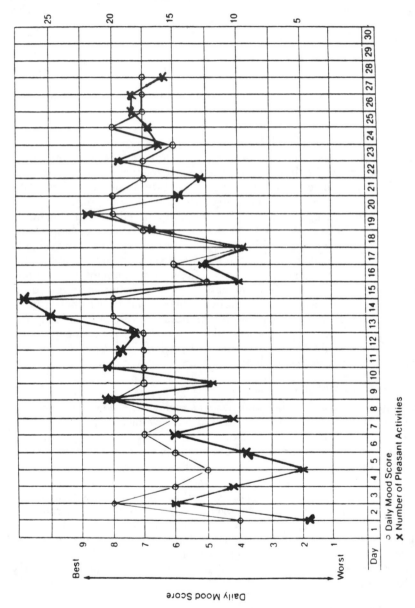

Figure 4-1 Liz's mood and pleasant activities graph.

ent their plans. Several women discussed their ideas in detail, but others were much more reticent. Liz, who had a cold, chatted with the group before the session began but remained silent during the session. Although it was clear that she felt physically ill, her score on the BDI, which the students filled out as a posttreatment measure, dropped from 29 (at the beginning of treatment) to 0.

When the session was adjourned, the women lingered to wish one another good luck and exchange phone numbers. They then dispersed.

Follow-up Assessment

On her posttreatment assessment form, Liz wrote, "I feel very encouraged with my attitude toward everything since taking this course. I am more aware of the many factors involved in controlling depression, and, although I cannot pinpoint what caused my depression, I now definitely have some tangible ways of coping with my problem."

Liz returned for follow-up appointments one and six months later. On both occasions, her status was excellent. Her BDI scores were 0 and 3 at one and six months, respectively. After both follow-up diagnostic interviews she was determined to be no longer clinically depressed. Indeed, her interviewer wrote, "She seems happy—has a job and social contacts, is realistic about the future, and doesn't brood. She has had one or two occasions of feeling down, not lasting more than a day."

At the six-month class reunion, Liz said she was continuing to use techniques from all units of the course: relaxation, pleasant activities, cognitive modification, and social skills. Her job was going well, and she was continuing in her efforts to renovate her house.

Since the reunion, Liz's instructors have seen her informally several times. Liz continues to feel in control of her life, and she speaks enthusiastically about her job. She invited the instructors to the art studio for a tour, which she conducted with obvious pride. Quite recently, Liz was promoted to the position of associate head instructor. At this writing, 1½ years later, Liz is continuing to maintain the gains she made during the Coping with Depression Course.

SPECIAL PROBLEMS

Leader Qualifications

Working with depressed individuals in a Coping with Depression Course creates special challenges. The instructor must have not only clinical skills and a sensitivity to group process, but also a knowledge of behavioral techniques and the ability to teach those techniques. Because of the diverse skills required, and perhaps because of previous experiences within a more traditional treatment framework, new in-

structors may be uncertain as to whether their role is that of therapist or teacher. To be sure, the two roles have commonalities. Therapists
and teachers both view the persons they help as capable of and responsible for change; they also strive to facilitate learning by creating conditions conductive to change. But there are differences as well.
Therapists are able and willing to deal intensively with a client's
agenda. The therapeutic contract (especially regarding length of treatment) may be relatively open-ended. For teachers, however, a major
goal is to communicate a body of information. They thus, tend to
follow a prearranged agenda, and their contracts with students are
well defined and time-limited.

It is our position that instructors who lead Coping with Depression
Courses are more teachers than therapists. Their major responsibilities are to impart information, teach skills, and facilitate group discussions. That is not to say that expertise in clinical assessment and
therapy are irrelevant to leading a course. Quite the contrary, instructors must have a solid grounding in both. Situations may arise, such
as students engaging in emotional self-disclosure or threatening suicide,
which necessitate the use of skills more commonly applied in therapeutic than in academic settings.

The behavior of instructors needs to be flexible—sometimes didactic,
sometimes therapeutic, but always facilitative. Especially at the beginning of the course, instructors must not only impart a great deal of
information; they must also act as orchestrators, actively ensuring that
all students have grasped the "rules" of the course and are contributing appropriately to the sessions. In addition, they must be sensitive
to changes in the clinical status of the students. Later, as students
begin to interact more, instructors may become less directive, encouraging students to help one another, rather than look to the instructor
for guidance. Active student participation not only maximizes learning;
it also enhances students' sense of competence.

For the complex role of instructor of a Coping with Depression
Course, specialized training is highly recommended. Our experience
in training therapists to conduct these courses indicates that it is essential for future leaders to take the course from someone trained to
conduct it.

Problem Client Behaviors

Depressed clients define themselves in passive and pessimistic ways.
They also view themselves as lacking easily pinpointable problems.
They will let you know that they are having serious difficulties (e.g.,
interpersonal, marital, occupational problems), but they fail to con-

nect these difficulties to their depression. Assistance to clients in making the association between their current problems and their depression and having them commit themselves to achieving a change in behaviors are of the greatest importance.

Despite the best efforts of instructors, problems can nevertheless arise. Students may miss sessions, arrive late, or neglect assignments. They also may fail to comply with group process guidelines by talking in a depressed manner, criticizing other students, monopolizing the group, or maintaining total silence.

It is advisable for an instructor to restate course ground rules or to try, in session, to shape appropriate behaviors. If shaping does not work, the instructor may decide to arrange for an individual consultation with the student. In consultation, the instructor can determine the reasons for the problem and then help the student find solutions. Some situations lend themselves to straightforward interventions. For example, it may be determined that the student lacks the requisite skills for doing the coursework. Special tutoring would then be appropriate. Alternatively, a student may have excellent academic skills but need special encouragement to follow through on assignments. Often, selecting a less threatening activity, or selectively reinforcing whatever has been accomplished can be quite helpful. Although a student may not be doing a perfect job on the homework assignments, *any* effort is more than what he or she attempted for their depression prior to the course. The Coping with Depression Course presupposes a certain level of motivation. Clients have to be interested in terminating their depression and in achieving something better. They have to be willing to try *something*. We have found that most depressed clients are willing, and it is the instructor's responsibility to see that client's expectations and goals are realistic.

Other problem client behaviors are less easily rectified and require more creative problem-solving on the part of the instructor and student. Some students engage in lengthy discussions about material, which is, at best, only loosely related to the focus of the class. Their talk is tangential and can interfere with the aims of the course (to train skills that will help students control their depression). For this reason, the "runaway" tangential talker must be discouraged. A "house rule" we state at the beginning of the course is: "Do your part to give everyone equal air time. Try not to overtalk, but, at the same time, make sure that you are heard." This rule can be repeated, restated, and reframed as needed.

Depressed persons also commonly talk at length about their problems and how difficult their lives are. Another "house rule," then, is: "Don't talk depressed talk. Use the group for support and feedback, but avoid depressed talk." Instructors can often "reframe" depressed statements from students. Difficult situations can be reinterpreted as opportunities to use new skills. Negative input from others can be reframed as an opportunity to exercise assertiveness and see how it works. A tense day at work can be seen as an opportunity to practice on-the-spot relaxation skills. A negative thought can be an opportunity to notice how one thinks and to substitute a more positive or constructive thought.

The possibility of marital or family distress, or serious alcohol or drug problems, may interfere with a student's performance. At such times the instructor may find it appropriate to help the student decide whether additional intervention might be helpful. Depressed students also may report serious suicidal thoughts or gestures. If a suicidal student is not already under another therapist's care, the instructor should be prepared to offer referrals. Not all students will need additional support, but those who do (especially those in immediate danger of self-harm) should definitely receive additional help.

A certain percentage (approximately 20%) of people treated with any treatment do not improve following treatment and can be considered nonresponders. Nothing helps nonresponders. Altering tasks, changing reinforcers in the group, and providing extra help or personal attention simply do not impact on these individuals. The nonresponder becomes discouraged after five or six sessions because most of the other participants are very clearing improving. Instructor and student alike perceive the student's complaint, "This course is not working. Nothing helps, I'm wasting your time and my time." A nonresponder's lack of progress may be due to a number of reasons: (1) low motivation, (2) low expectations regarding improvement, (3) a poor match between client and treatment, or (4) too many stressful and aversive events going on in the participant's life. Several of the strategies just discussed may be employed, but it is important for the instructor to provide this student with hopeful avenues of additional resources. The last thing a depressed person needs is another failure experience.

Whatever client problem behaviors are encountered, the instructor should not attempt to impose an ultimatum to the student that says, in effect, "shape up or ship out." Research on the relationship between client behaviors and successful treatment outcome is sparse. Student in-group behavior may or may not generalize, and care should be taken regarding how much pressure is brought to bear on the noncompliant student. Noncompliant students can and do improve. For example, a socially isolated woman in Liz's course who attended most of the sessions but patently refused to do what she called the "diddly" homework actually improved a great deal. She attributed the positive changes to both the social interaction afforded by the group format and the instructor's having been so "nice" to her. Had the instructors insisted on better compliance, the woman might have felt forced to drop out of the course and would not have benefited at all. Students' noncompliance must be handled cautiously, and always with the students' best interests in mind.

SUMMARY

Depression is a pervasive and debilitating emotional disorder, prevalent in a large proportion of any clinician's caseload. This chapter presents material relevant to the proper identification, assessment, and treatment of clinical depression. A multifaceted disorder, depression must be assessed and treated in a multifaceted manner. Assessment should incorporate differential diagnosis, functional analysis, and ongoing evaluation of treatment effectiveness. Treatment should employ a variety of cognitive-behavioral techniques tailored to the individual's depressive constellation.

The Coping with Depression Course, derived from years of treatment and research at the University of Oregon's Depression Research Unit, illustrates such a multifaceted approach. The course is a highly structured, time-limited, skills training program that can be offered in an individual or group treatment modality. Viewing depression within a social-learning perspective, depressed persons are assumed to have learned maladaptive patterns of behaviors and cognitions that can be unlearned with the structure of the Coping with Depression Course. A detailed case example is presented.

REFERENCES

Antonuccio, D., Lewinsohn, P. M., & Steinmetz, J. Identification of therapist differences in a group treatment for depression. *Journal of Consulting and Clinical Psychology,* 1982, *50,* 433–435.

Bandura, A. *Social learning theory.* Englewood Cliffs, N.J.: Prentice-Hall, 1977.

Beck, A. T. *Depression: Clinical, experimental, and theoretical aspects.* New York: Harper and Row, 1967.

Beck, A. T., Rush, A. J., Shaw, B. F., & Emery, G. *Cognitive therapy of depression.* New York: Guilford Press, 1979.

Beck, A. T., Ward, C. H., Mendelson, M., Mock, J., & Erbaugh, J. An inventory for measuring depression. *Archives of General Psychiatry,* 1961, *4,* 561–571.

Beck, A. T., Weissman, A., Lester, D., & Traxler, L. The measurement of pessimism: The hopelessness scale. *Journal of Consulting and Clinical Psychology,* 1974, *42,* 861–865.

Bellack, A. S., & Hersen, M. Chronic psychiatric patients: Social skills training. In M.

Hersen & A. S. Bellack (Eds.), *Behavior therapy in the psychiatric setting.* Baltimore: Williams & Wilkins, 1978.

Blaney, P. H. Contemporary theories of depression: Critique and comparison. *Journal of Abnormal Psychology*, 1977, *86*, 203–223.

Brown, R., & Lewinsohn, P. M. A psychoeducational approach to the treatment of depression: Comparison of group, individual, and minimal contact procedures. University of Oregon mimeograph, 1979.

Burgess, E. The modification of depressive behaviors. In R. Rubin & C. M. Franks (Eds.), *Advances in behavior therapy*, 1968. New York: Academic Press, 1969.

Burglass, D., & Horton, J. A scale for predicting subsequent suicidal behavior. *British Journal of Psychiatry*, 1974, *124*, 573–578.

Ellis, A., & Harper, R. A. *A guide to rational living.* Cal.: Wilshire, 1961.

Endicott, J., & Spitzer, R. L. A diagnostic interview, the schedule for affective disorders and schizophrenia. *Archives of General Psychiatry*, 1978, *35*, 837–844.

Farberow, N. L. Assessment of suicide. In P. McReynolds (Ed.), *Advances in Psychological Assessment*, Vol. 5. Cal.: Jossey-Bass, 1981.

Fuchs, C. Z., & Rehm, L. P. A self-control behavior therapy program for depression. *Journal of Consulting and Clinical Psychology*, 1977, *45*, 206–215.

Gambrill, E., & Richey, C. An assertion inventory for use in assessment and research. *Behavior Therapy*, 1975, *6*, 550–561.

Grinker, R. R., Miller, J., Sabshin, M., Nunn, R., & Nunally, J. C. *The phenomena of depressions.* New York: Hoeber, 1961.

Grosscup, S. J., & Lewinsohn, P. M. Unpleasant and pleasant events, and mood. *Journal of Clinical Psychology*, 1980, *36*, 252–259.

Hamilton, M. A rating scale for depression. *Journal of Neurology, Neurosurgery, and Psychiatry*, 1960, *23*, 56–61.

Hamilton, M. Development of a rating scale for primary depressive illness. *British Journal of Clinical and Social Psychology*, 1967, *6*, 278–296.

Hathaway, S. R., & McKinley, J. C. *The Minnesota Multiphasic Personality Inventory Manual.* New York: Psychological Corporation, 1967.

Hersen, M., Bellack, A. S., & Himmelhoch, J. M. Treatment for unipolar depression with social skills training. Unpublished manuscript, 1980.

Kranzler, G. *You can change how you feel.* Eugene, Oreg.: RETC Press, 1974.

Lazarus, A. A. Learning theory and the treatment of depression. *Behaviour Research and Therapy*, 1968, *6*, 83–89.

Lettieri, D. J. Research issues in developing prediction scales. In C. Neuringer (Ed.), *Psychological assessment of suididal risk.* Springfield, Ill.: Charles C. Thomas, 1974.

Lewinsohn, P. M. Activity schedules in the treatment of depression. In C. E. Thoreson & J. D. Krumboltz (Eds.), *Counseling methods.* New York: Holt, Rinehart, & Winston, 1976.

Lewinsohn, P., Antonuccio, D., Steinmetz, J., & Teri, L. The coping with depression course: A psychoeducational intervention for unipolar depression. University of Oregon, mimeograph, 1982.

Lewinsohn, P. M., & Atwood, G. Depression: A clinical-research approach. The case of Mrs. G. *Psychotherapy: Theory, Research and Practice*, 1969, *6*, 166–171.

Lewinsohn, P. M., & Grosscup, S. J. Decreasing unpleasant events and increasing pleasant events: A treatment manual for depression. Unpublished mimeograph, University of Oregon, 1978.

Lewinsohn, P. M., & Lee, W. M. L. Assessment of affective disorders. In D. H. Barlow (Ed.), *Behavioral assessment of adult disorders.* New York: Guilford Press, 1981.

Lewinsohn, P. M., Muñoz, R. F., Youngren, M. A., & Zeiss, A. M. *Control your depression.* Englewood Cliffs, N.J.: Prentice-Hall, 1978.

Lewinsohn, P. M., Steinmetz, J., Antonuccio, D., & Teri, L. Social-learning treatment of depression: The coping with depression course. University of Oregon, 1982.

Lewinsohn, P. M., & Talkington, J. Studies on the measurement of unpleasant events and relations with depression. *Applied Psychological Measurement*, 1979, *3*, 83–101.

Lewinsohn, P. M., & Teri, L. Selection of depressed and non-depressed subjects on the basis of self-report data. *Journal of Consulting and Clinical Psychology*, 1982, *50*, 590–591.

Lewinsohn, P. M., Teri, L., & Hoberman, H. Depression: A perspective on etiology, treatment, and life span issues. In M. Rosenbaum & C. M. Franks (Eds.), *Perspectives on behavior therapy in the eighties*, in press.

Lubin, B. *Bibliography for the depression adjective check lists: 1966–1977*. San Diego: Educational and Industrial Testing Service, 1977.

MacPhillamy, D. J., & Lewinsohn, P. M. The pleasant events schedule: Studies in reliability, validity, and scale intercorrelations. *Journal of Consulting and Clinical Psychology*, 1982, *50*, 363–380.

MacPhillamy, D. J., & Lewinsohn, P. M. *A scale for the measurement of positive reinforcement*. Unpublished mimeograph, University of Oregon, 1971.

McLean, P. Therapeutic decision making in the behavioral treatment of depression. In P. O. Davidson (Ed.), *The behavioral management of anxiety, depression, and pain*. New York: Brunner/Mazel, 1976.

McLean, P. & Hakstian, A. R. Clinical depression: Comparative efficacy of outpatient treatments. *Journal of Consulting and Clinical Psychology*, 1979, *47*, 818–836.

Muñoz, R. F., & Lewinsohn, P. M. The cognitive events schedule. Unpublished mimeograph, University of Oregon, 1976.

Paykel, E. S., Meyers, J. K., Dienelt, M. N., Klerman, G. L., Lindenthal, J. J., & Pepper, M. P. Life events and depression: A controlled study. *Archives of General Psychiatry*, 1969, *21*, 753–760.

Perris, C. The distinction between bipolar and unipolar affective disorders. In E. S. Paykel (Ed.), *Handbook of affective disorders*. New York: Churchill-Livingstone, 1982.

Radloff, L. The CES-D scale: A self-report depression scale for research in the general population. *Applied Psychosocial Measurement*, 1977, *1*, 385–401.

Raskin, A., Schulterbrandt, J. G., Reatig, N., Cook, T. H., & Odle, D. Depression subtypes and response to phenelzine, diazepam, and a placebo. *Archives of General Psychiatry*, 1974, *30*, 66–75.

Rehm, L. P. Assessment of depression. In M. Hersen & A. S. Bellack (Eds.), *Behavioral assessment*. Oxford: Pergamon Press, 1976.

Rehm, L. P. & Kornblith, S. J. Behavior therapy for depression: A review of recent developments. In M. Hersen, R. M. Eisler, & P. M. Miller, (Eds.), *Progress in behavior modification*, Vol. 7. New York: Academic Press, 1979.

Rush, A. J., & Beck, A. T. Behavior therapy in adults with affective disorders. In M. Hersen & A. S. Bellack (Eds.), *Behavior therapy in the psychiatric setting*. Baltimore: Williams & Wilkins, 1978.

Rush, A. J., Beck, A. T., Kovacs, M., & Hollon, S. Comparative efficacy of cognitive therapy and imipramine in the treatment of depressed outpatients. *Cognitive Therapy and Research*, 1977, *1*, 17–37.

Sanchez, B. C., Lewinsohn, P. M., & Larson, D. Assertion training: Effectiveness in the treatment of depression. *Journal of Clinical Psychology*, 1980, *36*, 526–529.

Seitz, F. A behavior modification approach to depression: A case study. *Psychology*, 1971, *8*, 58–63.

Spitzer, R. L., Endicott, J., & Robins, E. Research diagnostic criteria. *Archives of General Psychiatry*, 1978, *35*, 773–782.

Steinmetz, J., Antonuccio, D., Bond, M., McKay, G, Brown, R., & Lewinsohn, P. M.

Instructor's manual, Coping with depression. Unpublished mimeograph, University of Oregon, 1979.

Steinmetz, J. L., Lewinsohn, P. M., & Antonuccio, D. O. Prediction of individual outcome in a group intervention for depression. *Journal of Consulting and Clinical Psychology*, in press.

Stuart, R. B. Operant-interpersonal treatment of marital discord. *Journal of Consulting and Clinical Psychology*, 1967, *33*, 675–682.

Teri, L., & Leitenberg, H. Assertion training in the treatment of clinical depression. Paper presented at the annual meeting of the Association for Advancement of Behavior Therapy, San Francisco, 1979.

Teri, L., & Lewinsohn, P. M. Comparative efficacy of group vs. individual treatment of unipolar depression. Paper presented at the annual meeting of the Association for Advancement of Behavior Therapy, 1981.

Teri, L., & Lewinsohn, P. M. Modification of the pleasant and unpleasant events schedules for use with the elderly, *Journal of Consulting and Clinical Psychology*, 1982, *50*, 444–445.

Weissman, A., & Beck, A. T. Development and validation of the Dyfunctional Altitude Scale. Paper presented at the annual meeting of the Association for Advancement of Behavior Therapy, Chicago, 1978.

Wells, K. C., Hersen, M., Bellack, A. S., & Himmelhoch, J. H. Social skills training in unipolar nonpyschotic depression. *American Journal of Psychiatry*, 1979, *136*, 1331–1332.

Wolpe, J., & Lazarus, A. A. *Behavior therapy techniques*. New York: Pergamon Press, 1966.

Youngren, J. A., & Lewinsohn, P. M. The functional relationship between depression and problematic interpersonal behavior. *Journal of Abnormal Psychology*, 1980, *89*, 333–341.

Youngren, M. A., Zeiss, A., & Lewinsohn, P. M. *Interpersonal events schedule*. Unpublished mimeograph, University of Oregon, 1975.

Zeiss, A. M., Lewinsohn, P. M. & Muñoz, R. F. Nonspecific improvement effects in depression using interpersonal skills training, pleasant activity schedules, or cognitive training. *Journal of Consulting and Clinical Psychology*, 1979, *47*, 427–439.

Zung, W. W. K. A self-rating depression scale. *Archives of General Psychiatry*, 1965, *12*, 63–70.

5

Somatic Disorders

Donald Williamson, Elise E. Labbé, and
Stanford W. Granberry

SOMATIC COMPLAINTS are among the most frequent presenting problems of outpatients seen at medical and psychological clincs. According to the U.S. Department of Health and Human Services, complaints of headache accounted for an estimatcd 18,341,923 office visits during 1977 and 1978 (NAMCS, 1981). Also, it has been estimatcd that 10–25% of the American population suffers from some type of sleep disturbance (Goldberg & Kaufman, 1978). Furthermore, 23 million Americans are thought to be affected by essential hypertension (National Centcr for Health Statistics, 1969). In the past, treatment of somatic disorders has been the province of general medical practice. In recent years, however, other health care professionals—including psychologists, psychiatrists, nurses, and social workers—have developed a new approach to treating somatic problems based on a biobehavioral model of health and behavior (Engel, 1977; Williamson, Waters, & Hawkins, in press). This model emphasizes the biological, environmental, and behavioral influences on health and physical problems. This new approach to treating somatic complaints has led to the development of a number of behavioral treatment approaches that are directed at modification of either the biological, environmental, or behavioral determinants of the disorder.

The purpose of this chapter is to describe the assessment and treatment of the most common somatic disorders in adult outpatients. These disorders are (1) head pain, including migraine, muscle contraction, and mixed headache, and temporomandibular joint (TMJ) pain, (2) cardiovascular disorders, including essential hypertension and Raynaud's syndrome, (3) gastrointestinal disorders, including peptic ulcers and irritable bowel syndrome, and (4) sleep disorders, emphasizing insomnia.

ASSESSMENT

Careful assessment of the patient's problem is essential for formulation of a treatment plan. Assessment should continue throughout treatment. Assessment during treatment will provide information concerning effectiveness of treatment and will help to determine whether changes in the treatment plan should be made. Assessment after treatment will allow the therapist to determine whether therapeutic benefits have been maintained. The patient should be asked to come in for booster treatment or reevaluation if followup assessment indicates a return of somatic symptoms.

Evaluation of somatic disorders usually requires four modes of assessment: interview, self-monitoring, self-report inventories, and psychophysiological assessment. First, one or more interviews are usually required in order to properly diagnose the somatic disorder and to formulate the case in terms of a behavioral analysis. During this pretreatment period, the patient is usually instructed to self-monitor the somatic symptoms in order to ascertain the relationships among environmental, cognitive, and behavioral events associated with the occurrence of somatic complaints. Such self-monitoring should be continued throughout treatment and follow-up in order to evaluate treatment outcome. Before treatment the patient is often asked to complete several self-report instruments in order to evaluate the significance of general personality features, depression, and so on. In many cases, it is advisable to use psychophysiological assessment procedures in order to evaluate physiological changes that occur during treatment. The following subsections outline the details of these four modes of assessment.

Interview

Patients with somatic disorders may present a wide array of problems: medical, emotional, and social. The interviewer needs to determine the extent of the patient's problems and influence they have on the somatic disorder to be treated. Patients with somatic disorders may be experiencing considerable anxiety, and symptoms associated with anxiety are often present. The interviewer should thus assess both medical and behavioral aspects of the disorder.

The initial stages of the interview should include a detailed analysis of the presenting problem. Questions concerning the length of the somatic symptom(s) as well as typical frequency, duration, and intensity of the symptoms should be asked. As a general rule, most patients will have received a medical diagnosis by a physician. It is important to independently evaluate the patient's symptom pattern, however, since it is imperative that you feel confident of the diagnosis. In order to properly diagnose common somatic disorders, the therapist must ask specific questions regarding the presence or absence of particular symptoms. Table 5-1 summarizes the most important presenting symptoms for diagnosing the disorders discussed in this chapter.

For example, in cases of head pain, one must distinguish among the diagnoses of migraine, muscle contraction, and mixed headache versus TMJ pain. Questions should focus on the location of pain (e.g., unilateral versus bilateral, neck and shoulders versus forehead), the quality of pain (e.g., throbbing versus constant bandlike pressure), and typical antecedents of head pain (e.g., stressful events, certain foods, menstrual cycle). From these interview data, diagnosis of the somatic disorder is usually possible. If there is any question regarding the diagnosis, however, referral to the proper medical specialist is mandatory.

There will be some patients whose somatic complaints are best conceptualized in terms of operant learning (Fordyce, 1976). Sometimes somatic complaints may have developed as result of some physical condition and then may be maintained by reinforcement contingencies (Cinciripini, Williamson, & Epstein, 1981; Epstein & Cinciripini, 1981). For most patients with somatic disorders, both physiological and environmental factors interact to maintain the symptom; thus it may be difficult to determine which factor has the most influence. If at all possible, postulating the extent of operant control of the symptoms can be extremely helpful in choosing the best treatment package. This information will help determine whether operant procedures, e.g., coping skills such as assertiveness training, anxiety management skills such as relaxation training, or stimulus control procedures, should be included in the treatment package for best results.

In order to determine the influence of environmental events on the symptoms, questions concerning antecedents and consequences of the symptoms, as well as patient's behaviors that maintain or exacerbate the disorder, should be asked. Several important questions concerning antecedent events can be asked. What, if any, environmental events precede or initiate the pain or problematic physiological response?

Table 5-1 Guidelines for Differential Diagnosis of Common Disorders

Class of Disorder	Diagnosis	Presenting Symptoms for Diagnosis	Symptoms Contraindicated for Diagnosis
Head pain	Classic migraine	1. Unilateral locus of pain 2. Description of pain severe and throbbing or pulsating 3. Prodromal symptoms, e.g., visual disturbances before headache 4. Possible nausea and vomiting 5. Episodic attacks 6. Family history of migraine 7. Ingestion of foods containing tyramine often initiating headache, e.g., cheese, seafoods 8. For women, headaches often increase during menses, reduce or disappear during pregnancy and menopause 9. Relief after sleep 10. Tenderness in affected areas for several days after the headache	1. Description of pain: constant with bandlike tightness 2. Bilateral locus of pain 3. Pain locus near jaw or ear, with bruxism or jaw popping
Head pain	Common migraine	1. Locus of pain is more often bilateral than unilateral 2. No clearly defined prodromal phase 3. All other symptoms similar to classical migraine	1. Prodromal symptoms 2. Description of pain: constant bandlike tightness 3. Pain locus near jaw or ear with bruxism or jaw popping
Head pain	Muscle-contraction headache	1. Diffuse or bilateral locus or pain that usually begins in either suboccipital or frontal areas of the head 2. Description of pain—constant bandlike tightness or pressure around the head or stiffness or soreness in the neck	1. Prodromal symptoms 2. Description of pain—pulsating or throbbing 3. Unilateral locus of pain 4. Pain locus near jaw or ear with bruxism or jaw popping 5. Nausea and vomiting

Head pain		3. Possible tinnitus, vertigo, and lacrimation occurs when pressure is applied 4. Pain intensity—mild to severe 5. Frequency varies widely	1. Pain locus near jaw or ear with bruxism or jaw popping 2. Clearly migraine or clearly muscle-contraction headaches
	Mixed headache	1. Pulsating or throbbing pain and, or at other times, bandlike tightness or pressure 2. Bilateral or unilateral locus of pain 3. Other symptoms of both migraine and muscle contraction headache	
Head pain	TMJ pain	1. Locus of pain over masseter muscles near ear 2. Pain may extend over the face, head, and neck 3. Often associated with jaw dysfunction 4. Teeth grinding (bruxism) may occur at night, occasionally during the day 5. Chronic pain and hypomobility of the mandible 6. Tension of masseter muscles with increasing tightness or tension; may also throb or pulsate 7. Muscle spasms 8. Jaw popping	1. Unilateral or bilateral head pain only in frontal or temporal areas of head 2. Nausea and vomiting 3. Prodromal symptoms 4. Spontaneous or traumatic dislocation of joint 5. Chronic mandibular hypomobility—painless restriction of jaw movement 6. Temporomandibular arthritis

(continued)

Table 5-1 *(continued)*

Class of Disorder	Diagnosis	Presenting Symptoms for Diagnosis	Symptoms Contraindicated for Diagnosis
Cardiovascular	Hypertension	1. ≥160 mm Hg or more systolic 2. ≥95 mm Hg or more diastolic	1. Elevation directly attributed to an organic or physiological problem
Cardiovascular	Raynaud's disease	1. Locus of pain; hands, feet, and sometimes face and tongue 2. Description of pain: episodes of subjective coldness and/or numbness 3. Possible discoloration of the skin; three-stage color change: blanching, cyanotic blue, and finally bright red 4. Low skin temperature in hands and feet 5. Duration minutes to hours 6. In severe cases, necroses, gangrene, ulceration may occur	1. Occurs only in extremely cold weather 2. Vascular symptoms due to some other physical disorder, e.g., lupus 3. Symptom onset after a trauma (e.g., pneumatic hammer disease) 4. Presence of scleroderma 5. Presence of vascular or anatomical abnormality resulting in ischemia
Sleep disorder	Insomnia	1. Complaints of disturbed sleep combined with complaints of daytime fatigue 2. Complaints include extended latency to sleep onset, excessive minutes or wakefulness during night, early morning awakenings, excessive number of awakenings during night	1. Anuresis 2. Diagnosis of other symptoms of depression 3. Use of stimulates such as coffee, diet pills, etc. 4. Narcolepsy 5. Sleep complaint is secondary to some illness 6. Sleep apnea—respiratory pauses during sleep more than 10 seconds in duration 7. Nocturnal myoclonous—repetitive muscular jerks occurring in the lower limbs at sleep onset and during sleep 8. Nocturnal bruxism

Gastrointestinal	Peptic ulcer	1. Medical assessment indicating erosion in the lining of the gastrointestinal tract caused by excess secretion of hydrochloric acid and pepsin 2. Ulcer can occur at any point in the tract where secretions come in contact with the lining—duodenum, stomach, and esophagus 3. Pain in upper abdomen, when the stomach is empty 4. Pain relieved by ingestion of food	1. Spastic colon 2. Painless diarrhea 3. Constipation 4. Ulcer-directly attributed to an illness or use of certain drugs such as aspirin
	Irritable bowel syndrome	1. Major complaints are (1) abdominal discomfort, described as a stabbing pain, gas, or cramps and (2) a change in bowel function with either diarrhea, constipation, or alternating episodes of both 2. Associated symptoms may include headache, weakness, flushing, palpitations, or lethargy 3. Symptoms often occur after eating and frequently coincide with periods of stress	1. Symptoms related to other organic symptoms or illness 2. Ulcers 3. Abdominal pain relieved by ingestion of food

Sometimes the patient has noted certain events consistently occur prior to an attack. Sometimes certain stimuli, such as foods, odors, or light may trigger an attack. Does rest or an argument with an important person precede somatic complaints? Further assessment through self-monitoring can often assist the interviewer to evaluate the influence of specific antecedent events on symptom reports.

In order to assess consequences of reporting symptoms, questions concerning the consequences of somatic complaints should be asked. Is the patient receiving a great deal of attention or favors from family, friends, or work colleagues when reporting illness? Does the patient escape from aversive situations because of somatic complaints? Questions concerning antecedents and consequences of the patient's response must be tactfully asked. For example, instead of asking, "Do you think you have a headache so you can get out of work?", one can ask, "How often do you feel your headache pain is related to avoiding work frustration?" Another example is "Do you ever get angry at your family, and then experience stomach pain?" This can be rephrased as "When you get angry at the family does your stomach pain worsen?" Questions about nutrition and diet, assertiveness, and coping skills can allow the therapist to determine whether a patient's lifestyle is contributing to the severity of the somatic complaint. For instance, does a person with hypertension use unnecessary amounts of salt? Prior attempts at psychological treatments and the type of treatment should be noted. If traditional psychological treatments have been tried, reorientation toward a behavioral approach during initial stages of assessment is warranted. The interviewer should also create and reinforce positive expectancies of treatment benefits during the interview.

The interviewer should assess the person's strengths as well as weaknesses. What assets does the patient have that will be useful in the treatment process? For example, a person who is well organized in daily routine, is more likely to reliably complete self-monitoring assignments and practice self-control skills at home. Some patients may have to be instructed and reinforced on how to manage their time so that the treatment can be effective. Assessment of the patient's family and social systems also is necessary. Will the family encourage or sabotage the treatment plan? For example, will the family be quiet in the evening so that mother can practice relaxation? Interviewing of family members is often helpful in order to evaluate the reliability of the patient's self-report.

From the medical history, the most recent medical examination should be noted. Any patient who has not had a medical examination within the past year should be asked to have one completed before further assessment is made. If a medical examination has recently been performed, the interviewer should request a copy of the report from the physician.

All medication used by the patient should be noted. Purpose, usage, side effects, and effectiveness of the drugs should be discussed with the patient. If questions related to medication usage are noted, contact with the patient's personal physician should be made.

It often is necessary to use additional assessment procedures in order to confirm the medical diagnosis and behavior analysis of the disorder. In particular, self-monitoring self-report inventories, and psychophysiological assessment procedures can be used for this purpose.

Self-Monitoring

Self-monitoring can be a very valuable tool in assessing somatic disorders. Figure 5-1 illustrates a self-monitoring record for a headache patient. The basic format of this record could be used for most somatic complaints, especially for disorders involving pain or discomfort. From this self-monitoring procedure, the patient's headache activity can be assessed in terms of frequency, severity, and duration. Also, environmental influences and behavioral responses to headache pain can be evaluated. In the example shown in Figure 5-1, a moderately severe headache (which lasted from before lunch to after dinner) was reported. The patient reported that time pressure at work preceded the headache and that his response was to take two aspirins. From a behavior analytic perspective, it is significant that environmental stress preceded the headache and that his response was to take two aspirins. From a behavior analytic perspective, it is significant that environmental stress preceded the headache and that the patient remained at work rather than leaving work to rest. The latter piece of data can be construed as evidence against the hypothesis that negative reinforcement—that is escape from a stressful work environment—is a major factor in the maintenance pain reports.

When self-monitoring procedures are used, it is important to keep the following principles in mind:

- Design neat, easy-to-follow self-monitoring records.
- Discuss in detail the rationale for using self-monitoring and the procedures involved in the self-monitoring task.
- Always examine the self-monitoring records at the time the patient returns them to you so that his or her behavior is reinforced and so that you can discuss the events summarized on the self-monitoring record.

Name_____

Date_____

Pain Rating Scale

0 = No headache (HA)
1 = Very mild HA, aware of it only when attending to it
2 = Mild HA, could be ignored at times
3 = Moderate HA, pain is noticeably present
4 = Severe HA, difficult to concentrate, can do undemanding tasks
5 = Extremely intense HA, incapacitated

Instructions: Rate your headache pain at each of the four times shown below. If any medications are taken, record the *name* and *quantity* of medication taken. Also, specify the events occurring before onset of the headache and your response to the headache.

	Pain Rating	Medication Intake	Events Before HA	Your Response to HA
Breakfast	0		Hurried to get to work	
Lunch	2	2 Aspirins	Much pressure to get work done	Stayed at work and tried to ignore HA
Dinner	3		Finally got work done	
Bedtime	0			

Figure 5-1 A self-monitoring record for a typical headache patient.

- In cases of noncompliance with your requests, reemphasize the importance of self-monitoring and discuss possible solutions to the problems that led to noncompliance.
- Remember that continued self-monitoring throughout treatment and follow-up is very useful for purposes of evaluating outcome.

Self-Report Inventories

Self-report inventories are most useful in assessing psychological and health problems related to the patient's presenting complaint(s). In principle, any valid self-report instrument might be useful in this regard. We have found that the Minnesota Multiphasic Personality Inventory (MMPI), depression inventories, and general medical and health questionnaires are the most commonly used self-report inventories for patients with somatic disorders.

MMPI

The MMPI can be used as a screening device for cases in which there are questions concerning the presence of certain psychiatric (e.g., schizophrenic) or personality (e.g., hysterical personality) disorders. As a general rule, most patients with somatic disorders will show elevations of MMPI scales 1(Hs), 2(D), and 3(Hy), the so-called neurotic triad.

Depression Inventories

Many patients with somatic disorders are significantly depressed. Often the depression may be a result of the chronic discomfort produced by the somatic disorder. In other cases depression may be the primary diagnosis. Use of relatively short depression inventories such as the Beck Depression Inventory [(BDI) (Beck, Ward, Mendelson, Mock, & Erbaugh, 1961)] or the Depressive Adjective Checklist [(DACL) (Lubin, 1965)], often provide very important information concerning the severity of the depression. Also, periodic assessment of depression by use of these inventories is often useful for evaluating changes in depression over the course of treatment.

Medical/Health Questionnaires

Many patients have an extensive medical history that can be quite perplexing to thoroughly assess during an interview. In such cases, we have found that questionnaires designed to survey most significant medical or health problems can provide a very efficient means of obtaining this information so that the interview can focus on the patient's current somatic problems.

Psychophysiological Assessment

Clinical use of psychophysiological assessment has been used very infrequently until recent technological advances in biomedical engineering led to the production of reasonably priced, easy-to-use psychophysiological recording equipment. In general the equipment required for psychophysiological assessment falls into two classes: polygraph recorders and biofeedback/physiological data acquisition packages. Although polygraph equipment allows for the greatest versatility, its use requires more training, and it is generally more expensive. For these reasons, most outpatient clinics that treat somatic disorders have chosen to purchase biofeedback/physiological data acquisition packages. The quality and sophistication of this type of equipment is rapidly improving and prices are remaining reasonable.

The most common use of psychophysiological assessment is for evaluating specific physiological changes during relaxation, biofeedback, or stress testing. The most frequent responses to be measured in psychophysiological assessment are (1) skin temperature—usually measured from a finger and generally considered to be an indirect measure of peripheral blood flow; (2) heart rate—the number of ventricular contractions over a period of time (e.g., one minute), generally a good measure of emotionality, stress, and so on; (3) blood pressure—usually measured using a blood pressure cuff and stethoscope, although an indirect measure called *pulse wave velocity* has been recently developed; (4) electromyogram (EMG)—commonly measured from the frontal area of the forehead, although the EMG of any muscle group can be recorded; generally regarded as a good measure of muscle tension in a selected muscle group; (5) vasomotor response (VMR)—usually recorded using photoplethysmography from a finger or the temporal artery (in migraine headache patients); regarded as a direct measure of blood flow in a specific vascular bed; and (6) electrodermal responses—includes skin resistance, skin potential (SP), and skin conductance; measures sweat gland activity and is generally regarded as the best indicator of sympathetic arousal.

- Adaptation phase (10 minutes): after electrodes or transducers are attached, the patient is asked to sit quietly for 10 minutes in order to allow for adaptation to the laboratory and reduction of physiological arousal due to environmental factors.
- Baseline phase (5 minutes): the subject continues to sit quietly for 5 minutes; physiological data during this baseline phase are used for evaluating changes during later phases.
- Relaxation or biofeedback phase (15–25 minutes): the subject is instructed to relax, using a specific procedure (e.g., progressive

muscle relaxation) or biofeedback to modify a specific physiological response.

- Stress phase (2–15 minutes): subjects are exposed to a stress test designed to produce significant physiological arousal. Common stress tests include mental stressors (e.g., mental arithmetic or an oral intelligence test), painful stressors (e.g., cold pressor task or sustained occlusion of blood flow by use of a blood pressure cuff), and imaginal stressors (e.g., imagined stressful events).

In our research on headaches, we have used relaxation phases of 25 minutes and a 12-minute oral intelligence test designed to create time pressure to answer questions correctly. As an example of the results of the assessment procedure, Figure 5-2 illustrates the physiological changes observed for adult headache patients during relaxation and stress testing. Subjects in the relaxation group had received a six-week group relaxation program. Subjects in the control group met weekly to discuss headaches, life events, and so on. Therefore, it was expected that during the relaxation phase, the relaxation group would show greater reductions of physiological arousal in comparison to the control group. As shown in Figure 5-2, the relaxation group did tend to lower arousal as evidenced by heart rate deceleration, lowered EMG, and lowered skin potential amplitude. During stress testing physiological arousal was produced in both groups as evidenced by substantial increases of heart rate, EMG, and skin potential. These data are typical of those derived from the psychophysiological assessment procedures described earlier.

Summary

Assessment of somatic disorders prior to treatment must include evaluation of physical symptoms for diagnostic purposes, the influence of the patient's environment and behavior on somatic complaints, and general psychological and health factors. From this assessment, a treatment plan should follow. Assessment of treatment outcome should include self-monitoring of somatic symptoms. Psychophysiological assessment is often included in order to objectively monitor physiological changes during treatment.

TREATMENT APPROACHES

The most well-established therapeutic approaches used for somatic disorders are biofeedback and relaxation training. Both of these approaches generally combine self-control procedures so that patients

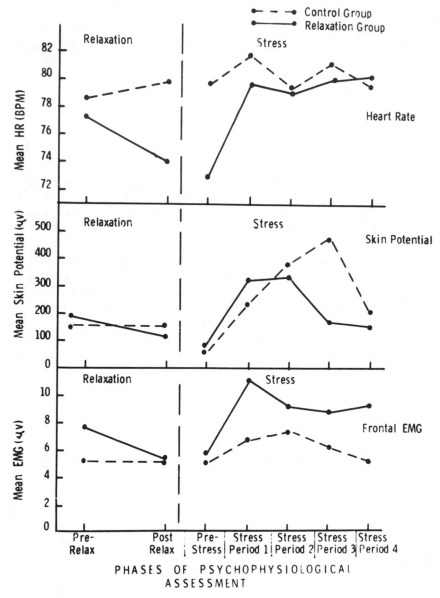

Figure 5-2 Psychophysiological changes during relaxation and stress testing.

can develop control over somatic symptoms in natural environment. The following subsections describe the methodology of these approaches and summarize current research finding concerning effectiveness of these interventions with the major somatic disorders.

Biofeedback

General Methodology

Any type of biofeedback requires a specially designed laboratory or clinical environment. An ideal biofeedback environment should include two rooms so that psychophysiological recording equipment can be physically separated from the patient's room. The environment should be sound-attentuated and equipped with a comfortable recliner and a sink for cleaning electrodes and the patient's skin. Also, light dimmer switches should be sufficiently dim that lighting can be controlled.

Most clinical biofeedback systems are specially designed to enable the clinician to amplify the biofeedback signal, filter electrical noise, and eliminate artifacts as a result of movement. The most important features of a good system include (1) the capability of providing visual and auditory feedback, (2) the capability of providing analogue feedback (i.e., feedback that changes as a direct function of the physiological response), and (3) the capability of modifying the sensitivity of the feedback signal.

If psychophysiological recording equipment is also desired, important features are the ability to calibrate the amplification of the physiological response, a permanent record of the data (e.g., digital print-out), and an electrical output that can be monitored in order to check the accuracy of the recording.

When conducting a biofeedback session, the therapist should give the client instructions regarding the response to be modified, such as increase in skin temperature and the manner by which biofeedback informs the client of response changes. For instance, as the pitch of the auditory feedback becomes higher, your skin termperature is increasing. Most clinicians also give clients suggestions that have been found to be helpful in learning to control a particular response. For example, the client may be instructed to "pay attention to the feelings of warmth in your hand and fingers as the feedback signal changes; learn to associate the feelings with changes in the feedback." Also, suggestions for relaxing imagery or recommendations against "trying too hard" are often provided. There are differences of opinion concerning the utility of coaching the subject during biofeedback sessions. We have found that with some patients who experience initial difficulty in modifying the response, coaching to relax and thinking of pleasant imagery is sometimes helpful. Once the person has obtained at least some control over the response, however, we usually leave the patient's environment so that he or she can pay very careful attention to the feelings associated with response changes.

There are no standards for the frequency and duration of treatment sessions; however, we have found that at least for the first month of treatment, sessions should be scheduled twice per week. Typical biofeedback sessions last from 20 to 40 minutes, with at least a 5-minute period of self-control with feedback at the end of a session. In most cases, homework assignments are given to practice a specific relaxation procedure (e.g., progessive muscle relaxation or autogenic training, or to practice biofeedback using a portable biofeedback device).

Skin Temperature Biofeedback

Table 5-2 summarizes the effectiveness of skin temperature biofeedback as a treatment for migraine headache, mixed migraine/muscle-contraction headache, and Raynaud's syndrome. As can be seen, skin temperature biofeedback is quite effective for all these disorders, although long-term controlled research concerning mixed headache and Raynaud's disease has not been reported.

Clinical applications of skin temperature biofeedback often combine autogenic training (Schultz & Luthe, 1969) with the biofeedback procedure. Autogenic training assists the client in the discrimination of interoceptive cues, such as heaviness of arms and warmth of the hands and fingers, associated with relaxation. Using repetitive covert autogenic phrases such as, "My hands are getting warmer and warmer. . . . I am at peace," the client learns to associate feelings of warmth with changes in the biofeedback signal so that evantually simply repeating the autogenic phrases comes to elicit the hand warming response.

For headache patients, the temperature probe or thermistor is usually placed on the distal portion of an index finger. Although many researchers prefer to place the thermistor on the nondominant hand, this practice has no well-established empirical basis. For Raynaud's patients, the thermistor is usually placed on affected areas of the hands or feet, such as the fingers or toes. It has been established that modification of peripheral blood flow by means of skin temperature biofeedback is localized in only the immediate area surrounding the thermistor. For Raynaud's syndrome patients, therefore, it is advisable that the thermistor placement be moved (e.g., from hand to hand) either across or within treatment sessions.

When treating either headache or Raynaud's syndrome patients, the therapist must stress the importance of home practice. We generally

Table 5-2 Biofeedback Treatment of Somatic Disorders

| Treatment | Disorder | Percentage of Patients Improved* | | Pertinent Studies | |
		At End of Treatment	At Follow-Up	Controlled Group Experiments	Single-Case Studies
Skin temperature biofeedback	Migraine headache	60–80	40–60	Blanchard et al. (1978), Silver et al. (1979)	Johnson and Turin (1976)
	Mixed headache	30–50	?	Blanchard et al. (1979), Blanchard et al. (1980)	
	Raynaud's syndrome	60–80	?	Jacobson et al. (1979)	Surwit (1973)
EMG biofeedback	Muscle-contraction headache	60–90	50–80	Budzynski et al. (1973), Haynes et al. (1975)	Epstein & Abel (1977)
	TMJ pain	60–80	60–80	Gessell (1975), Carlsson & Gale (1977)	
Cephalic VMR biofeedback	Migraine headache	60–85	60–80	Bild and Adams (1980), Friar and Beatty (1976)	Feuerstein and Adams (1977)
	Mixed headache	?	?		Feuerstein et al. (1976), Sturgis et al. (1978)
Skin resistance biofeedback	Essential hypertension	Percentage of patients improved has not been reported; mean decrease in systolic BP from 20–26 mm Hg; mean decrease in diastolic BP 14–17 mm Hg	Mean decrease in systolic BP 15–22 mm Hg; mean decrease in diastolic BP 13–15 mm Hg	Patel (1976), Patel and North (1975)	

*Percentage of patients improved is based on representative finding from a number of studies reporting on the response of individual subjects to the present program.

125

instruct patients to practice at least once daily for 20 minutes. After control of skin termperature has been achieved, we instruct headache patients to utilize the hand-warming skill at the onset of prodromal symptoms in the case of classical migraine or at the earliest signs of headache in the case of common migraineurs (patients who do not experience prodormal symptoms). Using this strategy, we have witnessed the abortion of headaches in both the laboratory and the natural environment.

EMG Biofeedback

Table 5-2 summarizes the results of treatment studies with the use of EMG biofeedback for muscle-contraction headache and TMJ pain. Controlled research concerning the treatment of both disorders is now fairly well established. In general, researchers have reported a high degree of success with the use EMG biofeedback as a treatment for both disorders.

The most common electrode placement for EMG biofeedback is the frontal area across the forehead (Williamson, Epstein, & Lombardo, 1981). In cases of headache with a pain locus in the neck, shoulder, or back of the head, however, biofeedback from the trapezius or sternomastoid muscles may be more appropriate. For TMJ pain patients, EMG electrodes are most commonly positioned over the masseter (jaw) muscles.

Electromyographic biofeedback is used to assist the patient in learning to relax muscles that have become chronically contracted and thus very painful. Home practice of relaxation is very important for effective treatment of these disorders. Therefore, we often train patients in progressive muscle relaxation in order to provide an easy-to-follow relaxation procedure for home practice. Once patients have learned to relax their muscles, we instruct them to pay attention to slight changes in muscle tension so that relaxation in the natural environment can be used to "nip muscle pain in the bud." We have found that by using this self-control type of relaxation, most patients can learn to prevent most muscle pain from worsening. In most cases, therefore, head pain is greatly reduced in terms of frequency, duration, and intensity.

Cephalic Vasomotor Response Biofeedback

Table 5-2 summarizes the major treatment outcome research concerning cephalic VMR biofeedback. This treatment procedure has been found to be effective for both migraine headache and mixed headache. Only reports of single cases have been published for mixed headache, however; therefore, conclusions regarding degree of effectiveness of this intervention as a treatment for mixed headache must be made cautiously.

Cephalic VMR biofeedback provides binary (yes/no) feedback concerning the amplitude of pulses measured from the temporal artery. Since migraine headache is in part caused by extreme vasodilation of the extracranial arteries, training to constrict these arteries (the temporal artery is one extracranial artery commonly involved in migraine) is a logical treatment for migraine. Cephalic VMR biofeedback is usually conducted so that a feedback signal such as a light or tone remains on as long as the pulse amplitude remains below a certain criterion. This criterion can be gradually lowered so that greater vasoconstriction can be shaped during the treatment session. Using this procedure, the patient is instructed to constrict the temporal artery by learning to keep the feedback sigal on.

This treatment procedure is somewhat more complicated than most other biofeedback procedures. At present, no commercial cephalic VMR biofeedback packages have been marketed. The clinician or experimenter must thus design the biofeedback system using polygraph equipment for measuring VMR. Required components include AC and DC preamplifiers, voltage threshold comparators, and digital logic for programming the feedback signal. Interested readers may wish to closely examine the methodology described in the studies cited in Table 5-2 for cephalic VMR biofeedback.

One interesting feature of cephalic VMR biofeedback is that the procedure is designed to enable the patient to constrict cephalic vessels during the early stages of migraine headache. You may recall that for skin temperature biofeedback, clinical findings suggest that the hand-warming skill is best implemented during the prodromal or preheadache phase of migraine headache. This difference in the use of these two procedures suggests that they may operate by different physiological mechanisms. Also, one might speculate that cephalic VMR biofeedback might be most effective for common migraineurs.

Skin Resistance Biofeedback

Biofeedback of skin resistance in combination with a variation of yoga meditation has been found to be the most effective biofeedback treatment for essential hypertension (Blanchard & Miller, 1977). As shown in Table 5-2, this treatment package has been found to produce long-term reductions of blood pressure that are of sufficient magnitude to be regarded as clinically significant. Given the generally weak effects of blood pressure biofeedback as a treatment for essential hypertension (Seer, 1979), these findings are especially impressive.

This treatment package involves training hypertensives in passive yoga meditation exercises for home practice. In the clinic, patients are trained to raise skin resistance by use of biofeedback. Increases in skin resistance are associated with lowered sympathetic arousal and a generally relaxed state. Given the general effectiveness of consistent home practice of relaxation (discussed in the next section), one must question the importance of including skin resistance biofeedback as a part of the treatment package for essential hypertension.

Relaxation

In recent years relaxation training has received increased attention as a primary or adjunctive treatment procedure for a variety of somatic complaints and psychophysiological disorders. Behavior therapists frequently employ relaxation training since it requires no special equipment, is relatively time- and cost-efficient, and has demonstrated effectiveness for numerous somatic complaints and disorders.

At present, there is no one commonly accepted procedure for conducting relaxation training. In fact, the term "relaxation training" is frequently used in a general way to describe a class of different procedures for training clients how to relax. The variety of different procedures used to teach relaxation is well illustrated by a recent review article. Hillenberg and Collins (1982) surveyed 12 psychology journals from 1970 to 1979 and found a total of 26 distinct relaxation training procedures reported. Among the more commonly cited procedures were progressive relaxation (Jacobson, 1938), autogenic training (Schultz & Luthe, 1969), and the relaxation response (Benson, 1975).

The primary difference among relaxation approaches lies with the procedure or methodology used to achieve a relaxed state. Some procedures, such as progressive muscle relaxation, require patients to actively tense and relax specific muscle groups in order to achieve relaxation. Other relaxation procedures, such as meditation or autogenic training, involve passive concentration on a cognitive device (e.g., a mantra or a set of phrases designed to elicit relaxation). Basic and clinical research comparing the effects of these different relaxation procedures have found that all produce very similar subjective and psysiological changes. Also, treatment outcome research comparing different relaxation procedures, has revealed no significant differences in overall effectiveness. Furthermore, evidence suggests that biofeedback and relaxation are equally effective for treating somatic disorders.

Table 5-3 summarizes the results of treatment outcome studies concerning relaxation treatment of somatic disorders. For various types of head pain (i.e., headache and TMJ pain), relaxation training has been well researched. With the expection of mixed headache, relax-

Table 5-3 Relaxation Treatment of Somatic Disorders

Disorder	Percentage of Patients Improved*		Pertinent Studies	
	At End of Treatment	At Follow-Up	Controlled Group Experiments	Single-Case Studies
Migraine	60–80	40–70	Blanchard et al. (1978), Silver et al. (1979)	Gessel & Alderman (1971), Carlsson & Gale (1977)
Muscle-contraction headache	60–85	50–80	Haynes et al. (1975)	Tasto & Hinkle (1973), Blanchard et al. (1980)
Mixed headache	20–40	20–30	Hutchings & Reinking (1976), Williamson et al. (1981)	
TMJ pain	55–75	50–75	Gessel (1975)	Brady et al. (1974)
Essential hypertension	30–80	30–80	Stone and Deleo (1976), Taylor et al. (1977)	
Raynaud's syndrome	65–100	60–100	Surwit et al. (1978)	Stephenson (1976), Grabowski (1971)
Insomnia	30–70	25–70	Borkovec & Fowles (1973), Nicassio & Bootzin (1974), Haynes et al. (1974)	Coates & Thoresen (1979), Weil & Goldfried (1973)
Peptic ulcer	Unknown	Unknown	Chappell et al. (1936)	Aleo & Nicassio (1978)
Irritable bowel syndrome	75–100	75–100		Mitchell (1978), Youell & McCullough (1975)

*Percentage of patients improved is based upon representative findings from a number of studies reporting on the response of individual subjects to the treatment program.

ation training has been found to be a very effective treatment procedure for these disorders. Recent research from our laboratory has indicated that many cases of mixed headache do not respond well to relaxation treatment.

Research concerning relaxation treatment of hypertension has indicated that significant reductions of blood pressure can be achieved if patients regularly practice relaxation at home. It should be noted, however, that many hypertensives must be continued on at least low dosages of antihypertensive medications following relaxation treatment.

Relaxation treatment of Raynaud's disease has been found to be very effective and comparable in efficacy to skin temperature biofeedback. Many authorities in this area now believe that either relaxation or biofeedback should be prescribed for Raynaud's disease patients before suggesting more serious interventions, such as a sympathectomy.

Relaxation can often benefit insomnia patients. However, recent research has suggested that careful evaluation of the patient's lifestyle and general habits (drug habits, daytime activities, etc.) are essential for proper formulation of a treatment plan for these patients (Coates & Thoresen, 1979).

Treatment outcome research concerning relaxation treatment of peptic ulcer is almost nonexistent. A very early study by Chappell, Stefano, Rogerson, and Pike (1936) is the only group study ever reported for this disorder. Presently, insufficient data have been presented to evaluate the degree of effectiveness of relaxation treatment of peptic ulcer.

Several recent single-case studies have been reported for relaxation treatment of irritable bowel syndrome. Although no controlled group outcome studies have been published, preliminary findings have suggested that relaxation is a promising treatment for this disorder.

As noted earlier, despite the methodological differences among various relaxation procedures, effects of these different procedures are quite similar. On the basis of these findings, we have developed a general relaxation training program that incorporates procedures from progressive muscle relaxation and passive meditation. We have found this approach to be quite effective for producing deep relaxation in the overwhelming majority of cases. This procedure has three stages: initial relaxation procedure, shortened relaxation procedure, and relaxation as a self-control procedure. The following subsections describe general methodology of relaxation training for each of these three stages.

General Methodology

Relaxation training is best conducted in a quiet, comfortable room without distracting stimuli or interruption. A couch or recliner is ideal for patient comfort, but the procedure can be administered in a comfortable chair. Before conducting relaxation, the therapist should practice the administration of the instructions until the delivery is fluid and confident. It may be helpful for the therapist to practice the relaxation exercises to become more aware of how the procedure works and how relaxation feels.

Prior to beginning relaxation training it is important to determine whether the patient is able to comfortably perform the procedure. For example, the patient may have an old whiplash injury or arthritis that will become painful during the procedure. If the patient has a medical or physical condition which counterindicates tensing of certain muscles, the therapist can adapt the training procedure to accommodate the patient's problem or resort to a procedure requiring less physical activity.

In our experience, relaxation can be effectively learned in four to six sessions lasting 30–60 minutes per session. Home practice of once or twice per day for 15–20 minutes per session is usually assigned as homework.

We have found it very useful to tape-record the initial relaxation session so that the patient can play the relaxation tape at home during practice sessions.

Initial Relaxation Procedure

Prior to beginning the procedure, the therapist should offer some introductory instructions about the procedure in order to provide realistic expectations regarding the steps of relaxation. An example of such instructions follows.

I am going to teach you how to relax. This is a simple way to feel more relaxed and comfortable. With practice you will become better and better at obtaining his relaxed feeling. In a way, this is like learning how to ride a bicycle. At first, you had to learn each step, how to get on the cycle, how to stay balanced and how to pedal. With practice you become more and more comfortable at riding the bicycle. After a while it was such a natural feeling that you didn't have to concentrate on how to do it and just enjoyed riding and how relaxed you felt. Once we start I am going to ask you to tense certain muscles and then relax them, let them go loose. We start with your hands and then move on to your arms, then shoulders, face, etc. I want you to tense the muscles tightly but not so tight you hurt yourself. Do not try to force yourself to relax, just let the relaxation occur naturally as you follow the procedure. If you feel relaxed after this first session that is a good sign that you are learning the procedure quickly; if you don't feel more relaxed this first or second time that is O.K. With practice you will learn to relax at your own pace.

Step 1:   First I want you to lie (or sit) comfortably without your arms or legs crossed.

Step 2:   Search your body and find any muscle groups that are tense and compare how they feel to muscle groups that are relaxed; think for a few seconds how different they feel and how pleasant the relaxed muscles feel.

Step 3: Close your eyes. Now take a deep, slow breath. Hold it (5–10 seconds). (Repeat this instruction for a total of three times). Watch the patient; monitor the rate of breathing and keep note of progress in slowing the breathing until it is smooth and natural.

Step 4: Now, raise both arms about 6 inches off your lap. Hold it (5–10 seconds). (Repeat this instruction for a total of three times.) Relax; notice how comfortable it feels to relax your arms.

Step 5: Now raise your arms and make a fist. Hold it (5–10 seconds). (Repeat this instruction for a total of three times.) Relax, and lower your arms. Notice the different feelings associated with muscular tension and relaxation.

Step 6: Now raise your arms again, clench your fists, and tighten your arm muscles. Hold it (5–10 seconds). Relax and lower your arms. (Repeat this instruction for a total of three times).

Step 7: Now without tensing any other muscles, tense your shoulders forward. Hold it (5–10 seconds) Relax. (Repeat this instruction for a total of three times). Now tense your shoulders back.

Step 8: Now rest your chin on your chest and tense your neck muscles. Hold if (5–10 seconds) Relax. Now turn your head left and tense your neck muscles. Hold it. Relax. Now turn your head to the right and tense your neck muscles. Hold it. Relax.

Step 9: Now frown hard. Wrinkle your brow. Feel your face muscles tense. Hold it (5–10 seconds) Relax.

Step 10: Now clench your jaw tight. Hold it (5–10 seconds) Relax.

Step 11: Now push your tongue against the roof of your mouth. Hold it (5–10 seconds) Relax.

Step 12: Now tense your back and chest. Hold it (5–10 seconds) Relax.

Step 13: Now tense your stomach muscles. Hold it (5–10 seconds) Relax.

Step 14: Now tense your buttocks. Hold it (5–10 seconds) Relax.

Step 15: Now raise your legs about 6 inches. Hold it (5–10 seconds) Relax.

Step 16: Now tense your thighs. Hold it (5–10 seconds) Relax.

Step 17: Now tense your calves. Hold it (5–10 seconds) Relax.

Step 18: Now tense your feet. Grip your shoes with your toes. Hold it (5–10 seconds) Relax.

Step 19: Now that you have relaxed your muscles, let's deepen the relaxation through pleasant imagery. Try and imagine the following scene as vividly as possible. Imagine lying on a beautiful, white sandy beach. It is very peaceful. You can hear the ocean, with the waves breaking on the shore. You can see the waves, the white foam, rushing in, rushing out, rushing in, rushing out. The sky is blue, the sun is shining, warming the skin of your hands and arms. You can feel them warming, gradually warmer and warmer. White clouds are floating across the sky. There is gentle breeze; you can hear the rustling of the wind in the palms, in the sea oats. It's such a beautiful scene. Relax, relax. It's so peaceful; so calm (continue for 1–4 minutes).

Step 20: Now that we have completed the relaxation session, follow my instructions as I count from 1 to 3. One: open your eyes. Two: take a deep breath. Three: Stretch your arms and legs.

After the patient is again oriented, talk to him or her about how relaxed they feel. Determine whether there are still areas that are tense and revise treatment accordingly to allow for additional relaxation of those muscle groups.

Shortened Relaxation Procedure

Usually within two or three weeks the patient can become deeply relaxed by using this initial relaxation procedure. The therapist can then introduce a modified version of the procedure. In the streamlined version, the client relaxes four large muscle groups instead of individual muscle groups. The four muscle groups are (1) hands and arms, (2) shoulders, neck, and face, (3) chest, back, and abdomen, and (4) legs and feet. Completion of tensing and relaxing of muscles is followed by relaxation through pleasant imagery.

Instructions for tensing and relaxing these four muscle groups should combine the instructions used for the longer relaxation procedure. Approximately 15–30 seconds should separate each instruction. It is useful to provide suggestions related to relaxation during these intervals, with comments such as "You are so peaceful and calm, you don't even have to try and relax; just let it happen naturally."

Relaxation as a Self-Control Procedure

Once the patient can elicit relaxation within five minutes, self-control training can begin. The first step is called *relaxation by recall.* The patient is instructed to elicit the physiological responses associated with relaxation by simply concentrating on the sensations associated with these responses, such as warmth in the hands and fingers, heaviness in the arms, and slow rhythmic breathing. Covert repetition of autogenic phrases by the patient is often helpful for eliciting this relaxation response. An example of autogenic phrases is: "My arms are getting heavier and heavier. My arms are getting heavier and heavier. I am at peace. My hands are getting warmer and warmer. My mind is relaxed. I am calm."

Once the patient has mastered relaxation by recall (usually within one week), the next step is training in the use of relaxation to manage stress, anxiety, or specific somatic symptoms associated with emotionality. This procedure has many similarities to systematic desensitization. Also, it often is called *anxiety* or *stress management training* in other published literature. The first step is to establish a hierarchy of situations and cognitions that consistently elicit anxiety or somatic symptoms. This hierarchy should include about 15 items that are ordered from low to high anxiety ratings. The next step is to relax the patient and present the hierarchy items (in order, one at a time) in the clinic. The therapist should try to elicit an anxiety reaction by vividly describing the situation or cognitions and by having the patient practice reducing this anxiety by means of self-control relaxation. Initial presentations should be short, thereby enabling the patient to reduce anxiety very easily. As treatment progresses, presentations should become longer and more intense (i.e., more anxiety provoking). When the patient is able to consistently control emotional responses in the clinic, homework assignments for management of anxiety, stress, or somatic symptoms in the natural environment are provided. For example, a patient with a diagnosis of irritable bowel syndrome may be instructed to self-monitor stress so that minor stress reactions can be identifed before excessive arousal occurs. The patient is instructed to elicit relaxation in the natural environment during these episodes so that the arousal and subsequent somatic symptoms can be prevented or at least substantially reduced in intensity.

By using this three-stage relaxation procedure, most patients are able to gain substantial control over somatic symptoms. Total duration of treatment is usually about three to four months.

Common Problems Encountered with Relaxation Training

Some problems may occur in conducting relaxation training. It is important to observe patients closely as they perform the procedure. Some patients may overdo tensing and cause soreness or injury. Some patients may experience performance anxiety about their degree of success with relaxation. Preliminary assessment indicating that the patient worries about how well he or she is performing should cue the therapist to be alert for this potential problem. Performance anxiety may be identified by slow progress in learning the relaxation procedure or by physical signs of anxiety, including sweating, increased pulse, breathing, or swallowing. Direct discussion about performance anxiety and encouragement to let relaxation occur naturally often eliminates this problem.

Another problem that often occurs is difficulty with vividly imagining a relaxing scene. The therapist can evaluate this skill by asking the patient to describe in detail the imagined scene. The therapist should be alert for descriptions involving not only visual aspects of the scene, but sounds, smells, and tactile sensations as well.

Selection of a relaxing scene by the therapist may present problems. The particular scene may not be especially pleasant or relaxing to the patient and may, in fact, be aversive because of unpleasant memories associated with the scene (severe sunburn at the beach, hay fever in the springtime, etc.).

A similar problem may arise when the patient is bothered by intrusive thoughts during relaxation. This problem usually occurs during initial relaxation sessions with extremely anxious patients. We have found that patience and assurance that relaxation will naturally occur is the best solution for this problem. Usually, within a short period of time the patient will begin to master the technique and intrusive thoughts will no longer be problematic.

Summary

Relaxation training has been successfully applied to a wide variety of somatic disorders. Careful assessment and individualized planning of treatment is essential for using relaxation for such patients. Also, training patients to actively use relaxation as a self-control procedure is very important for maximizing treatment effectiveness.

EXAMPLE

The following case study is presented in order to illustrate the assessment and treatment of somatic disorders in adults. A case involving headache was chosen because these types of cases are often seen in outpatient medical and psychological clinics.

CASE STUDY

Preliminary Information

Ms. Jacobs was a 35-year-old, white, married female who was referred to our clinic by her physician for assessment and treatment of headache.

Initial Interview

Therapist: Hello, Ms. Jacobs, I am Dr. Williamson, a member of the psychology faculty at LSU and a staff member of the Psychological Services Center. From the referral information that I have received, I understand that you have been suffering from severe headaches. Could you tell me a little about your head pain—where it hurts, how it feels, and so forth.

Patient: Well, for about the last year I have been having very frequent headaches that are just excruciating. They are so bad that I can't get any work done and I really am afraid to do almost anything because I might have a headache. The headache usually starts right over my right eye. Sometimes the pain is just there, and other times it spreads all along the right side of my head. When it does that, I really know I'm in for a bad one. My doctor says that they're probably migraine headaches.

T: Do you ever have headaches on the left side of your head or on both sides of your head?

P: No, not really. At least the bad ones are always on the right side. I guess I might have had a few minor headaches across my forehead, but they're so infrequent that I'm not really concerned with them. Also, in comparison to the other headaches, they aren't really that painful and don't bother me that much.

T: How often do you have these mild headaches that are painful across your forehead?

P: Oh, maybe once or twice per year.

T: How often do the severe headaches occur; especially recently, like in the past six months?

P: Often. It's hard to say, because they kind of vary.

T: Over the course of a month, about how many severe headaches would you average?

P: I would say about 8 or 10.

T: Do you usually have at least one per week?

P: Yes, it's a rare week that I don't have a headache.

At this point the therapist is beginning to suspect that the patient's headaches are probably migraine and that muscle-contraction or other types of headache (the mild headaches across the forehead) are not of clinical significance. Therefore, questions regarding migraine become more focused.

T: Would you describe your head pain as constant or more throbbing in quality?

P: Definitely throbbing—like a knife jabbing me in the head with every pulse beat.

T: Do you ever have warning signs that signal you that a headache is about to begin?

P: You know, I do. Most of the time, about 15–30 minutes before my headache, I start feeling kind of dizzy and I can see little stars, little shiny spots before my eyes. Several times my vision got real blurry and I swear it seems that there were things that disappeared if I looked at them just so.

T: Do you mean that if you focused your eyes, there were blind spots in your visual field?

P: I guess so; I never thought of it that way.

T: Do you ever feel nauseous or vomit before or during a headache?

P: Yes, I almost always feel nauseous and sometimes I throw up after my headache begins. Several times after I vomited, I felt better.

T: After the headache, is the pain location kind of sore and tender?

P: Yes, I hate to have to comb my hair on the right side after I have had a headache.

T: Well, Ms. Jacobs, it sounds as though you are having migraine headaches. Has anyone else in your family ever been diagnosed as having migraine headaches?

P: Not that I know of. My Mom used to have some bad headaches. She called them "sick headaches," but I don't think she ever went to the doctor for them.

T: Have you been able to identify any events in your life or things that you do that seem to cause a headache?

P: Well, sometimes when I drink wine or a mixed drink, I seem to have a headache the next day. But now, I just don't drink very often and I still have headaches.

T: How about pressure, tension, or stress? Do they ever seem to trigger a headache?

P: I used to think so, but I'm not so sure now. Often I seem to have headaches on the weekend, when I am most relaxed.

T: Are your headaches better, worse, or about the same in recent months?

P: Well, I believe I had my first bad headache when I was about 15 years old. I had about one or two per year until about a year ago. Over the past year, they seem to have gotten worse and worse.

T: Do you mean that they have become more frequent or more intense?

P: Mostly more frequent, but maybe a little longer also. It's hard to say.

During the remainder of the interview, it was learned that Ms. Jacobs has been employed as a bookkeeper for the past two years. She has two teenage daughters and a husband of 15 years. She describes their marriage as satisfactory. No specific stressors or precipitating circumstances were identified for headaches. Also; no other significant problems other than mild depressive episodes were identified. Therefore, further assessment for the purpose of screening and treatment planning were instituted.

Further Assessment

Screening for significant psychological problems was accomplished using the MMPI. Testing indicated clinical elevations of scales 1, 2, and 3, the "neurotic triad." Further assessment using the BDI suggested that the patient's depression was moderate, but not of serious clinical significance. Medical records obtained from her physician indicated that all other medical problems that could have caused headache had been ruled out. Also, these records documented a four-month trial of vasoconstrictor medication (Cafergot) for migraine that was partially successful. Side effects from the medication, however, including dizziness, nausea, and cold chills, led to a recommendation that alternative treatment should be sought. This recommendation resulted in a referral to our clinic.

Self-monitoring data indicated that Ms. Jacobs was experiencing one to three headaches per week. They usually were quite intense, reaching a peak rating of either four or five, and usually lasted for about 8–16 hours. Assessment of antecedent conditions suggested that she was under considerable time pressure at work and at home, and that these stressors may have been associated with headache. However, no systematic consequences of reporting head pain were noted.

Psychophysiological assessment indicated that Ms. Jacobs had great difficulty relaxing and was very reactive to stress testing. In particular, elevations of heart rate and skin resistance and excessive peripheral vasoconstriction were noted during stress testing.

Case Formulation

On the basis of the assessment data, it was concluded that Ms. Jacobs was suffering from classic migraine headache. Depression was considered to be mild and probably secondary to the discomfort and inconvenience of recurrent head pain. No specific stressors or other antecedent conditions were identified for headache. However, MMPI and self-monitoring data suggested that Ms. Jacobs tended to worry and became anxious over day-to-day matters.

From this formulation, a treatment plan for a combination of skin temperature biofeedback and relaxation training was developed. Given the success of skin temperature biofeedback for aborting headaches, this procedure was included in order to train Ms. Jacobs to directly control headaches by using the hand-warming technique during predromal periods. Relaxation was included in order to provide a useful technique for managing anxiety and stress on a daily basis. Cognitive interventions to modify worrying and "catastrophizing" were also to be used later in treatment. Treatment was scheduled for sessions twice per week, one for skin temperature biofeedback and one for relaxation training over a five-week period. Over the last five weeks of treatment, only one session per week was to be scheduled, and skin temperature biofeedback was to be used in these sessions. Naturally, modification of these plans were to be made, depending on progress in treatment. Assessment of depression was to be continued over the course of treatment in order to evaluate changes in this problem area. Also, posttreatment psychophysiological assessment was planned in order to evaluate physiological changes due to relaxation and stress.

Course of Treatment and Treatment Outcome

Prior to treatment, three weeks of baseline self-monitoring data indicated that Ms. Jacobs was averaging about two headaches per week. Skin temperature biofeedback and relaxation training progressed without major difficulties. By the fourth week, Ms. Jacobs' skin temperature was increasing by about 1°C, and she was showing good signs of relaxation. No significant changes in headache activity were noted until about the fifth week of treatment. Over the last month of treatment she experienced only two headaches. Follow-up data over a three-month period indicated that she generally experienced about one headache per month and that the intensity and duration of these headaches were reduced in comparison to baseline. Assessment of depression during follow-up indicated considerable improvement. Ms. Jacobs was now able to plan enjoyable activities without fear of having a migraine headache. She was quite pleased with the outcome of treatment. Plans for telephone follow-up were made at 6 and 12 months following treatment.

SUMMARY

Outpatient behavioral treatment of somatic disorders in adults is a new area of clinical practice and research. Although much work remains, considerable progress has been made to date. The treatment procedures of biofeedback and relaxation training are the most well developed methods now used for somatic disorders. Current clinical research data reveal that these methods have been empirically validated as useful interventions for a majority of the major somatic disorders. On the basis of these findings, it now appears promising that these interventions can be further validated by clinical usage in outpatient clinics.

REFERENCES

Aleo, S., & Nicassio, P. Auto-regulation of duodenal ulcer disease: A preliminary report of four cases. *Proceedings of the Biofeedback Society of America*, 9th Annual Meeting. Denver, 1978.

Beck, A. T., Ward, C. H., Mendelson, M., Mock, J. E., & Erbaugh, J. K. An inventory for measuring depression. *Archives of General Psychiatry*, 1961, *4*, 53–63.

Benson, H. *The relaxation response*. New York: Avon Books, 1975.

Bild, R., & Adams, H. E. Modification of migraine headaches by cephalic blood volume pulse and EMG biofeedback. *Journal of Consulting and Clinical Psychology*, 1980, *48*, 51–57.

Blanchard, E. B., Ahles, T. A., & Shaw, E. R. Behavioral treatment of headaches. In M. Hersen, R. M. Usler, & P. M. Miller (Eds.), *Progress in behavior modification*, Vol. 8. New York: Academic Press, 1979.

Blanchard, E. B., Andrasik, F., Ahles, T. A., Teders, S. J., & O'Keefe, D. Migraine and tension headache: A meta-analytic review. *Behavior Therapy*, 1980, *11*, 613–631.

Blanchard, E. B., & Miller, S. T. Psychological treatment of cardiovascular disease. *Archives of General Psychiatry*, 1977, *34*, 1402–1413.

Blanchard, E. B., Theobald, D. E., Williamson, D. A., Silver, B. V., & Brown, D. Temperature biofeedback in the treatment of migraine headaches: A controlled evaluation. *Archives of General Psychiatry*, 1978, *35*, 581–588.

Borkovec, T. D., & Fowles, D. Controlled investigation of the effects of progressive relaxation and hypnotic relaxation on insomnia. *Journal of Abnormal Psychology*, 1973, *82*, 153–158.

Brady, J. P., Luborsky, L., & Kron, R. E. Blood pressure reduction in patients with essential hypertension through metronome-conditioned relaxation: A preliminary report. *Behavior Therapy*, 1974, *5*, 203–209.

Budzynski, T. H., Stoyva, J. M., Adler, C. S., & Mullaney, D. J. EMG biofeedback and tension headache: A controlled outcome study. *Psychosomatic Medicine*, 1973, *35*, 484–496.

Carlsson, S. G., & Gale, E. N. Biofeedback in the treatment of long-term temporomandibular joint pain. *Biofeedback and Self-Regulation*, 1977, *2*, 161–171.

Chappell, M. N., Stanfano, J. J., Rogerson, J. S., & Pike, F. H. The value of group psychological procedures in the treatment of peptic ulcer. *American Journal of Digestive Diseases*, 1936, *3*, 813–817.

Cinciripini, P. M., Williamson, D. C., & Epstein, L. H. Behavioral treatment of migraine headaches. In J. M. Ferguson & C. B. Taylor (Eds.), *The comprehensive handbook of behavioral medicine*, Vol. 2, New York: SP Medical and Scientific Books, 1981.

Coates, T. J., & Thoresen, C. E. Treating arousals during sleep using behavioral self-management. *Journal of Consulting and Clinical Psychology*, 1979, 47, 603–605.

Engel, G. L. The need for a new medical model: A challenge for biomedicine. *Science*, 1977, 196, 129–136.

Epstein, L. H., & Abel, G. G. An analysis of biofeedback training effects for tension headache patients. *Behavior Therapy*, 1977, 8, 37–47.

Epstein, L. H., & Cinciripini, P. M. Behavioral control of tension headaches. In J. M. Ferguson & C. B. Taylor (Eds.) *The comprehensive handbook of behavioral medicine*, Vol. 2, New York: SP Medical and Scientific Books, 1981.

Feuerstein, M., & Adams, H. E. Cephalic vasomotor feedback in the modification of migraine headache. *Biofeedback and Self-Regulation*, 1977, 2, 241–254.

Feuerstein, M., Adams, H. E., & Beiman, I. Cephalic vasomotor and electromyographic feedback in the treatment of combined muscle contraction and migraine headaches in a geriatric case. *Headache*, 1976, 16, 232–237.

Fordyce, W. E. *Behavioral methods for chronic pain and illness*. Saint Louis: Mosby, 1976.

Friar, L. R., & Beatty, J. Migraine: Management by trained control of vasoconstriction. *Journal of Consulting and Clinical Psychology*, 1976, 44, 46–53.

Gessel, A. H. Electromyographic biofeedback and tricyclic anti-depressants in myofacial pain–dysfunction syndrome: Psychological predictors of outcome. *Journal of American Dental Association*, 1975, 91, 1048–1052.

Gessel, A. H., & Aldermann, M. M. Management of myofacial pain dysfunction syndrome of the temporomandibular joint by tension control training. *Psychosomatics*, 1971, 12, 302–309.

Goldberg, P. & Kaufman, D. *Natural sleep*. Emmaus, Pa.: Rodale Press, 1978.

Grabowski, M. J. The effects of hypnosis in hypnotic suggestion on the blood flow in the extremities. *Polish Medical Journal*, 1971, 10, 1044–1051.

Haynes, S. N., Griffin, P., Mooney, D., & Parise, M. Electromyographic biofeedback and relaxation instructions in the treatment of muscle contraction headaches. *Behavior Therapy*, 1975, 6, 672–678.

Haynes, S. N., Woodward, S., Moran, R., & Alexander, D. Relaxation treatment of insomnia. *Behavior Therapy*, 1974, 5, 555–558.

Hillenberg, J. B., & Collins, F. L. A procedural analysis and review of relaxation training research. *Behaviour Research and Therapy*, 1982, 20, 251–260.

Hutchings, D. F., & Reinking, R. H. Tension headaches: What form of therapy is most effective? *Biofeedback and Self-Regulation*, 1976, 1, 182–190.

Jacobson, A. M., Manschreck, T. C., & Silverberg, E. Behavioral treatment for Raynaud's disease: A comparative study with long-term follow-up. *American Journal of Psychiatry*, 1979, 136, 844–846.

Jacobson, E. *Progressive relaxation*. Chicago: University of Chicago Press, 1938.

Johnson, W. G., & Turin, A. Biofeedback treatment of migraine headache: A systematic case study. *Behavior Therapy*, 1975, 6, 394–397.

Lubin, B. L. Adjective checklists for measurement of depression. *Archives of General Psychiatry*, 1965, 12, 57–62.

Mitchell, K. R. Self management of spastic colitis. *Journal of Behavior Therapy and Experimental Psychiatry*, 1978, 9, 269–272.

National Ambulatory Medical Care Survey (NAMCS): 1981 Summary United States. U.S. Department of Health, Education and Welfare, Public Health Service, Health Resources Administration, National Center for Health Statistics. Rockville, Maryland, 1981.

National Center for Health Care Statistics. *Blood pressure of adults by age and sex, United States 1960–1962*. U.S. Department of Health, Education and Welfare, 1969.

Nicassio, P., & Bootzin, R. A comparison of progressive relaxation and autogenic training as treatments for insomnia. *Journal of Abnormal Psychology*, 1974, *83*, 253–260.

Patel, C. Reduction of serum cholesterol and blood pressure in hypertensive patients by behavior modification. *Journal of the Royal College of General Practitioners*, 1976, *26*, 211–215.

Patel, C. & North, W. R. S. Randomized controlled trial of yoga and biofeedback in management of hypertension. *Lancet*, 1975, *2*, 93–95.

Seer, P. Psychological control of hypertension: Review of the literature and methodological critique. *Psychological Bulletin*, 1979, *86*, 1015–1043.

Schultz, J. & Luthe, W. *Autogenic therapy*, Vol. 1, New York: Grune & Stratton, 1969.

Silver, B. V., Blanchard, E. B., Williamson, D. A., Theobald, D. E., & Brown, D. A. Temperature biofeedback and relaxation training in the treatment of migraine headaches. *Biofeedback and Self-Regulation*, 1979, *4*, 359–366.

Stephenson, N. L. Two cases of successful treatment of Raynaud's disease with relaxation in biofeedback training in supportive psychotherapy. Paper presented at the seventh annual meeting of the Biofeedback Research Society, Colorado Springs, Colorado, February 1976.

Stone, R. A., & Deleo, J. Psychotherapeutic control of hypertension. *New England Journal of Medicine*, 1976, *294*, 80–84.

Sturgis, E. T., Tollison, C. D., & Adams, H. E. Modification of combined migraine—muscle contraction headaches using BVP and EMG biofeedback. *Journal of Applied Behavior Analysis*, 1978, *11*, 215–223.

Surwit, R. S. Biofeedback: A possible treatment for Raynaud's disease. In L. Birk, (Eds.), *Biofeedback: Behavioral medicine*. New York: Grune & Stratton, 1973.

Surwit, R. S., Pilon, R., & Fenton, C. H. Behavioral treatment of Raynaud's disease. *Journal of Behavioral Medicine*, 1978, *1*, 323–335.

Tatso, D. L., & Hinkle, J. E. Muscle relaxation treatment for tension headache. *Behaviour Research and Therapy*, 1973, *11*, 347–349.

Taylor, C. B., Farquhar, J. W., & Nelson, E. Relaxation therapy and high blood pressure. *Archives of General Psychiatry*, 1977, *34*, 339–342.

Weil, G., & Goldfried, M. Treatment of insomnia in an eleven-year-old child through self-relaxation. *Behavior Therapy*, 1973, *4*, 282–284.

Williamson, D. A., Epstein, L. H., & Lombardo, T. W. EMG measurement as a function of electrode placement and level of EMG. *Psychopysiology*, 1980, *17*, 279–282.

Williamson, D. A., Monguillot, J., Jarrell, P., Cohen, R. A., & Pratt, J. M. Controlled evaluation of a self-help relaxation program for the treatment of headache. Paper presented at the annual meeting of the Association for Advancement of Behavior Therapy, 1981.

Williamson, D. A., Waters, W., & Hawkins, M. Physiological variables. In R. Nelson & S. Hayes (Eds.), *Conceptual foundation of behavioral assessment*. New York: Guilford Press, in press.

Youell, K. K., & McCullough, J. P. Behavioral treatment of mucous colitis. *Journal of Consulting and Clinical Psychology*, 1975, *43*, 740–745.

6

Alcoholism

David M. Lawson

THE CONFUSION SURROUNDING the definition of alcoholism is so great, and its associated theoretical concepts so varied, that an Expert Committee of the World Health Organization recommended that the term "alcoholism" itself be abandoned. Fortunately, however, there is sufficient overlap among various descriptions of the disorder that a recognizable yet indistinct clinical picture emerges. The most general feature of this disorder is a pattern of alcohol consumption that causes impairment in physical, social and/or occupational functioning. Considerable variation is present in both the patterns of alcohol usage and the nature and extent of the resulting impairment. Drinking may occur daily; it may be restricted to weekends or may occur episodically with interposed periods of abstinence lasting weeks or months. Typically, there is a history of repeated, unsuccessful attempts to reduce or to stop drinking, a perceived dependence on alcohol to enhance pleasure or reduce discomfort, and a personal sense of helplessness or "loss of control" stemming from the persistence of drinking despite recognition of its adverse consequences. Virtually every aspect of individ-

Acknowledgment is due to Ms. Catherine Bond, who, under the author's supervision, treated the patient described in the case description, and to Ms. Lorry Spady, who assisted in the preparation of the manuscript.

ual functioning may be impaired to varying degrees by excessive alcohol consumption. Drinking may interfere with or end marital and other social relationships; it may result in absenteeism, reduced job performance, job loss, and associated economic difficulties; it may contribute to accidents and criminal behavior; and it may seriously compromise health. The least ambiguous clinical features that characterize the most severe form of the disorder are signs of what is sometimes referred to as "alcohol addiction." These signs, tolerance and withdrawal, occur only following prolonged excessive alcohol consumption, and they vary in proportion to the amount, frequency, and duration of drinking. Tolerance refers to the diminished effect obtained by repeated consumption of a fixed dosage of alcohol or the greatly increased dosage required after repeated alcohol consumption to achieve the desired effect. Withdrawal is a syndrome that occurs following cessation or reduction of drinking and that may include tremor, profuse sweating, nystagmus, muscle cramps, hyperreflexia, and occasionally seizures, disorientation, confusion, and vivid hallucinations (delirium tremens).

Two divergent models of alcoholism have very profound and very different implications for treatment. In what has become known as the *traditional model* (Pattison, Sobell, & Sobell, 1977), alcoholism is viewed as a progressive and irreversible disease of unknown genetic or physiological etiology manifest by an irresistible compulsion to drink and an inability to control alcohol consumption once it is initiated. The implications of this model are clear: drinking is determined by factors beyond the individual's control; inpatient treatment is no less appropriate than outpatient treatment; abstinence is the only appropriate treatment goal; and complete recovery is impossible. By contrast, the behavioral model assumes that drinking is a socially acquired, learned pattern of behavior; that it is a continuous rather than a dichotomous variable; and that alcoholism is a diagnostic label assigned to those whose drinking habits result in adverse personal consequences. From this perspective, alcoholism is determined by the interaction of environmental and personal variables and is, therefore, most appropriately treated on an outpatient bases. Abstinence and controlled drinking are equally legitimate treatment goals, and recovery depends on the acquisition of new patterns of behavior.

Although many questions regarding the nature and treatment of alcoholism remain unanswered, there is growing empirical support for the assumptions of the behavioral model. Undoubtedly, the most important finding from the clinical perspective is that individuals diagnosed as alcoholics improve significantly as a result of treatment. It is with faith in the promise of these findings, and the expectation that future research will confirm the efficacy of behavioral procedures, that the following guidelines for the assessment and treatment of alcoholism are presented.

CLINICAL ASSESSMENT

From a behavioral perspective, the distinction between assessment and treatment is an artificial one. Information gathering about the client should be conducted concurrently with treatment to permit an ongoing evaluation of the effects of therapy, which is essential for clinical decision making. Prior to implementation of any therapeutic procedure, however, the clinician must determine the extent of the drinking problem, the client's motivation for treatment, and the variables that influence the client's alcohol consumption. On the basis of this information, decisions will be made regarding the goal of treatment, selection of a treatment strategy, and outcome measures to be used. Following a brief discussion of each of these basic areas of assessment, clinically useful assessment methods for alcohol abuse are presented.

Assessment Areas

In assessing the extent of the client's problem, it is important not only to know how long he or she has been drinking in an abusive manner and what previous attempts, if any, have been made to modify alcohol consumption, but also to know the extent to which such drinking habits are affecting day-to-day activity. Abusive drinking can result in adverse consequences in virtually every area of an individual's functioning: health, marital, and social relationships, vocational activity, and economic and legal status. It is highly likely, in fact, that a problem in one or more of these areas occurred or intensified in a client's recent history and served as a stimulus to seek treatment. The client may, for example, have been treatened with separation or divorce from a spouse or with termination by an employer, may have been warned by a physician about medical risks associated with continued alcohol consumption, may have injured himself, or may have been charged with a criminal offense while intoxicated.

Obtaining information regarding the extent of a drinking problem not only permits an understanding of the client's current life circumstances, but is also of value in determining his or her motivation for treatment. To the extent that clients' social environments have imposed contingencies on them that govern their access to important reinforcers and support their treatment goals, they will likely be highly motivated to change their drinking habits. Unfortunately, however, many alcohol abusers are referred for treatment long after access to many meaningful reinforcers has been permanently withdrawn. The divorced alcohol abuser who is unemployed and rejected by his former friends is a case in point. Clients in such circumstances often dwell on what they have irrevocably lost as a consequence of their drinking. In assessing the motivation of such clients to modify their drinking, however, it is important to identify the reinforcers that may still be accessible and contingent on the client's improvement. The clinician's focus must, therefore, not only include the losses already sustained by the client, but more importantly, the losses that may yet occur in the absence of any improvement and the gains to be realized if improvement occurs.

Another major objective of the initial assessment is to identify the variables functionally related to alcohol consumption. Abusive drinking does not occur randomly. Rather, it is presumed to be lawfully related to a potential host of variables, and knowledge of these relationships is the key to the selection of the optimally effective treatment. It is useful in the functional analysis of drinking problems to classify potentially relevant variables as either internal or external. The former includes covert self-statements, physiological states, mood, and beliefs and expectations regarding the effects of alcohol—in other words, any cognitive, affective, or somatic condition of the client. External variables include social and environmental cues, such as the presence of drinking companions, a liquor advertisement, or a disapproving comment or expression from others. In temporal perspective, variables exercising the greatest influence over drinking are likely to be present shortly before, during, and shortly after drinking occurs. The fact that many alcoholics persist in drinking despite warnings of potentially catastrophic, long-term consequences is attributed by behavioral clinicians to the relatively greater influence of more subtle and more immediate antecedents and consequences. It is, therefore, particularly important to obtain detailed information regarding the client's drinking episodes. To facilitate further the identification of controlling variables, it is useful to contrast the circumstances surrounding abstinence or controlled drinking with those surrounding abusive drinking. This usually draws into sharper focus the role of important factors that might be overlooked if the clinician were to focus exclusively on abusive drinking episodes. Additional information regarding the functional analysis of alcohol consumption can be found in Sobell and Sobell (1981).

Information regarding the extent of the client's drinking problem is also necessary to determine the appropriate goal of treatment. For more than 20 years, a controversy has raged regarding the legitimacy of controlled drinking as a goal in the treatment of alcohol abusers. Initially, even reports of controlled drinking outcomes following abstinence-oriented treatments were severly attacked. Adherents of the traditional disease model, believing that alcoholism is both irreversible and characterized by a loss of control over drinking, argued that those who appeared to engage in nonproblematic drinking following treatment could not have been alcoholics in the first place. In the unlikely event that controlled drinking did occur following treatment, they argued, it was merely a prelude to a complete relapse. Successful treatment was assured only as long as the alcoholic avoided the first drink.

In the years since this controversy first erupted, more than 100 studies have documented successful controlled drinking outcomes by a significant minority of alcoholics (Sobell & Sobell, 1982). As a result, the objective of much current research has been to determine valid guidelines for assignment of clients to either abstinence or moderation-oriented treatment. In the absence of such empirically derived criteria, Miller and Caddy (1977) proposed a list of rationally derived contraindications for both treatment goals. They recommended against moderation for clients (1) whose health would be jeopardized by even small amounts of alcohol, (2) who are personally committed to abstinence or for whom there are social sanctions against moderation, (3) who have a history of pathological intoxication or severe withdrawal symptoms, (4) whose medication would be hazardous if combined with alcohol, and (5) who are successfully abstaining or who have failed in previous moderation-oriented treatment programs. Abstinence was considered an inappropriate goal for clients (1) who found it unacceptable, (2) whose social environments sanction against abstinence or fail to support it, (3) who have a shorter history of problem drinking, (4) who have not experienced severe withdrawal symptoms, and (5) who have failed in previous abstinence-oriented treatments.

Since these guidelines were published, empirical support for them has begun to accumulate. Specifically, it has been demonstrated that patients who request moderation-oriented treatment fare better in such programs than in abstinence-oriented treatments, and that the patients who achieve moderation initially consume less alcohol, report fewer symptoms of alcoholism, and have a briefer history of problem drinking than do those who are unsuccessful. In addition, successful controlled drinkers are more likely to be younger, and female, and are less likely to regard themselves as "alcoholics" or to have a familial history of alcoholism than are those who fail to moderate their drinking. To date, however, the majority of the relevant research is correlational in nature and derives from studies in which controlled drinking outcomes were reported following abstinence-oriented treatments. Matching of clients with treatment goals, therefore, will continue to involve a measure of clinical judgment until such time as the predictor variables have been validated in controlled research and the optional prediction equations for them have been determined.

Before a particular treatment strategy can be selected, it also is essential to assess treatment-relevant client and environmental variables. Some types of information are relevant to almost any potential treatment; these include the extent of clients' social contacts exclusive of their drinking companions, and the effective reinforcers for them and the availability of these reinforcers in the immediate environment. Some treatment strategies, however, will assume certain characteristics of the client, or the environment, or both, and these must be assessed before treatment is proposed. Bibliotherapy materials, for example, would be of little value to an illiterate client, and stimulus-control strategies would be impossible to implement if the client were to remain a bartender!

The final objectives of pretreatment assessment are to select appropriate outcome measures and to obtain a baseline. Obviously, some measure of alcohol consumption will be included, and various means of assessing it are described below. Less obvious, perhaps, is the necessity to select outcome measures of variables functionally related to the client's problem drinking. It may, for example, be appropriate to assess the client's social skills, marital adjustment, mood, and problem-solving skills. Assessment in these areas is particularly important in view of the research findings that improvement in drinking habits are not necessarily related to improvements in other areas of the client's functioning (Gerard, Saenger, & Wile, 1962). In addition, assessment of other drug usage is essential to ensure that improvements in drinking habits do not covary with increased usage of other substances that may be equally or more detrimental to the client (Miller, P. M., 1980). Recommendations regarding assessment in these related areas can be found in other chapters of this volume and in Hersen and Bellack (1981).

Assessment Methods

In an extensive review of assessment methods for alcohol abuse, W. R. Miller (1976) noted that the bulk of the research consisted of studies in which a single assessment strategy has been used in an attempt to differentiate alcoholics from nonalcoholics. Some investigators had used self-report instruments and others, behavioral observations or physiological measures in the quest for a valid and reliable diagnostic criterion for alcoholism. Three major problems with this approach, as Miller pointed out, are that it assumes (1) a high degree of uniformity among those labelled "alcoholics," (2) assumes primacy of the particular assessment strategy employed, and (3) reduces an already unduly limited amount of information about alcohol abusers to a dichotomous classification. The approach recommended by Miller and espoused by most behaviorally oriented clinicians (Foy, Rychtarik, & Prue, 1981; Miller, P. M., 1981; Nathan & Lipscomb, 1979) avoids the use of diagnostic labels, conceptualizes problem drinking as a continuous variable, and uses multimodal assessment, including self-report and behavioral and physiological measures. In this section, clinically useful examples of each of these types of measures are briefly described and their strengths and limitations noted.

The most clinically useful structured interview for the behavioral assessment of alcohol abuse is Marlatt's (1976) Drinking Profile. It is appropriate for inpatients or outpatients and includes closed- and open-ended questions regarding family and employment status, drinking history and current drinking practices, physical sequelae of drinking, motivation for treatment, and expectations for treatment outcome. In addition, there are sections that relate to drinking settings and companions, beverage preferences, and affective consequences of drinking that utilize a card-sort assessment technique. Altogether the instrument is 14 pages long and takes approximately one hour to administer. Scoring is straightforward. Responses to many of the items are expressed quantitatively, and for those that are not, a manual describing reliable coding categories and scoring rules is available. A complementary follow-up questionnaire has even been developed to assist in the evaluation of treatment outcome.

Like all direct self-report measures, however, the Drinking Profile is subject to distortion resulting from inaccurate recall, faking, and failures to observe relevant events. Recent research (Polich, 1982), in fact, indicates that whereas alcohol abusers provide accurate reports of abstinence and major, alcohol-related events such as hospitalizations, their current drinking practices are often underreported. In summary, the Drinking Profile provides detailed information relevant to all the assessment areas discussed previously. It is especially valuable for a functional analysis of alcohol consumption but should be used in conjunction with other assessment methods.

Although several alcoholism scales have been developed (Miller W. R., 1976), none is more valuable for a behavioral assessment than the Alcohol Use Inventory [AUI (Wanberg, Horn, & Foster, 1977)]. Unlike other questionnaires that have been developed by differentiating between alcoholic and nonalcoholic criterion groups, the AUI is based on a multidimensional model of alcohol abuse and a series of factor-analytic studies. The instrument itself includes 147 forced-choice items, which relate to styles of alcohol consumption, and adverse consequences and perceived benefits of drinking and that are divided into 22 empirically derived scales. The AUI scales have a median test–retest reliability of 0.81 and internal consistency reliability of 0.75 (Wanberg, Horn, & Foster, 1977) and have been shown to differentiate among outpatients, first-admission inpatients, and "chronic severe" inpatients who had previous histories of treatment for alcoholism. The predictive validity of the scales has been demonstrated to the extent that pretreatment scores discriminate between abstinent and nonabstinent groups at six-month follow-up. Original scale standardization was conducted on 2261 problem drinkers, including both men and women who, for the most part, were voluntarily admitted (94%) for short-term inpatient treatment at the Fort Logan Mental Health Center. Additional norms for other subgroups of alcohol abusers are also available.

Many of the AUI scales are directly relevant for a functional analysis of drinking. There are scales that focus on the circumstances of drinking (e.g., Gregarious versus Solitary Drinking, Drinking Following Marital Problems), the anticipated effects of drinking (e.g., Drink to Improve Sociability, Drinking to Improve Mental Functioning and Mental Benefit, Drink to Change Mood), the topography of drinking (e.g., Quantity of Alcohol Used, Obsessive-Compulsive Drinking, Continuous, Sustained Drinking), and the cognitive (e.g., Postdrinking Worry, Fear and Guilt, Psychoperceptual Withdrawal), social (e.g., Social-Role Maladaptation, Drinking Provokes Marital Problems), physical (Psychophysical Withdrawal), and behavior (Loss of Behavior Control when Drinking) consequences of drinking. There are also scales that relate to other drug usage and to previous treatment for alcoholism. Subscale scores do not substitute for a detailed intake interview or more extensive behavioral assessment of problems related to alcohol consumption; however, they do assist in the identification of factors functionally related to drinking and provide quantitative measures of them.

Although research is necessary to explore further the clinical utility of the AUI, it has been suggested that some subscale scores may be useful in decision making regarding inpatient or outpatient treatment (Alcohol-Use Disruption) and the appropriateness of anxiety reduction techniques (Anxiety Related to Drinking). It is noteworthy in this regard that a recent factor analytic study of the 16 AUI primary scale scores (Skinner, 1981) has led to the development of a 29-item Alcohol Dependence Scale that has been shown to predict drop-out from treatment and to be associated with patients' expected outcome following abstinence-oriented or controlled drinking treatment (Skinner & Allen, 1982).

Self-monitoring of alcohol consumption is generally introduced toward the end of the first session and continued throughout treatment. It not only provides an objective index of improvement and a basis for clinical decision making, but can also facilitate a functional analysis of the patient's drinking behavior (Miller & Mastria, 1977; Sobell & Sobell, 1973) and serve as the basis for a self-control approach to treatment (Miller & Muñoz, 1976). The patient may be instructed to record the date and time at which drinking occurs; the type and amount of beverage consumed; the setting in which drinking occurred, including drinking companions, if any, and antecedent and consequent behaviors, thoughts, or feelings. In addition, monitoring urges to drink that are resisted by the patient can facilitate a functional analysis if drinking episodes occur infrequently and can aid in the identification of responses that successfully compete with drinking. Unfortunately, there is no practical method of validating self-reports of daily drinking habits (Sobell, 1978). It is, therefore, particularly important to supplement them with additional assessment methods (Brownell, 1982; Polich, 1982; Sobell, Sobell, & Vander Spek 1979).

Although direct observations of drinking have been conducted in the natural environment (Kessler & Gomberg, 1974, Rosenbluth, Nathan, & Lawson, 1978), the practical limitations of this assessment methodology have led to the development of a host of analogue drinking measures (Nathan & Briddell, 1977). Unfortunately, analogue drinking measures such as those obtained in simulated barrooms and living rooms or in research laboratories or hospital wards are usually equally impractical or inappropriate for the clinical assessment of outpatient alcoholics. As a result, clinicians typically rely on friends, relatives, or coworkers of their clients to provide observational data of their drinking. P. M. Miller (1981) cautions, however, that such collateral observers must be selected judiciously to maximize objectivity of reporting and to avoid the possibility that the observers themselves do not inadvertently provoke the client's drinking. Collateral observers should also be selected on the basis of the amount of contact they have with the client, since there is suggestive evidence that those with the greatest contact provide the most accurate reports (Miller, Crawford, & Taylor, 1979; Maisto, Sobell, & Sobell, 1979).

Even with appropriately selected collateral observers, it is unlikely that self- and collateral reports will be in perfect agreement. The available research, in fact, suggests that (1) correlations between self- and collateral reports, although generally positive, can range between .06 and .92; (2) collaterals are as likely to underestimate as to overestimate client reports of drinking; (3) agreement is greater for reports of abstinence and readily discriminated alcohol-related events such as hospitalization; and (4) factors such as interviewer skill and a client's knowledge that collateral sources will be contacted may increase agreement between self- and collateral reports (Maisto, Sobell, & Sobell, 1979; Miller, Crawford, & Taylor, 1979; Polich, 1982). The only exception to this general caveat regarding collateral sources is when there is a therapeutic contract that specifies that drinking may occur only in the presence of the observer. P. M. Miller (1972), for example, established a behavioral contract in which a client's wife agreed to refrain from criticizing her husband's drinking, provided it occurred only in her presence at specified times of the day and did not exceed a limit that had been mutually agreed on. Evidence of the husband's drinking at other times, such as observations of friends, impaired behavior, or liquor on his breath, resulted in a monetary fine.

An objective but indirect measure of drinking that is also widely used in research is blood alcohol concentration. Because there is a constant ratio between the concentration of alcohol in the breath and in the blood, sophisticated breath-testing instruments permit a precise estimate of blood alcohol concentration that, in turn, is positively related to acute alcohol impairment and the amount consumed (Lovell, 1972). Many such instruments, however, have been developed for use in research and in the criminal justice system and, as a result, are highly accurate but prohibitively expensive for occasional use in clinical settings.

Fortunately, however, inexpensive portable breath-testing devices are now commercially available and provide relatively accurate estimates of blood alcohol concentration immediately after testing. Perhaps the best known of these instruments is the Mobat SM-6, which is manufactured by Luckey Laboratories (7252 Obsun Road, San Bernadino, California 92404). In essence, a breath sample is collected in a balloon, which is then connected to a tube through which a predetermined volume of expired air passes before a volumetric bag attached to the other end of the tube becomes fully inflated. Inside the tube are three rings of a chemically treated gel that changes in color from yellow to green on exposure to alcohol. The Mobat SM-6 permits blood alcohol level estimates in the range of 0–30 mg percent with an average error of approximately ±4 mg percent (Sobell, & Sobell, 1975) at a cost of less than $1.25 per test. Another practical feature of the Mobat SM-6 is that patients and others who may be involved in treatment can be easily instructed in its use. It not only serves as an objective treatment outcome measure, therefore, but can also be used as a feedback device by the client during a drinking episode and to resolve disputes regarding the occurrence and amount of drinking.

When breath-testing instruments are used as detection devices, however, no inference can be made regarding the amount consumed without knowledge of the time course of drinking, because the metabolism of alcohol will begin almost immediately after it is consumed. A client could, therefore, easily evade detection by discontinuing a drinking episode in sufficient time to allow the alcohol he had consumed to metabolize (approximately one hour per SEC consumed). It is for this reason that breath tests are usually administered on an unscheduled basis. To facilitate the interpretation of blood alcohol levels, a computer program (Matthews & Miller, 1977) and a slide-rule device (Compton & Vogler, 1975) are available that transform blood alcohol levels into consumption measures and vice versa while taking into account the passage of time since alcohol was consumed and individual client characteristics such as weight and sex.

Attempts to identify a longer-lasting biological index of alcohol consumption that would reflect drinking patterns over a period of weeks have focused attention on the liver enzyme, gamma-glutamyl transpeptidase (GGT). Although serum levels of GGT are significantly elevated for several weeks after drinking (Lamy, Baglin, Weill, & Aaron, 1975), they also are elevated as a result of a variety of physical disorders and other drug usage. Moreover, significant GGT elevations characterize only 55% of healthy, untreated alcohol abusers who are otherwise drug-free (Garvin, Foy, & Alford, 1981). Insofar as GGT indicates the extent of probable liver damage, however, it is of value in (1) screening clients for controlled drinking programs (Reyes & Miller, 1980); (2) increasing the patient's motivation for treatment; and (3) monitoring improvement in liver function among patients with elevated pretreatment GGT levels. (Garvin, Foy, & Alford, 1981; Reyes & Miller, 1980).

Archival records provide another potentially valuable indirect measure of alcohol consumption. Records of employment status, absenteeism from work (especially following weekends and paydays), arrests, driving charges, and hospitalizations have all been used as treatment outcome measures (Sobell, 1978). Although the client's written consent must first be obtained before such archival records can be requested, it is noteworthy that clients themselves can provide paycheck stubs to substantiate self-reports of employment (Miller, P. M., 1981).

TREATMENT TECHNIQUES

In a recent, comprehensive review of treatments for alcohol abuse, Miller and Hester (1980, p. 108) concluded that "No treatment method has been shown to be consistently superior to the absence of treatment or to alternative treatments in a sufficient number of well-controlled studies to warrant 'established status.' The corollaries to this statement are that therapists working with alcohol abusers must be skilled in a variety of different treatment techniques and adopt a flexible approach to ensure that treatment is individually tailored to the needs of the patient. Miller and Hester also noted that "extensive and intensive interventions are no more effective in general than are more minimal treatments" (Miller & Hester, 1980, p. 108–110). Accordingly, they recommend the selective use of a limited number of techniques that focus primarily on drinking before implementation of comprehensive, broadband treatment programs.

A variety of treatment techniques are described in this section, all of which have some empirical support and that, in various combinations, would be appropriate for any particular alcohol abuser. All these techniques can be viewed as serving one or more of the following treatment objectives indentified by Miller and Foy (1981): (1) to educate the patient about the nature of alcohol abuse and the effects of alcohol consumption, (2) to teach alternative coping skills that clients could use in situations that formerly led to drinking, (3) to modify directly the situational and topographical parameters of drinking, (4) to decrease the immediate reinforcing effects of drinking; and (6) to rearrange contingencies in the client's natural environment so as to maximize reinforcement for abstinence or controlled drinking. In addition, a final overview is included of some recently developed, but as yet untested techniques, designed to minimize the likelihood of relapse.

Alcohol Education

Although few, if any behaviorally oriented clinicians would rely exclusively on alcohol education as a treatment for alcoholism, many incorporate educational components in their treatment programs. The purpose for including an alcohol education component is twofold: (1) it prepares clients for treatment by disabusing them of their misconceptions regarding the nature of alcoholism and the effects of alcohol and by providing an alternative conception to the traditional model of alcohol abuse, and (2) it enhances clients' motivations for treatment by informing them of potential adverse effects of alcohol abuse and by describing promising treatment approaches. What little research there is on the effects of alcohol education programs with clinical populations supports its use for these purposes (Uecker & Solberg, 1973).

The content and format of alcohol education programs can vary substantially. Vogler, Weissbach, Compton, and Martin (1977), for example, instructed their patients in the physiological and behavioral effects of alcohol, the etiology of alcohol abuse, and the use of the Alco-Calculator (Center of Alcohol Studies, Rutgers–The State University) to estimate blood alcohol concentration. Miller and Muñoz (1976) included a definition of controlled drinking, drinking norms, and information regarding the degrees of impairment associated with various blood alcohol concentrations, the alcohol content of various beverages, and other factors that influence blood alcohol concentration. Similarly, a variety of formats have been used to communicate this information including bibliotherapy materials, videotape, and lectures. In a comparison of these methods in an inpatient setting, Stalonas, Keane, and Foy (1979) found that videotaped presentations were the most effective.

Alternative Coping Skills

In an analysis of relapse episodes among 70 alcohol abusers, Marlatt and Gordon (1980) found that the vast majority of relapses (74%) occurred in response to negative emotional states, interpersonal conflict, and social pressure to resume drinking. It is, therefore, not surprising that skill training programs that develop alternative responses to these antecedents of drinking have been found to be effective in treatment outcome research. What follows is an overview of the specific coping skills that have been targeted in programs for alcohol abusers and the training techniques that have been used to develop them.

Assertiveness training is very often included in alcoholism treatment programs and has occasionally been used as the primary component of treatment. "Assertiveness" refers to the direct and appropriate verbal and nonverbal expression of both positive and negative thoughts and feelings and includes a wide variety of behavior such as refusing unreasonable requests, responding to criticism, offering compliments, initiating conversations, and requesting changes in the behavior of others (Gambrill, 1978). Eisler, Hersen, and Miller (1974), for example, described a 34-year-old male night clerk who, despite a long drinking history, had been abstinent for several months prior to his promotion as motel manager. A functional analysis of his drinking episodes following his promotion identified three antecedent situations, each of which required an assertive response: (1) requesting housekeeping staff to clean the motel rooms more thoroughly; (2) refusing salesmen who wanted him to make unnecessary purchases; and (3) handling unreasonable complaints made by motel patrons. Following acquisition of appropriate assertive responses to these situations, the patient was reported to have been able to cope with the demands of his new job more effectively and without resort to alcohol.

In view of Marlatt and Gordon's (1980) findings that many relapses occur in response to direct social pressure to resume drinking, it is especially important that patients be trained to refuse drinks asser- tively. In the drink refusal training program developed by Foy, Miller, Eisler, and O'Toole (1976), two therapists and the client played three specific situations in which the client was offered a drink. During each interaction, the therapists assumed the roles of "friends" or relatives who insisted that the client drink with them and who persisted even after he or she had initially refused. After a baseline was established, the patient was taught to emit five target behaviors: (1) to request his companions to refrain from insisting that he drink in the role-played situation and in the future; (2) to suggest thay they engage in an activ- ity other than drinking; (3) to redirect the conversation to a topic un- related to alcohol; (4) to look directly at his companions while he was speaking to them; and (5) to use his voice, facial expression, and hand gestures in a convincing manner. Although this program effectively established assertive drink refusal skills, which were maintained at a three-month follow-up, no published study has yet evaluated its con- tribution to successful treatment outcome.

Two variations of drink refusal training are noteworthy. The first is that it can be used with clients whose goal is moderation as well as with those whose goal is abstinence. P. M. Miller (1975b), for example, adapted the procedures for refusal of the second or third drink and, once the clients became proficient, they role-played the situation af- ter actually consuming one or two drinks. A second variation is to uti- lize a group training format and to cast group members rather than therapists in the "pusher" role. It is commonly observed that alcohol abusers themselves play this role more convincingly, which in turn makes the role-played situation more realistic.

Another approach to alternative skills training is the problem-solving skills training program developed and validated by Chaney, O'Leary, and Marlatt (1978). The focus of their treatment was on four general situations that had been selected on the basis of Marlatt's (1978) ear- lier analysis of the circumstances associated with relapse: those in which the patient was (1) frustrated and unable to express anger; (2) pressured by others to drink; (3) lonely, bored, depressed, or experi- encing other negative emotional states; and (4) experiencing a desire or urge to drink in the absence of any identifiable antecendent. Four specific examples of each of these problematic situations were pre- sented during the course of eight sessions, and patients were instructed to adopt a problem-solving approach in their response to each of them. More specifically, they were taught the following problem-solving pro- cedure developed by D'Zurilla and Goldfried (1971): (1) to accept that problems are an inevitable aspect of daily life, to recognize them when they occur, and to refrain from responding to them impulsively; (2) to define problematic situations specifically and to identify the personal goals that are thwarted by them; (3) to generate as many alternative responses as possible while suspending judgment regarding their effectiveness; (4) to select a response on the basis of its predicted short- and long-term consequences; and (5) to rehearse the response and assess whether the anticipated consequences are realized. Unlike assertiveness training and drink refusal training, in which specific coping responses are indentified for specific situations, problem solving provides a more general coping skill applicable to a wide variety of problematic situations. Although controlled-outcome research on problem solving has only just begun, the first such study revealed a significant reduction in the duration and severity of relapse episodes during the year following treatment (Chaney et al., 1978).

A common core of training techniques is used in assertiveness, drink refusal, and problem-solving training. First, the patient and therapist role-play several situations that exemplify those that precipitate drinking. This initial role-playing is often videotaped for the purpose of obtaining baseline measures of specific verbal and nonverbal components of behavior, such as duration of eye contact, facial expression, tone of voice, and requests for behavior change. Patients are then given specific instructions regarding these behaviors, appropriate responses are then modeled by therapists, and the situations are again role-played and videotaped. In addition to feedback from therapists and other patients, if the training is conducted in a group setting, videotape feedback may also be provided. When assertive and problem-solving responses are mastered in the treatment setting, patients are instructed to practice them between sessions to maximize their generalization to the natural environment. Postassessment can take the form of a role-play of the same or similar situations or less obtrusive measures either in the treatment setting or in the natural environment.

To the extent that excessive drinking is functionally related to marital discord, marital therapy is an appropriate treatment component and can be viewed as yet another example of alternative skills training. Most of the objectives of marial therapy for alcoholics are identical to those of most other behaviorally oriented marital therapy programs and include (1) increasing shared recreational activities; (2) increasing and reinforcing behaviors that connote caring and affection; (3) improving communication skills and scheduling "talking times," and (4) improving problem-solving skills. Detailed descriptions of these objectives and the associated training procedures are provided in Chapter 9.

One feature specific to marital therapy with alcohol abusers, however, is a behavioral contract that is usually written and signed by both partners and in which the alcoholic agrees to limit or abstain from or to take disulfiram. The spouse, in turn, agrees to refrain from making any comments relating to the alcoholic's past or future drinking. Such behavioral contracts may also specify social reinforcement of each partner by the other for compliance with the contract and response costs if it is violated (Azrin, 1976; Miller, 1972, 1978; O'Farrell & Cutter, 1981). Although marital skills training often is included in broad-spectrum treatment programs, there are relatively few outcome studies of its effectiveness as a primary form of treatment. There is, however, a consensus based on the available research that behavioral marital therapy is a promising form of intervention for alcoholism (P. M. Miller, 1978; Miller & Hester, 1980).

Modifying Situational and Topographical Parameters of Drinking

Whereas the procedures described above are intended to develop skills that enable alcohol abusers to cope effectively with problematic situations without resorting to alcohol, another approach to treatment is to teach them to modify the situational and topographical parameters of their drinking so as to reduce it to a nonproblematic level. Although this approach is appropriate only for a selected minority of alcoholics, it nevertheless has wide application in outpatient practice. This approach to treatment is probably best exemplified by the behavioral self-control training program described by Miller and Muñoz (1976). Their program teaches problem drinkers to identify factors associated with excessive drinking, such as the time of day, drinking companions, location, and moods; and to avoid drinking in their presence. In addition, a variety of self-control techniques are used to modify the amount and rate of alcohol consumption. These include self-monitoring, goal setting, self-reinforcement, drink spacing, and alternating alcoholic and nonalcoholic beverages.

Since behavioral self-control training also includes instruction in alternative coping skills and drink refusal training, it is impossible to determine the effects of stimulus control and rate reduction procedures along on the basis of the available treatment outcome studies. Recent treatment outcome research on behavioral self-control training is, however, relevant because of its implications for cost-effective outpatient treatment. According to the average improvement rates at one-year follow-up calculated by Miller and Hester (1980) for moderation-oriented treatments, the focused, behavioral self-control program conducted in 10 sessions is as effective as more extensive, multimodal treatments lasting twice as long. Moreoever, behavioral self-control training has been shown to be as effective in the treatment of nonaddicted problem drinkers in self-administered bibliotherapy format as it is in individual therapy (Miller & Taylor, 1980). There are, undoubtedly, those for whom the more extensive, professionally administered treatments are necessary, the the problem, as Brownell (1982) has noted, is one of achieving an optimal match between patient and treatment.

Making Alcohol Aversive

One of the earliest behavioral approaches to the treatment of alcoholism, aversion therapy, is based on the assumption that the apparent attraction alcohol has for the alcoholic can be reversed if the sight, small, and taste of alcoholic beverages are associated with a noxious stimulus. Over the years, a variety of aversive physical stimuli have been used in this paradigm, the most popular of which were electric shock and nausea-producing drugs. Although treatment with the latter has been associated with some of the most impressive abstinence rates ever reported, it has never been compared to a no-treatment control condition, nor is it discussed further here for it is administered only on an inpatient basis. Aversion therapy with electric shock, by contrast, has been the subject of considerable treatment outcome research, the results of which indicate that it produces a high dropout rate and is relatively ineffective. Not surprisingly, there is a growing consensus that electrical aversion therapy should be discontinued for the treatment of alcohol abuse (Nathan & Briddell, 1977; Nathan & Lipscomb, 1979; Wilson, 1978).

There is, however, one form of aversion therapy that can be used in outpatient settings and that is comparable in effectiveness to chemical aversion (Miller, W. R., 1982). In covert sensitization, patients are first relaxed and then instructed to imagine as vividly as possible a drinking scene in which they become nauseated and vomit after having consumed an alcoholic beverage. In the procedure described by Elkins (1980), detailed information is obtained about the typical circumstances of drinking in order to heighten the realism of subsequent nausea suggestions. Particular attention is also given in the verbally guided imaginal scenes to the patient's desire for alcohol and to the sensory and motor components of drinking. After patients have imagined themselves taking their first swallow, a detailed and disgusting description is given on the onset of nausea and vomiting, including suggestions of a foul-tasting vomitus moving up into the throat and out through the nose and mouth and other images of it floating in the beverage and running down the side of the glass. The scene ends with the patient running from the drinking setting, beginning to feel relieved, and, finally, washing up at home and feeling completely relaxed. In subsequent scenes, suggestions regarding nausea are associated with progressively earlier events in the drinking sequence, and relief is associated with the consumption on nonalcoholic beverages or engaging in pleasurable activities unrelated to drinking. After patients reliably report the sensation of nausea in response to suggestions, they are instructed to self-administer treatment trials both in the treatment setting and at home. In Elkins' (1980) study, as many as 50 scenes were presented in an average of 12 treatment sessions.

It is important to bear in mind when considering covert sensitization that it constitutes a treatment component rather than a treatment per se. As P. M. Miller (1976) noted, covert sensitization is best viewed as a self-control strategy that is useful in supressing alcohol consumption while patients are taught alternative coping response and therapeutic environmental contingencies are established.

Therapeutic Contingencies in the Natural Environment

Dozens of studies conducted in residential laboratories and hospital research wards during the 1960s and 1970s attest to the effectiveness of environmental contingencies in modifying the drinking behavior of alcoholics. Reinforcers as diverse as enriched ward environments, weekend passes and even access to alcohol itself, and punitive consequences such as brief social isolation and forfeiture of ward privileges were consistently shown to produce either controlled drinking or abstinence. The theoretical implications of these findings were obvious: alcoholics were not subject to an involuntary "loss of control" over their drinking. The clinical implications, however, were less clear for generalization of treatment effects depends entirely on the extent to which similarly effective environmental contingencies could be established in the natural environment. In recent years, several investigators have demonstrated that, with persistence and ingenuity, individually tailored therapeutic contingencies can be established to control drinking outside laboratory settings. Some of the simplest of these interventions, such as the marital contract described previously, were developed by Peter Miller. In another of P. M. Miller's studies (1975a), 10 chronic public drunkeness offenders who ordinarily had noncontingent access to community agency resources such as housing, employment, meals, cigarettes and nonessential medical care became ineligible to receive them for a five-day period if they were judged to be grossly intoxicated by agency staff or if their randomly scheduled breath tests revealed a blood alcohol concentration in excess of 10 mg%. As a result of this intervention, there were significant reductions in alcohol consumption and public drunkeness arrests and a significant increase in the number of hours the subjects were employed.

The most comprehensive contingency management program described in the literature is embedded within the multicomponent, community-reinforcement program developed by Azrin and his colleagues (Azrin, 1976; Azrin, Sisson, Meyers, & Godley, 1982; Hunt & Azrin, 1973). In addition to marital contracts for abstinence, such as those described previously, spouses were advised to refrain as much as possible from physical and social contact with the alcoholics in the event that they began to drink and, if necessary, to move out of the house until sobriety had been regained and the spouse had been requested to return. To encourage social interactions in the absence of drinking, a self-supporting social club was established in a former tavern where patients could invite their friends to dance, play cards, and engage in other recreational activities, but where alcoholic beverages were strictly forbidden. Any member showing any indication of drinking was denied admission. Less specific contingencies to maintain abstinence were also established.

Perhaps the most powerful contingency of the community reinforcement program was established through the "disulfiram assurance" component. The drug disulfiram is typically administered on a chronic basis and reacts with alcohol to produce an aversive physical reaction characterized by flushing, increased skin temperature, hypotension, and in more severe reactions, nausea, vomiting, and shock (Kwentus & Major, 1979). As a result, when disulfiram is taken, it serves as an effective deterrent to alcohol consumption, but it must be prescribed only for carefully selected alcoholics who are unlikely to experience a severe reaction by rapidly consuming a large amount of alcohol, and who are in adequate physical condition to tolerate a moderate disulfiram–alcohol reaction. The greatest limitation of disulfiram as a treatment adjunct, however, is noncompliance with self-administration. In the "disulfiram assurance" treatment component, alcoholics were instructed to take the medication at a regular time and place, and in the presence of a spouse, roommate, employer, or friend. Both the alcoholic and his monitor role-played solutions to situations in which the alcoholic wanted to discontinue the medication or in which the monitor wanted to discontinue his role in treatment. As a final resort, either could call the program counselor, who would contact the noncompliant partner to urge that the arrangement be reinstated.

At the six-month follow-up, the "disulfiram assurance" component alone was significantly more effective than traditional disulfiram treatment and resulted in near complete abstinence by married or cohabitating clients. Whether this finding justifies use of "disulfiram assurance" as a sole component of treatment for this group may well be a contentious issue that will be settled only after longer term follow-up data with a larger number of subjects are available. In the meantime, it is noteworthy that near total abstinence was achieved in single patients only through a combination of the broad-spectrum community reinforcement therapy and "disulfiram assurance" procedures (Azrin et al., 1982).

Relapse-Prevention Strategies

The final stage of outpatient treatment that Miller and Hester (1980) recommend for all patients is a relapse-prevention program. The most extensive program development in this area has been conducted by Marlatt and his colleagues and is based on his cognitive-behavioral model of relapse (Marlatt, 1978; Marlatt & Gordon, 1980). Several interventions derived from this model, including coping skills training, controlled drinking skills, and alcohol education already have been described in detail. Others, however, are unique to Marlatt's cognitive behavioral model and are described briefly below.

The first steps on the path to relapse, according to Marlatt, are cognitive antecedents. These include *apparently irrelevant decisions* (AIDS), such as deciding to keep liquor in the house for friends who may come by unexpectedly. Since a series of such AIDs may culminate in an overwhelmingly irresistible temptation, clients are trained to recognize them and to use their occurrence as a signal to reconsider their decisions, to accept personal responsibility for the outcome, and to recommit themselves to their treatment goals. At a later point on the path to relapse, alcoholics may feel a sense of deprivation resulting from a preponderance of externally imposed demands on their time and activities. In such circumstances they may be disposed to compensate by overindulging in alcohol. To reduce this risk, Marlatt recommends that alcoholics schedule a regular break during each day to engage in a pleasurable activity of their own choosing, which would serve the same function as drinking, but that would enhance their sense of self-efficacy. The final step leading to relapse in the cognitive behavioral model is the first drink following treatment. In contrast to most other treatments, the relapse-prevention approach realistically acknowledges the near inevitability of drinking following treatment and provides a cognitive coping strategy for dealing with it. In essence, Marlatt contends that the cognitive and affective responses of alcoholics to the first drink determine the amount of their subsequent drinking. To the extent that drinkers experience dissonance arising from their conflicting perceptions of themselves as abstainers who have just had a drink and to the extent that they attribute this "slip" to their own personal weaknesses rather than to external factors, they fall victim to what Marlatt refers to as the *abstinence violation effect* (AVE). Under these circumstances, the likelihood of a full relapse occurring is greatly increased. If, however, alcoholics construe the event as an opportunity to learn more about the factors affecting their drinking rather than as evidence of personal failure, they are more likely to regain control of their drinking. To prepare clients to respond in this manner, Marlatt recommends that they (1) be forewarned about the AVE, (2) rehearse a relapse episode either in imagination or overtly without actually drinking, and (3) carry with them a wallet-sized card that specifically prompts an adaptive cognitive interpretation of the first drink. Marlatt even goes so far as to recommend in extreme cases that the therapist schedule and supervise a "programmed relapse" during which clients actually consume a drink (if a relapse appears imminent, and if such a controlled exposure is deemed necessary to extinguish patients' maladaptive expectations concerning alcohol's effects).

Although the "programmed relapse" is viewed by some as an entirely unique procedure, it can be seen as an extension of the much less controversial exposure approach described by Blakey and Baker (1980). Unfortunately, like the exposure approach, Marlatt's relapse prevention strategies are yet to be systematically evaluated in controlled treatment outcome research. It is likely, however, that some of the procedures he advocates will be implemented if only on the basis of their intuitive appeal and the strong empirical foundation of his cognitive behavioral model of relapse.

CASE STUDY

Mr. D. L., a 35-year-old union negotiator employed in the construction industry, was referred by his physician for treatment of recurrent episodes of anxiety and depression, alcohol dependence, and reactive depression stemming from the recent termination of a romantic relationship.

The client was one of seven children who reported having a happy childhood and good relationship with his mother and siblings. His father, who was a self-employed contractor and often absent from the home, had had a drinking problem for which he sought help from Alcoholics Anonymous. At the age of 14 years, the client began to associate with older adolescents who spent much of their time drinking and partying, and he himself began to drink heavily. Mr. D. L. left school in the tenth grade and worked sporadically until he married at the age of 19. Two years later, he was sentenced to a year in prison for breaking and entering; shortly after his release, he and his wife separated and he took custody of their two daughters. During the years preceding his treatment, Mr. D. L. had held several different jobs in the construction industry and, for a short while, had been a partner in a private business venture. He enjoyed good relationships with both his daughters until six months before treatment, at which time his older daughter, who was 13, went to live with her mother. Two months before coming to treatment, his girlfriend had terminated their relationship of three years and Mr. D. L. had become depressed and had briefly contemplated suicide.

Mr. D. L. had a lengthy history of problem drinking beginning when he was 16 years of age, at which time he frequently engaged in barroom brawls that led to 10 arrests during a two-year period. He had also been charged twice during his late twenties for drinking and driving offenses. He reported, during a structured interview (Marlatt's Drinking Profile), that his drinking had also caused him to lose several jobs and to lose friends and had directly contributed to his separation from his wife and the dissolution of his more recent romantic relationship. In the month prior to their breakup, he apparently had spent considerable time drinking with his business associates and had on several occasions neglected to call or meet his girlfriend despite previous commitments to do so. Mr. D. L. also reported having repeatedly experienced hangovers, nausea, vomiting, the "shakes," and "blackouts" after drinking. Despite the lengthy history of problem drinking and its numerous adverse consequences for Mr. D. L., he had attended only a few Alcoholics Anonymous meetings and had not previously sought any other form of treatment.

Detailed information obtained during the structured interview and from self-monitored records was used in a functional analysis of Mr. D. L.'s drinking and episodes of mixed anxiety and depression. Two or three times each week, Mr. D. L. consumed 6–15 drinks with business associates, and on Saturdays and Sundays, he drank approximately 20 and 5 drinks, respectively. He also reported that he rarely drank at home, but most often in the evening while alone or with friends in a lounge or restaurant. Drinking, according to Mr. D. L., made him feel more socially at ease, especially when he was feeling "bored, lonely, and wanted someone to talk to." His ex-girlfriend had been the only woman with whom he had had a long-term relationship since his separation from his wife 12 years earlier, and he had no other close friends. In fact, apart from occasional reading, watching television, and preparing his evening meal, Mr. D. L.'s principal leisure activity was drinking in bars.

Approximately every six weeks, Mr. D. L. was overcome by feelings of nervousness and dysphoria that lasted one or two days, but that appeared to him to be unrelated to any precipitating environmental event. The first such episode occurred four years prior to treatment, on the dissolution of his business partnership, and subsequent episodes seemed to occur when he was experiencing a hangover and was engaged in particularly stressful labor negotiations. Following these episodes, he typically took diazepam for a few days and occasionally drank to calm himself.

As a result of this behavioral analysis, three treatment goals were identified:

(1) to reduce his drinking to a nonproblematic level; (2) to develop social relationships and recreational interests unrelated to drinking or work; and (3) to reduce the frequency and severity of his episodic anxiety and depression. Moderation rather than abstinence was selected as a goal because he had not suffered any medical disorder, delerium tremens, or seizures as a result of his drinking. Moreover, his social environment sanctioned against abstinence; he did not consider himself an "alcoholic," and he had explicitly expressed his desire to reduce his drinking. His physician, of course, approved of moderation-oriented treatment. It is noteworthy, however, that Mr. D. L. was not an ideal candidate for such treatment in that he had a family history of alcoholism and a lengthy history of excessive drinking with numerous associated life problems.

Following a two-week baseline period, during which his average weekly alcohol consumption was 65 drinks (see Figure 6-1), a behavioral self-control training program was initiated. The client was first instructed in the functional analysis of his drinking behavior and episodes of mixed anxiety and depression. Goal-setting strategies were introduced and a more detailed self-monitoring form was provided on which he specified his daily drinking goals one week in advance. Upper limits of three drinks per hour and four drinks per session were agreed on to ensure that his blood alcohol content (BAC) always remained well within the legal limit for driving. Rate-reduction strategies such as alternating alcoholic and nonalcoholic beverages and ordering regular drinks rather than "doubles" were proposed, as were stimulus-control strategies such as drinking with moderate rather than with excessive drinkers and in locations where he was least likely to exceed his self-imposed limits. Weekly consumption rates were plotted on a graph at each session and checks

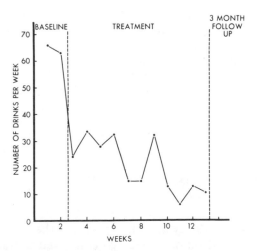

Figure 6-1 Weekly self-monitored alcohol consumption during baseline, treatment, and at three-month follow-up.

were made to determine whether he had exceeded his hourly and sessional limits. These self-control strategies were introduced during the sessions on weeks 2 and 3 and would, therefore, appear to account for the dramatic reduction in weekly consumption immediately following baseline.

During the subsequent three sessions, particular attention was focused on the development of new social relationships and recreational interests. After considering a number of alternatives, Mr. D. L. volunteered to coach a juvenile football team and enrolled in a night school course that ran two nights a week. On hearing a rumor that his ex-girlfriend was engaged to be married, he wanted to win her back, despite the fact that he had never been able to express his feelings toward her. Consequently, an entire session was devoted to assertiveness training. Instructions, modeling, role-playing, and therapist feedback were used in rehearsing his initial telephone contact with her and, in the event she accepted his invitation, in rehearsing their interaction at dinner. Within a few weeks, the relationship had been reestablished; Mr. D. L.'s girlfriend became a collateral source of information regarding his drinking during the latter portion of therapy.

Late in therapy, one session was devoted to the self-management of depression, despite the fact that the client had not scored in the clinical range on the Beck Depression Inventory (BDI). This session was intended to reinforce the patient's newly acquired conceptualization of depression and to prepare him for the possibility of occasional recurrence in the future. One episode of anxiety and depression had occurred during the course of treatment and had lasted "less than a minute." Unlike earlier episodes, however, Mr. D. L. attributed it immediately to environmental factors rather than to his own inadequacy. Apparently, after a series of lengthy and heated negotiation sessions a contract had been signed, but before the ink had dried, the company owner's wife began to question the terms of the settlement.

As Figure 6-1 illustrates, there was a clinically significant reduction in the patient's weekly alcohol consumption. Confirmation of the data provided during the latter sessions was obtained by Mr. D. L.'s girlfriend, who, by the final treatment session, was living with the patient. She also corroborated his self-reported abstention from cigarette smoking, which had occurred during the week of the eighth session. Tobacco and alcohol usage were unchanged at three-month follow-up, although the patient had gained weight. A notation in a Christmas card sent by Mrs. D. L. 1½ years after treatment indicated that the patient was continuing to drink in a nonproblematic manner.

ISSUES ARISING FROM ASSESSMENT AND TREATMENT

A host of issues inevitably arise in providing therapeutic services to alcoholics. Consideration has already been given to the most controversial and most frequently discussed issue, the relative merits of abstinence and controlled drinking as goals of treatment. What follows are brief guidelines for handling four less prominent but no less important issues: (1) the credibility of nonalcoholic therapists; (2) the rationale for collateral data sources; (3) noncompliance with instructions to self-monitor; and (4) the accuracy of self-monitored consumption data.

Perhaps because of the widespread reputation of Alcoholics Anonymous as a self-help organization and because of uncritical acceptance of its claims of therapeutic efficacy, some alcoholics assume that effective treatment can be provided only by a therapist who was once an alcoholic. This assumption, if unchallenged, can seriously jeopardize treatment effectiveness and should, therefore, be addressed at the outset in much the same manner as any other query regarding the therapist's qualifications. Do not depreciate the value of self-help approaches to treatment, but begin instead by providing personal information regarding clinical training, licensure, membership in professional associations, and other relevant personal experience. General findings in the research literature may also be presented: according to Miller and Hester (1980), nothing has been published in the last 11 years to change Covner's (1969) conclusion that "a history of alcoholism neither guarantees nor precludes counseling success" (Covner, 1969, p. 422). It may also be of value to examine the assumptions underlying this belief and to point out that other patients do not consider personal experience with their psychological disorder as a prerequisite for therapeutic effectiveness. Reference may also be made to previous successful treatment outcomes both in one's own clinical practice and in those of other nonalcoholics; and treatment may be offered with the understanding that the alcoholic, like any other patient, may terminate the therapeutic contract at any time. Ultimately, the therapist's credibility is established by his or her demonstration of technical expertise in the selection and implementation of treatment techniques and by willingness to enter into a genuine therapeutic relationship.

Direct observation of the patient's drinking behavior by collateral sources, such as friends, relatives, and employers, is the most practical, albeit imperfect, means of corroborating self-reports of drinking. Requesting the patient's consent to obtain this information, however, may be problematic because it may be construed as evidence of distrust or an invasion of privacy. To minimize these problems, the patient is usually informed at the outset, even before the establishment of a therapeutic relationship, that these measures are routinely required. Descriptions of the treatment program, including the involvement of collateral data sources may be included in brochures that are sent to patients prior to their first appointment or made available in the clinic waiting room. Admission to some treatment programs may even be, and often is, contingent on patient consent to provide names of significant others who could corroborate client self-reports of drinking. It is noteworthy that the use of such collateral sources not only yields additional assessment information, but is likely also to improve the accuracy of the assessment method used most extensively, self-report.

Two potential problems regarding the self-monitoring of drinking must routinely be anticipated: compliance and accuracy. To minimize noncompliance with requests to self-monitor, the clinician must first emphasize the importance of the information it provides and convey at the outset the expectation that monitoring will continue throughout the course of therapy. A form or index card with designated columns or spaces for the necessary information can be provided, and the use of abbreviations or codes can be suggested to simplify recording. In subsequent sessions, these records should be routinely reviewed and the client reinforced for maintaining them. The response cost associated with self-monitoring can also be reduced by minimizing the amount of information required. When the functional analysis is completed, for example, the client may be instructed to discontinue recording antecedents and consequences of drinking. If clients anticipate being self-conscious about their monitoring when drinking with others, they can be coached on how to respond to questions concerning their self-monitoring or on how to self-monitor unobtrusively (Miller & Muñoz, 1976). If, despite these strategies, a client fails to self-monitor, Mahoney's (1977) four-stage approach can be implemented: (1) emphasize the necessity of self-monitoring by asking specific questions about previous drinking episodes that could not be answered without reference to self-monitored records; (2) initially request only a minimal amount of information and gradually increase the amount required; (3) confront the client with the fact that failure to self-monitor seriously undermines the effectiveness of therapy; (4) make continuation of therapy contingent on the client's self-monitoring.

Several of the strategies recommended to promote compliance also enhance the accuracy of self-monitored data. To the extent that records are kept in a systematic fashion on a form that not only simplifies, but also prompts, recording of the target behavior, the accuracy of self-monitored data is likely to be increased (McFall, 1977). Accuracy is also likely to be enhanced by instructing the client to self-monitor either immediately before or immediately after taking the first sip of each drink and by using an explicit definition of what constitutes "a drink." W. R. Miller's (1978) Standard Ethanol Content (SEC) unit is particularly useful in this regard because it not only defines drinking precisely, but also establishes equivalents for beverages of varying alcohol content. In his system, one drink or one SEC equals 0.5 oz (15 ml) of absolute alcohol, which is the amount present in 12 oz (360 ml) of beer, 4 oz (120 ml) of table wine, 2.5 oz (75 ml) of fortified wine, and 1 oz (30 ml) of distilled spirits.

SUMMARY

Alcoholism is a complex, behavioral disorder with a myriad of behavioral, cognitive, affective, and physiological consequences. As a result, assessment must include measures not only of the consumatory behavior, but also of functionally related, interpersonal behavior and cognitive and affective states. Moreover, no single assessment method alone is adequate for this purpose. Clinically useful self-report measures, such as self-monitoring Marlatt's Drinking Profile and the Alcohol Use Inventory are available but need to be supplemented either by direct observation, by breath alcohol testing, or preferably by a combination of both. Since alcoholism constitutes a variety of syndromes rather than a unitary disorder with a single etiology, there is no single best treatment for it. Instead, individually tailored treatment programs consisting of combinations of empirically supported behavioral techniques, such as assertiveness training, self-management training, and contingency management, are recommended. Although recent research strongly suggests that intensive, short-term interventions focusing primarily on drinking are comparable in effectiveness to multicomponent programs that focus on a wide range of problems, there is no empirical basis for the differential assignment of patients to these different forms of treatment. In summary, it is abundantly clear that behavioral interventions produce clinically significant improvement in alcoholics. The major problem now before us is to determine the criteria for optimal matching of patient and treatment.

REFERENCES

Azrin, N. H. Improvements in the community-reinforcement approach to alcoholism. *Behavior Research and Therapy*, 1976, *14*, 339–348.

Azrin, N. H., Sisson, R. W., Meyers, R., & Godley, M. Outpatient alcoholism treatment by disulfiram and community-reinforcement therapy. *Journal of Behavior Therapy and Experimental Psychiatry*, 1982, *13*, 105–112.

Blakey, R., & Baker, R. An exposure approach to alcohol abuse. *Behavior Research and Therapy*, 1980, *18*, 319–326.

Brownell, K. D. The addictive disorders. In C. M. Franks, G. T. Wilson, P. C. Kendall, & K. D. Brownell (Eds.), *Annual review of behavior therapy: Theory and Practice* (Vol. 8). New York: Guilford press, 1982.

Chaney, E. F., O'Leary, M. R., & Marlatt, G. A. Skill training with alcoholics. *Journal of Consulting and Clinical Psychology*, 1978, *46*, 1092–1104.

Compton, J. V., & Vogler, R. E. Validation of the Alco-calculator. *Psychological Reports*, 1975, *36*, 977–978.

Covner, J. J. Screening volunteer alcoholism counselors. *Quarterly Journal of Studies on Alcohol*, 1969, *30*, 420–425.

D'Zurilla, R. J., & Goldfried, M. R. Problem solving and behavior modification. *Journal of Abnormal Psychology*, 1971, *78*, 107–128.

Eisler, R. M., Hersen, M., & Miller, P. M. Shaping components of assertive behavior with instructions and feedback. *American Journal of Psychiatry*, 1974, *30*, 643–649.

Elkins, R. L. Covert sensitization treatment of alcoholism: Contributions of successful conditioning to subsequent abstinence maintenance. *Addictive Behaviors*, 1980, *5*, 67–89.

Foy, D. W., Miller, P. M., Eisler, R. W., & O'Toole, D. H. Social skills training to teach alcoholics to refuse drinks effectively. *Journal of Studies on Alcohol*, 1976, *37*, 1340–1345.

Foy, D. W., Rychtarik, R. G., & Prue, D. M. Assessment of appetitive disorders. In M. Hersen & A. S. Bellack (Eds.), *Behavioral assessment: A practical handbook* (2nd ed.). New York: Pergamon Press, 1981.

Gambrill, E. D. *Behavior modification: Handbook of assessment, intervention and evaluation*. San Francisco: Jossey-Bass, 1978.

Garvin, R. B., Foy, D. W., & Alford, G. S. A critical examination of gammaglutamyl transpeptidase as a biochemical marker for alcohol abuse. *Addictive Behaviors*, 1981, *6*, 377–383.

Gerard, D. L., Saenger, G., & Wile, R. The abstinent alcoholic. *Archives of General Psychiatry*, 1962, *6*, 83–95.

Hersen, M., & Bellack, A. S. (Eds.). *Behavioral assessment: A practical handbook* (2nd eds.) New York: Pergamon Press, 1981.

Hunt, G. M., & Azrin, N. H. A community-reinforcement approach to alcoholism. *Behavior Research and Therapy*, 1973, *11*, 91–104.

Kessler, M., & Gomberg, C. Observations of barroom drinking: Methodology and preliminary results. *Quarterly Journal of Studies on Alcohol*, 1974, *35*, 1392–1396.

Kwentus, J., & Major, L. F. Disulfiram in the treatment of alcoholism. *Journal of Studies on Alcohol*, 1979, *40*, 428–446.

Lamy, J., Baglin, M. C., Weill, J., & Aaron, E. Gamma-glutamyl transpeptidase. *Nouvelle Presse Medicale*, 1975, *4*, 487–490.

Lovell, W. S. Breath tests for determining alcohol in the blood. *Science*, 1972, *178*, 264–272.

Mahoney, M. J. Some applied issues in self-monitoring. In J. D. Cone & R. P. Hawkins (Eds.), *Behavioral assessment: New directions in clinical psychology*. New York: Brunner/Mazel, 1977.

Maisto, S. A., Sobell, L. C., & Sobell, M. B. Comparison of alcoholics' self-reports of drinking behavior with reports of collateral informants. *Journal of Consulting and Clinical Psychology*, 1979, *47*, 106–112.

Marlatt, G. A. The Drinking Profile—A questionnaire for the behavioral assessment of alcoholism. In E. J. Mash & L. G. Terdal (Eds.), *Behavior therapy assessment: Diagnosis, design and evaluation*, New York: Springer, 1976.

Marlatt, G. A. Craving for alcohol, loss of control, and relapse: A cognitive-behavioral analysis. In P. E. Nathan, G. A. Marlatt, & T. Loberg, (Eds.), *Alcoholism: New directions in behavioral research & treatment*. New York: Plenum Press, 1978.

Marlatt, G. A., & Gordon, J. R. Determinants of relapse: Implications for the maintenance of behavior change. In P. O. Davidson & S. M. Davidson (Eds.), *Behavioral medicine: Changing health lifestyles*, New York: Brunner/Mazel, 1980.

Matthews, D., & Miller, W. R. Computer program for estimating blood alcohol concentration: Applications in therapy and research. Unpublished manuscript, University of New Mexico, 1977.

McFall, R. M. Parameters of self-monitoring. In R. B. Stuart (Eds.), *Behavioral self-management: Strategies, techniques and outcomes.* New York: Brunner/Mazel, 1977.

Miller, P. M. The use of behavioral contracting in the treatment of alcoholism: A case report. *Behavior Therapy,* 1972, *3,* 593–596.

Miller, P. M. A behavioral intervention program for chronic public drunkenness offenders. *Archives of General Psychiatry,* 1975, *32,* 915–918. (a)

Miller, P. M. Training responsible drinking skills in veterans. Paper presented at the American Psychological Association, 1975. (b)

Miller, P. M. *Behavioral treatment of alcoholism.* New York: Pergamon Press, 1976.

Miller, P. M. Alternative skills training in alcoholism treatment. In P. E. Nathan, G. A. Marlatt, & T. Loberg (Eds.), *Alcoholism: New directions in behavioral research and treatment.* New York: Plenum Press, 1978.

Miller, P. M. Theoretical and practical issues in substance abuse assessment and treatment. In W. R. Miller (Eds.), *The addictive behaviors: Treatment of alcoholism, drug abuse, smoking & obesity.* New York: Pergamon Press, 1980.

Miller, P. M. Assessment of alcohol abuse. In D. H. Barlow (Ed.), *Behavioral assessment of adult disorders.* New York: Guilford Press, 1981.

Miller, P. M., & Foy, D. W. Substance abuse. In S. M. Turner, K. S. Calhoun, & H. E. Adams (Eds.), *Handbook of clinical behavior therapy.* New York: Wiley, 1981.

Miller, W. R. Alcoholism scales & objective assessment methods: A review. *Psychological Bulletin,* 1976, *83,* 649–674.

Miller, W. R. Behavioral treatment of problem drinkers: A comparative outcome study of three controlled drinking therapies. *Journal of Consulting and Clinical Psychology,* 1978, *46,* 74–86.

Miller, W. R. Treating problem drinkers: What works? *The Behavior Therapist,* 1982, *5,* 15–18.

Miller, W. R., & Caddy, G. R. Abstinence & controlled drinking in the treatment of problem drinkers. *Journal of Studies on Alcohol,* 1977, *38,* 986–1003.

Miller, W. R., & Hester, R. K. Treating the problem drinker: Modern approaches. In W. R. Miller (Ed.), *The addictive behaviors: Treatment of alcoholism, drug abuse, smoking & obesity.* New York: Pergamon Press, 1980.

Miller, W. R., & Muñoz, R. F. *How to control your drinking.* Englewood Cliffs, N.J.: Prentice-Hall, 1976.

Miller, W. R., & Taylor, C. A. Relative effectiveness of bibliotherapy, industrial & group self-control training in the treatment of problem drinkers. *Addictive Behaviors,* 1980, *5,* 13–24.

Miller, W. R., Crawford, V. L., & Taylor, C. A. Significant others as corroborative sources for problem drinkers. *Addictive Behaviors,* 1979, *4,* 67–70.

Nathan, P. E., & Briddell, D. W. Behavioral assessment and treatment of alcoholism. In B. Kissin & H. Begleiter (Eds.), *The biology of alcoholism* (Vol. 5). New York: Plenum Press, 1977.

Nathan, P. E., & Lipscomb, T. R. Behavior therapy & behavior modification in the treatment of alcoholism. In J. H. Mendelson & N. K. Mello (Eds.). *The diagnosis and treatment of alcoholism.* New York: McGraw-Hill, 1979.

O'Farrell, T. J., & Cutter, H. S. G. Evaluating behavioral marital therapy for alcoholics: Procedures and preliminary results. Paper presented at Banff International Conference on Essentials of Behavioral Treatment of Families, March 1981.

Pattison, E. M., Sobell, M. B., & Sobell, L. C. *Emerging concepts of alcohol dependence.* New York: Springer, 1977.

Polich, J. M. The validity of self-reports in alcoholism research. *Addictive Behaviors,* 1982, *1,* 123–132.

Reyes, E., & Miller, W. R. Serum gamma-glutamyl transpeptidase as a diagnostic aid in problem drinkers. *Addictive Behaviors*, 1980, *5*, 59–65.

Rosenbluth, J., Nathan, P. E., & Lawson, D. M. Environmental influences on drinking by college students in a college pub: Behavioral observation in the natural environment. *Addictive Behaviors*, 1978, *3*, 117–121.

Skinner, H. A. Primary syndromes of alcohol abuse: Their measurement and correlates. *British Journal of Addiction*, 1981, *76*, 63–76.

Skinner, H. A., & Allen, B. A. Alcohol dependence syndrome: Measurement & validation. *Journal of Abnormal Psychology*, 1982, *91*, 199–209.

Sobell, L. C. Alcohol treatment outcome evaluation: Contributions from behavioral research. In P. E. Nathan, G. A. Marlatt, & T. Loberg (Eds.), *Alcoholism: New directions in behavioral research and treatment*. New York: Plenum Press, 1978.

Sobell, L. C., & Sobell, M. B. A self-feedback technique to monitor drinking behavior in alcoholics. *Behavior Research and Therapy*, 1973, *11*, 237–238.

Sobell, M. B., & Sobell, L. C. A brief technical report on the MOBAT: An inexpensive portable test for determining blood alcohol concentration. *Journal of Applied Behavior Analysis*, 1975, *8*, 117–120.

Sobell, M. B. & Sobell, L. C. Functional analysis of alcohol problems. In C. K. Prokop & L. A. Bradley (Eds.), *Medical psychology: Contributions to behavioral medicine*. New York: Academic Press, 1981.

Sobell, M. B., & Sobell, L. C. Controlled drinking: A concept coming of age. In K. R. Blankstein & J. Polivy (Eds.), *Self-control and self-modification of emotional behavior*. New York: Plenum press, 1982.

Sobell, M. B., Sobell, L. C., & VanderSpek, R. Relationships among clinical judgment, self-report and breath-analysis measures of intoxication in alcoholics. *Journal of Consulting and Clinical Psychology*, 1979, *47*, 204–206.

Stalonas, P. M., Keane, T. M., & Foy, D. W. Alcohol education for inpatient alcoholics: A comparison of live, videotape & written presentation modalities. *Addictive Behaviors*, 1979, *4*, 223–229.

Uecker, A., & Solberg, K. Alcoholics' knowledge about alcohol problems: Its relationship to significant attitude. *Quarterly Journal of Studies on Alcohol*, 1973, *34*, 509–513.

Vogler, R. E., Weissback, T. A., Compton, J. V., & Martin, G. T. Intergrated behavior change techniques for problem drinkers in the community. *Journal of Consulting and Clinical Psychology*, 1977, *45*, 267–279.

Wanberg, K. W., Horn, J. L., & Foster, F. M. A differential assessment model for alcoholism: The scales of the Alcohol Use Inventory. *Journal of Studies on Alcohol*, 1977, *38*, 512–543.

Wilson, G. T., Alcoholism & aversion therapy: Issues, ethics & evidence. In G. A. Marlatt & P. E. Nathan (Eds.), *Behavioral approaches to alcoholism*. New Brunswick, N.J.: Rutgers Center of Alcohol Studies, 1978.

7

Obesity

William J. Fremouw
Nicholas E. Heyneman

MOST CLINICIANS have repeatedly heard the plea "If I could only lose this weight my problems would be solved!" Sometimes the client is correct; problems of depression or social anxiety may be affected by the person's weight and self-perception associated with this weight. All clients require an individualized assessment and hierarchical identification of problems; however, therapists may agree with their client's view that treatment for obesity is an appropriate goal for outpatient care as the sole presenting problem or as an adjunct to therapy in other areas. To aid the clinician, this chapter defines basic terms in the area of eating disorders and then presents an outline for a multisession cognitive-behavioral treatment program for weight loss.

BASIC TERMS

With our emphasis on physical appearance, the bookstores and newspaper racks are stuffed with guides for diet regimens and exercise programs to treat obesity. Most individuals confuse the term "obesity" with "overweight." Obesity is the excessive amount of body fat. The average American adult male has 14% body fat, whereas the average adult female has 24% body fat (Stuart & Davis, 1978). Technically, any person whose body composition has excessive fat is obese. However, the direct assessment of body fat (i.e., obesity) is a technical and difficult process. The most rigorous procedure is hydrostatic weighting, in which a person is submerged in a known body of water to determine the amount of water displaced. Through conversion tables and equations, the amount of body fat is then calculated. This procedure is of limited use because of the expensive equipment required. A more practical approach to determining body fat is by measuring skinfold thickness with calipers from one to multiple sites on a person's body. This is a scientific procedure that measures the "pinch an inch of fat" definition of obesity popularized by a cereal company for defining obesity. Because caliper readings require extensive experience to produce adequate reliability, they seldom are used in defining obesity except for research studies. Therefore, most individuals and clinicians are left to define obesity by relying on traditional height-weight tables. These tables identify "ideal weights," which are not mean weights for an age group and height, but are the weights that represent the lowest mortality rates based on insurance company studies (Brownell, 1981).

According to height-weight tables, obesity is generally defined as a minimum of 20% above the ideal weight for the height. On the basis of this criterion, 30% of men and 40% of women between 40 and 49 years old are obese (Metropolitan Life Insurance Co., 1960). The sole reliance on height-weight tables can sometimes be misleading because the person may weigh above the ideal weight and not be obese (i.e., excessive in body fat content). Many athletes with well-developed musculature are overweight for their height. However, their actual body composition is under the norm for fat content. This apparent paradox occurs because muscle is representing a disproportionate amount of their body weight instead of fat, thus rendering them heavier than the ideal.

CLINICAL ASSESSMENT

Because most clients define obesity as the degree that they are overweight from a statistical norm, assessment of obesity generally begins with the measurement of the client's height and weight. This determines a person's pretreatment weight. The client and clinician can then establish an explicit treatment goal for weight loss. Generally, a weight loss of 1–2 lb per week is the maximum goal that can be sustained over a multiple number of weeks. Establishment of a weight loss goal merely determines the amount to be lost. This does not assess which eating and exercise behaviors are necessary to be changed to achieve this goal. The treatment for obesity requires assessment of specific behaviors that will lead to the change of body weight. Use of a daily self-monitoring food diary is the most commonly used procedure to assess eating habits. The diary contained in Figure 7-1 provides useful behavioral information about a client's eating patterns. The first step in the behavioral assessment of obesity is for the client to complete a daily food intake diary for at least one week. The diary in Figure 7-1 is the one used in most behavioral treatment programs, such as those of Stuart and Davis (1978) or Ferguson (1975). The diary contained in Figure 7-2 is a cognitively oriented diary used for a treatment program that focuses on change of cognitive and emotional antecedents and consequences to eating. Later sections of this chapter provide detailed instructions for use of this diary. The first week of a diary provides the behavioral data for the therapist to determine general patterns of eating.

Common eating patterns exhibited by clients include abstinence from eating until late in the day followed by periodic snacking until late evening. Another pattern involves eating three full meals plus several large snacks between meals. A third pattern, although not common,

Meals   Date_____

Day + Time	H	M	Time Eating	Where	Food + Quantity	Cal

Figure 7-1 Behavioral diary (H—hunger: 0 = none, 1 = slight, 2 = moderate, 3 = extreme; Cal = calories; M—mood: Depressed, Bored, Frustrated, Guilty, Happy, Neutral).

Snacks/Binges   Date_____

Day + Time Start/Stop	S/B	Situation	Stress	Prior to Eating			Food + Quantity + Calories	Following Eating			Control
				Mood	Self-statement	Rate −5 +5		Mood	Self-statement	Rate −5 +5	

Figure 7-2 Cognitive-behavioral diary (S/B = snack/binge; Stress; 0 = none . . . 7 = extreme; Control—0 = none . . .7 = extreme; Rate—−5 = extremely negative, +5 = extremely positive, 0 = neutral; M = mood: Bored, Depressed, Frustrated, Guilty, Happy, Neutral).

consists of eating three meals a day without snacking; however, the food choices for these meals are high in caloric value, such as breads, sweets, or protein items. This, of course, leads to an excessive amount of caloric intake for the person's maintenance needs. The number of calories consumed per day can be calculated by use of any popular calorie book. Most behavioral programs suggest that clients eat at least two meals (and ideally three meals) totaling 1200–1600 cal/day. Many clients feel that this is excessive and that they can lose weight only if they "starve" themselves. However, that is a short-term strategy and does not promote long-term habit changes that can be maintained. The person whose eating intake pattern does not show regular meals consumed thus requires the establishment of a goal to increase such regularity while keeping the total caloric intake at a moderate level.

Additional information derived from diaries include the situational antecedents, such as the location and activity engaged in while eating, as well as the duration of eating episodes. Each of these eating behaviors can be a target for habit change. The cognitively oriented diary shown in Figure 7-2 permits identification of maladaptive thoughts and feelings that precipitate and maintain snacking and binge episodes. The baseline assessment of type and frequency of these self-statements also helps to identify target behaviors for treatment. The treatment manual outlined in later sections primarily addresses these cognitive and emotional antecedents of between-meal consumption.

TREATMENT APPROACHES FOR OBESITY

There are a wide variety of weight reduction techniques currently available. In this next section we briefly discuss a few of these and then offer, in depth, a specific cognitive-behavioral treatment package and a case study designed to illustrate its use.

Behavior Modification

Behavior modification approaches to obesity are loosely based on the assumption that excessive weight is largely the result of maladaptive eating and exercise habits. Treatment follows from this by targeting the obese individual's eating style and the environmental cues associated with eating. The most prevalent topics covered in these programs are self-monitoring of eating, increasing exercise, preplanning snacks and meals, caloric information, reduction in the number of environmental cues associated with food by eating only in designated places, changing the rate of eating, and behavioral contracting for reduced caloric intake. Although behavior modification approaches offer some of the most currently effective strategies for weight loss (Stunkard & Mahoney, 1976), ironically, the basic assumption of a maladaptive pattern of eating by obese individuals has been seriously questioned by recent evidence (Mahoney, 1975). Nevertheless, at least some portion of this approach seems to be a component of nearly all successful weight-loss programs. Detailed behavior modification procedures are not given here as they are readily available from a variety of sources. The interested reader is referred to Ferguson (1975) or Stuart and Davis (1978).

Hypnosis

Hypnosis is one of the most requested contemporary treatments for obesity. Its appeal probably lies in the technique's almost magical mystic: the belief that the dieter need be resigned only to the command of the hypnotist and the pounds will disappear. This belief is false, of course; there is no magical cure to the problem of obesity. Hypnotic suggestions for weight loss vary considerably. They include aversive conditioning or the suggestion that food will make the individual nauseous, suggestions to decrease appetite, and even "hypno-analysis," a technique that purportedly uncovers deep-seated conflicts that may underlie the weight problem. There is little evidence to support the claim that hypnosis, as is currently practiced, is an effective treatment for obesity. In most studies the technique fails to produce weight loss comparable to behavior modification methods both at the conclusion of treatment and at follow-up. In those cases where hypnosis has been shown effective, its efficacy can be attributed to nonhypnotic factors, such as providing a structured program, a positive treatment expectancy, or simply encouragement for weight loss (Wadden & Anderton, 1982).

Other Currently Popular
Weight-Reduction Methods

There are currently a multitude of commercial weight-loss programs available to the consumer. These range from over-the-counter appetite suppressants to very expensive food programs. The active ingredient of the widely advertised appetite suppressant pills (phenylpropanolamine hydrochloride) is also one of the active ingredients in allergy and cold symptom relief medicines. Although the manufacturers attest to studies showing the drug's "clinical efficacy," we are not aware of any serious independent evaluations comparing these drugs with other currently available techniques.

There are numerous commercial weight-loss programs offering "guaranteed weight reduction." These programs generally provide clients with food or a list of permissible foods they may eat. These foods contain restricted caloric content and, assuming that these clients eat nothing outside the specified diet, they will lose weight. In fact, the programs often are established so that the client's fee is determined by the amount of weight actually lost. Fees vary but are usually quite expensive: $30.00/lb, not including food. The primary problem with these programs is maintenance of weight loss. Although the initial weight loss is guaranteed by restricted caloric intake, there usually are no skills taught to the client to maintain the reduced weight level once a "normal" diet is reinstituted.

A Cognitive-Behavioral Treatment Program for Obesity

Cognitive-behavioral treatments for obesity rest on the assumption that dysfunctional thinking may play a role in maintaining problematic eating episodes. The primary goal of such a program is thus to increase the clients' awareness of their thoughts, develop an understanding of how these thoughts can influence eating and exercise habits, and teach a method or increasing the frequency of positive coping thoughts designed to mediate desirable eating and exercise behaviors. In addition to these goals, the program emphasizes intervention for stress and negative moods as antecedents to eating problems, as well as techniques to help with the problem of "binge" eating. The program can be easily combined with some standard behavior-modification techniques. Of the various behavior-modification interventions available, we have found the following to be of value: (1) preplanning snacks, (2) eating only in designated eating places, (3) reducing eating cues ("stimulus control"), (4) eating slowly, and (5) behavioral contracting.

Our program involves a number of distinct components. First, a good deal of self-monitoring is required throughout. We have found reasonably good compliance when we elaborate on the rationale that before a behavior can be changed, it first must be accurately observed. "Homework" is an integral part of the program. As with self-monitoring, however, if this is preceded with a good rationale and positive expectancies, clients usually will be enthusiastically compliant. Generally, we do not present any nutritional dietary information. We have found that, for the most part, our clients are "experts" on nutrition and calorie contents of foods. They know what they should and should not eat; they simply do not "follow through." Because nutritional information is such a central aspect of weight loss, however, it is recommended that all clients be screened for this knowledge and that dietary education be provided if necessary.

Finally, we have all clients obtain approval from their family physicians before enrolling in the program. Needless to say, these doctors are usually very enthusiastic about the prospect of their patients losing weight. Beyond the wisdom of obtaining a medical consent, this procedure helps screen for unusual physical factors that may be involved in obesity, such as diabetes and hypothryroidism, as well as providing an added source of encouragement for the client.

The program is designed for one orientation session, six weekly sessions of active treatment, and three monthly follow-up sessions (a total of 10 sessions). Each session lasts about 1½ hours. We have found that the most cost-efficient procedure is to administer the program in a small group format (three to six persons), although the package can be administered individually or to large groups.

The group leader's "treatment manual" for this program is presented in the appendix at the end of this chapter. Although this manual is written in outline form for the leader, it can be provided to the clients as well.

CASE STUDY—SMALL GROUP

This case study is re-created here from a treatment group conducted by one of the authors to illustrate the use of the cognitive-behavior treatment package. Figure 7-3 summarizes weight-loss data during the program.

Three clients were enrolled in this group, which met in the evenings at a local community mental health center. Sally is a 50-year-old housewife who entered the program weighing 197 lb, or 62 lb overweight. Nancy is a 34-year-old personnel manager in a large corporation whose initial weight was 145 lb, or 15 lb overweight. Mary, who started the program at 162 lb, or 26 lb overweight, is 48 years old and is employed as a secretary.

Session 1 (Orientation)

Leader: Welcome to the weight reduction program. Tonight's meeting will serve two purposes. First, it will allow us all to get acquainted and for me to give you an overview of the program. I will also answer any questions that you may have. Second, you will learn how to self-monitor your eating and related thoughts and feelings. As you will soon see, this is a critical aspect of the program. This program is designed to teach you *skills* necessary to lose weight and keep it off. The important point to note here is that you will learn new skills to help in weight control. It's not a matter of "willpower," which suggests some unknown force that some people seem to have and others don't ("If I only had more will-power!"); to the contrary, anyone can use the self-management skills taught here. In fact, these same basic skills have been used to help people with a variety of problems, such as smoking, alcohol abuse, and even public-speaking anxiety. You may even be able to use what you'll learn here in other areas of your lives besides eating, such as exercising or just feeling more mastery over your life. The program will focus on what you are thinking and feeling (different mood, stress) as related to eating. As we will see, what you say to yourself makes a big difference in how you act. You will learn to recognize negative thoughts (we call them *self-statements)*, how they influence eating, and how to replace them with more positive self-statements that lead to desirable eating habits. You also will learn to balance the stressful demands on you (which often leads to frustration and overeating) with more positive time for yourself. We will discuss binge eating, new ways to think about it, and ways to help give you greater feelings of control over eating. Finally, we'll see how negative moods, such as boredom or depression, can mediate problem eating and ways to deal with these. The goal of this program is slow and steady weight loss. We do not expect you to lose more than about 1–1½ lb/week. The key is *maintenance* of weight loss, and we hope that you will be able to utilize the skills you learn for this.

There is then an informal discussion where clients can introduce themselves, get to know each other, and ask the leader questions. Clients

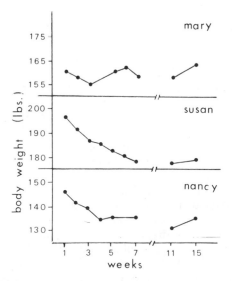

Figure 7-3   Weight-change data for three clients in the cognitive-behavioral treatment program.

are instructed in the logistics of the program (e.g., length and number of sessions, fees) and are strongly encouraged to try to attend all meetings. The next phase of this session is to explain the process of self-monitoring and to familiarize the group with the two eating diaries.

Leader: As I mentioned before, a critical part of this program is keeping the self-monitoring diaries. On these two diaries (one for meals and one for between-meal eating) you will keep track of everything you eat, the situation you eat in, and your thoughts and feelings associated with eating. This will required a good deal of effort. However, it has been our experience that although people find this recording difficult at first, it soon becomes more automatic—and it certainly is well worth the effort. As I said, there are two diaries: one labeled "meals" and one labeled "snacks and binges." Let's take a look at the meal diary. This diary is straightforward and may be very similar to ones you have filled out in the past. You are simply asked to record the day and time, a rating of hunger on a 0–3 scale (see bottom of diary), your predominant mood prior to eating, where you are eating, and a description of the food and quantity eaten. This description should be detailed enough to enable an observer to give a calorie estimate of the consumed food. For example, writing "eggs" would not be sufficient; instead, "two large scrambled eggs." "Pie" would also be incomplete; instead—"one-fourth of a 9-in. apple pie." Test yourself by going back over a diary and seeing if the descriptions are detailed enough so that you can reasonably estimate the calorie contents. Write down only your "meals" (breakfast, lunch, and dinner) on this diary. The snack and binge (SB) diary will probably be new to you since you are asked to monitor not only *what* you eat, but also what you are saying to yourself before and after you eat. Becoming aware of these "self-statements" may seem difficult at first—we don't normally think about thinking! However, with practice this will soon become more natural. You will use the SB diary *twice:* once just prior to eating, and once just after eating. Let's go through it to see how to fill it out. First, write in the date and the time you start eating. Where it says "stop," you'll fill in the time you finish eating—this lets you know how long you spent eating. In the next column where it says "S/B," write in a "S" or a "B" if you feel the eating episode is a snack or a binge. This distinction is left up to you—whatever you feel is a snack or a binge for you. Where it says "situation," write in where you are and what you are doing just prior to eating. This can be very brief, for example, "watching TV." In the column marked "Stress," put in a rating of your overall stress level just prior to eating. Use the scale printed on the bottom of the diary (0 = none, 7 = extreme stress). On the next part of the diary under "prior to eating" there are three columns— "mood": write in the first letter of the mood listed below the best describes your mood just prior to eating. For example, if you're feeling mostly bored, write in "B." The self-statement columns are the most important aspects of the diary. Here you are asked to write in the predominant statement you are saying to yourself just prior to eating. Pick out the one predominant thought that runs through your mind just prior to eating. For example, you might say something like; "I'm so bored, I think I'll have a snack," or "Oh, what's the use in dieting, I can't lose weight." Another example might be, "I feel like eating, if I eat an apple, I'll be satisfied and feel good about myself." Does that make sense to everybody?

Sally: I'm not sure I know what I'm thinking, how do I know what I'm saying to myself?

Leader: Just stop and ask yourself what you are thinking —in a sense—think out loud. It sounds hard because we're not used to doing this, but I think it will become easier than you realize.

Mary: I'm thinking a lot of stuff, what do I write down?

Leader: Write down that self-statement that you think to be the most important or most salient one. It is usually the one that just seems to pop up automatically when you ask yourself "what am I thinking?" In the next column, you are asked to rate the self-statement on a scale from –5 to +5, with 0 being neutral. To do this, simply think how negative or positive you consider the statement. This usually is the same as considering how much the self-statement will help or hinder your dieting goals. In the next column write in a description of the food you eat. This should be done with the same accuracy as the meal diary. Finally, the last section of the diary is to be filled out *just after* you've finished eating. Write in your mood, your self-statement, and a rating (–5 to +5 scale) of the self-statement. Also, rate your general feelings of control over eating on a 0–7 scale (0 = no control, 7 = extreme control) in the last column. So, for example, if you've just had a bad binge you might rate "control" as 0, no control. If, on the other hand, you just eaten a nutritious snack, you might rate "control" as 7."

Once this procedure is explained, the group then "practiced" by filling in information pertaining to recent eating episodes. The leader then checked these entries and provided feedback.

Session 2

At the beginning of every session the group weighs in. Any group member who loses weight is verbally complimented for this. If there is no weight loss or weight gain, it is important to model a coping statement for the client such as: "One week doesn't break a diet, I'll see what I can do to improve to next week." All three clients lost a fairly large amount of weight this week. Needless to say, the group was very pleased and enthusiastic. However, because a large weight loss (3–4 lbs) is common the first week, it is important to "innoculate" the group against unrealistic expectations that they will continue to lose equally large amounts of weight each week.

Leader: It is unlikely that you will continue to lose 3 + pounds per week. What you have lost is, for the most part, water-weight or "easy weight loss." We are hoping for a slow, steady weight loss of about 1–1½ lb/week. What is important is to learn those skills necessary to lose this weight steadily and keep it off.

The main purpose of this session is to give the rationale for the congitive-behavioral approach and to learn to identify negative self-statements and problem situations. As a convenient way to lead into this discussion, the group examined their SB diaries from the previous week. All clients understood the basic concept of cognitive self-monitoring; however, there were some omissions on the diaries. Mary, for example, forgot to rate her self-statements on a number of occasions. Constructive feedback was given for all deficiencies and praise was given for accurate monitoring. All clients recorded several negative self-statements during this week, which were used as examples when explaining the rationale. More representative problem situations and negative self-statements were generated and discussed by the group. Finally, the client's meal diaries were examined. All group members were eating three balanced, reasonable meals. They were praised for this and encouraged to continue. They were reminded that inadequate nutrition leads to problematic between-meal eating. For example, the person who binges and fasts experiences dramatically changing blood sugar levels, which often leads negative mood, fatigue, and hunger—all common antecedents to problem eating.

Session 3

The weigh-in this time showed that the group was still losing weight. A check of the diaries revealed all 3 clients to understand and be complying with the self-monitoring instructions and homework (list three problem situations and associated negative self-statements). This session was devoted to explaining the concept of the coping statement, with examples focusing on each client's listed problem situations and negative thoughts. As stated in the leader's manual, a good deal of time was spent discussing how coping statements could be useful in increasing exercise habits. Finally, the group discussed "alternative activities" to be used in conjunction with cognitive coping statements. Each client developed a list of five activities (see leader's manual) and was instructed to try to follow through with these activities for homework.

Session 4

Mary was absent for this session; both Sally and Nancy lost weight. We first reviewed their use of coping statements. Both clients appeared to understand the process and utilized coping statements effectively. In fact, they were quite imaginative in generating coping responses.

Nancy: I found that when I felt hungry I could tell myself, "My stomach feels hungry, that must be a sign I'm doing well on my diet."

The remainder of the session was spent discussing the "want/should" ratio, "self-time," and the "programmed binge." While the first two of these are relatively straightforward and explained in sufficient detail in the leader's manual, the "programmed binge" may require further elaboration.

Leader: Over the next three weeks we are going to do a series of three "programmed binges." Believe it nor not, this means I'll be asking each of you to eat some "forbidden food"! The reason behind this is quite simple: this is a way to increase your sense of control over eating. At first we'll make it relatively easy such as eating when you're not very hungry, or in an minimally enjoyable situation. We will make it progressively more "difficult" or realistic each time, building your sense of control over these situations. For this first binge, pick a somewhat difficult food-one of your "weaknesses." Then choose a time and place that will minimize the problem of hunger, negative mood, or excessive stress. Write each of these considerations (food, time, place, quantity) down on paper in the form of a contract between you and me stating that you agree to eat this food in the specified time, place, and quantity. Then we both will sign the "contract." While you are eating, I would like you to really notice the taste of the food as well as being very aware of the entire situation. That is, eat your food slowly, notice the taste, and think about your sense of control over eating. Be sure to use lots of coping self-statements before, during, and after eating (examples in the teacher's manual). We will discuss your experiences next week.

Session 5

All three group members were present this week. Mary arrived early to obtain the previous week's material, which she missed. She did not self-monitor for two weeks, saying that there was "too much stress at work and home, visiting relatives and a new boss." She weighed in at 161 lb, up 5 lb from the previous weigh in two weeks ago. We discussed the importance of keeping the diary and the difficulties involved given an extrastressful environment. It was apparent in our discussion that Mary was very upset with her performance and feeling hopeless about losing weight. She had, after five weeks, nearly returned to her preprogram weight. In our conversation she continually emitted negative self-statements, such as: "I just can't do it," "I'll never learn to control my eating." I pointed out these maladaptive statements she was making and how they were affecting her eating and exercise habits, even without her being aware of it. We discussed the coping statements we covered during session 3.

Nancy weighed in 1 lb heavier than last session, whereas Sally lost 2½ lbs. After going over the group's diaries, we discussed the first "programmed binge." Both Sally and Nancy were successful with this, and both responded, to their surprise, that they did not even feel like eating the entire amount for which they contracted. In fact, Sally said she had to force herself to even eat her contracted scoop of chocolate ice cream. The important part of the discussion, however, focused on their feelings of control over eating. Both reported a "7" in the "control" column of their diaries and said that it was a "very enjoyable" feeling.

This session was devoted to discussing the "Abstinence Violation Effect." After throughly explaining this phenomenon, it was discussed in terms of examples from each client. The group then contracted again for a "programmed binge," but this time choosing a situation that was slightly more difficult.

Session 6

Nancy was absent this session, Sally continued to lose weight, but Mary gained 1 lb. This session dealt with the effects of mood on eating. This meeting seemed particularity appropriate for Mary, who was feeling very stressed from problems at work and home, leading to feelings of frustration and depression. Her "failure" in terms of weight loss was also creating more negative moods. In this session we used the same basic process of identifying negative self-statements and replacing them with positive ones, but did so specifically in terms of negative mood statements. Three mood statements were targeted: depression, boredom, and anger as these were the predominant problem moods reported by the group. The group also contracted for a final "programmed binge."

Session 7

All group members were present; Sally and Mary lost weight, whereas Nancy had gained ½ lb. over the past two weeks. This session was devoted to a general review of the program materials. The group discussed making new commitments to work on each of the areas that had been presented.

Leader: The program is not over! In fact, it is just beginning. We have stressed all along that weight loss *maintenance* is the key, not simply weight loss. At least part of your weight loss over the past seven weeks is attributable to the mere fact that you reported into the group each week. Since you won't be doing that anymore, at least for a month, you can begin to really utilize the new skills you have learned. These skills will enable you to deal more effectively not only with eating, but in all areas of your life. Remember the feelings of control you experienced during your "programmed binges" and the self-esteem you felt when coping self-statements seemed to occur automatically. Keep up the good work!

Follow-Up Session

There were two follow-up sessions for this group: one at four weeks and the other at eight weeks following completion of treatment. These sessions were primarily group discussions, sharing problems and strategies, and individual "trouble-shooting." No new material was presented during these sessions.

Over the nine-week program, Nancy lost 6 lbs, Sally lost 18 lbs, and Mary gained 3 lbs. This variability appears to be typical of weight-loss programs, regardless of the treatment approach. This underscores the need for an individualized approach targeting the specific and unique needs of each client. At the same time, we have found it beneficial (and cost-efficient) to conduct treatment in a small group setting, allowing for discussion, group cohesion, and maximal generation of ideas and strategies. The emphasis of this program was on the teaching cognitive skills that hopefully will generalize beyond group sessions. Unfortunately, there are no long-term follow-up data on this program as yet available.

TREATMENT ISSUES

A therapist implementing a multisession group treatment approach for obesity should be sensitive to several potential issues that frequently emerge. In the following section we identify these issues and provide some suggestions or strategies to address them.

Therapist's Competence

"You've never been obese so you can't understand what it's like and how hard it is to lose weight." In most weight-loss programs the clients will question the credentials of the therapist to help them lose weight. If the therapist is overweight, they will question why or or she has not applied the techniques to himself or herself. If the therapist is average or below average weight, they will assume that he or she "can't understand what it's like." This is generally the first issue to emerge in a group, either directly through a confrontative statement or by a simple question. This type of theme is no different from any other client saying "You've never been divorced so you can't know what it's like" or asking "You've never been depressed so how can you understand me?" Although a therapist may not share the same behavioral problems that the client is experiencing, the therapist's training, experience, and clinical skill should permit him or her to be a trainer for the person to make changes of habits. It is generally very helpful for a therapist to share some area of self-control that is a challenge to the therapist. For example, the therapist may say: "No I've never had a weight problem, but I'm attempting to stop smoking. Therefore, I'm experiencing some of the same difficulties that you encounter in trying to keep data and change a very difficult habit." Prior to the first therapy group, the therapist should consider his or her own response to this very probable question and be comfortable when it is raised by the clients.

Treatment Effectiveness

"I think that all this behavior modification stuff is unnecessary. If someone wants to lose weight they will. If not, they won't. It's all just willpower." Or, "Why do we have to do this junk? Some of these diets can make you lose 10 lb. in a week, which is all we'll probably lose in the whole program." Over a multisession program, which is directed toward slow, steady changes in habits and weight, clients often become impatient with the rate of change. They are enticed by the tabloids promising to melt pounds off in just days. The therapist needs to remind the clients of the rationale, goals, and time frame for achieving these goals. If the clients have not accepted the treatment's rationale and approach, they will be dissatisfied with its implementation and will not be cooperative in their own behavior change program. These types of question suggest that the rationale has not been clearly explained and accepted by the clients. Therefore, the therapist should ask the group to restate the goals and explore the belief that it is all just "willpower." Unless the clients accept that they must make systematic and long-term changes in eating habits, they will not be cooperative in the multiple changes required for successful implementation of behavioral and cognitive behavioral programs.

Lack of Rapid Success

"I've been good all day and I get on the scale the next morning and I haven't lost weight. What's the use?" During the treatment program, most clients weigh themselves too often. They expect to see ½–1-lb weight losses each day. The person who looks for that each morning is bound to be disappointed. Therefore, therapists are to instruct clients not to weigh themselves more than twice per week to permit time for them to see a change in body weight. When the clients complain that they do not see change every day, remind them that they should not expect change daily. Consider asking them if they can remove their scale to reduce the likelihood that they will weigh themselves and be disappointed.

Too Busy to Change Behaviors

"My life is too busy now to do all this stuff. You're lucky I even get to the meetings." This type of statement can be expected from a client who is not completing homework and thus is probably not experiencing satisfactory weight loss. The statement "My life is too busy now" should alert the clinician that the person is not highly motivated to comply with homework assignments. During the first few sessions, it is essential that clients understand that changing habits takes a deliberate effort and that it must be a relatively high priority in their life to be successful. If a person is overwhelmed with other events, such as changing jobs, moving, new work responsibilities, the demands of keeping diaries and making other changes in aspects of their life may not be realistic. If a client says, "My life is too busy to do this stuff," then he or she is saying that he or she is too busy to lose weight at this time. Clinicians should point out that this may not be the proper time to implement a systemic long-term habit change program and that it may be better to postpone the weight-loss program until the client's life is not "too busy." If the client is habitually "too busy," the therapist may need to begin time management training to help the client regain some control of life before attempting to make these changes in eating habits. The second statement, "You're lucky I even get to the meetings," implies that the client is not taking responsibility for his or her own changes. The therapist is not lucky that the client got to the meeting. Ideally, the client is the lucky one who will benefit from the content of the meetings. The clients in a weight-loss program, as well as other programs, may externalize responsibility for the changes they must make. This type of statement should sensitize the clinician to this client's lack of commitment to change.

Sabotage

"My husband seems to want me heavy." Or, "I do my best to avoid snacking, but when my husband brings home cakes and cookies and eats in front of me. I can't help but eating some too." For most clients there are significant others in their lives who may interfere, sometimes explicitly, but more often covertly, with the habit changes attempted. These significant others may undermine the treatment program by suggesting high-calorie foods for meals and snacks, by eating in front of the client, or by openly disparaging the client's efforts to change. Depending on the degree of sabotage or lack of support, the therapist may need to help the client to rehearse assertive responses to reduce interference of these other people in the habit-change program. If stories of sabotage or lack of support emerge weekly with the same client, an assessment of the marital situation is warranted to determine whether this is just one battleground in a marital war. Support of other members in the group can often help the individual overcome the negative influence of these significant others or to develop alternative strategies for dealing with the bad eating habits of their family member.

Poor Attendance and Noncompliance with Homework

"I just didn't have a chance to get in last week and I forget to keep my diaries." Whenever this statement is heard, chances are high that the person has not lost weight during the preceding period and has not continued to work on a habit changes. Depending on the actual weight change over this period, the therapist can point out to the client how not attending the prior session or keeping the required diary may have slowed his or her progress. The therapist can reduce these problems by beginning the treatment program with an explicit contract that includes financial contingencies for both attendance and completion of homework.

In addition to the outpatient fee, the therapist can contract with the client to deposit a refundable amount of money for completion of program requirements. For a 10-session program, a deposit of $50 would permit the refund of $5 per week for attendance ($2) and completion of homework ($3). Although this explicit contract will not guarantee complete attendance, it will help to reduce nonattendance by providing a positive reinforcement for attendance in spite of any weight gain during that week.

Many people fail to attend weekly sessions when they have perceived that they have had "a bad week." They do not want to be weighed to learn that they have gained weight. This is unfortunate because these "bad weeks" provide ideal times to do problem solving with clients to identify which situations led to their overeating and inability to complete the habit change assignment. If clients come in only when they have been "good," the clinician is denied the data from the weeks that are most in need of modification. Therefore, clients must be reminded that attendance is the first and most important requirement for the weight loss program, followed by the completion of homework assignments. Changes in weight will follow if the client makes a good effort to meet with the therapist and attempt the habit changes. The ability to refund $5 per week for attendance and homework completion provides a positive reinforcement for the client, independently of whatever weight he or she has gained or lost during the week. Money not refunded because of nonattendance can be given as a bonus to these clients who have achieved the most systemic weight loss (i.e., lost weight the most number of weeks). It is strongly recommended that the weight loss program have a clear number of sessions and some type of financial contingency to increase attendance and homework compliance.

SUMMARY

Many clients in outpatient therapy request help for weight loss. Because obesity is a difficult problem to treat, the clinician must carefully assess the person's motivation to engage in a multiweek weight-loss program, the importance of weight loss at this point relative to other potential target behaviors, and the person's expectation that he or she can achieve weight loss through a behavioral or cognitive-behavioral approach. Although there are many well-written behavior-oriented treatment programs available, this chapter broadens these approaches by providing a congitive-behavioral treatment package, which integrates more recent views of self-control to supplement the standard behavioral programs available. The clinical issues outlined at the end of the chapter are especially important to working on a long-term problem such as weight loss. Hopefully, this chapter will help prepare an outpatient therapist to design and implement a successful outpatient weight-loss program. Do not expect miracles. The case study included in this chapter is very representative of the range of outcomes for typical outpatient clients. Clients lost from 18 lb to gaining 3 lb during the treatment phase. The clinician must carefully examine the differences between the successful and unsuccessful clients. Through this type of case review, the therapist's skills and techniques can be refined to help identify appropriate clients for long-term weight-loss programs as well as improved treatment delivery for those clients who previously did not benefit.

REFERENCES

Brownell, K. D. Assessment of eating disorders. In D. H. Barlow (Ed.), *Behavioral assessment of adult disorders*. New York: Guilford Press, 1981.

Ferguson, J. M. *Learning to eat: Behavior modification for weight control*. Palo Alto, Calif.: Bull Publishing Company, 1975.

Mahoney, M. J. Fat fiction. *Behavior therapy*, 1975, *6*, 416–418.

Metropolitan Life Insurance Company. Frequency of overweight and underweight. *Statistical Bulletin*, 1960, *41*, 4–7.

Stuart, R. B., & Davis, B. *Slim chance in a fat world*. Champaign, Ill: Research Press, 1978.

Stunkard, A. J., & Mahoney, M. J. Behavioral treatment of eating disorders. In H. Leitenberg (Ed.), *Handbook of behavior modification and behavior therapy*. Englewood Cliffs, N.J.: Prentice-Hall, 1976.

Wadden, T. A., & Anderton, C. H. The clinical use of hypnosis. *Psychological Bulletin*, 1982, *91*, 215–253.

Appendix: Cognitive Behavior Therapy
Package for Obesity

Lesson 1
Objectives:
1. Introduce concept of self-statements and describe importance in mediating behavior.
2. Learn to identify problem situations.
3. Learn to identify negative self-statements associated with
   these situations.
I. *What you say to yourself makes a difference* (introduction):
   A. Provide examples of how thought patterns can affect eating
   behaviors.
     1. You say to yourself: "Every other diet has failed and
      so will this one"—and then you stop at Baskin-Robbins.
     2. You eat two small cookies and say: "I blew it, I might
      as well eat the whole package."
     3. You see a piece of pie in the refrigerator, but you say:
      "I'll feel a lot better if I don't eat this"—and you don't.
   B. Explain the general process of how thoughts can influence
   behavior by describing the pattern shown in Figure 7-4.

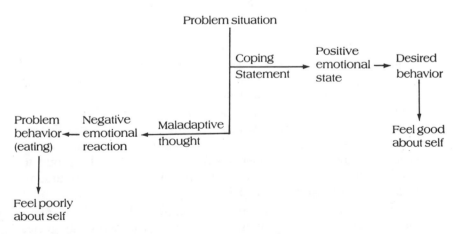

Figure 7-4   Flowchart of thought–behavior reflex.

C. To further illustrate, give the following examples:

Situation: You have just come home after a bad day and feel very busy, tired, and frustrated.

Maladaptive thought: "I can't diet now, I'm just too tired to work at it, besides, I always fail anyway."

Outcome: Feeling of being undesired, excessive eating, feeling bad about self.

Positive coping statement: "I'm in control. I don't have to overeat just because I'm down."

Outcome: Not eating and feeling better about self.

D. Explain that this program will teach this process one step a time so that maladaptive thoughts are quickly recognized and replaced by positive coping responses. Like any other new skill (e.g., driving a car), it may seem awkward at first but will soon become natural and easy.

II. The first step is to identify *specific* high-risk situations and likely maladaptive self-statements (before, during, and after eating) associated with those situations.

A. Provide the following example:

Situation: You are feeling bored watching television at night, you look in the refrigerator—there is half of a pie.

Maladaptive thoughts:

1. *Before eating:* "I'm so bored, it's just not worth dieting—I'll always be fat."
2. *During eating:* "I just blew it now—I might as well finish it off."
3. *After eating:* "I'm a failure. I have no control. I can't do anything right."

Explain how each of these statements is maladaptive: (a) leads to undesired, unnecessary eating; (b) leads to eating an excessive amount; (c) lowers feelings of control and self-esteem.

The emphasis should be on the *function* of the self-statement, that is, what consequences would follow each statement. For example, the statement "I blew it now, I might as well finish it off" would probably be followed by more eating. Ask the group to predict what consequences would follow each self-statement. Coach and prompt as appropriate.

It can be useful to point out *how* maladaptive self-statement works. Many such statements fall into the following categories of irrational thinking patterns:

1. *Arbitrary inference:* Drawing a conclusion without sufficient evidence; for example, "I have *no* control."
2. *Overgeneralization:* Unjustified generalization to similar cases; for example, "Diets *never* work for me."
3. *Self-fulfilling statements:* Expressing failure creates the failure; for example, "This diet is sure to fail."

B. *Practice:* Have the group practice identifying (1) *Specific* high-risk situations; (2) Maladaptive self-statements associated with the problem situations
C. Have each person identify three problem eating situations as associated maladaptive self-statements. Do not worry about coping statements for now. Situations and maladaptive thoughts should be specific.

Lesson 2
Objectives:
1. Generate coping responses for problem situations and substitute for maladaptive thoughts.
2. Identify alternate activities for emotional eating.

I. Generating and using positive coping statements:
A. Briefly review model presented in lesson 1 where an effective coping response to a problem situation can prevent undesired behavior (excessive eating).
B. Explain that repeated past exposure to problem situations followed by maladaptive thoughts and undesired eating has developed into a strong habit. It will require repeated exposures with coping statements to neutralize the habit.
C. Coping statements should be *short, clear, powerful,* and *meaningful* for the individual. They should be tailored to the specific problem situation. Examples of coping statements *before* the situation are:
1. "Just because there's food there, doesn't mean I have to eat it."
2. "I'm going to be successful this time."
3. "I'll feel better if I don't eat."

Examples of coping statements *during* the situation are:
1. "I'm doing very well."
2. "I feel hungry. I really must be losing weight and looking thinner."

    3. "I'm eating too much. If I stop now, I'll be alright."
    4. "It will only do more harm to keep eating."
Examples of coping statements *after* the situation are:
    1. "I did very well."
    2. "I can be successful if I'm just sensible about it."
    3. "That didn't work so well. What did I do wrong? I can do better next time."

D. Describe how positive coping statements can affect other behaviors besides eating (e.g., exercise). It is very important to emphasize exercise. Tell the group that research shows exercise habits to differentiate overweight from normal weight people more than eating patterns. All exercises should be undertaken only with medical approval. Examples of positive coping statements *during* exercise are:
    1. "This feels good."
    2. "My heart and lungs must really be getting stronger."
    3. "I can feel myself getting thinner and stronger."
    4. "I'll finish soon and I will be very pleased with myself."

Examples of coping statements *after* exercise are:
    1. "I got out today. Good job!"
    2. "I really did well today."

II. Alternative activities for emotional eating are:

A. In the same way that positive coping thoughts can be generated for problem situations, various alternative behaviors can be generated. Simply put, eating in response to a negative feeling or situation can be replaced with some nonfood activity. Because this kind of eating is a habit, it will, at first, require a conscious effort to engage in other nonfood activities. As with a new coping response, however, these new behaviors soon will become natural and spontaneous.

B. Generate possible alternative behaviors. All group members should make a list of such activities appropriate for them. Guidelines are as follows: (1) activity should be practical, (2) activity should last at least 10–15 minutes (then hunger will usually diminish), (3) the activity should be incompatible with eating (out of the kitchen!), (4) activity involving some conscious effort (e.g., making a telephone call is better than watching TV). Keep this list with you all the time and use the urge to eat as a cue to look at the list. Examples are hobbies, housework, phone calls, errands, letter writing, washing hair, taking a bath, paying bills, meditation, and exercise.

Lesson 3

Objectives:

1. Review use of coping statements.
2. Describe "want/should ratios" and "self-time" periods.
3. Introduce "programmed binge."

I. Review the use of coping statements:

A. Have group state problem situations, and then elicit potential coping responses. Outcomes associated with each response can be evaluated and the best one chosen. This should be done "cognitively" (with self-statements) and "behaviorally" (with alternative activities). Discuss how this approach (coping statements) can be useful in all daily activities, not just eating. Encourage use of these techniques in other life areas. Preface this session by stating that the lesson is to help in dealing with feelings of stress and pressure from everyday life—not just eating. These techniques can help to (1) deal with daily stress and (2) develop feelings of being more in control of one's life.

II. Describe the want/should ratio and the notion of self-time:

A. In many instances, eating (particularly binging) can be a reaction to high stress or feelings of personal deprivation associated with the self-statement "I need to do something for myself." These pressures can come from "shoulds"—things that everyone *has* to do such as enjoyable work or chores. If an individual feels too much pressure from "shoulds" and doesn't have enough "wants" (i.e., things a person *enjoys* doing and does for her or himself), then she or he may resort to eating (or binging) as a kind of escape.

B. Develop a list of "shoulds" and "wants." Items should be *specific*, and "wants" should be enjoyable and realistic. On examining these lists, the overall aim is to *balance* the want/should ratio. If there are too many "shoulds," add "wants" until a balance is achieved. Follow-through on doing the "wants!" (see item C).

C. Self-time can be used to help balance the want/should ratio. Self-time is also important as a way to increase one's sense of inner control. Self-time is an allotted time away from chores and tasks ("shoulds") for specified periods each day. During these times (which can be as little as 20 minutes, twice a day) one can relax and "forget" the stress of the day. For self-time to be most effective, the following guidelines should be used:

1. Decide on and set aside a *reasonable* amount of self-time for each day. *Always* follow through.
2. Stress the fact that the individual has *control* over own behavior—self-time is for the individual.
3. Stress the fact that self-time, as a relaxing experience, can help to counteract the problem of stress.
4. Self-time should be spent in some relaxing activity such as meditation, enjoyable reading, or simply imagining oneself in control and relaxed. External disturbances and stress should be ignored.

D. Have group members decide on *when* and *what* they will do for self-time and follow through for the week.
E. Some individuals may respond to "self-time" or "waits" log by saying that they simply have no time available to engage in these activities. It may be useful in these cases to briefly teach *time-management skills*. Have these individuals keep a special log of all their activities during all waking hours for at least three days. Entries should be made every ½ hour. Inspection of the log will reveal either available time or allow for rearringing the daily routine to accommodate self time.
F. (Optional.) Imagery training for self-time can be administered. Have all members relax and each imagine a positive, relaxing scene—becoming a part of that scene. Involve as many senses as possible. No food images!

III. Programmed "binging":
A. Programmed binging involves a group leader-group member contact where the member is asked to engage in eating a problematic food under specified conditions. The purpose for this procedure is to demonstrate that eating in a problem situation or a problem food can be controlled. Successful programmed binges increase sense of self-control.
B. The procedure for programmed binge is as follows:
1. Decide on a problem food, quantity of food, and time and place of eating. For the initial trial, a somewhat difficult food but a reasonable quantity should be chosen. Time and place should be chosen to minimize the problem of hunger, negative mood, or stress.

2. Eat the specified quantity of food *slowly*, noticing the taste and in the *absence* of other activities (e.g., TV).

3. An example of instruction in making positive coping statements *before eating* is "I can eat this without losing control"; *during eating*, "This food doesn't control me. I can stop anytime"; and *after eating*, "I was able to control myself very well. I'm doing just great!"

4. Discuss "binge" at the next session. If an individual notices a disinterest in eating while "binging" or cannot eat as much as specified, identify the techniques (e.g., self-statements) used successfully. Discuss feelings of control.

Lesson 4

Objectives:

1. Outline the "Abstinence Violation Effect" in order to innoculate against destructive personal attributions for "slips."

2. Programmed "binge" II.

I. The Abstinence Violation Effect (AVE):

A. Once a "slip" has occurred, that is, you have began to eat a "forbidden food," in many cases the disastrous maladaptive statement "I've already blown it, I might as well go all the way," can occur. . . ." Not only does this lead to feelings of not being in control, but also can lead to thoughts of *personal failure* ("I can't do anything right." "What a pig—I'm just no good."). It is *important* to realize the *complete falacy* of these statements! It is important to understand why there is sometimes this guilt and sense of failure.

B. *AVE* is the source of the feelings of guilt and failure. The AVE is a known psychological phenomenon that occurs when someone engages in a behavior that they are trying to avoid. For example, people trying to quit smoking will experience the AVE (and guilt and sense of personal failure) if they do smoke. Similarly, if you eat more than you want or when you don't want too, you feel the AVE.

C. The negative feelings of guilt and loss of control are *not* necessary! Steps to innoculate against these destructive feelings and to prevent worse eating.:

1. Realize that a "slip" is *not* unusual. It does *not* mean failure. In fact, "slips" are expected! By re-

alizing this, the "damage" can be minimized. Remember, one piece of cake is *not* all that bad! If you can realize this and stop, you will be alright!

2. The negative feelings of guilt do *not* mean you are a failure! They are to be expected, a part of the AVE.

3. You *do* have control over your urge to eat. By using the strategies you have learned, the urge will pass ("If I stop now, I'll be OK!")

4. Consider the "slip" as a *learning experience*, not a failure! What were the elements of the high-risk situation? What coping response could I have used? Remember, one slip *doesn't* mean you're a failure or cannot follow through on your diet. What you've learned from this experience can help you with the next!

5. Rehearse cognitive coping strategies that can be used next time this problem situation arises.

II. Programmed "binging" II:

A. Repeat programmed "binge," but increase (reasonably!) the risk by altering the situation. Instead of a benign, pre-planned snacktime, try a time when hunger or stress are slightly higher.

Lesson 5
Objectives:

1. Cognitive restructuring for specific negative moods.
2. Programmed "binge" III.

I. Negative moods are common antecedents to problem eating. Cognitive restructuring techniques can be applied to specific negative moods—not just for eating, but life stress in general.

A. For each of the following negative emotions, identify problem situations, examine associated negative self-statements, and generate coping responses:

1. Depression:
   a. Negative statements: "Everything is going lousy. I might as well eat. It's not worth it."
   b. Coping responses: "I'll feel better if I lose weight. . . . I'm in control; I don't have to overeat just because I'm down."

2. Boredom:
   a. Negative statement: "I'm bored. What's to eat?" "There's *never* anything to eat around here."

        b. Coping response: "I don't want to live to eat, what else can I do? I don't want to waste my life; I'm going to start doing things now."

    3. Anger:

        a. Negative statement: "I can't control it. . . . Eating will help me calm down."

        b. Coping response: "What am I angry about? I should express my anger directly, not by eating. . . . Eating won't make me less angry, it will just make me fat."

  B. Similar self-statements can be generated for other negative moods. It is important to remember the process of replacing the maladaptive thought with the positive coping statement. Bad thoughts can lead to bad behavior and mood; good thoughts, to good behavior and mood.

II. Programmed "binge" III.

  A. Repeat but increase (again reasonably!) "risk" by altering situation slightly.

Lesson 6

Objectives:

    1. Review program material:

        a. Cognitive model

        b. Coping skills (cognitive and alternate behavior)

        c. Wants/shoulds ratio and self-time

        d. AVE

        e. Results of programmed binge

(Optional.)

    2. If standard b-mod material was presented, review:

        a. Preplanning snacks

        b. Designated eating place

        c. Reduction of eating cues

        d. Eating slowly

        e. Contracting

    3. Discuss individual problems

I. Cognitive material:

  A. Discuss model (lesson 1).

  B. Briefly discuss coping skills (lesson 2).

  C. Construct new want/should ratios—new commitments to self-time (lesson 3).

  D. Briefly discuss AVE (lesson 4).

II. B-mod material:
     A.   Encourage the continued use of all behavioral strategies learned. Particularly work on the ones that seem *most difficult.*
III. Individual problems can be discussed with the group. Stress the importance of utilizing the techniques learned to deal with *all* streses of life—not just weight loss. Emphasize the importance of *self-esteem* and *self-efficacy.* Stress that the program is *not* over. The maintenance sessions are, in some ways, even more important than the treatment sessions. Weight loss maintenance is the key! Be positive; encourage success!

8

Sexual Dysfunction

Judith V. Becker and Linda J. Skinner

THE SEXUAL RESPONSE CYCLE of males and females consists of four stages: appetitive, excitement, orgasm, and resolution. During the appetitive stage, an individual may engage in sexual fantasies or have a psychological interest in or desire to be sexual. Psychological pleasure accompanied by physiological changes is characteristic of the excitement stage, whereas the orgasm stage is characterized by a peaking of sexual pleasure and a simultaneous release of sexual tension accompanied by rhythmic muscular contractions. During the final stage, that of resolution, an individual experiences a sense of well-being and muscular relaxation. Behaviors or physiological conditions that prevent an individual from engaging in sexual activity or deriving psychological and/or physical pleasure generally are categorized as sexual dysfunction and can disrupt any of the four stages of the sexual response cycle.

Sexual dysfunctions may be lifelong in duration or develop after a period of normal sexual functioning. Additionally, such problems may be generalized in that they are present in all sexual activities or interactions, or the problems may be situational in nature, such as being present only under specific conditions or with particular sexual partners. Finally, sexual dysfunctions may be total or only partial.

The authors wish to thank Joan Cichon, Thomassina Hoeppel, and Mary McCormack for their assistance in the preparation of the manuscript for this chapter.

Thus a male may experience a total lack of sexual desire or only diminished desire.

This chapter focuses on the diagnosis and treatment of sexual dysfunction in males and females. The topics discussed include the taking of a problem-oriented sexual history, techniques for differentiating organic from psychogenic sexual problems, the major sexual dysfunctions of males and females, behavioral strategies for treating sexual dysfunctions, and general issues confronting the clinician working with sexually dysfunctional patients.

A PROBLEM-ORIENTED SEXUAL HISTORY

The first step in diagnosing and treating a patient with a sexual problem is to obtain a problem-oriented sexual history. Unlike a general sexual history, a problem-oriented sexual history focuses only on the problem the patient currently is experiencing. A behavioral approach to the treatment of sexual dysfunctions does not necessitate obtaining an in-depth history of the patient's sexual development and practices. Instead, it is more efficacious to focus on the presenting problem. Numerous paper-and-pencil measures and models for taking a problem-oriented sexual history have been developed (Schiavi, Derogatis, Kuriansky, O'Connor, & Sharpe, 1979), whereas the sexual problem history format formulated by Annon (1976) is relatively simple for a clinician to follow. This history format covers five major areas: identification of the problem, onset and course of the problem, the patient's perception of causes and maintenance factors, previous therapy for the problem and outcome, and the patient's current therapeutic goals and expectations.

Obtaining a clear description of the presenting problem is the initial focus of a sexual problem history. When having a patient describe his or her problem, it is important to avoid the use of labels as patients frequently apply them erroneously.

Nicole was seeking therapy for a lifelong problem. When asked to describe the problem, she stated that she was "frigid." Since people use the term "frigidity" to describe a variety of problems, Nicole was asked to explain what she meant by "frigid." She indicated that she did become aroused and experienced both the physiological and psychological concomitants of arousal. However, she had never experienced an orgasm; thus, to Nicole, frigidity meant not being orgasmic.

An effective procedure for determining the exact nature of a sexual problem is to have patients describe in detail exactly what occurs whenever they attempt to be sexual. Since patients are often embarrassed or anxious when asked to provide such a description, it is important for the clinician to explain that people have not been socialized to discuss their sexual practices and, therefore, may experience some mild discomfort. However, the clinician should stress that such a thorough description is necessary in order to understand the nature of the presenting problem.

The second area that should be addressed when taking a sexual problem history is the onset and course of the presenting problem. The clinician should determine the age of the patient when the sexual problem first manifest itself and how long the problem has continued. Additionally, it is important to learn whether onset of the problem was gradual or sudden and if the patient remembers any particular events that occurred about the time of onset.

Marco indicated that he had been experiencing erectile problems for approximately 6 months. Prior to that time, he had experienced no difficulty obtaining an erection or maintaining an erection during penetration. During the intake interview, Marco revealed that he first had a problem obtaining an erection one evening when he attempted to have intercourse with a woman he had met at a bar. When asked to describe the evening, Marco reported that he had been drinking rather heavily that night. This information helped the clinician conclude that Marco's erectile problem was physiological rather than psychogenic in etiology and related to his consumption of alcohol.

The clinician also should assess the course of the sexual problem, including any changes in its intensity and whether it occurs under all circumstances or only under specific conditions. For example, Marco's erectile problems had not changed in intensity and occurred only when he had been drinking. Again, this information assisted in the determination that his problem was physiological. However, sexual problems with a gradual onset and following a different course may result in a diagnosis of an organic problem.

Stan was also referred for treatment because of an erectile problem. He reported that he had noticed a gradual decline in his erectile response. Furthermore, the problem was present when he masturbated as well as when he was with any sexual partner. Additionally, Stan felt that his problem was continuing to worsen. This history of onset and course of the problem caused the clinician to question if Stan's problem was organic rather than psychogenic in nature.

It is very important for a clinician to be aware of a patient's concept of what caused and continues to maintain a sexual problem. A clinician may save a considerable amount of time by allowing patients to comment on the etiology of the problem as they frequently are able to pinpoint the exact cause.

Cathy's presenting problem was that she was not orgasmic. Her history revealed that although she did experience orgasms through self-stimulation, she had never had an orgasm when she was with her sexual partner. When asked what she believed to be the cause of her problem, Cathy stated that her partner did not provide her with ample stimulation prior to penetration. As a result, she was not sufficiently aroused when they had intercourse.

Knowledge about a patient's concept of the cause and maintenance factors of a sexual problem may also explain a patient's response to therapy.

Mike had been experiencing erectile problems for four months. His history revealed that he and his wife had been having increasing marital problems for approximately one year and that their sexual encounters had decreased significantly during the last few months. However, Mike did not believe that their marital problems were related to his sexual problems. Instead, he reported that he had had a serious bout with the flu just around the time that he began to experience erectile problems, and he was convinced that this illness was the cause of his sexual problem. Despite the evidence that nothing was physiologically wrong, Mike continued to believe that his erectile problems had an organic basis. Consequently, he was resistive throughout therapy.

The fourth area that a clinician should address is the treatment history of the patient with respect to his or her sexual problem. Frequently, a patient will have contacted other professionals for assistance with a sexual problem. It is helpful to determine if the patient has participated in psychotherapy and, if so, the outcome of that treatment. Sometimes a patient will have spent a number of years in therapy for a sexual problem without obtaining any relief for that problem. Consequently, the patient may be somewhat resistant to treatment or believe that no therapy will help. Other patients may have made some progress during an earlier course of therapy. It is important to identify the successful components of previous treatment, focus on these with the patient, and incorporate some of these treatment strategies into the present therapy.

It is imperative to rule out any organic factors that may be instrumental in affecting the patient's sexuality. When asking about previous treatment, therefore, a clinician should determine whether the patient has had a previous medical evaluation and, if so, how recently it was performed, whether it was performed by a general practitioner or a specialist, (e.g., a urologist or a gynecologist), and what the results of the evaluation were. Additionally, it is important to know what form of treatment, if any, was prescribed and whether the patient is presently taking any medication. There are a variety of illnesses, medical conditions, and medications that interfere with sexual performance.

Detailed lists of these medical complications are available in the literature (Kaplan, 1974). In general, increases in sexual drive are associated with moderate doses of drugs that serve as a central nervous system stimulants, whereas decreases in sexual drive frequently accompany the use of depressants. Any type of medication that produces improvements in general health may be associated with restored sexual interests. The clinician treating patients with sexual dysfunctions should be aware of the impact various drugs have on sexual arousal. Unfortunately, the majority of research in the area of the effect of drugs on sexual arousal and performance has been conducted with males. Further research needs to be done on the impact of various drugs on females.

With the burgeoning interest in human sexuality and functioning, there has been a proliferation of books and articles in popular magazines describing self-help techniques for treating sexual problems. Consequently, many patients may have attempted to implement these techniques with varying degrees of success. It thus behooves the therapist to note exactly what techniques a patient has used, how these techniques were implemented, and the outcome of these efforts.

Never having experienced an orgasm in her life, Sylvie purchased a book describing how to become orgasmic. After reading the book, however, she was still unable to have an orgasm and, consequently, felt very frustrated. When asked how she implemented the steps outlined in the book, Sylvie indicated that she had skipped the first several chapters and had not followed the remaining steps in a systematic fashion. Instead, she was so intent on having an orgasm that she was not able to relax sufficiently and proceed at a slow enough pace that would allow her to have an orgasm. Using very similar techniques under the direction of a therapist, however, Sylvie now was successful in becoming orgasmic.

The final topic to be covered in a sexual problem history is identification of a patient's therapeutic goals and expectations about therapy. Although it is the patient's responsibility to identify the treatment goals, the therapist does have the responsibility of helping the patient hone and sharpen goals so that they are concrete and specific.

Gerry identified her one treatment goal as being able to enjoy sex more! With such a generalized goal, it is particularly difficult to determine appropriate therapeutic interventions, with progress difficult to rate. To help Gerry identify a more concrete and specific goal, the therapist asked her what she would like to be able to do or experience sexually after 10 treatment sessions that she was currently unable to do or experience. In response, Gerry indicated that she would like to feel less anxious when she and her partner engaged in mutual oral stimulation and that she would like to modify the content of some of her sexual fantasies.

It also is important to understand what expectations a patient may have about therapy. Unrealistic expectations may result in an unsuccessful outcome. For example, men who have a psychogenically based erectile dysfunction frequently are looking for some magical injection or medication that will automatically reverse the problem. A clinician should ensure that a patient is being realistic about the proposed therapy.

DIFFERENTIATING PSYCHOGENIC FROM ORGANIC SEXUAL PROBLEMS

Some sexual dysfunctions may be organic in origin. For example, more than 40 possible organic causes of erectile problems have been identified (Masters & Johnson, 1970). Prior to initiating sexual dysfunction therapy, a clinician should consider the possible role organic factors play in causing a patient's sexual problems. Such factors include congenital abnormalities, systemic diseases, vascular disorders, endocrine deficiencies, neurological disorders, and the use of prescribed medication or street drugs.

One potential contributory factor may be disturbances in the endocrine system. The complex relationship between psychological events, circulating hormonel levels, and sexual behavior has been debated for years. Recently, accurate methods of determining secreted levels of hormones have been established. Although the relationship between sexual activity and hormone level has been found to be complex, a number of studies have demonstrated a therapeutic response to testosterone replacement therapy with sexually dysfunctional hypogonadal males (Rose, 1972). Research also has found that there may be a relationship between chronically low testosterone levels and the development of sexual problems; however, this has not been a consistent finding (Raboch, Millan, & Starka, 1975; Raboch & Starka, 1973; Schiavi & White, 1976). Other researchers have demonstrated that testosterone levels may play an important role in female sexual functioning (Geobelsmann, Arce, Thorneycroft, & Mischell, 1974; Kaplan, 1974; Karney, Bancroft & Matthews, 1978; Money & Ehrhardt, 1972). Although the relationship between hormonal levels and development of sexual dysfunctions is not clearly understood, the possible contribution of hormonal disorders should be entertained.

Despite information obtained in the taking of a sexual problem history and the results of a medical examination, a clinician still may have difficulty ascertaining whether a sexual problem is psychogenic or organic in etiology. Recently, psychophysiological research has focused on sexual dysfunctions, with the results indicating promising applications in both diagnosis and treatment of sexual problems characterized by inhibited sexual excitement.

In males, inhibited sexual excitement is manifest by erectile problems that can take numerous forms, including an inability to generate any erection at all, an ability to obtain only a partial erection, loss of an erection immediately after it is generated, or loss of an erection at the point of penetration. Recently, a psychophysiological procedure has been developed that can be utilized by a clinician to assess objectively a patient's biological erectile capability. During rapid-eye-movement (REM) sleep periods, males experience penile erections known as *nocturnal penile tumescence* (NPT). Although these nocturnal erections appear to be present in normal males of all ages, they have been found to vary from night to night (Karacan, Williams, Thornby, & Salis, 1975). Initially, it was hypothesized that sexually dysfunctional males who did not develop nocturnal erections were experiencing an organically based problem whereas males who did develop nocturnal erections had psychogenic sexual problems (Karacan, 1970). More recently, however, research has shown that NPT measures are occasionally equivocal and that there is a group of males who cannot be diagnosed with any degree of accuracy using these measures (Abel, Becker, Cunningham-Tathner, Mittleman, & Primack, 1982). Since NPT measures, in and of themselves, have not been found to be accurate in all cases in differentiating organically from psychogenically based sexual dysfunctions, research currently is being focused on the use of adjunctive methods, including the measurements of penile blood pressure, perineal muscle activity, and penile rigidity.

A response analogous to NPT measures in males occurs during the REM sleep period in women. Using a vaginal photoplethysmograph, researchers have demonstrated the occurrence of vascular changes in vaginal responses during REM sleep (Abel, Murphy, Becker, & Bitar, 1979). Use of a vaginal photoplethysmograph has clinical potential in diagnosing organic-versus psychogenic-inhibited sexual excitement problems in women. To date, however, this potential has not been explored fully and further research is warranted.

BEHAVIORAL TREATMENT OF SEXUAL DYSFUNCTION

The efficacy of the behavioral model for the management of sexual dysfunctions has been well documented (Marks, 1981, 1981; Wright, Perreault, & Mathisen, 1977). Behavioral interventions are effective when applied to a variety of sexual dysfunctions as well as when directed at anxiety accompanying sexual activity (Brady, 1966; De Moor, 1972; Friedman, 1968; Haslam, 1965; Ince, 1973; Kaplan, 1974; Kraft & Al-Issa, 1967; Lazarus, 1963, Masters & Johnson, 1970; Semans, 1956; Wolpe, 1958; Wolpin, 1969). In addition, behavioral procedures can be used with couples or individuals with or without partners in individual, group, or self-treatment formats (Barbach, 1974; Ersner-Hershfield, 1978; Golden, Pierce, Heinrich, & Lobitz, 1978; Kaplan, Kohl, Pomeroy, Offit, & Hogan, 1974; Leiblum & Ersner-Hershfield, 1977; Leiblum, Rosen & Pierce, 1976; Reynolds, Price, & Hanrich, 1981). The application of various behavioral treatment interventions is presented in the discussion of each dysfunction.

SEXUAL DYSFUNCTIONS

The sexual dysfunctions presented below are the major sexual problems defined in the *Diagnostic and Statistical Manual of Mental Disorders* (APA, 1980).

Inhibited Sexual Desire

These sexual dysfunctions are characterized by a pervasive or persistent inhibition of sexual desire. Generally, a patient with such a presenting problem reports an absence of sexual fantasies and a lack of desire or interest in engaging in sexual activities. Some patients may indicate that this sexual dysfunction causes personal distress. Other patients may not be unduly bothered by the lack of sexual desire; however, their partners may experience great distress. The lack of sexual desire does not necessarily mean that the patient is nonsexual, as some patients with inhibited sexual desire may engage in sex occasionally and actually be responsive without desiring sex.

Prior to classifying a patient's presenting problem as inhibited sexual desire, a clinician should be sure that the patient is actually experiencing such decreased drive. Some people may not "realize" that their desire is "low" until they judge their desire for sex against comments made by friends or information read in magazine articles. Such patients frequently want to know what the norm or mean frequency is for sexual activity. Research indicates that the mean frequency depends on a variety of factors, including age, marital status, religious preference, and education. Whereas Kinsey and his associates (1948) found that the mean frequency of sexual contact was 2.34 times per week for American males up to the age of 85, 2.8 times per week for women under 30 years of age, and once every 12 days for women by the age of 60, the clinician should stress that there is a tremendous degree of variability, with some people having intercourse daily and others having it much less frequently.

It is also important to determine whether inhibited sexual desire is actually the primary problem or only the consequence of an underlying sexual problem. Frequently, a male with an erectile problem may "shut down" sexually and report having no desire for sex because of the difficulty he has had in effecting intercourse. Similarly, a woman with inhibited sexual excitement or an orgasmic problem may not find sex reinforcing and subsequently may lose all her desire for sexual interaction. In such cases, treatment directed at increasing sexual desire only will be ineffective in the long run. Rather, successful treatment of the underlying sexual problem will generally result in increased sexual desire.

For some patients, inhibited sexual desire is partner-specific.

Mike and Rosemary entered sexual dysfunction therapy as a result of the husband's apparently low sexual desire. While Rosemary wanted to have intercourse four times a week, Mike was satisfied having intercourse once a month. When Mike was interviewed separately, he reported that, while he lacked desire to be sexual with his wife, he masturbated at least three times a week, was extremely attracted to other women, and was desirous of being sexual with those women. When the couple's relationship was examined, it became apparent that Mike was using his lack of sexual desire for his wife to control their relationship and to punish her.

When inhibited sexual desire is found to be partner-specific, the clinician should carefully evaluate the total relationship.

Some of the organic factors causing inhibited sexual desire include acute and chronic illnesses, fatique, and malnutrition. A variety of neurological disorders may also cause a lack of desire. For example, patients with temporal lobe epilepsy frequently experience drastically reduced sexual desire (Blumer & Walker, 1975). Similarly, patients with Simmond's disease, Cushing's disease, chronic renal failure, and decreased gonadal hormones may experienced inhibited sexual desire. Finally, a number of substances may result in decreased sexual desire. For example, chronic alcoholism, which can produce irreversible liver damage and altered central nervous system (CNS) functioning, and the depression and marital problems concomitant with chronic alcoholism can contribute to an appetitive stage dysfunction. Drugs that have been implicated in the reduction of sexual desire include barbiturates in large doses; narcotics such as morphine, heroin, methadone, and codeine; a number of antipsychotic medications such as the phenothiazine, thioxanthene, and butyrophenone groups; the tricyclic antidepressants; and lithium carbonate.

In addition to organic causes, a variety of psychogenic factors may result in inhibited sexual desire. For example, patients may become less physically attracted to their sexual partners. Frequently, patients report that their partners' excess weight or poor hygiene has a negative impact on sexual desire. The boringness of the sexual routine also may contribute to a lack of desire. Over time, a couple may become quite routine and programmed in their sexual interactions, no longer exploring sexual alternatives. A lack of emotional intimacy in a relationship may also affect sexual desire, as may an extramarital or extrarelationship affair. Discovery that a spouse or sexual partner has been involved in such a relationship may result in inhibited desire. Additionally, a number of situational conditions, including job loss, financial problems, retirement, or difficulty with children may affect a person's level of sexual desire.

Perhaps one of the most common causes of inhibited sexual desire is marital or relationship maladjustment. Partners who feel very angry and hostile, who are resentful of their partners, or who dislike their partners can experience a decrease in sexual desire. Consequently, a clinician may elect to work on the marital or relationship problems prior to initiating sexual dysfunction therapy or treat both issues concomitantly.

At the request of the wife, Diana and Peter were seen for therapy as a result of Perer's inhibited sexual desire for his wife. During the initial interview, the clinician learned that Diana and Peter were both in their early thirties, were employed, and had been married for 12 years. Diana wanted children, but Peter was sterile, and the couple did not wish to consider adoption. They had been high-school sweethearts, and neither of them had had other sexual partners. Diana reported that Peter had been very desirous of her when they were dating and that they had frequently enjoyed foreplay while engaged. However, they did not have penile–vaginal intercourse prior to marriage. After they were married, Diana noticed a change in their sexual relationship in that she became more desirous of sex than Peter. This problem was noticed approximately two years into the marriage and has become worse with the passage of time. While Diana wanted to have sex three times a week, she and Peter were having sexual relations approximately once each month.

Diana and Peter had seen a therapist several years earlier. However, they both felt that his therapy not only did not help their sexual problem, but actually caused other problems for them as each session was spent with the two of them arguing. They had also separated previously but both were miserable while living apart.

In an individual session, Peter revealed that he masturbated at least three time per week. No medical problems or organic factors were found that would interfere with his desire for sex.

When asked what they saw as the cause of the presenting problem, Peter readily reported that Diana's constant comments about how many weeks it had been since they had been sexual angered him and resulted in his refusal to be sexual with her at all. He felt that if his wife would stop making such comments he would feel more comfortable in making approach behaviors. Diana indicated that Peter's refusal to have sex with her made her feel that he did not love her. Their treatment goal was to have the same level of desire for sexual interaction.

In a case such as this, the clinician needs to point out that rarely do people have the same sexual drive and that the strength of the male and female sexual drives differs at various ages. Additionally, throughout the course of a relationship, partners are not always desirous of sex at the same time and, consequently, compromise is necessary. Moreover, lack of effective communication would be discussed. For example, Diana would be encouraged to ask Peter what his lack of sexual desire meant and if, in fact, he was communicating to her nonverbally that he no longer cared for her. The importance of compromise would also be addressed. In the above case, Peter had difficulty initiating sex but once a sexual interaction was under way, he had no difficulty with erection or ejaculation. When asked if there were any behaviors that would make sex more exciting for him, Peter indicated that he would like them to engage in different sexual behaviors, including acting out some of his sexual fantasies. For one week, therefore, Diana was asked not to initiate any sexual interactions or remind her husband that she wanted to be sexual; Peter was asked to initiate sexual behavior and share one of his sexual fantasies with his wife. Further therapy sessions would focus on how to communicate sexual and emotional wants and needs. If, when treating a psychogenic inhibited desire dysfunction, a clinician meets with constant resistance from one or both partners, the therapist should assume that the sexual problem is not the primary problem in the relationship on the contrary, there is a severe degree of marital disharmony that must be addressed before the sexual dysfunction can be treated.

Inhibited Sexual Excitement

These dysfunctions are characterized by persistent and recurrent inhibitions of sexual exitement during sexual activity. Erectile difficulties represent inhibited sexual excitement problems in the male, whereas this category of problems is manifest by difficulties with vaginal lubrication and swelling in females.

Erectile problems may be primary, secondary, or situational. A male with a primary erectile problem has never achieved an erection that allows vaginal penetration, whereas one with a secondary erectile problem has been able to generate an erection at least once that allowed penetration but has since lost that ability. A diagnosis of a situational erectile problem indicates that a male is able to achieve an erection under one set of conditions, such as with one partner, but not under a different set of conditions, as with a different partner.

When evaluating a patient with an erectile problem, it is imperative that the clinician differentiate organically from psychogenically caused problems. The various organic causes of erectile problems have been discussed at length in the literature (Masters & Johnson, 1970; Munjack & Oziel, 1980). In approximately 90% of the cases, the etiology of an erectile dysfunction will be psychogenic (El Senoussi, Coleman, & Tauber, 1959; Johnson, 1968; Roen, 1965). In some cases, however, the dysfunction may be due to both organic and psychogenic factors. To help make a differential diagnosis, the clinician should ask the patient if he has night or morning erections or if he is able to generate an erection when masturbating, viewing erotic films or reading erotic literature, or with particular partners. Additionally, any medications the patient is taking should be noted. If a patient is able to achieve an erection, the clinician should ask the patient whether he loses it at the point of penetration, how long he is able to maintain an erection, and whether the erection is full or partial. If identification of the etiology is still not clear, the patient should be referred for further evaluation, such as the monitoring of NPT measures.

A 34-year-old, happily married male, Don was referred to a sex therapist by his general practitioner. His presenting problem was the complete absence of an erection. About two years earlier, he noticed that his erections were less firm and that he was losing his ability to generate an erection. Additionally, Don was experiencing retrograde ejaculation. About six months previously he had stopped having morning erections and had been unable to generate any erection for about 4 months, even though he continued to desire sex. His history also revealed that he was diagnosed as having diabetes when he was 22. Although his history was very consistent with that of an organically based erectile dysfunction, Don participated in NPT studies with a diagnosis of an organic problem subsequently made. A medical evaluation revealed diabetic neuropathy.

The treatment of an organic erectile dysfunction is the use of one of two types of penile implant (Nellans, Naftel, & Stein, 1976; Pearman, 1972; Scott, Bradley, & Timm, 1973; Small, 1976). The carrion is a small silicone prosthesis, one of which is surgically implanted into each corpora cavernosa. The advantages of this device are that the implantation is fairly simple and the device is relatively inexpensive. The disadvantages of this procedure are that occasional infection may necessitate removal of the device and the permanent erection caused by the device may be difficult to conceal.

The second type of implant is the Scott inflatable prosthesis. This prosthesis consists of paired inflatable silicone cylinders implanted within the corpora cavernosa and connected to a hydraulic pumping device implanted in the patient's scrotum. The fluid reservoir that is utilized in the pumping of pressure is inserted behind the rectal muscle. When the patient wishes to achieve an erection, he presses his scrotum, and when he wants detumescence to occur, he again presses his scrotum. With this device, concealment is assured, there is greater potential anatomically in terms of penis size during the achievement of erection, and more physiological functioning is possible. However, this prosthesis is relatively expensive, involves a generally complicated surgical procedure, and is more prone to mechanical problems.

The psychogenic causes of erectile failure can include the following: boredom with a sexual partner, failure to perceive a partner as attractive, fatigue, preoccupation with other aspects of one's life, fear about ejaculating too quickly, fear of disease or pregnancy, performance anxiety, a homosexual arousal pattern when one is attempting to function within a heterosexual relationship, inattention to sexual stimulation, continued anxiety or guilt stemming from the early childhood experiences of being punished when found masturbating and being given a strong warning about being sexual with girls, fear of hurting the female, and fear of damaging oneself.

Jim was good-looking medical student in his last year of school. His erectile problems began about six months ago. Although he continued to have morning erections and was able to achieve an erection during masturbation or while reading erotic literature, he was no longer able to generate an erection that allowed penetration. The first occurrence of his erectile problem was when he had been on a date with a woman to whom he was very attracted. They had gone out to dinner and during the course of the meal, he consumed quite a bit of wine. He remembered being very tired as he had been on call the night before. That night and on several subsequent occasions with the same woman, Jim was unable to achieve an erection. Similarly, he was unable to generate an erection when he attempted to have intercourse with a different woman.

Jim's ability to obtain an erection under several conditions suggests that his erectile problems were physiological and psychogenic and most probably related to fatique, alcohol consumption, and the fact that Jim was intent on having a very satisfactory sexual experience with the woman he was dating. His constant worry about the problem and his performance anxiety helped to maintain his problem.

The treatment of erectile problems is generally easier if the patient has a willing sexual partner to participate in therapy. However, treatment is possible without a partner's attendance.

Initially, the clinician should inform the patient that he is not alone in his problem and that, in fact, most men are unable to generate an erection sometime in their lives. A discussion of the cause and maintenance factors should follow. Thus Jim was told that his anxiety and worry were maintaining his problem. Generally, use of sensate focus exercise (Masters & Johnson, 1970) is recommended. For example, it was suggested to Jim that he make a date with the woman he liked and, when he felt like being sexual at the end of the evening, he explain to her that their sex did not succeed the last time as he was tired, and had consumed too much wine and had proceeded too quickly. He was to tell her that this evening he just wanted to massage and caress her in the manner that was pleasing to her and that he would like for her do the same to him. By doing this, they could learn about one another's bodies. He was instructed not to engage in any breast or genital caressing during this date. This date had gone well and he obtained a full erection but did not attempt penetration. A second date was arranged during which the couple engaged in genital caressing. In this treatment, penetration is allowed during later dates with the instructions that thrusting should not be attempted immediately, and when begun, should be very slow to ensure that the patient is able to maintain the erection.

For a patient who does not have a sexual partner or who is unwilling to engage in the graduated sexual response procedures with his partner, the same general technique should be used in combination with self-stimulation. That is, while masturbating, he should initially imagine himself caressing a woman and having an erection while doing so. He is instructed to change his fantasies gradually and not allow himself to ejaculate unless he is fantasizing about having a full erection when with a sexual partner.

The organic and psychogenic causes of inhibited sexual excitement in women are similar to those noted for men. In addition, a sexual assault is a causative factor for some women (Becker, Skinner, Abel, & Cichon, 1982). Treatment usually involves communication skills training, use of sensate focus exercises, and fantasy training to help a woman become aroused.

Inhibited Female Orgasm

These dysfunctions are characterized by the total absence of or a delay in achieving an orgasm. Like erectile problems, orgasmic dysfunctions may be primary, secondary, or situational.

Gerry, a 30-year-old woman who had been married for five years, was very desirous of sex, and was aroused during sexual interactions. However, she had never experienced an orgasm. Gerry indicated that she never engaged in self-stimulation as a youngster and grew up in a rather puritanical family. When evaluated, she was physically healthy and not taking any medication that would interfere with orgasmic responsiveness.

The most likely way for a woman to become orgasmic is through masturbation; consequently, any discomfort the patient may feel about exploring her own body should be discussed. In addition, the patient should be instructed to perform the Kegel exercises, a systematic program for exercising the pubococcygeus muscle, a muscle involved in orgasms (Kegel, 1952). Once the patient has mastered these exercises, she is placed on a masturbatory program that begins with a gradual exposure to her own body by a visual and tactile exploration of the body and moves toward focused genital touching (LoPiccolo & Lobitz, 1972). Use of sexual fantasies combined with stimulation is also taught. The clinician may recommend use of a vibrator if the woman is unable to have an orgasm when engaging in focused genital touching. Once the woman is able to have an orgasm through self-stimulation, she then teaches her sexual partner (using sensate focus exercises) the type of genital stimulation she requires to have an orgasm.

Secondary orgasmic problems are frequently related to marital or relationship discord, and these problems may need to be addressed prior to the initiation of sex therapy. The treatment interventions for secondary orgasmic problems parallel those used with primary orgasmic problems (Snyder, LoPiccolo & LoPiccolo, 1975; McGovern, Stuart, & Lo Piccolo, 1975).

There are no treatment interventions specific to situational orgasmic problems. Instead, the clinician must identify the specific inhibiting factors and then aid the patient in overcoming her anxiety through a gradual exposure approach.

The most frequent complaint of women experiencing an orgasmic problem is that they are not orgasmic through penile–vaginal intercourse. When becoming orgasmic through intercourse is a patient's treatment goal, the clinician should ensure that she and her partner are aware that the clitoris is the focus of sexual response in the female and that adequate stimulation both prior to and during intercourse is necessary. Additionally, the clinician may suggest various sexual positions that allow stimulation of the clitoris by the patient or her partner during intercourse. For women who are fearful of "letting go" during intercourse, systematic desensitization is appropriate. Finally, the patient should be told not to expect to have an orgasm every time she has intercourse, as research has shown that a minority of women are orgasmic regularly during intercourse (Hite, 1976).

Inhibited Male Orgasm

This dysfunction is characterized by persistent and recurrent inhibition of ejaculation subsequent to sexual arousal and may be primary or secondary in nature. Masters and Johnson (1970) reported that only

17 men of 510 couples treated exhibited inhibited male orgasmic problems, whereas other researchers indicate that this dysfunction is more common (Kaplan & Abrahms, 1958).

The cause of this problem can be psychogenic or organic, with organic factors including any form of disease or trauma that destroys part of the substrate subserving ejaculation. Additionally, the following drugs have been implicated in this disorder: heroin, morphine, methadone, Demerol (meperidine), Dilaudid (hydromorphone hydrochloride), codeine, barbiturates, Aldomet (methyldopa), reserpine, Hydergine (adrenergic blocker), Mellaril (thioridazine), Stelazine (tripluoperazine), Trilafon (perphenazine), Haldol (haloperidol), Marplan (isocarboxazid), Nardil (phenelzine), Tofranil (imipramine hydrochloride), and Elavil (amitriptyline hydrochloride).

Some of the psychogenic causes include fear of impregnating the female, fear of hurting the female, marital discord, loss of attraction for one's sexual partner, insufficient stimulation, and distraction when being sexual. Males who are able to ejaculate during oral or manual stimulation or under any conditions other than with a partner are experiencing psychogenic inhibited orgasm.

The treatment for this disorder is similar to that used for inhibited orgasm in females. The patient should be told that, when he masturbates, he should masturbate as quickly as possible to ejaculation while fantasizing that his penis is inside his partner's vagina and ejaculating. A second technique is to teach the patient and his partner sensate focus exercises. If the patient is able to masturbate in the presence of his partner, he is instructed to place his partner's hand over his so that she can see how much touching he requires. He should then place his hand over hers while she masturbates him to ejaculation. Finally, she should sit astride him and stimulate him, eventually putting his penis in her vagina when he reaches the point of ejaculatory inevitability. If a man is uncomfortable ejaculating in the presence of his partner, systematic desensitization is used to help him become more comfortable in her presence.

Premature Ejaculation

This dysfunction is characterized by persistent and recurrent absence of voluntary control over ejaculation, with the result that a male ejaculates before he wishes to do so. This is the most frequent sexual complaint seen in clinics and one of the easiest to treat, with the success rate being as high as 98 percent (Masters & Johnson, 1970). Organic causes are extremely rare for this dysfunction. Instead, it is primarily a learned behavior in that many men did not learn to control the rapid ejaculation usually found in young males. Other contributory psychogenic factors include anxiety about ejaculating too quickly, having a partner with a sexual dysfunction, abstaining from sex for prolonged periods of time, and fatigue.

The treatment of premature ejaculation involves discrimination training and the reduction of anxiety. One successful intervention is the stop– start technique (Semans, 1956). This procedure involves having the patient lie on his back while his partner strokes his penis. The patient focuses on the pleasurable feelings resulting from the stroking of his penis and the sensations that precede his urge to ejaculate. When he feels that he is about to ejaculate, he signals his partner to stop the stimulation. The patient should start and stop at least four times before he allows himself to ejaculate.

A second procedure, the "squeeze" technique (Masters & Johnson, 1970), can be done in conjunction with the start–stop technique. In the "sqeeze" technique, the patient's partner is taught to place her thumb on the frenulum of the penis and her first and second fingers on opposite sides of the head of the penis. When the patient feels that he is going to ejaculate, the partner squeezes for up to 5 seconds and then releases the penis for up to 30 seconds. This procedure should only be used on a full erection and be discontinued as the patient gains control over ejaculation. The clinician should let the patient know that initially some "accidents" may occur and that practice will improve his ability to discriminate when ejaculation is imminent.

The clinician may also suggest that the patient increase frequency of sexual contacts leading to orgasm and ejaculation, so that he does not continue to delay his contacts for fear of ejaculating prematurely. Finally, the patient may be instructed to fantasize about ejaculating inside his partner whenever he masturbates to ejaculation.

Vaginismus

This dysfunction is characterized by involuntary spasms of the musculature of the outer one-third of the vagina that prevents penetration. This problem can be diagnosed by a physical examination. Some women who are anxious about sex may experience muscular tightening and some pain during penetration, but these women do not have vaginismus.

Vaginismus can be primary, secondary, or situational in nature. However, primary vaginismus is by far the most prevalent form seen.

Numerous organic factors may cause vaginismus, including Crohn's disease, diverticulitis, lower urinary tract infection, smegma under the clitoral hood, irritation of the clitoris due to trauma, infection, chemicals, episiotomy scars, an intact or partially intact hymen, pelvic inflammatory disease, ectopic pregnancies, cysts and tumors of the ovaries, other neoplasms, vaginal infections, insufficient vaginal lubrication, and a shortened vagina. Additionally, a woman with dyspareunia may experience pain in response to attempted intercourse and develop vaginismus secondary to the pain of intercourse.

Factors that play a role in the psychogenic etiology of vaginismus include poor sexual techniques on the part of the male partner, anxiety, fear, guilt, and early childhood sexual experiences such as incest or rape.

At the age of 19, Debbie was the victim of an attempted rape during which the rapist was unable to effect penetration as he kept losing his erection. However, he repeatedly battered his semierect penis against her vagina. Prior to the assult, she had not engaged in sexual intercourse.

When Debbie was referred to treatment, she had been married for about four years. While she and her husband had enjoyed a significant amount of foreplay while engaged, neither of them had had other sexual partners.

When her husband attempted penetration on their honeymoon, Debbie experienced vaginismus. A physician she consulted was unable to perform a pelvic examination. The physician told her and her husband that Debbie merely had to make up her mind to have intercourse. Consequently, her husband thought that she was just being stubborn and really did not want to have sex with him. This problem had continued for the four years of their marriage.

Good results have been found by using systematic desensitization in the treatment of vaginismus. A particularly successful procedure is the Haslam technique (Haslam, 1965), which involves the systematic insertion of dilators of graduated sizes. A similar procedure in which the patient and her partner use a set of dilators in the privacy of their own home has also been found to be effective (Masters & Johnson, 1970), as has a variation in which the patient or her partner inserts tampons and fingers until penile penetration can be effected (Kaplan, 1974). The clinician may suggest that the patient gently stroke her genitals and clitoris during the insertion procedure. Additionally, the clinician may recommend that penile penetration be effected with the partner lying on his back and the patient controlling the actual insertion and subsequent movement.

Dyspareunia

This dysfunction is characterized by persistent and recurrent genital pain and can occur in both males and females. Since physical pain is the characteristic of this sexual problem, it is imperative that any organic pathology be ruled out by the physical examination. Once organic factors have been eliminated, the clinician should investigate the patient's fear and/or anxiety underlying dyspareunia. Systematic desensitization has been found to be successful in the treatment of dyspareunia.

CASE STUDY

Rick and Nicole had been married for five years when they entered therapy, in their late twenties. They had no children but hoped to have a child in the near future. For the most part they considered their marriage to be very happy.

Whereas Rick had had sexual experiences with other partners, Nicole had had no previous sexual partners. Her first intercourse occurred about four months prior to their marriage. Nicole stated that she and Rick had gone to a party and later went to his apartment, where they had intercourse. Because she had been drinking that night, Nicole was unable to remember whether the experience was pleasurable.

The presenting problem was that Rick and Nicole were unable to engage in penile–vaginal intercourse. The onset of the problem was four years previously. At that time, Nicole began getting a series of vaginal infections that made intercourse extremely painful, and, consequently, they temporarily suspended sexual interactions. When they began being sexual again, attempts at intercourse were not successful, and for the last six months they had not attempted intercourse. Their means of sexual interaction was limited to Nicole fellating Rick. Their therapeutic goal was to be able to engage in and enjoy penile–vaginal intercourse.

A gynecological examination revealed that Nicole had no organic problems. Additionally, Rick did not have any erectile problems.

Session 1

Most of this session focused on obtaining a sexual problem history from Nicole and Rick. The rest of the time was spent giving them an overview of their problem. Although Nicole may have experienced dyspareunia when they were having intercourse, it was not possible to decide whether she still had this problem since they had not had intercourse recently. However, she was currently experiencing inhibited sexual desire and excitement.

Therapist: Let me begin by telling you that research indicates that 50% of all couples experience some form of sexual problem at some point in their lives. I think it might be helpful for you to know that you are not alone.

Nicole: I'm really glad to hear that. I thought that we were the only ones. I don't want to lose Rick because of these problems I am having.

T: That's a very common fear when there is a sexual problem within a relationship. You might want to check that out with Rick now by asking him what his intentions are in terms of remaining in this relationship.

N: Are we going to stay together?

Rick: Of course. You know I love you very much, and that is why I am here—to see if we can't work out this problem.

T: I believe your current problems stem from the pain you experienced during intercourse when you had the vaginal infections. Pain became associated with sex, and, consequently, you no longer wanted to engage in a behavior that was painful. Also, you shut down sexually because it was a very painful experience and you lost your desire to engage in sex. This frequently happens when a person engages in something that produces pain. Whenever they think about that behavior, they think about the pain, and then they soon stop thinking about the behavior.

N: Is that why I pull away whenever Rick touches me or tries to hug me?

T: Exactly. Rick's touch brings back memories of when he touched you in the past and that touching lead to intercourse. Now I think that the two of you have made a valiant effort to try to correct the problem. But even though you have tried, what you have been doing has not worked. But I think that with this therapy, you two will be able to make good progress.

Session 2

This session focused on what behaviors may be arousing to Nicole. Rick was able to remember particular behaviors that she once liked. However, Nicole had forgotten completely. To help Nicole get back in touch with her body, sensate focus exercises were introduced.

T: I don't want you to attempt intercourse until I say so. Instead, I want you to engage in a series of exercises. The first exercise is a hand caress. Some time when you have at least 30 minutes of relaxing time, I want the two of you to spend time just caressing, rubbing, and massaging each other's hands. For 15 minutes, one of you will caress the other's hands. For 15 minutes, one of you will caress the other's hands, then you switch roles. Toss a coin to decide who will be the first receiver. When you are caressing each other's hands, talk about how it feels.

N: That sounds really silly. How will it help our sexual problem?

T: What has happened in your relationship is that neither of you is now comfortable touching and it is important that you do touch. But not sexual touching. By just massaging hands, you can be comfortable knowing that it would not lead to intercourse.

Session 3

Rick and Nicole had practiced the exercise twice and reported that it had gone quite well. An upper-body caress exercise was explained.

T: This week I want you to do an upper-body caress. That means caress each other's head, neck, arms, shoulders, and chest. This should be done just like the hand caress—taking turns again.

R: Does that include breasts?

T: Breasts are okay, but don't focus just on them. Remember to caress the whole upper body.

N: Is this going to lead to intercourse?

T: Again, I don't want you to attempt intercourse until I say so.

Session 4

The upper body caress exercises were discussed.

N: I really enjoyed it. It feels good to have Rick touch me again. I forgot how nice it can be.

R: It's been a long time and it does feel good.

T: This week practice a lower-body caress. Again taking turns, caress each other's legs, feet, buttocks, and genitals. But don't limit the caress to just one body part. Try this twice this week.

Session 5

Nicole had been unable to do this exercise. As soon as Rick put his hand close to her genitals, she became extremely anxious.

N: I was so upset –all I could think of was that Rick was going to try to have intercourse and I wasn't ready. I couldn't focus on the touching. All I could think of was how I didn't want to have intercourse yet.

Session 6

Only Nicole came to this session.

T: There are some things that our bodies can't do at the same time. For example, we can't be anxious and relaxed simultaneously.

N: But I become anxious even when I don't want to.

T: Yes. But you can use a technique to bring on relaxation. Then, at the first signs of anxiety, you can begin to relax.

Nicole was taught standard relaxation procedures and encouraged to practice them.

T: Now, when you are relaxed, move your hand down toward your genitals and imagine that it is Rick's hand. If you begin to feel anxious, stop and begin relaxing again. Do this at least twice this week.

Session 7

Both Nicole and Rick attended this session. Nicole reported that she was able to relax better.

N: I can touch my genitals without feeling much anxiety, but when I pretend it's Rick's hand, I start to feel anxious.

T: When that happens, stop thinking of Rick's hand. Again relax and then move your hand toward your genitals while focusing on the sensations again. As good feelings continue, intersperse thoughts of Rick's hand with thoughts of the pleasure you are enjoying.

Session 8

N: I'm feeling very comfortable imagining Rick's hand touching my genitals. It sounds pretty good.

R: It sure does.

T: Then try the lower-body massage again. But remember that it is important not to push it. If it takes a little time, it's okay. But don't attempt intercourse yet.

Session 9

R: The exercise was a greater success than imagined.

N: It sure was. We both became so aroused, and we had intercourse and it was very pleasurable.

T: Did you have any discomfort?

N: No, no pain. Just good feelings. We had intercourse later that week, and it was even better.

T: That's great. It is important to realize, however, that if you develop any kind of vaginal itching or genital infection, you should not attempt to engage in sex. Wait until it clears up entirely before you resume having intercourse.

N: I'm feeling really good about our progress. Maybe we can put the sex therapy on hold for a while.

T: If you're both comfortable with that, it's fine with me. Remember that you can call me whenever you want or need to.

GENERAL ISSUES

A sexual problem should not be viewed as just a problem that one person has. Instead, such problems exist within a relationship, and, whenever possible, the couple should work on the problem together. However, it should be noted that sexual dysfunction therapy is possible when the patient participates in treatment without his or her sexual partner.

The relationship factor in sexual dysfunctions is particularly apparent when the sexual difficulties experienced by one partner result in difficulties in the other partner. For example, a woman married to a man who is unable to effect penetration because of erectile difficulties may develop vaginismus. A clinician should be sensitive to the possibility of both parties in a relationship experiencing sexual difficulties.

Although a couple's presenting problem may be sexual, a clinician should routinely evaluate the level of marital or relationship adjustment. The presenting sexual problem may really be a symptom of more serious marital problems that require therapeutic intervention before the sexual problems are addressed.

It is advisable for a clinician to contract for a limited number of therapy sessions at the beginning of treatment. This procedure adds structure to the treatment and helps to motivate the patient to work actively on his or her sexual problem. However, a clinician should amenable to renegotiate when necessary.

Sometimes patients are not diligent in doing their homework assignments between therapy sessions. When that happens, the clinician should reinforce the patient for whatever part of the assignment was done. Additionally, the clinician should share with the patient the fact that this sometimes does happen, as people experience both approach and avoidance conflicts when dealing with sexual problems.

Resistance to homework assignments is frequent when women are participating in a masturbatory training program. Some women are fearful of touching themselves sexually. In such cases, the clinician should acknowledge that the patient is uncomfortable but that dealing with her sexual problem requires that she experience some anxiety. Additionally, the clinician should modify the treatment program, primarily by slowing it down, so that the discomfort or anxiety experienced by the patient is limited.

Finally, some sex therapists believe that dysfunctional patients are most apt to show improvement if they participate in therapy with male and female co-therapists. However, research evidence does not demonstrate that a male-female therapist team has any advantages over a single therapist (Marks, 1981).

SUMMARY

An individual can experience sexual problems related to any of the stages of the sexual response cycle. Such problems can be caused by organic or psychogenic factors or a combination of these factors. Of the dysfunctions considered, only females experience vaginismus and premature ejaculation is restricted to males. However, inhibited sexual desire, inhibited sexual excitement, inhibited orgasm, and dyspareunia can be experienced by both males and females. Behaviorally oriented therapy has been found to be very effective in the treatment of sexual dysfunctions. This approach has the advantages of being flexible to meet the specific needs of the patient and can be utilized within a time-limited framework. Additionally, behavioral interventions allow the patient to assume a very active role in effecting the desired changes.

REFERENCES

Abel, G. G., Becker, J. V., Cunningham-Rathner, J., Mittleman, M., & Primack, M. Differential diagnosis of impotence in diabetics: The validity of sexual symptomatology. *Journal of Neurology and Urodynamics*, in press.

Abel, G. G., Murphy, W., Becker, J., & Bitar, A. Women's vaginal responses during REM sleep. *Journal of Sex and Marital Therapy*, 1979, *5*, 5–11.

American Psychiatric Association. *Diagnostic and statistical manual of mental disorders* (3rd Ed.). Washington, D.C.: Author, 1980.

Annon, J. S. *Behavioral treatment of sexual problems: Brief therapy.* Hagerstown, M.: Harper & Row, 1976.

Barbach, L. G. Group treatment or preorgasmic women. *Journal of Sex and Marital Therapy*, 1974, *1*, 139–145.

Becker, J. V., Skinner, L. J., Abel, G. G., & Cichon, J. Sexual symptomatology following sexual assault: Etiology and characteristics. Paper presented at the eighth annual meeting of the International Academy of Sex Research, Copenhagen, Denmark, August 1982.

Blumer, D., & Walker, A. The neural basis of sexual behavior. In D. F. Benson & D. Blumer (Eds.), *Psychiatric aspects of neurological disease.* New York: Grune & Stratton, 1975.

Brady, J. P. Brevital-relaxation treatment of frigidity. *Behavior Research and Therapy*, 1966, *4*, 71–78.

D. Moor, W. Vaginismus: Etiology and treatment. *American Journal of Psychotherapy*, 1972, *26*, 207–215.

El Senoussi, A., Coleman, D. R., & Tauber, A. S. Factors in male impotence. *Journal of Psychology*, 1959, *48*, 3–46.

Ersner-Hershfield, R. *The effects of couples vs. woman group treatment for female orgasmic dysfunction.* Paper presented at the annual meeting of the Association of Sex Therapists and Counselors, Memphis, April 1978.

Friedman, H. The treatment of impotence by brietal relaxation therapy. *Behaviour Research and Therapy*, 1968, *6*, 257–266.

Goebelsmann, U., Arce, J. J., Thorneycroft, I. H., & Mischell, D. R. Serum testosterone concentration in women throughout the menstrual cycle and following HCG administration. *American Journal of Obstetrics and Gynecology*, 1974, *119*, 445–452.

Golden, J. S., Pierce, S., Heinrich, A. G., & Lobitz, W. C. Group vs. couple treatment of sexual dysfunctions. *Archives of Sexual Behavior*, 1978, *7*, 593–602.

Haslam, M. T. The treatment of psychogenic dyspareunia by reciprocal inhibition. *British Journal of Psychiatry*, 1965, *111*, 280–282.

Hite, S. *The Hite report.* New York: MacMillan, 1976.

Ince, L. P. Behavior modification of sexual disorders. *American Journal of Psychotherapy*, 1973, *17*, 446–451.

Johnson, J. *Disorders of sexual potency in the male.* New York: Pergamon Press, 1968.

Kaplan, H. S. *The new sex therapy.* New York: Brunner/Mazel, 1974.

Kaplan, H. S. *Disorders of sexual desire and other new concepts and techniques in sex therapy.* New York: Brunner/Mazel, 1979.

Kaplan, A. H., & Abrahms, M. Ejaculatory impotence. *Journal of Urology*, 1958, *79*, 964–968.

Kaplan, H. S., Kohl, R. N., Pomperoy, W. B., Offit, A. K., & Hogan, B. Group treatment of premature ejaculation. *Archives of Sexual Behavior*, 1974, *3*, 443–452.

Karacan, I. Clinical value of nocturnal erections in the prognosis and diagnosis of impotence. *Medical Aspects of Human Sexuality*, 1970, *4*, 27–34.

Karacan, I., Williams, R. L., Thornby, J. I., & Salis, P. J. Sleep-related penile tumescence as a function of age. *American Journal of Psychiatry*, 1975, *132*, 932–937.

Karney, A., Bancroft, J., & Matthews, A. Combination of hormonal and psychological treatment for sexual unresponsiveness: A comparative study. *British Journal of Psychiatry*, 1978, *132*, 339–346.

Kegel, A. H. Sexual functions of the pubococcygeus muscle. *Western Journal of Surgery, Obstetrics, and Gynecology*, 1952, *60*, 521–524.

Kinsey, A. P., Pomeroy, W. B., Martin, C. E., & Gebhardt, P. H. *Sexual behavior in the human male.* Philadelphia: Saunders, 1948.

Kraft, T., & Al-Issa, I. Behavior therapy and the treatment of frigidity. *American Journal of Psychotherapy*, 1967, *21*, 116–120.

Lazarus, A. A. The treatment of chronic frigidity by systematic desensitization. *Journal of Nervous and Mental Disorders*, 1963, *136*, 272–278.

Leiblum, S. R., & Ersner-Hershfield, R. Sexual enhancement groups for dysfunctional women: An evaluation. *Journal of Sex and Marital Therapy*, 1977, *3*, 139–152.

Leiblum, S. R., Rosen, R. C., & Pierce, D. Group treatment format: Mixed sexual dysfunctions. *Archives of Sexual Behavior*, 1976, *5*, 269–274.

Marks, I. M. Review of behavioral psychotherapy II: Sexual disorders. *American Journal of Psychiatry*, 1981, *138*, 750–756.

Masters, W., & Johnson, V. *Human sexual inadequacy.* Boston: Little, Brown, 1970.

McGovern, K. B., Stuart, R. C., & LoPiccolo, J. Secondary orgasmic dysfunction: I. Analysis and strategies for treatment. *Archives of Sexual Behavior*, 1975, *4*, 265.

Money, J., & Erhardt, A. *Man and woman, boy and girl.* Baltimore: Johns Hopkins University Press, 1972.

Munjack, D. J., & Oziel, L. J. *Sexual medicine and counseling in office practice: A comprehensive treatment guide.* Boston: Little, Brown, 1980.

Nellans, R. E., Naftel, W., & Stein, J. Experience with the Small-Carrion penile prosthesis in the treatment of organic impotence. *Journal of Urology*, 1976, *115*, 280–283.

Pearman, R. O. Insertion of a Silastic penile prosthesis for the treatment of organic sexual impotence. *Journal of Urology*, 1972, *107*, 802–806.

Raboch, J., Millan, J., & Starka, L. Plasma testosterone in male patients with sexual dysfunction. *Archives of Sexual Behavior*, 1975, *4*, 541–545.

Raboch, J., & Starka, L. Reported coital activity of men and levels of plasma testosterone. *Archives of Sexual Behavior*, 1973, *2*, 309–315.

Reynolds, B. S., Price, S. C., & Hanrich, A. G. *The effectiveness of group treatment formats for the sexual dysfunctions.* Paper presented at the annual meeting of the American Psychological Association, Los Angeles, August 1981.

Roen, P. R. Impotence: A concise review. *New York State Journal of Medicine*, 1965, *56*, 2576–2582.

Rose, R. M. The psychological effects of androgens and estrogens: A review. In R. I. Shader (Eds.), *Psychiatric complications of medical drugs.* New York: Raven, 1972.

Schiavi, R. C., & White, D. Androgens and male sexual function: A review of human studies. *Journal of Sex and Marital Therapy*, 1976, *2*, 214–228.

Schiavi, R. C., Derogatis, L. R., Kuriansky, J., O'Connor, D., & Sharpe, L. The assessment of sexual function and marital interaction. *Journal of Sex and Marital Therapy*, 1979, *5*, 169–224.

Scott, F. B., Bradley, W. E., & Timm, G. W. Management of erectile impotence: Use of implantable inflatable prosthesis. *Urology,* 1973, *2,* 80–82.

Semans, J. H. Premature ejaculation: A new approach: *Southern Medical Journal,* 1956, *49,* 353–362.

Small, M. P. Penile prosthesis for the management of impotence. *Medical Aspects of Human Sexuality,* 1976, *10,* 92–92.

Synder, A., Lo Piccolo, L., & Lo Piccolo, J. Secondary orgasmic dysfunction: II. Case study. *Archives of Sexual Behavior,* 1975, *4,* 277.

Wolpe, J. *Psychotherapy by reciprocal inhibition.* Stanford, Calif.: Stanford University Press, 1958.

Wolpin, M. Guided imagining to reduce avoidance behavior. *Psychotherapy: Theory, Research and Practice,* 1969, *6,* 122–124.

Wright, J., Perreault, & Mathisen, M. The treatment of sexual dysfunction: A review. *Archives of General Psychiatry,* 1977, *34,* 881–890.

9

Marital Dysfunction

Gary R. Birchler

THE ASSESSMENT AND TREATMENT of marital dysfunction is most often performed in an outpatient setting such as a private practice or agency office. Referrals for marital therapy come from a number of sources and tend to be of a different composition for each treatment setting. Since clients' expectations, motivations, pyschological-mindedness, and socioeconomic status can vary tremendously, the clinician's treatment philosophy, assessment, and intervention techniques must take these variables into account. This chapter describes a behavioral-systems model that features the contemporary evaluation and treatment components of behavioral marital therapy (BMT). By design, the integrated systems approach is applicable to varying treatment populations.

BEHAVIORAL-SYSTEMS FORMULATION OF MARITAL DYSFUNCTION

There are two concepts derived from behavior exchange, social learning, and family systems theory that facilitate understanding of the nature of functional and dysfunctional marital relationships. The first concept relates to behavioral outcomes and the second to process issues, or how behaviors interact. First, when two people get married, both have the implicit expectation that they will get as much or more out of the relationship than they puts into it. That is, one's perceived or actual benefits of remaining in the marriage must be equal to or greater than the associated costs. These benefits and costs result from a combination of positive and negative outcomes, which are a function of implicit if not explicit behavioral exchanges. Positive outcomes relate to the quality and quantity of rewarding interactional exchanges; negative outcomes derive from displeasing or punishing interactions. Marital dysfunction exists when partners exchange relatively low rates or quality of pleasing behavior, or relatively high rates or an intense quality of displeasing behavior, or a combination of both. Ultimately, each partner's choice to remain married depends on the fit between one's expectations and experiences *in* the relationship versus one's perceived comparison levels of alternatives *outside* the relationship.

A second basic concept is that each partner's behavior in the relationship is largely determined by the eliciting stimuli and consequences provided for that behavior by one's spouse. Note that this does not necessarily imply a linear model of behavioral causation. Rather, in a circular and reciprocal fashion, each spouse's actions are being influenced by and are influencing the other spouse's actions. These notions of behavioral reciprocity and circular causality are complex in the sense that, in assessing the functional relationships withi a given marriage, the therapist must relalize that he or she is temporarily entering a complex action–reaction–action chain of events at an arbitrary point. This point usually is neither the beginning nor the end of an interactional process; it is a *punctuation point* determined by the timing of the therapist's observation. The art and science of contemporary BMT concern the therapist's abilities to identify, to interpret to the couple, and to help them modify the existing maladaptive and relationship-defeating interactional sequences. In summary, the extant quality of a marriage if determined largely by the functional nature of the positive and negative, circular, and reciprocal interactions that comprise it. A dysfunctional marriage is one in which, for one or both partners, the quantity and/or quality of negative interactions (costs) has significantly exceeded the positive interactions (benefits).

The obvious question in discussing a formulation of marital distress is that given most couples start out in a state of marital bliss, what goes wrong? One major problem relates to our culture's *myth of romance*. The expectations and interactional behaviors characteristic of courtship have too little to do with the tasks, goals, and realities of maintaining a long-term intimate relationship. Within a few days to a year or so "the honeymoon is over," and endurable intimacy becomes an elusive goal. Typically, it is achieved only through a couple's constant collaborative efforts to balance their idealized expectations with attainable realities.

Beyond the myth of romance, Jacobson and Margolin (1979) have summarized some of the most common antecedents of marital dysfunction. Some of these antecedents amount to deficiencies in relationship skills; others are developmental phenomena to which some marriages are particularly vulnerable.

Behavior change deficits.   Partners to an intimate relationship, not being identical people and having different needs and desires, inevitably attempt to change one another's behavior. Marital conflict can be defined as one partner's desire to change the behavior of the other in the face of noncompliance. A certain amount of marital conflict is inevitable, therefore, and it is not the conflict that is the problem but rather the partner's deficient conflict management—behavior change skills. Unfortunately, instead of relying on principles of shaping and positive reinforcement, distressed couples employ various punishment, coercive, and negative reinforcement procedures in attempting to force change in the relationship. A wife wants more attention and thus withholds sex until her husband complies. A husband terminates aversive yelling and screaming only after the wife complies with his demands. A wife increasingly nags her husband to get the screen door fixed, and his eventual compliance both terminates the nagging and reinforces nagging as a behavior change tool. All these aversive behavior change procedures, although perhaps somewhat effective in the short run, are ultimately deteriorative to the relationship.

Reinforcement erosion.   This phenomenon is the opposite of the cliche "variety is the spice of life." Long-term intimate relationships are naturally vulnerable to satiation and habituation effects. Behaviors and activities that once were novel and stimulating eventually lose their reinforcement value. Distressed couples typically present for treatment, indicating few or no rewarding activities in common. They often describe a restricted if not outright avoidant style of interacting. In contrast, happy couples effectively work at developing new individually and mutually rewarding activities that serve as enhancing stimuli for the relationship.

Family rules: lacking or rigid.   Deficiencies in the couples' ability to develop or alter the normative structure of their relationship may be important antecedents to marital dysfunction. Rigid rules of interaction or role, such as "no expression of anger" or "husband is the breadwinner; the wife, the domestic" may be destructive by their very nature or because they cannot be effectively changed as is necessary in the face of life event contingencies.

Skill deficits.   Clearly, the maintenance and endurance of a quality marital relationship are in part a function of the couple's abilities to accomplish certain relationship goals, such as communicating and problem solving, obtaining and keeping a job, maintaining a home, raising children, handling finances, and maintaining a satisfying sex life. Some couples naturally acquire these skills before or within the relationship; many do not.

External stressors.   Certainly we know that some relationships are vulnerable to changes in the external environment that are out of the control of the partners. Common stressors are major physical and mental disabilities, chronic unemployment, a sexually attractive third party, and interference from in-laws. Clearly, these and similar external factors can change the cost-benefit ratio of a relationship such that its viability is threatened.

Affiliative versus independent preferences.   As Jacobson and Margolin (1979) indicate, this particular antecedent is not only common, it also provides the potential for unrelenting marital conflict. At the time of presentation for treatment, these partners appear to have diverse if not opposite preferences and tolerances for intimacy. One partner acts greatly deprived and resentful about alleged unmet needs for intimacy; the other appears uninterested in, if not aversive to, high rates of spousal contact. Unfortunately, the prognosis for improvement in such cases is guarded.

In summary, marital dysfunction is viewed as a disorder originating primarily within the interaction of the relationship. Entry into and exit from marriage is dependent on each partners' experience of the cost—benefit ratio of negative—positive interaction outcomes. Interpersonal skills relating to communication, problem solving, conflict resolution, relationship enhancement, and the development of a balance between individuals' desires for dependence and independence account for critical variance in the formulation of marital distress.

BEHAVIORAL-SYSTEMS MARITAL THERAPY: THE MODEL

The assessment and intervention components of a model developed over the past several years by the author are represented in Figure 9-1. The approach follows a behavioral framework similar to most contemporary programs in BMT (Jacobson & Margolin, 1979; Liberman, Wheeler, deVisser, Kuehnel, & Kuehnel, 1980; Stuart, 1980; Weiss, 1980) The evaluation phase features multimodal assessment procedures, three or four conjoint clinical interviews, a comprehensive marriage assessment battery, and observed samples of couple conflict resolution. The culmination of the evaluation phase is a written and verbal presentation of the therapists' formulation of the couple's distress followed by a discussion of methods and goals for treatment should they choose to begin therapy.

The treatment phase features three rather standard components of BMT. These are interventions that follow directly from the antecedents of marital dysfunction described above. Most couples benefit from development of individual and mutually rewarding activities, development of support and understanding skills through basic communication training, and the acquisition of skills associated with problem solving, management conflict, resolution, and behavior change.

The third intervention phase pertains to termination and follow-up: maintenance of treatment gains, use of follow-up or booster sessions, and post-treatment assessment. One innovative aspect of this model is the anticipation of blocks to progress during the course of the assessment and treatment. Certain forms of "resistance" are virtually expected, and intervention options stand ready for implementation. The following sections present issues related to the general practice of outpatient BMT and detailed procedures of this author's behavioral-systems approach.

Clinical Assessment

The evaluation phase is a critical initiation into the therapeutic process. The three major objectives are to gather comprehensive diagnostic information, to establish trust and rapport with the clients, and to orient them in the language and theoretical perspectives of the therapeutic approach. The accomplishment of these objectives sets the stage for the treatment phase.

The reader should realize that most couples are either naive to the

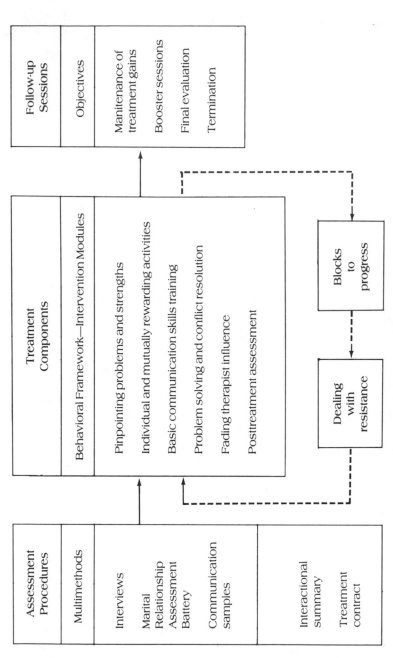

Figure 9-1 Behavioral-systems marital therapy: assessment and intervention components. (From Birchler, G. R. Behavioral-systems marital therapy. In J. P. Vincent (Ed.), *Advances in Family Intervention, Assessment and Theory* (Vol. 3). Greenwich, Conn.: JAI Press, in press; and from Spinks, S. H., & Birchler, G. R. Behavioral-systems marital therapy: Dealing with resistance. *Family Process*, 1982, *21*, 169–185. With permission.)

therapy process or, for better or worse, they have certain expectations about it. In any case, most couples respond best when they have a rather explicit understanding of what will occur in the sessions and how the objectives will be accomplished. Toward this end, at the first meeting, the clients are told of three major objectives of the first evaluation session (noted as E-1). First, it must be determined how the clients individually and collectively decided to initiate professional contact. Who referred them, whose idea was it to come, and what was the precipitating event? Second, the therapist would like to hear, from each partner's point of view, a presentation of their concerns, their perceptions of problem areas, and their goals for treatment. At this early point, the therapist establishes the principle that in a long-term, intimate relationship it is each partner's *right* and each partner's *responsibility* to assert his or her concerns and desires. If this important premise breaks a family rule, such as the "wife does not speak unless spoken to," either the rule must be modified or the couple must be referred to a therapist not so committed to an egalitation approach such as BMT. The third objective of E-1 is to mutually decide at the end of the 1–1½-hour session whether to continue the evaluation phase. The therapist begins by summarizing what he or she learned so far and outlinging the remaining objectives and procedures of the evaluation phase. The latter presentation typically is stated:

What the two of you need to decide at this point is whether you would like to continue and complete the evaluation phase. It would consist of two or possibly three more sessions where my job would be to learn as much about your relationship strengths and weaknesses as possible. Your part would be to provide the information. If you choose to continue, I'll ask you each to complete a series of inventories designed to help us all learn about your relationship. This will save several hours of interview time. Also, next week I would ask you to provide me with a live sample of how you communicate with one another. Effective communication is critical to a satisfying relationship and I want to see *how* you can go about it. In our last evaluation meeting I will present you with written and verbal feedback concerning my assessment of your relationship. Including the prospects and recommendations for change. Remember, if you decide to commit yourselves to completion of the evaluation phase, you are not being asked to *change* anything. We may or may not begin therapy to make some changes; that will be decided later. So, you can decide now, discuss it alone for a few minutes or even over the next few days, and let me know. In any case, I think it was a wise decision to seek some assistance and I would be happy to work with you further.

This strategy features a preview of things to come and the promise of an evaluative service that does not imply blame, the need for immediate change, or a long-term commitment to either therapy or the relationship. Under such conditions, this type of contract has resulted in over 95% of the couples deciding to at least complete the evaluation phase. Most couples immediately decide to continue. If so, each partner is given a battery of inventories to complete independently before the next session.

One of the strengths of BMT is its multimethod assessment strategy. Information from several sources is used to develop and confirm diagnostic hypotheses about the dysfunctional marriage at hand. Four different methods can be employed; the author routinely uses the first three.

Initial Interviews

As suggested above, three to four evaluation sessions are typical. During this period the therapist has the following tasks: (1) formulate hypotheses about family rules, roles, myths, and individual and relationship patterns of self-defeating behavior; (2) identify the relationship's major communication skill deficits; (3) identify the significant conflict areas and the couple's past attempts at resolution; (4) form a solid therapeutic relationship with the clients; and (5) set priorities for intervention.

These tasks are accomplished by the therapist(s) employing the following interviewing skills:

• Model good listening and validation behavior. That is, be empathic to each person, paraphrase, summarize, and validate or acknowledge each person's justifiable point of view.

• Involve both partners in their rights and responsibilities to participate in the evaluation process, that is, to assert their concerns and disclose their feelings.

• Establish control of the sessions in an empathic but firm manner. Follow an investigative agenda while allowing appropriate room for clients' idiosyncracies and styles of presentation. Exude confidence and competency by being assertive and setting limits when necessary.

• Allow for measured ventilation of feelings. There is an optimal balance between allowing partners to exchange so much hostility and anger such that destructive interaction begins to escalate, in contrast to allowing no expression or ventilation of anger with the result that clients do not feel heard and understood. If hostility and anger are inevitably in the offing, it is suggested that clients be directed to talk to the therapist and not directly to their partner. This allows for more therapist control in that she or he can periodically allow equal time for each partner to talk.

• Describe the system in interactional terms and foster a collaborative set. The idea is to avoid attribution of blame to individual partners but rather, to implicate the conjoint relationship as dysfunctional. The change in perspective is not an easy one for some couples. It generally takes the therapist several sessions to accomplish this task. However, this is a critical transition in clients' cognitions that can tremendously enhance their prospects for improvement.

Self-Assessment Inventories

There are several reasons for using paper-and-pencil assessment instruments. They provide an economical way to gather diagnostic information on the clients' own time. They provide data from the clients' point of view that can be different from conjoint interview data. Printed inventories also aid in the goal of indoctrinating the clients in the language and orientation of the treatment approach. Last but not least, they provide a source of pretreatment data that can be compared to posttherapy measures of change.

A number of behaviorally oriented instruments provide both clinical and normative information. One commercially available instrument is the Marital Precounseling Inventory by Stuart and Stuart (1973), currently offered by Research Press, Inc., Champaign, Illinois. In addition, the author has participated in the development of several assessment instruments and has combined them with standard instruments such as the Locke-Wallace Marital Adjustment Scale to comprise a package called the Marital Relationship Assessment Battery (MRAB). The MRAB consists of the following seven self-report inventories that are to be completed independently by each spouse. These descriptions indicate the kind of information deemed important in the assessment phase of BMT.

Locke-Wallace Marital Adjustment Scale. This scale devised by (Locke and Wallace (1959), is a commonly used self-report measure of global marital satisfaction. General areas of agreement and disagreement on major topics within the relationship are indicated. Empirically derived scale scores discriminate maritally distressed from nondistressed couples.

Marital Status Inventory. In this scale, prepared by Weiss and Cerreto (1975), 14 true–false questions assess the degree to which each spouse has sought dissolution of the relationship.

Areas of Change Questionnaire. In this questionnaire, devided by Weiss and others (Weiss & Birchler, 1975; Weiss, Hops & Patterson, 1973), 34 areas of typical marital conflict are assessed by analyzing couples' requests for behavior change in self and spouse.

Self-Description Inventory.   Designed by Wahler (1968), this is a self-report questionnaire including three scales designed to assess individuals' sense of self-esteem, psychological distress, and physical symptoms. The SDI helps indicate individuals' tendencies toward depression, anxiety, denial, and somatic preoccupation.

Responses to conflict.   Birchler (1977) prepared this scale as an index of the proportion of performance and opportunity that partners perceive self and spouse to engage in maladaptive responses to marital conflict.

Inventory of Rewarding Activities.   Birchler (1979) and Weiss, Hops, and Patterson (1973) devised this questionnaire to assess the types and proportions of recreational activities engaged in alone, with spouse only, with spouse and other adults, with family, and with others (excluding spouse) over the previous four weeks. A section on time distribution also indicates what percentage of the previous week was spent working, sleeping, and engaging in rewarding or nonrewarding activities.

Summary of current important issues.   To complete the MRAB, each spouse lists in order of importance his or her perception of the four most significant relationship and personal strengths and weaknesses.

Other Scales.   Many other instruments are also available that provide quantitative scores and clinically useful information, wuch as the *Dyadic Adjustment Scale* (Stuart, 1980) and the *Marital Happiness Scale* (Azrin, Naster, & Jones, 1973).

Communication Samples

A very important part of a behaviorally oriented marital therapy is to obtain a sample of interaction behavior. We have learned from existing research [see review chapters in Birchler (1979) and Jacobson and Margolin (1979)] that the communication and problem-solving skills demonstrated by distressed relative to nondistressed couples are significantly different. Observation of marital conflict interaction by means of live or videotaped methods, therefore, is extremely useful diagnostically and highly recommended as a pre–posttherapy outcome measure. On the basis of information obtained in the initial interview and from a preliminary screening of the MRAB, it is fairly easy to determine several areas of marital conflict that the couple can discuss. Research has shown that couples are most likely to become involved and demonstrate diagnostically useful patterns of communication when moderate-to-high levels of conflict exist. Without necessarily choosing the most explosive or emotion-laden topic, therefore, one or two issues of sufficient relevance and intensity should be assigned so that the interaction is likely to be active and representative. The couple is asked to spend about 10 minutes attempting to resolve the identified problems. They are told that they may not solve the problem in 10 minutes, but that the therapist is interested in observing how they go about it.

At this point a number of collection and interpretive procedures are possible depending on the setting and objectives of the task. Ideally, the therapist could leave the room and videotape the negotiation that could be evaluated for both diagnostic and baseline assessment purposes. With research in mind, a variety of coding systems have been developed to interpret and quantify videotaped interactions. The most prominent scoring system is the Marital Interaction Coding System (MICS). It was developed at the University of Oregon in the 1970s and requires trained coders. The MICS features 30 verbal and nonverbal codes that are summarized into the following behavioral categories: Problem Solution, Problem Description, Positive Verbal, Positive Nonverbal, Negative Verbal, and Negative Nonverbal. The interested reader is referred to Wieder and Weiss (1979) for more details about the MICS.

Although videotape recording certainly enhances the clinical and research utility of this procedure, live observation of conflict resolution also offers a complementary perspective to the verbal and written self-reports obtained during the evaluation period. Short of an elaborate analysis such as the MICS, it is possible to develop one's own coding system which serves a clinical if not research-oriented function. The therapist can informally use a checklist of behaviors to assess the interaction. A simple analysis might consist of making tally marks for each partner next to certain verbal, nonverbal, facilitative, and nonfacilitative communication behaviors (see Tables 9-1 and 9-2). One's checklist might also include interaction behaviors, such as dominance of speech, whether the problem was solved, and indicators of partners' general positive and negative affect. Communication samples can be obtained intermittently throughout the course of therapy for assessment and feedback purposes.

Spouse Observation

A fourth type of data is spouse observation of behavioral exchanges in the natural environment. These data sometimes are difficult to obtain in practice. The spouse observation procedure was developed at the University of Oregon and has since become a rather standard assessment-treatment procedure in BMT. It consists of asking partners to observe and record at home the actual spousal actions and re-

Table 9-1 Basic Communication Skills: Complementary Facilitative and Nonfacilitative Behvaiors

Facilitative Skills	Nonfacilitative Behaviors
Message Sender	
Exhibit positive nonverbal behaviors: eye contact, smiles, etc.	Minimize negative nonverbal behaviors.
Use "I" statements: be responsible for yourself.	Avoid "you" statements that imply blaming.
Selective self-disclosure of feelings: consider impact on listener.	Avoid extremes of "silent treatment" or "let it all hang out".
Use perception checking and clarifying questions.	Do not make assumptions that intent equals impact.
Listener	
Exhibit positive nonverbal behaviors: eye contact, supportive gestures.	Minimize negative nonverbal behaviors: inattention, grimaces, etc.
Paraphrase, reflect, and perception check to understand sender.	Do not respond before listening or react defensively prematurely.
Validate and empathize with sender's feelings, "feelings are fact".	Do not discount, disqualify, or deny sender's feelings.

From Birchler, G. R. Behavioral-systems marital therapy. In J. P. Vincent (Ed.), *Advances in Family Intervention, Assessment and Theory* (Vol. 3). Greenwich, Conn.: JAI Press, in press. With permission.

actions that are pleasing or displeasing to one another. These data can be noted in diary form, on prepared checklists or even by using IBM scoring sheets amenable to computer analysis. In baseline form, the therapist obtains a profile of pretreatment positive and negative behavioral exchanges that may be used to indicate specific areas for improvement. With repeated measurements it is possible to monitor the nature of behavioral exchanges over the course of therapy. Since research has indicated that up to 70% of the variance in couples' marital satisfaction scores can be attributed to the day-to-day behavioral exchanges, this innovative procedure may be used instrumentally to remediate marital dysfunction. However, spouse observation can be problematic because client compliance with detailed daily record-keeping assignments is not always adequate.

Feedback and Interactional Summary

Data derived from the above three or four assessment methods provide a wealth of information to consider in diagnosing a couple's marital dysfunction. Two objectives in the final evaluation session are to provide assessment information back to couple in a way that makes sense to them and to decide on initiation of treatment or termination of the case. To economize on time and provide clients with something concrete, the author has developed a partially individualized written

Table 9-2   Problem-Solving Skills: Complementary
Facilitative and Nonfacilitative Behaviors

Facilitative Skills	Nonfacilitative Behaviors
Message Sender	
Select and maintain focus on a single issue at a time.	Avoid sidetracking, kitchen-sinking, and gunnysacking.
Describe complaints and request changes in terms of behavior.	Do not assassinate other's character or assail other's personality.
Phrase behavior change requests positively.	Do not make indictiments negatively.
Propose present- and future-oriented solutions.	Minimize recounting and rehashing past problems and solutions.
Ask for listener's ideas for change.	Do not insist on always having it your way.
Listener	
Reinforce sender's openness and willingness to engage you.	Do not punish or ignore sender's attempts to problem-solve.
Seek to understand your contribution to the problem.	Minimize denial or defending your contribution to the problem.
Elicit disclosure of feelings and details of request for change.	Try not to cut off expression of feelings, ideas for change.
Offer counterproposals for change or resolution	Avoid an inflexible response or offer "yes–but" resistance.

From Birchler, G. R. Behavioral-systems marital therapy. In J. P. Vincent (Ed.), *Advances in Family Intervention, Assessment and Theory* (Vol. 3). Greenwich, Conn.: JAI Press, in press. With permission.

report to summarize findings from the MRAB. Major findings from the MRAB first are verbally summarized to the partners, who are instructed in further interpretation of the detailed report. Then, data from all sources of assessment are integrated into what is called the *interactional summary*. In most cases marital distress is described as a function of (1) interactional rather than individual problems; (2) behavioral skill deficits, mutual misunderstanding, and miscommunication rather than traitlike or intrapsychic personality attributes; and (3) misplaced and neglected priorities rather than malice or apathy. The interactional summary is individualized in the sense that examples of these phenomena are taken from the couple's own multimethod evaluation data. Moreover, the language, perceptual, and intellectual levels at which the feedback is given are necessarily matched to the clients' levels of function and understanding.

Problems, Goals, and Treatment Contract

The treatment contract is the result of first identifying sets of individual and relationship problems and then translating them into specific goals for improving the relationship. Obviously, there may be individual problems that either transcend the relationship or inherently require treatment before relationship therapy can be successful. Examples include acute alcoholism, drug abuse, psychosis, severe character disorder, and major medical problems. In most cases, problem resolution or stability in these areas is a prerequisite condition for effective marital therapy.

Concerning marital dysfunction per se, it may be useful to consider three major problem areas. First, couples may have critical structural or situational problems. That is, there may be too little or too much direct interpersonal proximity for intimacy to be viable. Frequently, partners have too little access to one another. Both people may work or otherwise be so preoccupied as to "pass each other in the night" going from one activity to the other. Structurally, there simply is insufficient time and physical access to relate to one another and do all the things necessary for maintenance of a satisfactory relationship. Other couples spend too much time together, particularly if retired, disabled, or suffering from chronic unemployment. They try to meet all their personal needs through the relationship. Whether continually underfoot or dependently smothering one another, these couples also benefit from structural or situational remediation. Second, there are interactional *process* difficulties that relate to *how*, and in a sense of a behavioral functional analysis, *why* partners interact in certain ways. Communication, support and understanding, and problem-solving and conflict-resolution skills are implicated here. Remediation focuses on couples' general lack of learning and their relationship-defeating patterns of interaction. *Third,* beyond the structural and process issues, there are usually certain *content* problem areas that benefit from therapeutic attention. Typically these include sex and affection, parenting, household management, finances, dealing with in-laws, and so on.

In sum, marital dysfunction and thus the goals of treatment can be related to *whether and how much* partners interact (structure), *how* and functionally *why* they interact as they do (process), and *what* they interact about (content). The treatment contract is designed to specify objectives and goals in these three areas and to estimate treatment procedures and time frames to accomplish them.

Treatment Modules and Modalities

The treatment techniques associated with behavioral-systems marital therapy are designed to rapidly help clients identify and modify marital dysfunction related to structural, process, and content variables. Obviously, a certain percentage of couples initiate treatment not to save the marriage, but to end it. Occasionally, these couples survive as a marital therapy unit past the evaluation process. However, the motivation and commitment necessary for following through with the very active therapy process soon separates the ambivalent and relationship-ending couples from those interested in strengthening the marriage.

Treatment is conceptualized in three standardized stages, each with three major objectives. As mentioned earlier, blocks to progress in these three stages are anticipated and dealt with by a variety of therapist interventions. Depending on the nature and progress of the couple, therefore, various modules and modalities of intervention are differentially applied. For example, some couples have relatively effective process skills in their repertoire, but structurally there is too little access to one another to nurture intimacy and actually solve problems. Other distressed couples have relatively few structural problems, but they suffer from skill deficits related to process and/or content. The behavioral-systems approach, emphasizing comprehensive assessment and active, systematic intervention, is designed to strengthen and remediate the particular problem areas specific to each relationship.

Initial Stages of Treatment

The purpose of this stage of therapy is to lay a solid foundation for couple interaction before addressing major behavior change or content-area problems. In many cases this is the most critical phase of treatment. One major objective is to bring about a change in partners' mind set from *win–lose* to *win–win*. That is, most partners view their relationship dysfunction or their personal discontent as a result of the attitudes and behaviors of their spouse. Blame is attributed to the spouse, but very infrequently to oneself. The inherent tendency of couples to cross-complain and blame one another for their marital problems establishes a win–lose mind set that is often refractory to relationship change. An early therapist intervention priority, therefore, is to bring about a *collaborative set* in the attitudes and behaviors of the couple (Jacobson & Margolin, 1979). The continually reinforced message is that (1) marital problems are a dysfunction of relationship interaction; (2) for better or for worse, both partners contribute to the relationship's current status; and (3) both partners will have to focus on changing themselves more so than changing one another in order to gain lasting improvements. Establishment of an enduring collaborative set is sometimes achieved over a few treatment sessions. Often it requires a more persistent effort. Sometimes, it is unattainable. Therapists can indoctrinate the couple in the interactional view of relationship dysfunction by emphasizing the perspective of reciprocal and circular causality, by reframing presenting problems and spouses' ongoing complaints into interactional terms, and by the design of homework assignments. When this major transitional goal of establishing a collaborative set is accomplished, it usually is readily apparent. Whether this occurs early or later in the therapeutic process, subsequent progress is often more rapid and satisfying.

Individual and Mutually Rewarding Activities

A second early objective is to modify any existing problems in the area of individual and mutually rewarding activities. Here, structural issues are addressed along with the assignment of a series of consciousness-raising priority-setting exercises. If indicated, one or both partners may be helped to develop some independent social, recreational, or vocational activities that provide relief from, and/or external stimulation into, the relationship. Similarly, therapists almost always help partners to reset structural priorities and to increase access to one another so that personal intimacy has a chance to develop. The therapist's role is to provide assistance in the form of encouragement, rationale, and graded activity assignments.

More specifically, two types of intervention are commonly employed to sensitize and encourage a strong caring commitment: caring activities and mutually rewarding activities. During the first treatment session (T-1), the caring activities assignment is given. This technique was originated by Richard Stuart (1980). In this somewhat modified technique, partners are given a checklist of 20 potential spouse-emitted caring behaviors that can be used as a worksheet for generating individualized caring behaviors, which if performed by the spouse, would be experienced as especially caring. Examples include: "initiates going for a walk with me," "says I love you," "brings me breakfast in bed," and "pays me a compliment." The completed lists are edited by the performing partner and therapist to ensure that the following criteria are met. Selected behaviors are (1) definitely nonproblem areas; (2) defined in small, repeatable units; (3) not too expensive or time-consuming; (4) of high caring or romantic value; and (5) things the performing spouse would at least be comfortable if not enjoy doing for the recipient. Performing partners are then given the final lists and asked to agree to do at least five of the caring activities over the next week.

Usually, this exercise is debriefed and updated weekly for a period of two to four weeks. The objectives are to orient the partners to the necessity and impact of positive caring exchanges (in a distressed relationship where most attention is usually devoted to negative exchanges) and to build a caring foundation from which one can later address significant relationship problems. In addition, this exercise is excellent in assisting the therapist to discover early in therapy whatever resistance or blocks to progress might likely be encountered. Not uncommonly, partners have considerable difficulty collaborating on this apparently simple, very specific assignment. The way in which sabotage occurs is instructive to the therapist.

The week after some success with caring activities has been achieved, couples are asked to initiate change on a somewhat larger scale by periodically engaging in a substantial mutually rewarding activity, such as a dinner out, a picnic, an evening at a play, or a movie, or an overnight stay. These assignments must be designed to fit the motivation and competence levels of the couple at a given point in time. Moving too fast does not accomplish the objective of increased relationship quality time.

Basic Communication Skills Training

The third early therapeutic objective is to help partners acquire and employ basic communication skills. Meeting this objective usually takes two to four weeks of considerable in-session and homework practice. Table 9-1 presents the facilitative and nonfacilitative skills associated with basic communication. Some couples also profit from adjunctive bibliotherapy, such as the use of *A Couple's Guide to Communication* (Gottman, Notarius, Gonso, & Markman, 1976) or the *Problem Solving Manual* from Jacobson and Margolin's book (1979). Through the use of therapist instruction, modeling, behavioral rehearsal, coaching, videotape feedback, and homework assignments, partners are trained to send short clear messages that are verbally and nonverbally congruent with their own thoughts and feelings. In the listening role, spouses are trained to express interest and understanding nonverbally through the use of good eye contact and attentive gestures and to respond verbally with clarifying questions, paraphrasing, and validation of feelings.

Basic communication skills training progresses most effectively when the therapist follows a hierarchial plan based on the couple's existing skills and deficits. In general, for basic training purposes, it is the skill acquisition that is important, not so much the content of the discussion. However, many variables, such as content, can adversely affect the skill acquisition process. For example, the premature discussion of an emotional-laden topic usually interferes with skill acquisition. The author has identified 10 variables that seem to interact in an interesting and complex way to influence a particular couple's progress. Generally, it is recommended that therapists vary the in-session tasks and home-work assignments along the following dimensions in order to reach an optimal balance of relevance and challenge for the couple and success in skill acquisition. The order of progression within dimensions is from a to c as shown in Table 9-3; there is no particular significance in the order of the 10 dimensions.

Table 9-3   Development of Communication Skills

Length of speech
   Single speech
   Single message
   Multiple thought-feeling message

Complexity of content
   Simple, inconsequential topic
   Mild to moderate relationship topic
   Major relationship topic

Valence of affect
   Neutral affect expressed
   Positive affect expressed
   Negative affect expressed

Amount of emotional involvement
   Very little personal involvement likely
   Moderate personal involvement likely
   Intense personal involvement likely

Thoughts versus feeling expression
   Noncontroversial thought
   Mild to moderate thought, mild feeling
   Moderate to intense feeling

Nonverbal listening skills
   Close proximity, some eye contact
   Good eye contact, some supportive gestures
   Full-spectrum attentive behavior

Verbal listening skills
   Parroting, simple repeating
   Paraphrase and reflection
   Reflection and validation of feelings

Selection of topics readiness
   Therapist decides topic
   Topic negotiated by therapist and couple
   Couple decides topic

Therapist coaching
   Extensive interruption, instruction, and shaping
   Moderate coaching, as needed for major feedback
   Minimal therapist involvement

Behavioral Rehearsal
   Mostly in session with extensive supervision
   In and out of session with monitoring supervision
   Mostly out of session with minimal supervision and review

To conclude, the beginning stages of treatment have been successful when partners behaviorally demonstrate the existence of a collaborative set, establish or strengthen individually and mutually rewarding activities, achieve substantial success along the 10 communication training dimensions, listed in Table 9-3, and demonstrate—at least under optimal conditions—the facilitative versus nonfacilitative skills presented in Table 9-1. At that point they are ready to begin problem solving and thus move into the middle stages of therapy.

Middle Stages of Therapy

Although some overlap occurs between the beginning and middle stages of treatment when the gains made in the beginning of therapy are continually monitored and reinforced, the primary objectives of the middle stage are to teach general techniques of problem solving and conflict management (process) and to achieve remediation of specific marital problems (content) through methods of acceptance or behavior change.

Problem Solving

Partners typically come to treatment with a variety of complaints. The most frequent problems are in the areas of communication (i.e., quantity-, quality-, access- and skill-related issues), sex and affection, finances, children, in-laws, trust versus jealousy, and personal habits. Often, after achieving the objectives of collaborative set, individually and mutually rewarding activities and basic communication skills, many such problems no longer exist or acquire as much importance. This occurs particularly with respect to such relationship issues as sex and affection, trust versus jealousy, general resentment, and the expression of hostility. However, most couples still have specific conflict areas that need attention. They cannot be resolved simply by feeling better about each other; increased skills are required to effect resolution. Table 9-2 presents the conceptualization of the facilitative and nonfacilitative sender and listener behaviors associated with problem solving per se. Clients become acquainted with these skills, identify their own particular strengths and deficiencies, and then learn new problem-solving techniques. As was the case for basic communication skills training, therapists are active teachers: instructing, modeling, coaching, and reinforcing appropriate behaviors.

One very effective, though be no means original, systematic approach to problem solving is outlined below. Couples are taught to apply this model to increasingly difficult problems: first in-session and then at home on their own. There are five distinct steps in the model, as shown in Figure 9-2.

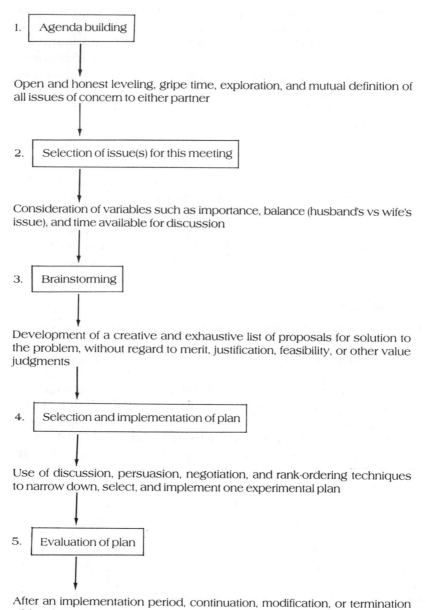

1. | Agenda building |

Open and honest leveling, gripe time, exploration, and mutual definition of all issues of concern to either partner

2. | Selection of issue(s) for this meeting |

Consideration of variables such as importance, balance (husband's vs wife's issue), and time available for discussion

3. | Brainstorming |

Development of a creative and exhaustive list of proposals for solution to the problem, without regard to merit, justification, feasibility, or other value judgments

4. | Selection and implementation of plan |

Use of discussion, persuasion, negotiation, and rank-ordering techniques to narrow down, select, and implement one experimental plan

5. | Evaluation of plan |

After an implementation period, continuation, modification, or termination of the plan

Figure 9-2   Problem-solving model flowchart.

In order to follow the model, outlined in Figure 9-2, couples are forced to break their usual maladaptive patterns of problem solving. With therapist guidance, this model is highly successful for most marital problems. It is taught not as something that must be used on every problem-solving occasion, but as an optimal and effective tool. During training, couples begin with the easier problems and progress over a few weeks to the most difficult relationship issues. In this manner, content-related problems are systematically addressed. The objective is for the couple to experience relief and resolution of specific problems while learning general techniques of problem solving.

Conflict Management

Dysfunctional conflict management can be represented by one of three general types of couples: conflict-avoiding, conflict-generating, and those who alternate conflict avoidance with eventual blow-ups. Occasionally, discord is so content-specific that resolution of a particular problem (e.g., childbearing) obviates the need for more extensive intervention. However, it is more likely that dysfunctional couples will profit from general training in conflict management skills. Developmental social learning processes and family rules influence individuals in certain ways of dealing with anger and conflict. It is not anger itself that is destructive; the feeling is inevitably a human condition. Rather, the forms of expression are what stimulate people into relationship-defeating patterns of interaction.

Couples who collaborate to avoid conflict and who have rules against the expression of anger and negative affect tend to suffer from intraindividual maladies such as anxiety and depression, psychosomatic symptoms, and lack of excitement and passion for spouse and life. The therapeutic challenge in these cases is to encourage and teach such individuals to identify and express such feelings in ways that produce understanding, validation, and safe conflict resolution.

Couples who collaborate to incessantly generate conflict present quite differently. The constant uproar paradoxically and simultaneously seems to be a representation of and a barrier to intimacy. The therapeutic goal is to teach partners to use their high-energy levels productively in first identifying and then resolving the basic problems. Conflict-generating interaction is rarely "much ado about nothing." Rather, it results from a combination of inadequate problem identification (i.e., hidden agendas) and problem-solving skill deficits. With conflict-generating couples, usually, existing conflict must be controlled before the couple can acquire new problem-solving skills. In such cases, partners are taught to arbitrarily terminate escalating sequences of interaction by taking a "time-out" from one another and by deferring the discussion to a later time. If necessary, the time-out may extend until the next therapy session. This type of limit-setting intervention is especially important where the potential for violence exists or the nature and frequency of conflict sabotages all other therapeutic relationship improvement.

Behavior Change Techniques

The behavioral approach emphasizes the use of social learning principles to change behavior. When indicated, couples are taught both the rationale and the interpersonal skills associated with positive reinforcement, shaping, punishment techniques (and the associated drawbacks), and extinction. For example, it is not uncommon for a wife to express a critical need for more help around the house or for a husband to insist on more sexual initiation from the wife. When these behaviors emerge, however, they may be treated as too little or too late. The point is that relationships in the midst of change are very vulnerable to one partner's failure to shape new behavior in the other. There is a tendency to extinguish or punish allegedly desired behavior.

In addition to teaching couples the principles and applications of social learning theory, many also benefit from more formalized training in negotiation skills and behavioral contracting. Several methods have been described in the recent BMT literature (Jacobson & Margolin, 1979; Stuart, 1980; Weiss, Birchler, & Vincent, 1974), and the interested reader is referred to these. What the negotiation training and behavioral contracting procedures feature in common are (1) an equitable "right and responsibility" philosophy of addressing relationship problems, (2) a focus on specific behavioral exchanges, and (3) a method of implementation that includes accountability and facilitative contingencies for behavioral performance and/or the lack of it. Once again, during this phase of therapy, both process (how) and content (what) issues are addressed. It is this integration of systematic intervention into content and process issues that forms the *art* of BMT.

Blocks to Progress—Dealing with Resistance

In the traditional behavioral formulation of marital therapy, the phenomenon of *resistance* has usually been conceived as a failure in case management. That is, the therapist has not paid sufficient attention to clients' competence and motivational factors in directing the case. More recently, however, rather specific *blocks to progress* in BMT have been described in the literature (Spinks & Birchler, 1982; Weiss, 1980), and the term *resistance* has appeared. It should be noted that resistance is not seen as inevitable as some theories would suggest, but rather is a problem to be addressed in some cases.

First, let us briefly outline the observable indications of blocks to progress as one pursues the assessment and treatment objectives represented in Figure 9-1.

Acting Out Between Sessions

In this category one can include repeatedly missed sessions or tardiness, failure to do or complete homework, and the phenomenon of repeated crises between sessions that serve to sidetrack the proposed agenda.

Blocks to Communication Skills Training

There are three observable indications of resistance during basic skills training: (1) some otherwise able couples demonstrate a *persistent* inability or unwillingness to learn simple communication skills (e.g., active listening); (2) after some couples have previously demonstrated good basic communication skills, they may enter a phase where there is constant generation of minor conflict issues that block further progress; and (3) there is the phenomenon of "wheel spinning," where the couple demonstrates a persistent inability to discuss a specific issue and reach an understanding or satisfactory resolution, even though they generally possess good communication and problem-solving skills.

Regression—Emergence of Original or New Symptoms

This is an interesting form of resistance in which there is a return of a chief complaint or reemergence of original symptoms (e.g., anxiety, depression) *after* major progress has been made. One variation of this is the sudden emergence of new symptoms of anxiety, phobia, headaches, or depression after substantial therapeutic progress has been made. The emergence of such symptoms is believed to be functional in terms of the relationship and the progress of therapy.

Lack of Maintenance and Generalization of Treatment Gains

Two final forms of resistance fall into this category. First, there may be the persistent failure of one or both partners to reinforce formerly requested behavioral changes. There may even be evidence of mild to moderate punishment of the alleged desired behavior. Second, the couple may demonstrate significant improvement in communication and problem-solving skills without enduring generalization to exchanges of affection or increases in subjective marital satisfaction.

Explanation for Blocks to Progress

The above 10 indications of blocks to progress emerge with some regularity in the application of BMT. Depending on one's theoretical orientation, there may be a variety of reasons for resistance and the indications thereof. From a behavioral-systems viewpoint, the following five hypotheses are useful in conceptualizing the blocks to progress. The major cause of difficulties, as mentioned earlier, is the therapist's *failure in case management* according to principles of social learning. For example, the therapist assigns the couple to take a weekend vacation for two when there is little evidence that they could manage a 15-minute nontalking walk around the block. The therapist's failure to adequately assess and shape the desired behavior would probably result in disaster on the weekend. Therapists must direct sessions and homework assignments with a full understanding of clients' present capabilities and motivations to perform.

Difficulties also are likely when one of the partners or the therapist is *breaking a normative rule* of the relationship. Certain objectives represent threats to implicit or explicit rules. For example, suppose that the implicit rules were: "No direct expression of anger or negative affect." It the therapist encouraged such self-disclosure too forcefully, considerable resistance might be encountered. No doubt similar rules require modification in most distressed relationships; however, a certain amount of resistance is likely to be encountered.

Fairly often a block in therapeutic progress is reached when a *hidden agenda* exists. That is, a critical issue has not been identified, discussed, and/or resolved. Hidden agendas, such as "I really want out of this marriage" or "I don't want to be closer and more affectionate with you because it will place too much pressure on me to perform sexually," are usually beyond the scope of clients' awareness. When they exist, however, they can subtly but effectively inhibit therapeutic progress.

In some cases clients are aware of critical issues (e.g., an affair where partners have ongoing suspicions or residual feelings) but collaborate to avoid confronting and resolving the problem because they have *catastrophic expectations* about the outcome. The issue thus remains covert and the associated resentment and fears prevent further progress in other areas.

Finally, it is soon evident to couples that marital therapy requires significant amounts of energy and requires significant personal and interpersonal changes. In some cases, one or both partners perceive that *the effort required to bring about the necessary attitudinal and behavioral changes is too costly.* This is not necessarily an inappropriate conclusion unless the partners remain in therapy and their actions reflect resistance as outlined above.

Therapist Intervention Options

In this model, given that the therapist detects a significant or repeated pattern of resistance, six major intervention options have been developed so far. With the exception of *interpretive modeling,* these planned deviations from the standard behavioral framework are not original to the field of marital therapy. However, the choice of intervention can be made according to the degree of persistence or the particular kind of block to progress. In order of presentation, the following procedures incur increasing amounts of time, complexity, and/or potential side effects. For practicality, therefore, it is suggested that they be applied in sequence or for specific indications.

Exploration of Cognitions and Emotions

This technique is the simplest to perform and is indicated when the therapist is unsure of the reasons for the observed resistance. Independently, partners are encouraged to offer their reasons as to why certain blocks to progress have emerged. Clients' thoughts and feelings are elicited and validated, and the issues that are identified are addressed. Supportive confrontation of the observed resistance behavior often suceeds in pinpointing and resolving the existing problems.

Relabeling or Qualified Interpretation

This technique is indicated when the therapist has a solid hunch about the reasons for the hindrance to progress. Relabeling is designed to facilitate identification and discussion of underlying or unspoken issues or feelings. The interpretations are "qualified" in the sense that therapist tact and suggestion are emphasized rather than direct stipulation or confrontation. Clients are given plenty of room to either entertain or reject the therapist's interpretations. This technique has its origins in several literatures: family systems, cognitive-behavioral, and psychodynamic. Given a certain behavior or pattern of behavior that suggests resistance (e.g., repeatedly arriving late for sessions), the therapist proposes an explataion for the behavior alternative to the one presented by the clients. When such reframing is done in a tactful and supportive way, it often succeeds in helping to identify and solve the obstructive issues.

Interpretive Modeling

The third resistance intervention option is more sophisticated than the former two. It is ideally suited for co-therapists. Its application is indicated when therapists strongly suspect that certain hidden agendas or catastrophic expectations are preventing therapeutic progress.

To employ the technique, co-therapists (or a single therapist with one of the clients) model self-disclosure, constructive confrontation, and risk-taking in an attempt to explore and elicit hidden agendas or unlabeled obstructive issues. Good sending and listening skills are modeled as the difficult topics are broached. The couple (or the other partner) is asked to carefully observe the role-play interaction and to entertain, accept, or reject its various aspects. Following this demonstration, partners are instructed to engage one another to correct, clarity, and further discuss the issue. In the author's experience, couples rather enjoy the therapists' attempt to role-model the clients. Moreover, partners often experience a sense of relief as obstructive issues are addressed that were formerly unrecognized or unmentionable (Spinks & Birchler, 1982).

Antisabotage Procedures

This technique is designed specifically to break resistance associated with homework assignments. Given that assignments are made with clients' motivation and ability levels in mind, some couples nevertheless repeatedly fail to complete or follow through with their agreed-on homework. The antidote (i.e., antisabotage procedures) consists of therapists allotting 15–20 minutes in a given session to systematically anticipate, identify, and help the couple modify high-probability resistance behaviors that could prevent their compliance with assignments (Birchler & Spinks, 1980).

Paradoxical Techniques

In the behavioral-systems model, these next two antiresistance techniques are reserved for last-resort efforts. Although the use of paradox, such as "going with the resistance," "prescribing the symptom" is not incompatible with the behavioral approach (Birchler, 1981), it is a sophisticated if not risky strategic maneuver. After more straightforward interventions have failed, however, the use of paradox may be indicated. The technique consists of the therapist first providing a plausible rationale and then prescribing a set of symptoms, behaviors, or exercises that function to put resistive clients into a therapeutic bind. Paradoxical prescriptions can help therapists gain leverage over resistance behavior in that if clients *resist* (e.g., do not engage in symptomatic behavior), they are breaking a maladaptive behavioral pattern. If they *comply* (i.e., follow the instructions), they are breaking the resistance-to-therapist pattern. Although strategic maneuvers of this sort have apparently had rather dramatic results (e.g., Papp, 1980; Soper & L'Abate, 1977), they have not been empirically validated and should be used only with caution and supervision.

Individual Confrontation

When the above conjoint interventions fail to remediate the obstructions to progress, separate interviews are conducted in order to explore each partners' feelings, hidden agendas, and commitment to remaining and changing in the relationship. When appropriate, partners are confronted with the relationship or self-defeating behaviors are identified and specific plans are made to remediate the problems. Infrequently, it is necessary to postpone treatment while clients consider their options.

It should be noted that all the above intervention options may be used alone, sequentially, or in combination to facilitate the remediation of significant blocks to therapeutic progress. When they all fail following skillful application, the therapist and clients may well resign themselves to terminating the therapy, if not the marital relationship.

Final Stages of Therapy

The final stages of therapy are fairly straightforward. There are three objectives that do not require much elaboration.

Diminution of Therapist Influence

It should be clear that the treatment approach features very active therapist intervention. During the final few weeks of treatment, therefore, attention must be given to fading the therapist's influence and turning over the course of events to the clients. Increasing responsibility for decisionmaking about homework and the in-session agenda is given to the couple.

Posttherapy Marital Relationship Assessment

At the second to last or last regular session, a final conflict resolution communication sample is obtained, and the couple is given a posttherapy Marital Relationship Assessment Battery to complete. These two assessment procedures provide objective data to complement the therapist's and clients' subjective impressions of relationship improvement.

Booster Session

Part of the last two sessions is devoted to reviewing and reinforcing the gains of therapy and to developing a plan for maintaining and/or improving on them. In particular, in order to extend the influence of therapy and to provide an opportunity for follow-up assessment, a "booster" session is scheduled usually six to eight weeks after the last regular weekly meeting. Since this procedure serves preventive, maintenance, and long-term assessment functions, it is highly recommended.

Finally, the handout shown in Figure 9-3 is given to the couple, and they are encouraged to periodically review and strengthen these critical relationship maintenance areas.

I. Communication
    A. General contract
        1. Most important is to make sure that you have easy access to your partner, one-on-one, to express feelings, hopes, fears, and maintain supportive contact.
        2. This contact seldom occurs by itself or through good intentions alone. One or the other of you must take the initiative to make these discussions happen.
        3. It is best to get in the habit of having a quality "talk time" on a fairly regular basis. For some couples, establishing certain rituals or "traditions" is very helpful. For example, at least once a week after the children are in bed, instead of TV, or before retiring, have a "talk time" along with a drink and a snack.
    B. Problem solving
        1. Think of yourselves *on the same team* in this relationship. If you find that you cannot successfully "edit" or drop the problematic issue on your own in a reasonably *short* period of time, take it to your partner for discussion and resolution.
        2. Solving relationship problems in their early stages is always easier than after aggravations and emotions build up.
        3. You each have a right and a responsibility to ask your partner to help resolve relationship issues.
        4. Negotiate or follow structured problem-solving procedures if you cannot quickly reach mutually satisfactory solutions.
        5. It is often helpful to separate the feeling expression and listening-validation process from the practical, solution-oriented problem-solving process.
        6. If necessary, *agree to disagree* and perhaps come back to the problem at another time.
II. Mutually rewarding activities
        1. It is important to establish (discover, develop) at least some mutually rewarding couple activities—*just the two of you.*
        2. Such activities may include dinners out, movies, concerts, plays, walks around the block or at the beach, picnics, hobbies, classes, and home projects. Find something regular and fun that you both enjoy doing together.
        3. One very successful idea has been for partners to alternate taking each other on surprise "dates." For example, husband makes all the arrangements to take wife on an outing that *she* would like some time during the months of January, May, and September; wife takes husband on a surprise date in March, July, and November.

III. Affection and sexuality
   1. These subjects are seldom discussed, and unsatisfactory patterns and feelings may continue for years.
   2. Open the lines of communication about demonstration of affection and your sexual relationship. Do not make assumptions about your partner's desires and inhibitions in this important relationship area. Be open and assertive in *discussing* your ideas regarding both the quantity and quality of affectionate and sexual activities.
   3. Be open to at least trying novel activities. Regarding sex, it is very helpful to keep the experience stimulating; therefore, be willing to vary the setting, positions, and activities of your sexual experiences.
   4. To revitalize this aspect of your relationship, you might well consider experimenting with special effects, such as lotions, powders, attractive clothing, magazines, pictures, reading material, films and vibrators: "Try it, you might like it!"
IV. Independent activities
   1. Although your partner can provide considerable rewards to you, it is equally important that you can serve yourself (and your relationship) by engaging in some independent rewarding activities.
   2. Perhaps once or twice a week, but on some regular basis, it is helpful if you participate, without your partner, in such activities as volunteer work, sports (active or spectator), classes, hobbies, and occasional weekend or even extended vacations.
   3. Your marriage, hopefully, will last for a long time. There should be room in it for the development of your interests and experiences apart from your spouse. If not abused in terms of time, frequency, or equal opportunity, the existence of independent activities strengthens most marriages.
V. Family quality time
   1. The process of *communication*, sharing ideas, and listening to and validating the feelings of your children is probably *more important* than providing an endless number of "activities" for them to do or "things" for them to play with.
   2. Establish opportunities for both parent–child "talk times" and full family discussions about life, hopes, fears, and family/household management issues.
   3. Also, full family activities are important, such as picnics, trips, sports events, home projects, or games. It is often advisable to "turn off the TV" so that family members can enjoy each other. The idea of an occasional "family home evening" is a good one to facilitate mutual enjoyment of the people in your family.
VI. You Must Make It Happen!
   1. To reiterate, these things tend *not* to happen on their own. *Somebody* must get the attention of their loved ones and organize and facilitate these activities. That's not bad or abnormal; it's just necessary.

Figure 9-3   Ideas for maintaining gains of marital therapy.

CASE STUDY

A brief case description is provided to outline in some detail a typical presentation and clinical intervention. Some representative verbatim therapist–client exchanges are also included.

Initial Interview

Linda and Tom were referred to the VA Mental Health Clinic by a friend who knew of the Family Mental Health Program. They are in their early thirties, have been married for six years, and have two daughters, aged two and four. It is the second marriage for Tom, a boiler repairman and mechanical engineer, and the first for Linda, who is currently occupied as a housewife and mother. During the initial clinical interview (E-1) the co-therapist team attempted to pinpoint presenting complaints and the precipitating event leading to the initiation of therapy. The answer to the sometimes very important question, "Why are you seeking help now?" (i.e., the precipitating event), was that Tom has recently admitted to having an affair with a young woman he had met during his rather extensive car-racing activities. Tom claimed that since the birth of their second child (whom he explicitly did not want but whom Linda had borne anyway), Linda's role had become almost exclusively one of mothering instead of being a wife (i.e., a loving sexual partner). With their dyadic and sex life faltering, Tom became more involved with racing activities, met an attractive, seductive girl, and succumbed to the affair over a period of several months. Beset with guilt and increasingly incompatible roles, however, he finally told Linda of the affair.

Linda, claiming that management of the young children and house required a huge amount of her time, asserted that Tom did not appreciate her responsibilities. He was very unhelpful with these tasks and, while spending less and less time at home, he became more and more demanding and resentful about their lack of sexual activity. Linda, in a fairly unemotional presentation, indicated that she felt hurt, angry, and abused regarding the affair. Nevertheless, the decision to seek professional help was primarily Tom's in that he wanted to "make or break" the marriage in order to relieve his ambivalence and frustration.

To summarize the content of E-1, the presenting complaints from Tom were: inability as yet to emotionally divorce himself from his lover, lack of affection and sex from Linda, Linda's tendency to spend more money than they had, and Linda's excessive attention to children and house, to his exclusion. Current relationship strengths that Tom noted were effective, loving parents, and basic caring and love for one another. Linda cited the major problem areas as: Tom's general lack of commitment to her and the family by way of attitude and actions, the quantity and quality of sexual interaction, and a desire for a reduction in the one or two nights a week and most of every other full weekend Tom devotes to racing. Strengths noted by Linda were: their mutual caring for one another, good senses of humor, and being good parents. At the end of E-1 an agreement was made by all to complete the evaluation process. The MRAB was distributed and the baseline results, obtained within one week, are listed in Table 9-4. The posttherapy scores also are indicated for later reference.

Marital Relationship Assessment Battery

Very briefly, the pretherapy data in Table 9-4 indicate that both partners are distressed and dissatisfied with the relationship; Tom significantly more than Linda (item 1 in Table 9-4). Tom has seriously entertained the idea of separation and divorce and initiated some such discussions outside the rela-

Table 9-4 Pre- and Posttherapy Results of the Marital Relationship Assessment Battery

	Pretherapy		Posttherapy	
Item	Tom	Linda	Tom	Linda
1. Locke-Wallace score	47	85	104	116
2. Marital Status Inventory	7	3	7	3
3. Self-Description Inventory				
Self-esteem	6.46	5.33	6.07	5.61
Psychological distress	1.00	3.36	1.77	3.19
Physical symptoms	0.19	1.25	0.65	1.06
4. Areas of Change Questionnaire	6	6	9	5
5. Response to Conflict Scale				
Self-appraisal	2.83	1.00	2.11	0.82
Spouse appraisal	1.42	3.08	1.18	2.40
6. Inventory of Rewarding Activities				
Proportion of activities				
Alone	55%	20%	27%	15%
With spouse only	22%	28%	31%	35%
With spouse and other				
adults	19%	18%	14%	14%
With family	2%	21%	17%	20%
With other adults,				
not spouse	2%	13%	11%	16%
Time distribution				
Working	24%	5%	24%	10%
Sleeping	25%	33%	28%	35%
Rewarding activities	32%	9%	22%	21%
Neutral or nonrewarding	20%	52%	26%	34%
7. Sexual Activity				
Worry about sex (0–8 scale)	0	5	2	4
Frequency of intercourse				
(past month)	5	15	9	9
Spouse initiated (–3 to				
+ 3 scale)	+ 3	–1	+ 2	0

tionship; Linda has taken significantly fewer steps toward divorce (item 2). In terms of self-attributions of self-esteem, psychological tension and anxiety, and physical symptoms (item 3), Tom demonstrates a pattern that strongly suggests denial and minimization of the negative aspects of these dimensions. Generally, such a pattern suggests one is likely to deny or rationalize one's own contribution to marital difficulties and to emphasize the faults of one's partner. In contrast, with the exception of a slightly elevated physical symptoms score, Linda's self-descriptive result fall within the "average" range and indicate no major problems or denial of problems in these areas.

The Areas of Change Questionnaire scores (item 4) fall within the range for nondistressed couples. This unusual finding suggests that relationship dissatisfaction has not spread sufficiently to affect multiple areas of interaction. The major areas of change that were indicated reflected a balance between the partners: less demand for sex on the part of Tom, Tom engaging in fewer sexual relationships outside the marriage, Linda becoming more responsible for finances, Linda engaging in more affection, sex and attention from Tom, and a desire for Tom to work late less often.

The Response to Conflict scale (item 5) indicated that Linda viewed both partner's response to conflict as within the normal range, whereas Tom perceived both of them as responding in a maladaptive fashion. He indicated high levels of active (e.g., complaining, swearing, criticizing) and passive responses to conflict (e.g., ignoring, refusing to talk about it, crying and leaving the scene). This difference in perception suggests at least that Tom is more frustrated than Linda with their style of conflict resolution and perhaps that the actual response levels are too high. If the latter is the case, conflict resolution skills will become targets for specific intervention.

The Inventory of Rewarding Activities (item 6) can be interpreted in several ways. The gross indicators are, however, that during the past month, Tom has engaged in a majority of elective activities alone. His results suggest relative deficiencies in elective activities with spouse, family, and independently of spouse. This pattern is largely the consequence of Tom's long-term withdrawal from family and his more recent withdrawal from friends and "lover." Linda's proportions of elective activities are more generally appropriate for a satisfied marriage. However, both partners' low "spouse only" proportions are of concern. Regarding time distribution, in a typical 168-hour week, note that Tom sleeps an average of only 6 hours a night. He also claims a solid proportion of rewarding activities. In stark contract to Tom and consistent with other available data, Linda indicates very little rewarding time and an overwhelming amount of neutral or nonrewarding activities: 78% of her waking hours! Such significant behavioral discrepancies between partners reliably function as major determinants of marital dissatisfaction.

Finally, data about sexual activity (item 7) confirm that sex is a major problem area. Whereas Tom characteristically denies that sex is a personal concern, he nevertheless indicates a low monthly frequency and calls for significantly more initiation by Linda. In contrast, Linda does admit to worrying about sex, indicates a desire for Tom to initiate requests less frequently, and claims a fairly high monthly frequency. Interestingly, the discrepancy and direction of Tom and Linda's estimates of sexual intercourse the previous month are typical for distressed couples. Wherever the truth lies, it seems that "sex-deprived" husbands often underestimate; "put-upon" wives often overestimate the frequency of sexual activity.

In summary, the MRAB documents the level and nature of marital dysfunction. For this couple, although the indicators are somewhat mixed, there is certainly sufficient self-reported distress to warrant marital therapy.

Communication Sample

The 10-minute videotaped communication sample was obtained at the outset of E-2. The conflict issue selected for problemsolving was Tom's involvement in racing activities. Here is a representative sample of their interaction.

Tom: What is it about my racing?

Linda: It's just that you spend so much time at it. Last night you worked on the car, tonight you have a meeting and then you will be gone all weekend.

T: Yes, but this is an important race and then there won't be another one until Long Beach. [three weeks later.] Besides you're invited to come.

L: I know, but I am not able to manage those kids all day by myself and at night you would rather party anyway than be with us. Last time you said you would be home by six and you got home at midnight.

T: I know. I already told you I'm sorry about that? We get so wired all day that it's hard to leave without having a few beers and winding down. What's wrong with that?

L: Nothing! I want you to have a good time, but you promised you would come home early. And when you come home that late you are too tired the next day to do anything with us.

T: [Said with disgust.] Well, maybe I should quit racing, but it's the only fun thing I do!

L: [With resignation.] No . . . you need an outlet, but the kids and I need some time with you too.

At this point, the pattern was set. The remainder of the discussion went similarly round and round. This couple is conflict-avoidant. Little direct anger was expressed throughout the interaction; however, they concurred during debriefing that they probably would not have carried on such a discussion at all at home. As it was, they spent most of their time describing the problem and summarizing their own positions. There was minimal evidence of understanding one another, expression of feelings, or problem solution. Unlike many couples, however, they did manage to stay on the topic, achieve a balance of talk time, and demonstrate fair-to-good nonverbal sending and listening skills. Unfortunately, their natural pattern at home is to withdraw from potential conflict discussions even before reaching the level of wheelspinning problem description evident in the observed sample.

Treatment Goals and Modalities

By the end of the evaluation period, good rapport had been established between therapists and clients, there was a consensus on the problems and goals of therapy, and a treatment contract was set for ten sessions. Goals and intervention methods are indicated below in the tentative order of approach. Note that the goals in italics are system issues. They tend to be process goals identified by the therapists and are not necessarily stated explicitly to the clients. Although process goals may be critical to the remediation of marital dysfunction, they are rarely the overt content-type complaints that couples present (see Table 9-5).

Table 9-5   Treatment Plan for Tom and Linda

Goals	Interventions
1. Establish collaborative set	Persuasion and didactic instruction in systems thinking; homework assignments that require and reward couple collaboration; therapist reinforcement for teamwork
2. Increase contact time for Tom and Linda; Tom and family	Negotiation and structured homework assignments, e.g., caring activities, mutually rewarding couple and family activities
3. Increase couple communication skills	Basic communication skills training in session; graded assignments at home—assigned reading, discussion, and exercises.
4. Increase Linda's independent rewarding activities	Negotiated resource allocation, e.g., money for babysitters; homework assignments
5. Increase problem-solving and conflict-resolution skills	In-session training in problem-solving and conflict-management skills; structured homework
6. Resolve financial management issues	Apply problem-solving skills; establish budget
7. Increase Tom's father role and decrease his "sex-deprived, errant husband" role; increase Linda's wife role and decrease her "overburdened mother-housewife" role	Systematic assignments above that foster one role over the other; therapist reinforcement of role shifts; techniques of dealing with resistance
8. Increase quality of sexual interaction	Graded assignments, e.g., caring activities; structured exercises, e.g., sensate focusing; communiation skills about sexual interaction
9. Resolve Tom's ambivalence about wife versus lover	A planned and eventual consequence of all the above

Treatment Progress and Resistance

At the outset both Tom and Linda seemed motivated to improved their marriage. While admitting to some emotional ambivalence about being with wife versus lover, Tom indicated that he wanted to stay with the family and make the marriage more rewarding. He had terminated self-initiated contacts with his lover. Since she was the daughter of his favorite racing couple, however, he could not guarantee that he would never lay eyes on her again. At the time, Linda characteristically accepted this situation without protest, believing that it would be unreasonable to expect Tom to give up his racing hobby and close friends to obviate potential contact with his *ex*-lover.

In any case, Tom and Linda made very good early progress. In fact, with only an average amount of direction, encouragement, repeated assignments, and reinforcement by the therapists, they did quite well through the beginning stage of therapy and part way through the middle stage. The difficulties arose when goal 7 (in Table 9-5) was broached through explicit focus on treatment goal 8. Treatment session number six (T-6) had ended with an assignment extending goal 2 into sexual interaction. On a given day, Tom agreed to come home by 5 P.M., to shower, and to help Linda feed and bed the kids by 8 P.M. That would leave about three hours for them to have a nice, jointly prepared dinner, to relax for awhile, and then to engage in a pleasurable sexual encounter.

The therapists suspected that if major resistance were going to emerge, it would be associated with movement toward increased intimacy (i.e., confronting the risk of rejection) through a sexually oriented assignment. The therapists carefully designed the assignment to be successful, therefore, stopping just short of employing a full anti-sabotage procedure (see above). The therapists' concerns were well founded. After the customary small talk, session T-7 began like this:

Female therapist: Well, how did your week go?

Tom: [Somewhat subdued] Not too good. About Thursday night . . . we did fine until after dinner. [Pause.]

Male therapist: What happened?

Tom: Nothing. We watched TV for awhile and Linda fell asleep on the couch as usual so I want to bed. Nothing has changed.

MT and FT: [Both look at Linda.]

Linda: I thought we had a nice evening, but after dinner Tom started watching TV and looked real comfortable over there in his chair, so I sat down on the couch and before I knew it I fell asleep. When I heard Tom going to bed I got up to join him but by that time he was mad and wanted to go to sleep.

MT: [Introducing some humor, incredulously] You mean to say that you got that close to having a super evening and at the critical moment after dinner you both dropped the ball?

Tom: I guess so, but Linda. . . .

MT: [Interrupting, not terribly surprised, but sensitive to their collusion to block progress and deciding to try a reframing, confronting tact.] Wait a minute, Tom . . . but Linda, but Tom, but Linda . . . it will not be productive to try and blame this on each other. The point is, you *both*, without saying so, apparently decided that having sex would be too risky, too scary. Perhaps you'd be too vulnerable to performance pressures or rejection. As far as I can see, there's no reason to get on each other's case about this. You're in it together! What do you think, Suzanne?" [Looking at female therapist.]

FT: It sure does look that way. Tom, what were you expecting to happen when you sat down in your chair to watch TV?

Tom: I thought Linda might ask me to come sit by her on the couch. . . .

FT: [Interrupting.] And Linda, what did you expect when you sat down to watch TV?

Linda: I thought Tom would finish his program and then turn off the TV so we could do something together. . . .

FT: [Interrupting.] So you both were waiting for the other person to initiate the affection and when they did not, Linda, you fell asleep and Tom, you played "I told you so" and then got mad. From then on you never did get back together to enjoy your evening, right? [Both nod their heads.] So perhaps we should spend some time this session talking about *why* following through with sex and affection was too difficult for *each* of you and what we can do this next week to make things work out better.

MT: Yes, you almost had a super evening. You're very close to jumping over this little hurdle and solving this problem. [Reframing the problem as "little" despite the powerful collaborative resistance to change.]

From there, further *exploration of cognitions and feelings* indicated that Linda was still a little unsure of herself as a competent sexual partner and thus was reluctant to initiate affectionate interaction. At the same time, she became aware of lingering, if unexpressed, resentment about Tom's affair. She wanted to be given special attention and to be seduced. In Tom's case, he was still vulnerable to their old interaction pattern and his self-defeating thinking style: "If Linda really cares about me, knowing that I want sex and affection, she will initiate it; I'm tired of always having to be the initiator." In addition, Tom admitted that although he had no contact with his girlfriend, he still occasionally experienced strong feelings for her. The therapists pointed out that such expectations and emotions were likely to cause relationship problems, particularly when left nonverbal (i.e., as hidden agenda). The remainder of the session was devoted to the careful design of another romantic evening together with encouragement to explicitly discuss their ongoing feelings and expectations.

Between sessions, the therapists discussed the likelihood that Tom's unresolved feelings for his girlfriend were functioning as a powerful hidden agenda. Even though their general communication and problem-solving skills had significantly improved, the therapists realized that the couple's conflict-avoidance style of interaction would make it difficult for either of them to bring up and work through the issue of the past affair. Accordingly, an interpretive modeling intervention was planned for the next session, if appropriate.

Interpretive Modeling

The couple returned for T-8 having completed successfully their sexual interaction assignment early in the week. However, a second more spontaneous sexual encounter went awry. Once again, each partner waited for the other to initiate sexual contact, and each became resentful and withholding of attention and affection when it did not occur. Therefore, about 20 minutes into the session the therapist decided to do the interpretive modeling sequence:

MT: OK, it's clear that while you've made some very excellent progress in the improvement of your relationship, you seem to get stuck when it comes to improving your sexual interaction. Suzanne and I have some hunches about what might be going on and we'd like to role-play the two of you discussing the problem.

FT: I will play Linda, Gary will play Tom, and we would like you to observe what we say and how we say it. Try to keep an open mind and entertain the possibility that what we are saying is correct.

MT: Once we finish you can each correct or reject anything that we have guessed about. Remember that we're *speculating* about what's going on.

Male therapist as Tom [MT (Tom)]: This is hard for me to say, and especially because I care a lot about you and want our marriage to work . . . but I still have a lot of mixed up feelings about Roxanne. [Girlfriend.] I think sometimes they get in the way of my total commitment to making this therapy work.

Female therapist as Linda [FT (Linda)]: [Said softly and seriously.] You are saying that it is hard for you to give 100% to us because you still care for Roxanne. But you want our marriage to work and you still care a lot about me.

MT (Tom): Yes. I've tried to forget all about her, but her parents are my best friends in racing and I couldn't bear to give that up. I think they are uncomfortable around me too because they liked Roxanne and me together, but I don't want that to interfere with you and me. Anyway, I think I've got to get this resolved before we can really make it.

FT (Linda): I have to admit, it really hurts to hear you talk this way. But I guess I have suspected that you are still confused because sometimes you withdraw and I do not understand why. It is better that we talk it out than keep it inside. Not knowing how you feel has made it difficult for me. I really do want to change from being a "supermom" and housewife to being a wife and good sexual partner to you, but I do not think I have done very well. I have let my feelings about Roxanne and racing keep me from doing my part to make things better. In some ways I am complacent and comfortable the way things are, except that I know you are dissatisfied with our sex life.

MT (Tom): You're saying that my mixed feelings hurt you, that you have experienced my distance and confusion, that we should talk about it and that you also are aware that you've not given 100% to our improvement because of your resentment about Roxanne and racing.

FT (Linda): And that part of me is fearful of becoming more of a sexual wife and giving up my supermother role.

MT (Tom): Well, I'm not sure yet what to do about this, but I feel a little better that we've got it out in the open. I'm certainly not comfortable going on with these mixed feelings.

FT (Linda): Me either. As much as the alternatives scare me, I would rather have you as a full time husband and father or not at all.

MT: [Breaking role.] OK, what do you think? [Looking at both Linda and Tom.]

Tom: [Hesitating as Linda smiles and nods.] That's about right.

MT: What would you change—or how about if the two of you take it from here and endorse or modify what we've said.

Tom: [Turning to Linda.] I wouldn't change too much of what Gary said. I know I can't have it both ways. That's why I came here in the first place. I also know that I don't want to lose you and the kids, and that . . . really . . . it wouldn't work with Roxanne anyway. I think I need to have a talk with her once and for all. [Linda looks noticeably more concerned after Tom's last sentence.]

FT: Tom, before you problem-solve, let's stay with the feelings awhile. How about your reaction, Linda, to what we did?

Linda: Well . . . I really can't argue with what you said [looking at Suzanne, almost tearful]. Over the past few weeks I can feel it when I retreat to the children . . . I know I should reach out to Tom . . . I want to and when I do he is responsive. Maybe too responsive. It scares me. . . .

FT: Is it more comfortable when Tom reaches out to you?

Linda: Yes, because then I knew he cares. Except when he just wants sex. Then I feel pressured and used.

FT: [Paraphrasing in part to interrupt the impact of the last, potentially sidetracking statement.] So, recently you have become aware of when you are withdrawing into the mother role, you experience both success and fearful feelings when you initiate affection, and you are more self-assured when Tom expresses affection toward you.

Linda: [Nods her head in assent.]

FT: So, once again we see that communication is critical. You both really do care about each other. And with the insecure feelings that you both have, you have been taking one step forward and one step backward.

MT: [Noting the lateness of the hour.] It seems to me that the main thing you two need to do is to figure out how to translate your positive feelings and affection for one another into action. Tom, you had an idea about how to begin resolution of this problem.

Tom: [Looking a little puzzled.]

MT: About a meeting with Roxanne.

Tom: Oh yes, I'd like to go talk with her and get things cleared up.

Linda: What do you need to clear up?

Tom: Well . . . not knowing what she's thinking makes me uncomfortable around her parents and about ever bumping into her at the races.

MT: [Wanting the agenda very explicit about any such meeting.] What would you want to accomplish at such a meeting? What would your message be to Roxanne?

Tom: Well, I'd like to get it understood that as far as a close relationship goes between us, it's over. That I want my marriage to work. That I want to visit and do things with her parents, but it doesn't mean anything about us.

Linda: So you plan to keep on racing as often?

Tom: Sure, at least the rest of this year while I'm track coordinator. How about you and the kids getting more involved? They're old enough now to go along.

MT: [Interrupting to keep focus.] OK, let's solve one problem at a time. So, Tom, you're planning to have a talk with Roxanne to clear up mutual expectations. Does that make sense to you, Linda?

Linda: Yes, if it will help get us back together.

MT: Well, you're already back together. Hopefully, this will help you both get past this difficult issue and on with your life together.

The session ended with a final review of the meeting plan and with assignments to further monitor and discuss this issue throughout the week. The following week Tom reported an anxiety-provoking and yet successful meeting with Roxanne, and both Tom and Linda appeared relieved and reenergized to continue with therapy.

The final three meetings progressed well as the couple continued to negotiate about and practice new patterns of sexual interaction. The therapeutic emphasis was on *mutual* responsibility for initiation of and response to sexual behaviors. Tom learned that in exchange for less frequency (e.g., two to three rather than five encounters per week) that quality could be improved in terms of Linda's responsiveness, enthusiasm, and active participation. Moreover, with modest decreases in Tom's working late and racing activities, there was increased contact time available for the full gamut of relationship business. This included sex and affection, sometimes initiated by Linda.

Posttherapy Assessment and Follow-Up

The posttreatment communication sample reflected increased collaboration and assertiveness during conflict resolution by both partners. The MRAB posttherapy results are presented in Table 9-4. These data suggest significant improvements in many of the relationship indicators, with the exception of the Areas of Change Questionnaire, which was not in the distressed range at the outset. At six-week follow-up, both partners claimed that they reviewed the "maintaining gains" guidelines biweekly and sometimes made adjustments in their activities. According to the pre- and posttherapy communication samples, therefore, the MRAB data and subjective estimates of change in marital satisfaction at six-week follow-up, significant relationship improvement seemed to occur.

SUMMARY

This chapter has presented a model of behavioral-systems assessment and intervention for marital dysfunction. The initial focus was on multimethod assessment, which indicates the appropriate emphasis to be placed on several available treatment modules: the development of individual and mutually rewarding activities; basic communication skills training; problem solving and conflict management; behavior change strategies; and, when indicated, content-oriented interventions such as financial planning, parenting skills training, and sex therapy.

The treatment approach was described as following a behavioral framework except with major or repetitive blocks to progress emerge. These identifiable blocks to progress or resistance phenomena were categorized into therapist- and client-generated behaviors that can usually be modified by intervention techniques ranging from *exploration of cognitions and feelings* through *interpretive modeling* to the more manipulative or confrontive strategies such as *paradox* and *individual sessions.*

This chapter closed with a brief case description that included pre- and posttherapy assessment data and representative therapist–client interactions. Behavioral marital therapy in general and communication and problem-solving skills training in particular have been shown to be effective in several outcome studies [see Birchler (1979) and Jacobson and Margolin (1979) for review chapters]. Moreover, the approach is especially suited to the outpatient setting. For further knowledge in this area, the interested reader may wish to pursue the clinical literature on behavioral marital therapy (Jacobson & Margolin, 1979; Liberman et al., 1980; Stuart, 1980; Weiss & Birchler, 1978) or its behavioral-systems integrations (Barton & Alexander, 1981; Birchler & Spinks, 1980; Spinks & Birchler, 1982; Weiss, 1980).

REFERENCES

Azrin, N. H., Naster, B. M., & Jones, R. Reciprocity counseling: A rapid learning-based procedure for marital counseling. *Behaviour Research and Therapy*, 1973, *11*, 365–382.

Barton, C., & Alexander, J. F. Functional family therapy. In A. S. Gurman & D. P. Kniskern (Eds.), *Handbook of family therapy*. New York: Brunner/Mazel, 1981.

Birchler, G. R. A multimethod analysis of distressed and nondistressed marital interaction: A social learning approach. Paper presented at Western Psychological Association Meeting, Seattle, Washington, April 1977.

Birchler, G. R. Inventory of rewarding activities. Unpublished manuscript, University of California Medical School, San Diego, 1979.

Birchler, G. R. Communication skills in married couples. In A. S. Bellack & M. Hersen (Eds.), *Research and practice in social skills training*. New York: Plenum Press, 1979.

Birchler, G. R. Paradox and behavioral marital therapy. *American Journal of Family Therapy*, 1981, *9*, 92–94.

Birchle, G. R. Behavioral-systems marital therapy. In J. P. Vincent (Eds.) *Advances in Family Intervention, Assessment and Theory* (Vol. 3). Greenwich, Conn: JAI Press, in press.

Birchler, G. R. & Spinks, S. H. Behavioral-systems marital and family therapy: Integration and clinical application. *American Journal of Family Therapy*, 1980, *8*, 6–28.

Gottman, J., Notarius, C., Gonso, J., & Markman, H. *A couples guide to communication*. Champaign, Illinois: Research Press, 1976.

Jacobson, N. S., & Margolin, G. *Marital therapy: Strategies based on social learning and behavior exchange principles*. New York: Brunner/Mazel, 1979.

Liberman, R. P., Wheeler, E. G., de Visser, L., Kuehnel, J., & Kuehnel, T. *Handbook of marital therapy*. New York: Plenum Press, 1980.

Locke, H. J., & Wallace, K. M. Short-term marital adjustment and prediction tests: Their reliability and validity. *Journal of Marriage and Family Living*, 1959, *21*, 251–255.

Papp, P. The Greek chorus and other techniques of paradoxical therapy. *Family Process*, 1980, *19*, 45–57.

Soper, P. H., & L'Abate, L. Paradox as a therapeutic technique: A review. *International Journal of Family Counseling*, 1977, *5*, 10–21.

Spinks, S. H. & Birchler, G. R. Behavioral-systems marital therapy: Dealing with resistance. *Family Process*, 1982, 169–185.

Stuart, R. B. *Helping couples change*. New York: Guilford Press, 1980.

Stuart, R. B., & Stuart, F. *Marital Precounseling Inventory*, Champaign, Ill.: Research Press, 1973.

Wahler, H. J. The self-description inventory: Measuring levels of self-evaluative behavior in terms of favorable and unfavorable personality attributes. *Journal of Clinical Psychology*, 1968, *24*, 40–45.

Weiss, R. L. Strategic behavioral marital therapy: Toward a model for assessment and intervention. In J. P. Vincent (Ed.), *Advances in family intervention, assessment and theory* (Vol. 1), Greenwich, Conn.: JAI Press, 1980.

Weiss, R. L., & Birchler, G. R. Areas of change questionnaire. Unpublished manuscript, University of Oregon, Eugene, 1975.

Weiss, R. L., & Birchler, G. R. Adults with marital dysfunction. In M. Hersen & A. S. Bellack (Eds.), *Behavior therapy in the psychiatric setting*. Baltimore: Williams & Wilkins, 1978.

Weiss, R. L., Birchler, G. R., & Vincent, J. P. Contractual models for negotiation training in marital dyads. *Journal of Marriage and the Family*, 1974, *36*, 321–330.

Weiss, R. L., & Cerreto, M. The marital status inventory: Development of a measure of dissolution potential. *American Journal of Family Therapy*, 1980, *8*, 80–86.

Weiss, R. L., Hops, H., & Patterson, G. R. A framework for conceptualizing marital conflict, a technology for altering it, some data for evaluating it. In F. W. Clark & L. A. Hamerlynck (Eds.), *Critical issues in research and practice: Proceedings of the fourth Banff international conference on behavior modification*. Champaign, Ill.: Research Press, 1973.

Wieder, G., & Weiss, R. L. Marital interaction coding system—II. Unpublished manuscript, University of Oregon, Eugene, 1979.

Part III

PROBLEMS IN CHILDHOOD

10

Anxiety-Based Disorders

Thomas H. Ollendick

THE PRACTICE of behavior therapy with children who evince fear and anxiety has a long tradition in clinical psychology (Jones, 1924a, 1924b; Watson & Rayner, 1920). However, the focus on children as a *special* group with unique needs is a relatively new advancement in clinical behavior therapy (Ollendick & Cerny, 1981; Ollendick & Hersen, 1983). All too frequently, behavioral clinicians have applied assessment strategies and treatment procedures found to be useful with adults to children in an indiscriminate fashion, irrespective of developmental considerations. Such practices, which at times ignored affective and cognitive processes characteristic of children at varying age levels, frequently met with failure. In response, behavioral clinicians have begun to modify existing assessment procedures and treatment strategies and have designed more age-appropriate and innovative ones for children. Such developments, although in their early stages of development, have already advanced our understanding, prediction, and control of child behavior in the clinical setting.

The purpose of the present chapter is to examine the current status of anxiety disorders in children in light of these emerging developmental considerations. In pursuing this goal, we examine practices and issues related to diagnosis, assessment, and treatment. Further, these practices are illustrated with actual clinical material; special problems encountered in the assessment and treatment of such children are identified and addressed throughout this chapter. Quite obviously, a chapter such as this cannot claim to provide an index to all the literature or issues in this area. Rather, the objective is to present an overview of major considerations and problems that lead to an awareness of the complexities and subtleties associated with the outpatient treatment of anxiety disorders in children.

DIAGNOSTIC CONSIDERATIONS

The *Diagnostic and Statistical Manual (DSM-III)* (APA, 1980) distinguishes among three principal types of anxiety disorders of Childhood: separation anxiety disorder, avoidant disorder of childhood, and overanxious disorder. Anxiety is the predominant clinical feature in all three categories; however, the anxiety is focused on specific situations in the first two categories and generalized to a variety of situations in the third category.

The essential feature of separation anxiety disorder is the presence of excessive anxiety on separation from persons, places, or surroundings to which the child has become closely attached. For example, a child may become highly anxious when it is necessary to leave home or safe surroundings (e.g., to run an errand, attend summer camp, and, in some instances, attend school). The anxiety frequently reaches panic proportions and is characterized by perspiration, complaints of difficult in breathing, and heaart palpitation. Children frequently appear fearful and apprehenisve and report being afraid that some harm might befall them or the significant others to whom they are attached. Duration of the disturbance is extended, and the reaction is well beyond that evidenced at specific developmental levels.

Similar clinical features are evident in the avoidant disorder of childhood category. That is, the child is highly anxious, fearful, and apprehensive, and displays heightened physiological arousal. In contrast, however, the anxiety is centered around contact with strangers. Frequently, the child becomes fearful and anxious in the presence of strangers: both adults and peers. Consequently, age-appropriate socialization skills do not develop, and the child appears unassertive as well as avoidant of social interactions. As with separation anxiety disorder, the avoidant reaction must be extended in duration (at least six months) and well beyond that normally expected at specific developmental levels.

In contrast to both of the above categories, the essential feature of overanxious disorder is excessive worrying and fearful behavior that is not focused on a specific situation or object (such as separation from a parent or entering a new social interaction). The child worries unrealistically about future events, is preoccupied with past behaviors, is overly concerned about being evaluated, and is in need of excessive reassurance or comfort. Further, the child reports a variety of somatic complaints (e.g., headaches or stomachaches), is highly self-conscious, and is unable to relax. As with the other anxiety disorders, the reac- tion must be relatively long term in duration (i.e., at least six months). Developmental guidelines are not indicated however, since pervasive anxiety is not expected to be present or characteristic at any age level.

In addition to these three primary types of disorders, *DSM-III* rec- ognizes the presence of phobic disorders in children that are not sub- sumed under the categories of separation anxiety or avoidant disorders mentioned above. The essential feature of such disorders is a persist- ent and irrational fear of a specific object, activity, or situation that results in an active avoidance of the dreaded object, activity, or situa- tion (the phobic stimulus). Among such specific fears are those of small animals, heights, the dark, and closed spaces. Although not explicitly stated in *DSM-III*, it is implied that these excessive fears are not age- or stage-specific and that they, too, are extended in duration.

Although these anxiety disorders in children appear relatively well defined and circumscribed, several conceptual and practical issues are raised by them. Probably the most critical questions are related to the reliability, validity, and clinical utility of these diagnostic cate- gories. How reliable and valid are they? How useful are they? Ideally, a classification scheme should provide information about the relation- ship of the specific disorder to different etiologies, treatments, and long- term prognostic statements. Quite simply the state of affairs in child psychopathology in general, and anxiety disorders in particular, is not sufficiently refined to permit such specificity [see Quay (1979) for a thorough discussion of classification issues]. Several authors have com- mented on the low interrater reliabilities for the various subvarieties of anxiety disorders in children and the proliferation of diagnostic cat- egories in *DSM-III* (e.g., Cantwell, Russell, Mattison, & Will, 1979a, 1979b; Mattison, Cantwell, Russell, & Will, 1979; Rutter & Shaffer, 1980). In general, the findings of these studies show a high level of agreement for broad diagnostic categories such as the anxiety disorders, but rather low reliability for the finer subdivisions within these gen- eral groupings. These findings, as well as those related to the validity of the various subcategories (Harris, 1979), call into question the clini- cal utility of such diagnostic practices.

As noted most clearly by Achenbach (Achenbach, 1966, 1980, Achen- bach & Edelbrock, 1982), the foregoing considerations argue for a taxonomy of child disorders based on empirical methods rather than nosological ones. Utilizing the statistical procedure of factor analysis,

Achenbach and his colleagues have consistently found that child behaviors, both deviant and normal, can best be described according to
two major dimensions, labeled externalizing (e.g., hyperactivity, aggression) and internalizing (e.g., anxiety, withdrawal). Within these
general "broad-band" categories, more specific "narrow-band" syndromes have been empirically derived, including syndromes of anxiety and social withdrawal. As with DSM-III, however, subvarieties of
anxiety disorders in children have not been reliably nor consistently
identified with these empirical procedures. Moreover, age and sex
differences have been found for some of the syndromes, affirming the
importance of developmental considerations when examining child
behavior disorders (Achenbach, 1978, 1979; Achenbach & Edelbrock,
1979).

What is the practicing clinician to conclude from this state of affairs?
On the one hand, *DSM-III* proposes a variety of anxiety disorders in
children that, at least intuitively, appear to make conceptual sense.
On the other hand, factor-analytic studies and those studies that examine the reliability and validity of specific subgroupings according
to *DSM-III* indicate that such intuitive and conceptual structures are
not always supported. As clinicians, we have all occasionally worked
with children who fit nicely into the various nosological categories;
unfortunately, we have also worked with a greater number of children who do not fit nicely into these categories. Illustratively, in our
work with "school-phobic" children, we have come to appreciate the
complexities and subtleties associated with such seemingly straightforward a disorder (Ollendick & Mayer, 1983). Over the past 11 years,
we have worked with 37 school-phobic children. All these children
evidenced a fear of school that was unrealistic, inappropriate, and
persistent. Further, in all cases, this unwarranted fear led to an avoidance of the school situation and a refusal to attend school. Aside from
common school avoidance behaviors, the children presented quite diverse scenarios as to precipitating events and associated clinical
features. In a retrospective attempt to classify these children according to *DSM-III* criteria, we (as "experts") assigned 13 of the 37 children to the separation anxiety disorder category (all feared separation
from a parent as well as school), 5 of the 37 children to the avoidant
disorder of childhood category (all feared entering new interpersonal
situations as well as school), 10 of the 37 children to the overanxious
disorder category (all worried excessively about future events, being
evaluated, and about how well they had done in the past, in addition
to specific fears about school), and the remaining 9 to the phobic disorder category (all had fears related specifically to a particular event
in the school setting itself). When we subjected these categorical place-

ments to a reliability review, however, we obtained only moderate correspondence with our "expert" assignments (about 60%). The most commonly cited reason for difficulty in making reliable assignments was the observation that a majority of cases shared elements across all four of the diagnostic categories. For example, it was not uncommon for a given child to express fear of separation from his or her mother, fear of meeting new classmates, and a specific fear of a particular school event. Overall, such a child appeared generally anxious as well, clouding the clinical picture even further. Our attempts to categorize these children along *DSM-III* guidelines were less than satisfactory, unless we used multiple categories of assignment.

Nonetheless, it should be recalled that all these children avoided school and refused to attend. In addition, all these children were described by parents and teachers as being anxious and exhibiting a high degree of somatic complaints on Achenbach's Child Behavior Checklist (see "Clinical Assessment" section below). Further, they all reported a high degree of fear in both school and nonschool situations on the revised Children's Fear Survey Schedule (Ollendick, 1978). Clearly, these children were anxious and fearful, and fit both *DSM-III*'s generic category of anxiety disorders of childhood and the empirically determined broad-band factor of internalized behavior described by Achenbach and others. Further, although they fit the narrow-band factors of anxiety and somatic complaints described by Achenbach, greater specificity was not possible, at least not reliably so.

On the basis of these findings, as well as others extant in the literature, it appears safe to conclude that practicing clinicians, as well as clinical researchers, are not always able to accurately categorize individuals into specific subcategories, such as those outlines in *DSM-III*. Although such diagnostic precison is currently lacking, there is sufficient consensus that a broad-band category of "anxiety disorders" exists, from both nosological and empirical standpoints. Further, children can be accurately placed into such a category from both perspectives, and meaningful treatment decisions can be made on the basis of those assignments.

CLINICAL ASSESSMENT

It is evident that anxiety disorders in children are complex and that they do not represent a unitary syndrome. Anxiety may result from a variety of causes and my be "explained" by a variety of theoretical construct. The factors that are considered relevant to a thorough clinical assessment vary according to one's theoretical persuasion. From a behavioral perspective, anxiety is viewed as a learned response that has specific cognitive, physiological, and behavioral referents. When exposed to potentially aversive stimuli (e.g., being critized, being hurt, being left alone), anxiety is experienced and escape responses are evidenced; that is, aversive events produce behaviors that lead to the termination of such unpleasant events. After a limited number of exposures to the threatening stimuli, and resultant escape from them, the child learns to circumvent the aversive stimuli by aboiding them altogether. Such avoidance responses are subsequently reinforced by the reduction in anxiety that was previously experienced when the child was exposed to the aversive stimuli. Unfortunately, the child cannot always avoid the aversive stimuli, and anxiety results. Such anxiety responses can be acquired vicariously, as well as through direct experiences (e.g., Bandura, 1969).

Although anxiety and fear can be learned according to the specific principles of classical, vicarious, and operant conditioning as suggested above, they are probably maintained by complex, interactive processes that involve each of the principles (Ollendick, 1979). For example, once a child has learned to be anxious around strangers and fearful of interpersonal relationships, this reaction might be maintained by periodic traumatic events (e.g., being ridiculed by a peer), observing another child's anxious behavior (e.g., seeing another child rejected by the teacher), and/or receiving an inordinate amount of attention from significant others (e.g., comforting by the parent). Of course, it also is probably that such anxious behaviors were acquired in the first place through multiple sources of conditioning. The important conclusion to be drawn here is that anxiety disorders are acquired and maintained through an interactive combination of conditioning processes. Such a conclusion has clear implications for clinical assessment and treatment.

Assessment of the anxious child from a behavioral perspective is undertaken in the sections that follow. Three specific strategies are described: the behavioral interview, self-report and other-report rating forms, and behavioral observation procedures. Although physiological measurement is recommended and has been used frequently in the measurement of anxiety in adults, it has been used less frequently with anxious children. Accordingly, use of this measure, although recommended, is not reviewed here.

The Behavioral Interview

In general, the behavioral interview has three primary purposes: (1) to establish a positive relationship with the child and his or her family, (2) to obtain specific information about the anxious behavior and its antecedent and consequent conditions, and (3) to determine the larger social and cultural context in which the behavior occurs. The development of a positive relationship helps to maximize the chances that the child and his or her family will openly and honestly share their concerns and that reliable and valid information will be obtained. Basic helping skills, including empathy, warmth, and genuineness, appear to facilitate rapport and to make the interview a less threatening experience for child and family alike (aspects of this approach are illustrated in the extended case description presented later).

In interviewing young children and their families, problems frequently arise because of the child's limited verbal repertoire, incomplete understanding of the reason and purpose of this interaction and frequent fear of new and strange places. These considerations are especially critical for the anxious child who often appears shy, timid, and fearful fo what might happen in the "doctor's office." When interviewing such children, it is frequently necessary to simplify questions by phrasing them in concrete and specific terms. Such a practice requires skill and patience: skill in using words and phrases the child will understand and patience in clarifying, rephrasing, and restating questions until they are understood. In those instances where the child is seemingly unable to describe the anxiety-eliciting events, instructing the child to image what "goes on" when he or she is anxious frequently is helpful. Such a procedure is illustrated by Smith and Sharpe (1970) in their assessement of a school-phobic child and by Ollendick and Gruen (1972) in the assessment of a highly anxious child who feared bodily injury. For example, Smith and Sharpe instructed their child to image in minute detail a school day, beginning with his awakening to his going to bed that evening. He was assisted in this process by specific questions about concrete events, such as what he was wearing, whom he was with, how he felt, and where he was. During this imaginal process, he was closely observed for behavioral symptoms of fear: flushing of the skin, increased motor movement, vocal tremors, and crying. On the basis of these observations, it was determined that specific school classes produced greater amounts of anxiety. In particular, it was observed that the child was anxious when called on to recite in these classes and ridiculed by his peers. This procedure was instrumental in ruling out separation from mother as a contributing source of the school phobia. When the child visualized leaving his mother, no signs of anxiety were produced, an observation later confirmed by parent report and behavioral observation.

During the interview, verbal and nonverbal behaviors of the family members also are noted and are used to formulate a conceptualization of the family context in which the anxiety occurs. In addition, parent-report, sibling-report (when siblings are present and included in the interview), and self-report data are solicited. Such data contain first-hand reports about antecedent and consequent conditions, as well as familial involvement in the development and maintenance of the anxious behaviors. In general, a thorough interview should also provide information about the early precursors to the anxiety behavior, topographic features characteristic of it (duration, intensity, and frequency), and the resources withing the child and family to deal with it. Information obtained from the interview should be viewed as tentative; it is only the beginning phase of the assessment process.

As with all assessment strategies, clinical interviews share problems related to reliability and validity. Quite obviously, full treatment of these issues is beyond the scope of this chapter. Two precautions are necessary, however. First, retrospective child and parent recollections may be distorted and may be lacking in reliability and validity. For example, Chess, Thomas, and Birch (1966) have shown that parents inaccurately recall that certain behavior problems emerged at times that coincided with those predicted by popular theories. These observations have direct bearing on the clinical utility of information obtained during the interview. Second, although the reliability and validity of general recollections are suspect (as indicated above), recent evidence suggests that parents and children are reliable and accurate reporters of current, specific information about problematic behaviors (e.g., Herjanic, Herjanic, Brown, & Wheatt, 1975). Specification of precise behaviors that are occurring (and the conditions under which they are occurring) thus is likely to produce more reliable and valid information than are general descriptions or recollections of previous events.

In summary, the behavioral interview is viewed as an important and necessary first step in the assessment process. Although problems remain with the reliability and validity of the information obtained, such problems can be partially offset by fostering a positive relationship with the child and his or her family and by focusing the interview on specific, current events. Although some parents and professionals advise against interviewing the child along the lines indicated here (due to possible iatrogenic effects—e.g., "let's not discuss it in front of her, it will probably only make matters worse"), in our own practice we routinely interview the child (regardless of age) *prior* to proceeding with any formal assessment or treatment. We use this procedure for ethical reasons and to obtain the explicit cooperation of the child. Although iatrogenic effects occasionally do occur, we prefer to address them as they develop rather than jeopardize the cooperation and involvement of the child in the clinical process [see Ollendick & Cerny (1981) for an extended discussion of this issue].

Rating Forms

In general, two types of rating instrument have been used to assess anxiety in children: (1) self-reports of attitudes, feelings, and behavior, and (2) other reports of the child's behavior. Although both types of rating have specific limitation, they each provide valuable information about the child and about his or her behavior in comparison to that of other children. Such normative comparisons can be used to determine the developmental appropriateness of the child's behavior (Ollendick & Ollendick, 1982) and to demonstrate the social validation of behavior change following treatment (Kazdin, 1977). These ratings also can be used as outcome measures to determine treatment efficacy. They can be administered prior to intervention, at postintervention, and at predetermined follow-up intervals to assess both specific and generalized behavior change. A further potential advantage of administering such forms is that further research might show that response to specific anxiety-reduction treatments (e.g., systematic desensitization, self-instructional training) is related to "subtypes" of anxious children as determined by patterns of responding on these scales (Ciminero & Drabman, 1977). This latter function, although largely untested at this time, is an especially important one in the pursuit of the "best" treatment.

A variety of self-report measures of anxiety and fear have been developed for use with children (Barrios, Hartmann, & Shigetomi, 1981; Ollendick, 1979; Ollendick & Mayer, 1983). The most frequently used self-report scales are the Children's Manifest Anxiety Scale (Castaneda, McCandless, & Palermo, 1956) and its recent revision (Reynolds, 1980; Reynolds & Richmond, 1978, 1979), the State-Trait Anxiety Inventory for Children (Spielberger, 1973), the Fear Survey Schedule for Children (Scherer & Nakamure, 1968) and its recent revision (Ollendick, 1978; Ollendick, 1982), and the Children's Fear Survey Schedule (Ryall & Dietiker, 1979). The two anxiety scales are useful in identifying overall levels of anxiety, whereas the fear survey schedules are instrumental in delineating specific fear stimuli as well as providing an overall index of "fearfulness." We limit our discussion here to Spielberger's State-Trait Anxiety Inventory and to our revision of the Fear Survey Schedule for Children. We have found these two scales most useful in our own clinical practice.

The State-Trait Anxiety Inventory, developed for school-age children, consists of 20 items that measure "state" anxiety and 20 items that measure "trait" anxiety. The state anxiety form is used to assess how the child "feels at this moment." The form measures the more generalized aspects of anxiety and can be employed productively as a before, after, and follow-up device. The scales have been widely researched

and possess adequate psychometric properties, including acceptable reliability and validity.

The Fear Survey Schedule for Children—Revised (Ollendick, 1978,
1982) is most useful for identifying specific fear stimuli that are related to the child's anxious behavior. In the revised scale, designed to
be used with school-age children, the child is instructed to rate his or
her fear level to each of 80 items on a three-point scale. Children are
asked to indicate whether a specific item (e.g., have to go to school,
being punished by father, snakes, the dark) frightens them "none at
all," "some," or "a lot." Although still in its experimental form, initial results indicate that this revision is reliable and valid. For example,
we have used the scale to discriminate between school-phobic children,
and to differentiate phobic youngsters whose fear of school appears
related to separation anxiety (e.g., ghosts, death, getting lost, my parents criticizing me, having my parents argue, being alone, dark places)
from those whose fear appears to be due to specific aspects of school
(e.g., taking a test, being teased, and making mistakes). The use of the
scale in working with school-phobic youngsters is described in greater
detail by Ollendick and Mayer (1983).

In general, these self-report instruments have proved useful in determining the overall level of anxiety in the child and in identifying
specific antecedent stimuli associated with the anxious behaviors. In
addition, the scales appear useful as process and outcome measures
of treatment efficacy. Furthermore, although sufficient data are not
yet available, initial indications suggest that individual response pattern to the scales might be related to differential treatment modalities.

As with self-report forms, other-report rating forms are useful in determining overall levels of anxiety in children. In this approach, members of the family or significant others (e.g., teachers) are asked to fill
out checklists or rating forms regarding the child's level of anxiety or
fear. A variety of scales are available (Ollendick & Cerny, 1981);
however, we have found the Child Behavior Checklist (Achenbach, 1978;
Achenbach & Edelbrock, 1979) and the Louisville Fear Survey Schedule for Children (Miller, Barrett, Hampe, & Noble, 1972) to be the most
useful with anxious children. The Child Behavior Checklist, which has
served as the basis for the factor analytic work of Achenbach and his
colleagues described earlier, is comprised of both social competency
and behavior problem items. The social competency items assess the
child's participation in activities (e.g., sports, hobbies, chores), social
organizations (e.g., clubs, number of friends, behavior with peers and
adults), and school (grades, placement, promotions). Response to these
itmes is scored on a three-point scale, that reflects both the quantity
and quality of competance-related behaviors. These item are especially

sensitve to social skill deficits—deficits that frequently are present in anxious children. The behavior problem scale of the checklist consists of 118 items, each rated on a three-point scale as to how well it describes the child (e.g., not true, somewhat or sometimes true, and very true or often true of the child). Importantly, the scale provides factor scores for various syndromes, including those characterized by anxiety and somatic domplaints. Items such as "too fearful or anxious," "fears certain animals, situations or places, other than school," "fears going to school," "nervous or tense," and "vomiting, throwing up" are included. When the behavior problem items are combined with the social competency items, a well-rounded description of the child's strengths and weaknesses is provided. Normative date are provided for each sex of child in each of three age ranges (4-5, 6-11, and 12-16), allowing for specification of important developmental and gender differences. Further, it possesses sound psychometric qualities, is both reliable and valid, and, through its various forms, can be filled out by both parents and teachers.

Another reliable and valid scale that can be completed by parents and teachers is the Louisville Fear Survey Schedule for Children (Miller et al., 1972). This scale is comprised of 81 items that cover an extensive array of fears found in children and adolescents. Each item is rated on a three-point scale: no fear, normal or reasonable fear, and unrealistic fear. As with the self-report of fear scales (e.g., the Children's Fear Survey Schedule—Revised), responses to specific fear items can be used to "subtype" fearful children. For example, in a study of school-phobic children, Miller et al. (1972) reported that 32 of 46 children had a specific fear of some aspect of the school situation itself, whereas the remaining 14 had a primary fear of separation. This latter group of children appears to fit *DSM-III*'s separation anxiety disorder category, whereas the former group appears to fit the phobic disorder category. Thus, Results from this instrument can be used to identify specific subtypes of fearful children, a function similar to that reported by us for the Children's Fear Survey Schedule—Revised (Ollendick & Mayer, 1983).

Like the behavioral interview, self-report and other-report rating forms serve a limited but important function in the assessment of anxiety and fear in children. They provide potentially meaningful data about a child's adaptive and problem behaviors, including specific worries and fears. Futhermore, the scales have the potential of describing classes of behavior (subtypes) that may respond differently to different treatment strategies. Although additional research is needed to more firmly establish their reliability, validity, and clinical utility, there is no doubt that these various instruments hold considerable promise and that they are a welcome addition to the thorough assessment of anxiety and fear in children.

Behavioral Observation

Direct observation of the child's behavior in the setting in which it occurs is the hallmark of behavioral assessment. Within this tradition, assessment has ranged from unobtrusive observation in the natural setting to direct observation in laboratory settings that simulate those settings (Lick & Katkin, 1976). Such observations provide a direct sample of the child's behavior and are the least inferential of date collection methods. As we have suggested elsewhere, however, behavioral observation procedures should not necessarily be viewed as "better" than the other methods we have already described (Ollendick & Cerny, 1981). Rather, such observations should be viewed as complementary to the other methods, with each providing valuable information about the child's behavior.

In behavioral observation systems, a behavior or set of behaviors that are indicative of anxiety are operationally defined, observed, and recorded in a systematic fashion. In addition, the events that precede and follow the anxious behaviors are recorded and subsequently used in developing a specific treatment program. This approach, applied to a clinical case, in nicely illustrated in Neisworth, Madle, and Goecke's (1975) behavioral assessment of a young girl's separation anxiety in a preschool setting. These authors observed that whenever the mother left her daughter at school, the young girl began to cry, sob, and scream until her mother returned to retrieve her. After being comforted, the mother would try to leave her daughter once more and, of course, the daughter would begin to cry and scream again. Such a pattern suggested that the daughter's "separation anxiety" was being maintained by, and possibly resulting from, the attention provided by mother. More importantly, for our purposes here, the separation anxiety was operationally defined as a set of observable behaviors (crying, sobbing, and screaming), and these behaviors were systematically observed throughout baseline, treatment, and follow-up phases. Further, these observations suggested a specific treatment (differential reinforcement plus shaping) that was based on the antecedent (preschool setting) and consequent (attention from mother) conditions under which the behaviors occurred.

In a similar view, Ayllon, Smith, and Rogers (1970) conducted extensive and systematic behavioral observations in the home of a school-phobic girl, who had been absent from school for an extended period of time. In this case, the mother left for work about one hour after the girl (Valerie) and her siblings left for school. Although the siblings went to school without incident, Valerie was observed to "cling" to her mother and refused to go to school. "Valerie typically followed her mother around the house, from room to room, spending approximately 80 percent of her time within 10 feet of her mother. During these times, there was little or no conversation" (Allyon et al., 1970, p.128). On leaving for work, the mother took Valerie to a neighbor's apartment for the day (she had long abandoned any hope of Valerie returning to school). When the mother left the neighbor's apartment, however, Valerie ran after her. Observations revealed that this pattern continued, with Valerie "following her mother at a 10-foot distance." Often the mother found it necessary to return Valerie to the neighbor's apartment. This daily pattern usually ended with mother "literally running to get out of sight of Valerie" so that she would not follow her to work.

At the neighbor's apartment, it was subsequently observed that Valerie was free to do whatever she pleased for the rest of the day. As noted by Ayllon et al. (1970, p. 129) "Her day was one which would be considered ideal by many grade school children—she could be outdoors and play as she chose all day long. No demands of any type were placed on her." Since Valerie was not attending school, the authors designed a simulated school setting in the home to determine the extent of anxiety or fear toward academic tasks and to differentially assess these effects vis à vis separation ones. Little or no fear was evinced in the simulated setting, suggesting that her refusal to attend school was related to her mother's attention and to the reinforcing environment of the neighbor's apartment, where she could play all day. Accordingly, a shaping and differential reinforcement program, similar to that reported by Neisworth et al. (1975), was successfully implemented. Importantly, the detailed behavioral observations led directly to specific and efficacious intervention.

In addition to these highly individualized assessment practices, Glennon and Weisz (1978) have described a more general observational scale of anxiety. After reviewing the literature, they developed a scale of 30 behavioral indices of anxiety (e.g., verbal expression of fear or worry, whining or whimpering, nail-biting, avoidance of eye contact, and rigid posture) that would likely be useful in measuring anxiety across diverse situations. Although adequate reliability and validity have not yet been reported, the system appears useful and highly promising as a clinical tool.

As with other types of assessment, behavioral observation procedures must demonstrate sound reliability and validity before their routine use can be endorsed. Whereas early behavioral-oriented clinicians proclaimed the value of direct observational systems based on their deceptively simplistic face validity, more recent behaviorists have enumerated a variety of problems related to their use in the clinical setting.

Among these problems are the complexity of the observation code, observer bias, observer drift, and the reactive nature of the observation process itself. For example, parents and teachers frequently report that the observations of therapists are not consonant with their own. When the child knows that he or she is being observed, specific behaviors change and are "reactive" to the presence of the observer. We have found that such reactivity can best be handled by scheduling extended observations, by having the parents (or some other agent in the setting) unobtrusively record the targeted behaviors, or by instructing the child to self-record his or her own behaviors (see Ollendick, 1981). We have found the latter practice of self-monitoring and self-recording useful and reliable with children as young as seven years of age. When the problems with direct behavioral observation procedures noted above are adequately controlled for, they represent one of the most elegant and productive assessment strategies.

In summary, behavioral observation in natural or simulated settings represent the hallmark of behavioral assessment. These strategies, which are not without their own special set of limitations, are a welcome complement to behavioral interviews and rating forms. They provide valuable information, which, when combined with that obtained from other sources, yield a potentially comprehensive as well as integrated "picture" of the anxious child. Such an integrated assessment is illustrated below in our detailed case description.

TREATMENT APPROACHES

In the present section, behavioral strategies commonly used in the reduction of anxiety in children are briefly described. Conceptually, these strategies are derived from principles of classical, vicarious, and operant conditioning. Although strategies based on each of these specific principles are presented, it should be understood from the onset that the most effective and durable treatments draw on all three sets of principles in a complex fashion. The use of such integrated approaches recognizes that anxiety, from the behavioral perspective, is acquired and maintained through an interactive combination of conditioning processes (Ollendick 1979).

Systematic Desensitization and Variants

Systematic desensitization procedures evolved from the early laboratory work of Pavlov and Watson and the subsequent application of this work to the clinical setting by Wolpe and others. In this paradigm, anxiety and fear are described as classically conditioned responses that can be unlearned through counterconditioning procedures. In counterconditioning, the anxiety-producing stimuli are presented in the presence of stimuli that elicit responses incompatible with anxiety. In this manner the anxiety is "counterconditioned" and inhibited by the incompatible response. In this procedure it is necessary to expose the individual to the anxiety-arousing stimuli (either imaginally or in vivo) for anxiety reduction to occur.

The first and most often cited account of counterconditioning principles applied to children's fearful behavior is that of Mary Cover Jones (1924b). She successfully treated a fear of rabbits in a 3-year-old boy, Peter, by exposing him to the feared rabbit in vivo and in the presence of food—a stimulus that elicited a positive response (i.e., eating). The pairing of a fear-producing stimulus with a stimulus that elicits a competing (or positive) response is, of course, the crux of systematic desensitization (Wolpe, 1958). Historically, systematic desensitization has typically employed the relaxation response as the competing, inhibiting response. Used most successfully with adults, systematic desensitization consists of three basic components: progressive relaxation training, development of a fear-producing stimulus hierarchy, and the pairing of items in the hierarchy with relaxation. Generally, the fear-producing stimuli are presented in imaginally (in the order of least to most anxiety-producing) while the individual is deeply relaxed. This part of treatment is the desensitization proper and leads to the inhibition of the anxiety response. As noted by Wolpe, it is imperative that the counterconditioning response (i.e., the relaxation, be sufficient to inhibit the anxiety at each step of the hierarchy. Although recent studies have questioned the active mechanisms and the necessary components of systematic desensitization, there is little doubt that it is an effective treatment procedure.

Variants of systematic desensitization, including in vivo desensitization (as originally used by Jones) and emotive imagery (in which feelings of self-assertion, pride, mirth, or affection are used as the anxiety-antagonistic response), have become increasingly popular with children (Hatzenbuehler & Schroeder, 1978; Ollendick, 1979; Ollendick & Cerny, 1981). These variants have evolved as a result of the acknowledged developmental limitations of children in being able to fully acquire the muscular relaxation response or in being able to adequately image the fear-producing stimuli. Although these limitations are evident, it much be recognized that not all fears and anxieties of children are amenable to in vivo treatment and that it is not always possible to gain therapeutic control over diverse counterconditioning agents. In response to this, recent efforts have been directed toward tailoring standard muscular relaxation procedures for children and toward using a variety of cues (e.g., sights, sounds, pictures) to help young children better image the anxiety-arousing events (Ollendick & Cerny, 1981).

In our own clinical practice, we frequently use a relaxation training script designed especially for children (Ollendick, 1978; Ollendick & Cerny, 1981). In this revised script, we have used words that are easily understood by young children and that capture and hold their attention. For example, in teaching the child to tense and relax facial muscles, the following script is employed: "Wrinkle up your nose. Make as many wrinkles in your nose as you can. Scrunch your nose up real hard. Good! Now you can relax your nose. Now wrinkle your nose up again. Wrinkle it up hard. Hold it just as tight as you can. Okay. You can relax your face. Notice that when you scrunch up your nose that your cheeks and your mouth and your forehead all help you and they get tight too. So when you relax your nose, your whole face relaxes too, and that feels good. . . ." We have found that 15- to 20-minute sessions produce the best results and that it is advisable not to introduce more than three to four muscle groups in any one session. Typically, a child can be trained in muscle relaxation in about three to four sessions. For those children who are anxious or fearful of some specific event, we use the relaxation response as the anxiety-inhibiting response in the standard desensitization format and then teach them how to remain relaxed when in the anxiety-producing situation (a procedure similar to that of cue-controlled relaxation training or anxiety management training used for adults). For those children who are more generally anxious and who are unable to specify the anxiety-producing stimuli with sufficient clarity, we use relaxation as a psychological "tranquilizer" and as an active coping strategy.

Although not truly a variant of systematic desensitization, flooding and implosion are also based on classical conditioning principles (extinction) and also require the child to be exposed to the anxiety-producing stimuli for anxiety reduction to occur. In contrast to the graduated approach of systematic desensitization, implosion and flooding entail prolonged exposure, either imaginal or in vivo, to the most anxiety-arousing stimuli. During these extinction procedures, the conditioned fear stimuli are repeatedly presented in the absence of the original unconditioned stimuli. In this manner, the individual learns that there is really nothing to be afraid of, and the anxiety response is weakened.

When using these procedures, it is critical that the conditioned anxiety-arousing stimuli be presented in the absense of the unconditioned aversive stimuli. For instance, if a child who is fearful of peer interactions were being treated in vivo by prolonged and direct exposure to a small group of children, it would be important to ensure that he or she not be ridiculed, bullied, or criticized by peers. Such occurrences would undoubtedly result in renewed conditioning. The child would avoid peers even more and and evince even greater arousal during their presence. This is an obvious risk that must be carefully considered before the use of such procedures can be endorsed. Perhaps because of these risks, very few clinical studies using these procedures have been reported with children (Graziano, 1975; Ollendick, 1979). Nonetheless, Marks (1975) reports that techniques based on flooding and implosion achieve consistently good results with adults; their continued use and systematic evaluation with children certainly seems warranted at this time.

In summary, systematic desensitization, relaxation training, emotive imagery, implosion, and flooding all represent potentially effective procedures for the treatment of conditioned emotional responses in children. Although problems with their use remain, most of these problems are obviated when attention is paid to special developmental factors that enhance their utility. Although much research remains to be conducted, they represent viable options and are a welcome addition to the practicing clinician's armamentarium.

Modeling

Treatments based on classical conditioning principles emphasize the role of direct learning experiences in the acquisition, maintenance, and reduction of anxieties and fears; however, those based on vicarious conditioning emphasize the role of observational learning or modeling (e.g., Bandura, 1968, 1969). Bandura has noted that:

> One of the fundamental means by which human behavior is acquired and modified is through modeling or vicarious processes. Research conducted within the broad framework of social learming theory provides considerable evidence that virtually all learning phenomena that result from direct experiences can occur vicariously, as a function of observing other people's behavior and its consequences for them.[*]

As with systematic desensitization and its variants, procedures based on vicarious conditioning have also been used to reduce anxiety and fear in both children and adults. Basically, modeling entails demonstrating nonfearful behavior in the anxiety-producing situation *and* showing the child an appropriate response for handling the feared

---

[*]From Bandura, A. Modeling approaches to the modification of phobic disorders. In R. Porter (Ed.), *Ciba Foundation Symposium: The role of learning in psychotherapy.* London: Churchill, 1968. With permission.

stimuli. Thus anxiety is reduced and appropriate skills are learned. After the demonstration, the child is then asked to imitate the performance of the model. Frequently, the child is then reinforced for displaying the appropriate behaviors.

Three types of modeling have been used: filmed modeling, live modeling, and participant modeling. Filmed modeling consists of having the child observe a graduated series of films in which a model exhibits progressively more intimate interaction with the feared object or setting, whereas live modeling consists of having the child observe a *live* model engage in graduated interactions with a *live* feared object or participate in real-life situations that are anxiety-producing. Participant modeling, on the other hand, consists of live modeling, physical contact with the therapist, and guided practice in the feared situation. That is, in addition to observing another interact fearlessly, the child also is provided physical and psychological support and direct contact with the therapist while performing the appropriate behavior. In general, research studies have shown that filmed modeling is effective in about 25–50 percent of cases, live modeling in about 50–67 percent, and participant modeling in 80–92 percent. [see review by Ollendick (1979)]. A clear ordering of effectiveness is evident in these figures: filmed modeling being least effective, live modeling intermediate, and participant modeling most effective.

The potential utility of these procedures is nicely illustrated in a clinical case study in which modeling and other procedures were used in the treatment of social withdrawal and fear of interpersonal relationships in a 6-year-old boy (Ross, Ross, & Evans, 1971). In this study, Ross et al. describe a child whose fear and avoidance of relationships with peers was so extreme that he actively avoided peers and refused to even watch symbolic presentations featuring young children. Prior to treatment, measures of prosocial interaction and avoidance behavior were obtained through behavioral observation procedures. Assessment revealed that the child "interacted" with peers less than once every five minutes (the average child in the classroom interacted approximately 11 times per five-minute period) and that he exhibited 52 avoidance behaviors during a 2½-hour observation period: "lowering eyes to avoid visual contact (4), withdrawing abruptly to avoid tactual contact (10), veering off suddenly on a circuitous route to avoid physical proximity (12), leaving a solitary activity upon arrival of a peer (9), ducking his head or turning away when a peer initiated verbal contact (8), running away when an adult advocated social interaction with peers (4), and hiding during large group social interactions (5)" (Ross et al, 1971, p. 276). Treatment was necessarily elaborate and consisted of the following strategies: establishing generalized imitative behavior, developing a strong relationship with the therapist, observing the therapist in live modeling with other children, looking through books at pictures of children interacting, participant modeling with the therapist, social reinforcement, and finally, practice in using the prosocial skills in situations other than the classroom. Counterconditioning (relationship, looking at pictures) and operant reinforcement (social reinforcement, reinforced practice) were thus used in addition to modeling (generalized imitation, observation, and guided practice). Following treatment, which was conducted during three 90-minute sessions a week for seven weeks, the child was observed to interact an average of 10 times during each five-minute observation period (a rate comparable to his peers) and to display only four avoidance responses over a 2½-hour posttreatment assessment (again, comparable to his peers). These gains in prosocial behavior and decreases in avoidant behaviors were maintained over a two-month period. Furthermore, they were observed to generalize to a playground setting where he was observed to "join ongoing play groups, initiate verbal contacts, and sustain effective social interactions, all with children who were complete strangers to him" (Ross et al., 1971, p.277). Clearly, significant changes were obtained following this rather elaborate treatment protocol.

In our own clinical practice with anxious and fearful chldren, we, too, have found it desirable to combine facets of counterconditioning and reinforced practice along with participant modeling an an integrated treatment sequence. Typically, when we use modeling procedures, we initiate treatment by focusing on the development of a positive relationship with the child and teach him or her relaxation skills as a coping strategy. The relationship and the relaxation are then used as anxiety-ihhibiting agents while the child is guided through a series of graduated interactions with the feared object. Participant modeling is used as the child first observes the therapist, then accompanies him or her (tags along), is involved in the interaction, and finally performs the feared interaction along. Feedback and reinforcement are provided at each step. We have found this procedure most useful with children who appear fearful of separation and avoidant of social interactions, although we have also used it with children who have specific fears and phobias.

Before leaving our discussion of modeling procedures, it is important to caution that many children who appear anxious do not possess the skills necessary to deal effectively with the feared object or situation. In such cases, the child might be more appropriately labeled skill-deficient rather than anxious or fearful. For example, a child who is fearful of interacting with others may not be aware of, nor have the necessary skills, to interact appropriately. Only thorough assessment will confirm the primary and secondary features. When a skill deficit is noted, however, clinicians might well invest their energies in skill acquisition procedures (e.g., social skills training).

In summary, modeling procedures also represent potentially effective treatment strategies for anxious and fearful children. An advantage of these procedures over standard systematic desensitization procedures is that they stress skill acquisition as well as anxiety reduction. Although considerable research remains to be conducted to identify the optimal conditions of modeling when used in the clinical setting (e.g., coping vs. mastery model, similar vs. dissimilar age and sex characteristics), there is a little doubt that it too is a welcome tool for the practicing clinician.

Positive Reinforcement Procedures.

In contrast to systematic desensitization and modeling, both of which asume that anxiety must be reduced or eliminated before the individual can overcome the feared situation, procedures based on the principles of operant conditioning make no such assumption. Elimination of anxiety or fear through direct or vicarious experiences is unnecessary from this perspective. Rather, operant procedures assume that simple acquisition of approach responses to the anxiety-producing situations is sufficient. Lick and Katkin (1976) have called this the *response-reinforcement model*. The basic premise of this model is that certain fears or anxieties may develop and are maintained by the consequences associated with them. Thus, one child's separation anxiety may result from excessive positive reinforcement, in the form of attention or affection, whereas another child's avoidant reaction to peers may result from the negative reinforcement received when he or she is able to escape unpleasant social situations. Both of these notions are similar to the concept of "secondary gain" used by dynamically oriented clinicains to account for persistent fears or anxieties. This model most forcefully calls for a thorough assessment of the positive and negative reinforcing stimuli that produce as well as maintain the anxious or fearful behaviors. If the anxiety reactions are being positively or negatively reinforced, interventions should be aimed at reducing the reinforcement value of the anxiety responses, not at reducing anxiety per se. Such conditions were evident in our earler descriptions of the separation anxiety cases studied by Ayllon et al. (1970) and Neisworth et al. (1975). In both cases, the children were observed to receive undue attention, comfort, and reassurance as a result of their "anxious" behaviors.

The utility of operant procedures is nicely illustrated in a case reported by Hersen (1970). In Hersen's study, broad-based operant procedures were used in the home, school, and clinic settings to treat a 12½-year-old school-phobic boy. Observations indicated that the mother in anadvertently reinforcing the boy's school refusal by showering him with attention and solace and that the guidance counselor similarly responded to his complaints once in the school setting. More specifically, the child frequently spent entire mornings in the counselor's office, during which time the counselor attempted to comfort him and alleviate his anxiety. The mother and the counselor were both instructed in operant strategies and informed to ignore his negative behaviors while profusely reinforcing positive, coping responses. For example, the counselor was requested to be supportive but firm in having him return to the classroom and to limit his own contacts with the child to five minutes. In addition to these efforts "out in the real world," the therapist also verbally reinforced his coping responses and ignored his maladaptive, fearful ones. The entire treatment program lasted 15 weeks; school refusal as well as the crying and complaining ceased in all three settings, and the child returned to school without incident. This comprehensive approach was both successful and relatively short term. The thorough functional analysis, similar to that described by Ayllon et al. (1970) and Neisworth et al. (1975), facilitated the development of an effective treatment program that was based largely on operant principles. Nonetheless, it is probable that treatment contained counterconditioning (e.g., positive relationship with therapist) and vicarious elements (e.g., modeling of other peers), as well as the more obvious operant ones.

In our own clinical practice with anxious and fearful children, we routinely combine operant procedures with those based on classical and vicarious principles. Such comprehensive treatment typically includes aspects of systematic desensitization, modeling, and reinforced practice. In addition to graduated exposure to the feared event, we use counterconditioning to reduce the intensity of the fear, participant modeling to demonstrate appropriate approach and interactive skills, and reinforcement to praise the child for the nonfearful behavior. Typically, counterconditioning consists of relaxation training or any of the variants previously discussed, including games, music, and a strong therapeutic relationship. Participant modeling consists of the guided demonstration of those skills necessary to interact with or approach the feared situation. Frequently, we have found that anxious children are deficient in the very skills needed to reduce the fear. Of course, such an approach also includes the counterconditioning effects of physical contact with the therapist during demonstration of the appropriate skills. Finally, we use social reinforcers as well as contingency contracts to reinforce the children for their nonfearful behaviors.

Recently, we have incorporated self-regulatory strategies into our procedure in an attempt to help the children gain even greater control over their own behavior. Studies by Kanfer, Karoly, and Newman (1975), and Graziano, Mooney, Huber, and Ignasiak (1979) demonstrate the utility of such procedures of children who are fearful of the dark.

In general, operant procedures are useful in the reduction of anxiety and fear in children. They appear to serve a primarily motivating function, and are useful in reinforcing initial responses as well as maintaining nonfearful responses once they are acquired. As with counterconditioning and modeling procedures, considerably more research is called for, especially if these procedures are to be used alone. When used in combination with these other procedures, however, they are well supported and of demonstrated clinical utility. As noted above, we have found such an integrated approach most useful in our clinical work. In the section that follows we illustrate this approach.

CS-1 CASE STUDY

The integrated assessment and treatment practices described above are illustrated here through the clinical case history of an 11-year-old highly anxious boy (Jimmy). Jimmy, the son of an accountant and elementary school teacher, had one sister, age 7. The family was of German-Catholic descent and resided in a small southeastern university town. The mother was an avid reader, while the father spent much of his leisure time working on manually oriented activities (e.g., repairing the home, tinkering with objects). Jimmy, on the other hand, was reported by his parents to be somewhat awkward and clumsy and to be uninterested in mechanical or manual activities. Her preferred to stay in the house and to read, much like his mother. Furthermore, he was described by both parents as "Mommy's boy." Jimmy's sister, on the other hand, was described as outgoing, highly sociable, and as well liked by the neighborhood children.

Jimmy and his parents were referred in mid-March by a middle-school guidance counselor because Jimmy had begun to miss school, to complain of stomachaches and headaches, and to appear "anxious or nervous most of the time." At school, he was described as a "loner," a child who had very few friends and who, at times, seemed "weird" or "strange." The counselor and teachers were most concerned with his lack of social interation and his peculiar "habits," including the making of funny noises and contorted facial grimaces. The counselor reported that these behaviors had increased gradually over the past six months since enrollment in the middle school. The only other information available at the time of referral was that Jimmy was doing poorly academically (he had just received three Ds and four Cs on his grade report). Prior to this school year, Jimmy had attended a neighborhood elementary school and had earned all Bs and As.

An initial interview was scheduled for Jimmy and his parents. Prior to the interview, the parents filled out a brief questionnaire regarding background information and the reasons for referral. The parents and Jimmy were then escorted to the interview room by the therapist. Verbatim aspects of that first interview follow:

Therapist: In our session today, I would like each of you to help me get a better understanding of the problems going on in your family. I understand that Jimmy is having some academic difficulty in school and that he seems anxious much of the time, and that you, Mom and Dad, are concerned about Jimmy and his problems. Perhaps there are other problems as well that I am not aware of. Each of you have a different view on these problems, so I would like to hear from each of you. Before we begin, I realize that it is sometimes difficult to share your concerns openly in a session like this; nonetheless, if you want me to assist you, I must hear from each of you . . . you need to tell me, as well as each other, exactly what's going on. OK. Do you have any questions before we begin? Who would like to start?

Mom: I can begin. We're so upset about Jimmy. He seems so different . . . like he's nervous all the time . . . he's just not the same Jimmy. Well, we've been meeting with the counselor at school. It seems that he is not relating well to other children and that his grades are getting worse and worse. He just got a terrible report card. He. . . . [The mother is interrupted by the therapist.]

T: So it sounds like things have not been going well for Jimmy. Jimmy, I'm wondering how you feel about the things Mom just said. Tell me in your own words what's happening [The therapist looks to Jimmy and touches him on the shoulder.]

Jimmy: I guess I'm not doing so well. . . .

T: Tell me more about that.

J: [No response. Jimmy looks down to floor, folds and unfolds his hands, and moves restlessly in the chair.]

T: It's hard to talk about it, isn't it, Jimmy? Maybe Dad can help us out here. Dad, tell me how it looks to you.

Dad: Well, I don't know. Sometimes I think Jimmy is a lot like me. . . . I didn't do well in school either and sometimes I like being alone. He. . . .

M: Well, John [Dad], this seems different. The counselor says that Jimmy's doing funny things like making noises and grunts and funny faces. Maybe that's why the kids don't like him. I know you like to be alone, too. But this is different.

D: He doesn't do that at home. At home he seems happy . . . he likes to read a lot and spend a lot of time in his room. I think he just prefers being alone.

T: Well, it sounds like the two of you might be seeing the problem a little differently. Let's come back to that later. Jimmy, tell me about your friends in school.

J: I have one . . . some kid named Eddie. That's it.

T: What do you like to do together?

J: Nothing in particular, not very much.

T: Tell me what you do at recess.

J: Go over and find a spot to sit down, or just walk around by myself. Eddie usually plays with someone else.

T: So you'd rather be alone at recess.

J: Sort of.

T: How do you feel when you are around other boys and girls?

J: Well . . . not too good.

T: I'm not sure what you mean.

J: Well . . . not so hot.

T: Not so hot?

J: Well, I just don't feel too good around them . . . sort of like I'd rather not be with them. They make me nervous.

T: How long have you felt this way?

J: Ever since I started middle school [which was about seven months ago].

T: So there's something about being in middle school that. . . .

J: Uh huh.

T: Mom and Dad, how do you see this? When did you first start to notice that Jimmy preferred to be alone?

M: Well . . . we thought everything was going pretty well at first. But then again, he never has been particularly outgoing personally. He has always been kind of a loner . . . maybe one friend or two, ever since he was little.

J: I did have one real good friend. His name was Patrick. I don't see him any more. He doesn't go to middle school.

T: It sounds like you miss him.

J: Yeah, he flunked fifth grade.

T: That's hard to lose a best friend. You probably did some neat things together.

J: Yeah.

D: What do you think, Doctor? Is Jimmy normal? Maybe he just misses his friend. He's a lot like me.

T: Certainly, a number of things are going on with Jimmy at this time. It's difficult for him to go to the new school and meet new friends. Also, he lost his best friend.

[This discussion continued for the next several minutes.]

T: Let's move on to how things are going in school. I understand that Jimmy has gotten sick at school. Tell me about that.

M: The school calls us because Jimmy got upset and his stomach started to hurt. I'm sure it hurt a great deal . . . those situations can really get you going. [Jimmy's mother briefly described her own school fears in the seventh grade.]

J: Hey, Mom, how about the time, the first time. Remember? The first time I was in the clinic?

M: I don't remember that.

J: Yes, you do. It was in September, September 3rd.

M: Did Daddy come and get you that day?

J: You both came.

D: That's right. I was home from work that day.

J: Do you remember what happened that night?

M: No, I don't. Do you, John?

D: No . . . I can't remember.

J: You don't remember when we came back from the grocery store and we heard explosions?

T: Jimmy, tell us what happened.

J: Well, uh . . . on our way home we heard these explosions and . . . uh . . . when we got home . . . uh . . . I went right into my room to check to see if my hamster was allright and . . . uh . . . I did something she wouldn't usually allow me to do. Pull her out by her tail. And . . . uh . . . I thought she had gone into hibernation and I went into the living room and showed her to Dad and he said she'd been dead for 30 seconds. [Jimmy appears very nervous, moving restlessly in his chair, stammering, and clutching his hands together.]

T: Tell us more about that.

J: I reached into where she usually slept and . . . uh . . . she . . . uh . . . and I poked at her and she didn't wake up. So I pulled her out by her tail and I didn't see her breathing.

T: Jimmy, picture that happening now. Can you imagine it?

J: Yeah.

T: How does it make you feel?

J: Just like the day at school . . . I was afraid . . . I started to cry. I didn't know what happened.

T: Picture her now. What color was your hamster?

J: She was golden. . . . I really liked her a lot . . . she was my best friend. [This dialogue continued for several minutes with Jimmy vividly describing this event in detail.]

T: Well, Jimmy, it's certainly understandable that you were upset that night. You had trouble at school, you heard the loud noises, and your favorite pet died. After that, your problems in school seemed to get worse. Is that right?

J: Yeah. It was like I didn't know what would happen next. I worry a lot. School makes me upset. I don't like to play with the other kids. Sometimes the teachers call on me, too. I don't like that. The kids laugh at me. [At this point Jimmy starts to cry in the session. His mother offers him a Kleenex while his father puts his hand on his shoulder.]

T: Well, Jimmy, you have shared a lot about yourself today. That's good. Sometimes, things seem pretty scary to you, and you are not sure what will happen next.

[The remainder of the first session was spent clarifying the presenting concerns and attempting to isolate antecedent and consequent events associated with them. The session ended with the therapist developing an initial contract with the family for further assessment and treatment.]

T: Well, we'll have to end our session today. I'm confident that we'll be able to assist you. Of course, a lot will depend on each of you and how hard each of you are willing to work. We'll need to do the following things. First, I would like you, Jimmy, to fill out these two forms [Spielberger State Trait Anxiety Inventory and the Children's Fear Survey Schedule—Revised]. These will tell me a little more about how you feel and the situations in which you feel that way. Second, I would like you, Mom and Dad, to complete this rating form together [Achenbach's Child Behavior Checklist] about Jimmy and his behavior. Third, I will be visiting the school to talk to your guidance counselor and your teachers, and to talk with you in school about how things are going. Fourth, I will have Jimmy record some things about his own behavior, and I will have you, Mom and Dad, record some things about your behavior also. We'll pinpoint these in our next session. Finally, in our next session, I'll review these forms with you and obtain more information, and then we'll map out a course of action. It's hard to tell exactly how long we'll be meeting, but it will probably be about 10 weeks. We'll meet once each week for about an hour. Do you have any questions about how we'll proceed or what will be involved? As we proceed, please feel free to make suggestions and to keep me informed as to how things are going.

Well, this has been a good session, especially for you, Jimmy. You seem like you really want to work on improving things. And Mom and Dad also want to help. That's good and a great start! OK. Let's stop for today.

As a result of this first session, Jimmy's problems were conceptualized as anxiety-related. In the session, he appeared highly anxious, fearful, and apprehensive. He seemed preoccupied with past events (e.g., his hamster's death, the loud noises), overly concerned about being evaluated (e.g., the other students making fun of him), in need of excessive reassurance (e.g., what will happen to me), and worried about future events. Furthermore, a variety of somatic complaints were evident (e.g., headaches and stomachaches), and he seemed unable to relax in the session (e.g., moving about in chair, folding and unfolding hands, etc.). This "picture" is most consistent with the more generalized overanxious disorder of childhood, although it should be noted that characteristics of separation anxiety (e.g., losing his best friend and his hamster, dependency on mother), Avoidant Disorder (e.g., entering a new social situation), and phobic disorder (e.g., fear of school) also were present. Such a picture reflects the typical scenario we encounter. Children we see do not fit nicely into simple or straightforward diagnostic categories. Nonetheless, Jimmy was anxious and fearful and clearly fit the more empirical classification of anxiety disorders described by Achenbach and others.

In the second session, the rating forms were reviewed and discussed with Jimmy and his parents separately. For the first part of the session, Jimmy was seen. On the State-Trait Anxiety Inventory for Children, Jimmy reported excessive anxiety to nearly every item on the trait scale (16 of the 20 items were marked "often"). For example, he reported "often" to the following items: "I worry about making mistakes," "I worry about things that may happen," "I get a funny feeling in my stomach," "I worry about school," and "I am secretly afraid." These scores placed him well above the normative sample and clearly in the anxious range (Spielberger, 1973). Similarly, on the state scale, Jimmy reported that he felt "very nervous," "very scared," "very frightened," "very mixed-up," and "not relaxed." Again, Jimmy's scores placed him in the highly anxious range. For the state scale, he was asked to describe how he felt, *at this very moment*, about himself and his school problems. Finally, on the Children's Fear Survey Schedule—Revised (Ollendick, 1978), Jimmy reported a multitude of fears that were related primarily to the social-evaluative factor (e.g., "giving an oral report," "looking foolish," "meeting someone for the first time," "being called on by the teacher," "having to go to school," "making mistakes," "taking a test"). Other excessive fears were less evident, although his total fear score was more than 1.5 standard deviation (SD) units above the normative sample. Clearly, he reported himself as being fearful in situations similar to those indicated on the anxiety questionnaires.

In the second part of the session, the Child Behavior Checklist (Achenbach, 1978) was reviewed with Jimmy's parents. Although the parents had some difficulty agreeing on specific items, they reported that his involvement in activities, social organizations, and school was minimal. Thus his social competency score was rated at about the fifth percentile—clearly well below that of Achenbach's normative sample. In addition, his parents agreed that it was "often true" that Jimmy was "anxious," "nervous," and "shy," that he "fears school" and "clings to adults," and that he has stomach problems," "pains," and "headaches." Although these individual items are drawn from various factors on the Achenbach profile, they all represent "internalizing" problems of an anxiety dimension.

In the last part of the second session, Jimmy shared his self-report results with his parents, who reported to Jimmy how they perceived him. The therapist mediated this discussion, encouraged the participants, and socially reinforced them for their efforts. By the end of the session, it was agreed that relaxation training would be initiated for Jimmy in the next session, that Jimmy would self-monitor the number of days he went to school and the number of times he was able to respond accurately when called on by his teachers (he was provided a handy index card for this purpose), and that the parents would self-monitor the amount of time each of them spent daily with Jimmy. This latter monitoring was initiated since one of the treatment goals was to increase the father's time spent with Jimmy and to indirectly reduce the amount of his solitary time. During the interval between the second and third sessions, the therapist was to visit the school, devise a behavioral observation system, and involve the school in Jimmy's treatment program.

At school, two teachers were recruited to assist in programming. One teacher had Jimmy in daily morning mathematics classes, and the other had him in daily afternoon reading classes. Both teachers shared "recess" duties on alternate days. These teachers were selected because of their interest in Jimmy. Representative samples of his behavior thus could be obtained during mornings and afternoons, as well as during structured (classes) and unstructured (recess) activities. The teachers unobtrusively recorded the number of times each called on him in class (they were instructed to call on him at least twice daily) and the number of recesses (20 minutes in length) in which he played with at least one other child. This latter assessment was intended to be a measure of generalization of treatment efficacy, resulting from reduced anxiety in social-evaluation situations. At this visit, the counselor also discussed Jimmy's grades and reported that he had missed an average of 2½ days of schools per week over the last month. She was asked to keep a record of his attendance and to report it weekly to the therapist. It was decided not to record the number of "weird" or "strange" behaviors in schools because of difficulties in operationalizing exactly what the teachers meant by these labels and because the treatment program was designed to reinforce positive behaviors and to ignore others.

In summary, the following measures were collected and reviewed during each successive session: (1) the State Scale of the State-Trait Anxiety Inventory, (2) Jimmy's self-monitoring of school attendance and the number of times he was able to respond accurately when called on by teachers in each class, (3) a recording of the number of times Jimmy responded accurately in class by the two representative teachers and the number of recesses he played with at least one other child, (4) the counselor's recording of school attendance and grades, and (5) the parent's recording of time spent individually with Jimmy at home.

At the third session it was revealed that (1) Jimmy's self-report of state anxiety remained high, (2) Jimmy had recorded that he went to school 3½ days and that he was able to answer the teacher correctly only twice, although he had been called on nine times by the mathematics teacher and five times by the reading teacher during that week, (3) the mathematics teacher recorded only one time that Jimmy answered correctly, whereas the reading teacher recorded none, and neither teacher had observed Jimmy play with another child during the three recesses for which he was present that week, (4) the counselor recorded 3½ days of school attendance, and (5) the mother reported that she spent an average of 62 minutes with Jimmy daily, whereas the father reported an average of only 7 minutes (these times were recorded between 5:00 P.M. and 7:30 P.M. nightly). As is evident, acceptable reliability was present for those measures where it was feasible to obtain such checks.

Treatment was multifaceted and included the following strategies spread over nine treatment sessions. Throughout treatment, the first part of each session was spent reviewing progress made on the various measures described above. Progress, or lack therof, was plotted on special graphs by Jimmy and his parents for those measures that they were recording daily. The therapist plotted the recordings from the school personnel and shared them with Jimmy and his parents. During the remainder of sessions 3–7, Jimmy was instructed in deep-muscle relaxation training and taught how to apply such training when he became anxious. Furthermore, a contract was negotiated between Jimmy and his parents so that he could earn points for purchasing a new hamster and special equipment for it (contingent on studying for 30 minutes each evening and attending school the next day). Also, his father was instructed to increase time with Jimmy each night by progressive weekly increments (up to 30 minutes a night) whereas his mother was to reduce her time concurrently (down to about 30 minutes a night). No specific contingencies were established in school; however, behavioral observations continued in this setting.

At the beginning of session 8, progress was once again reviewed. Overall, Jimmy appeared more relaxed in the session and was, by now, talking comfortably and freely about his experiences. Also, his self-report state anxiety was now at a normative level, although still in the upper range. Jimmy reported attending school every day (corroborated by counselor) and was able to answer the teachers' queries on 13 of 20 such prompted events for that week (teachers reported 15 of 20). Furthermore, the teachers reported that Jimmy had played with peers during two of the five recess periods that week. Finally, his mother and father were both spending approximately one half-hour per day with him, performing activities generated alternately by him or them. Clearly, progress had been made. Yet, Jimmy remained somewhat aloof at school, and his teachers reported that he still seems anxious and unsure of himself.

Accordingly, the teachers were now instructed to socially reinforce Jimmy whenever he responded correctly in class and to prompt and reinforce his social play at recess. These strategies were in effect across sessions 8–10 in addition to those previously described. At the 10th session, reports indicated that Jimmy had responded appropriately 17 of 21 times on the teacher's request, that he played with others at recess each day, and that he was appearing less anxious. Moreover, he had by now purchased his hamster and an elaborate set of equipment for him. A follow-up session was scheduled one month later.

At follow-up, Jimmy was readministered the Trait Anxiety Scale and the Fear Survey Schedule, and his parents completed the Child Behavior Checklist. Although Jimmy reported a moderate level of fear and anxiety, these estimates were now within the upper end of the normative distribution. Also, the parents reported on the Child Behavior Checklist that Jimmy was only "sometimes" anxious and nervous.

Overall, Jimmy's response to this treatment regimen was positive. Furthermore, multiple sources of assessment allowed us to determine the significance of change from Jimmy's own perspective as well as that of his parents and teachers. Finally, these reports of change were confirmed by actual behavioral change in the home and school settings. Although we cannot claim or illustrate this degree of success with all of our anxious clients (unfortunately), this case study highlights the diverse assessment and treatment procedures that are potentially useful in the outpatient treatment of anxious children. Whether all of these strategies were necessary is, of course, unknown. Each strategy, however, was used in an attempt to address "specific" areas uncovered through assessment. Although significant change may have occurred in the absence of such comprehensive assessment and integrated treatment, our clinical efforts have been guided by a philosophy that suggests that we provide our clients thorough as well as expedient clinical treatment. The diminished experimental rigor and finesse evident in such applications are typical of such interventions when applied in clinical settings (Ollendick & Cerny, 1981).

SUMMARY

In this chapter we have examined a number of issues related to the outpatient treatment of children who evince fearful and anxious behavior. Issues related to the diagnosis, assessment, and treatment of anxiety disorders in children were specifically addressed and illustrated in a clinical case study. Clearly, anxiety disorders in children are complex and do not represent a unitary syndrome. The complexity of these disorders is further complicated by specific developmental features of the growing child that necessitate special assessment and treatment practices. Several of these practices were reviewed and utilized in the clinical case illustration.

At this time, it seems safe to conclude that much remains to be learned about children and their special fears and anxieties. Our base of knowledge is continually increasing, and our resultant clinical practice, although unpolished and characterized by rough edges, appears highly promising. Surely, this area of study represents a significant challenge and one in need of further articulation.

REFERENCES

Achenbach, T. M. The classification of children's psychiatric symptoms: A factor-analytic approach. *Psychological Monographs*, 1966. *80*, 7 (Whole No. 615).

Achenbach, T. M. The child behavior profile, I. Boys aged 6–11. *Journal of Consulting and Clinical Psychology*, 1978, *46*, 759–776.

Achenbach, T. M. The child behavior profile: An empirically based system for assessing children's behavioral problems and competences. *International Journal of Mental Health*, 1979, *7*, 24–42.

Achenbach, T. M. DSM-III in light of empirical research on the classification of child psychopathology. *Journal of the American Academy of Child Psychiatry*, 1980, *19*, 395–412.

Achenbach, T. M., & Edelbrock, C. S. The child behavior profile, II. Boys aged 12–16 and girls aged 6–11 and 12–16. *Journal of Consulting and Clinical Psychology*, 1979, *47*, 223–233.

Achenbach, T. M., & Edelbrock, C. S. Taxonomic issues in child psychopathology. In T. H. Ollendick & M. Hersen (Eds.), *Handbook of child psychopathology*. New York: Plenus Press, 1983.

Ayllon, T., Smith, D., & Rogers, M. Behavioral management of school phobia. *Journal of Behavior Therapy and Experimental Psychiatry*, 1970, *1*, 125–138.

American Psychiatric Association. *Diagnostic and statistical manual of mental disorders (DSM-III)* (3rd ed.). Washington, D.C.: Author, 1980.

Bandura, A. Modeling approaches to the modification of phobic disorders. In R. Porter (Ed.), *Ciba Foundation Symposium: The role of learning in psychotherapy*. London: Churchill, 1968.

Bandura, A. *Principles of behavior modification.* New York: Holt, 1969.

Barrios, B. A., Hartmann, D. B., & Shigetomi, C. Fears and anxieties in children. In E. J. Mash & L. G. Terdal (Eds.) *Behavioral assessment of childhood disorders.* New York: Guilford Press, 1981.

Cantwell, D. P., Russell, A. T., Mattison, T., & Will, L. A comparison of *DSM-II* and *DSM-III* in the diagnosis of childhood psychiatric disorders: I. Agreement with expected diagnosis. *Archives of General Psychiatry,* 1979, *36,* 1208–1213. (a)

Cantwell, D. P., Russell, A. T., Mattison, R., & Will, L. A comparison of *DSM-II* and *DSM-III* in the diagnosis of childhood psychiatric disorders: IV. Difficulties in use, global comparison, and conclusions. *Archives of General Psychiatry,* 1979, *36,* 1227–1228. (b)

Castaneda, A., McCandless, B. R., & Palmero, D. S. The children's form of the Manifest Anxiety Scale. *Child Development,* 1956, *27,* 317–326.

Chess, S., Thomas, A., & Birch, H. G. Distortions in developmental reporting made by parents of behaviorally disturbed children. *Journal of the American Academy of Child Psychiatry,* 1966, *5,* 226–236.

Ciminero, A. R., & Drabman, R. S. Current developments in the behavioral assessment of children. In B. B. Lahey & A. E. Kazdin (Eds.), *Advances in clinical child psychology (Vol. 1).* New York: Plenum Press 1977.

Glennon, B., & Weisz, J. R. An observational approach to the assessment of anxiety in young children. *Journal of Consulting and Clinical Psychology,* 1978, *46,* 1246–1257.

Graziano, A. M. (Ed.). *Behavior therapy with children* (Vol. 2). Chicago: Aldine, 1975.

Graziano, A. M., Mooney, K. C., Huber, C., & Ignasiak, D. Self-control instruction for children's fear-reduction. *Journal of Behavior Therapy and Experimental Psychiatry,* 1979, *10,* 221–227.

Harris, S. L. *DSM-III:* Its implications for children. *Child Behavior Therapy,* 1979, *1,* 37–48.

Hatzenbuehler, L. C., & Schroeder, H. E. Desensitization procedures in the treatment of childhood disorders. *Psychological Bulletin,* 1978, *85,* 831–844.

Herjanic, B., Herjanic, M., Brown, F., & Wheatt, T. Are children reliable reporters? *Journal of Abnormal Child Psychology,* 1975, *3,* 41–48.

Hersen, M. Behavior modification approach to a school phobia case. *Journal of Clinical Psychology,* 1970, *26,* 128–132.

Jones, M. C. The elimination of children's fears. *Journal of Experimental Psychology,* 1924, *7,* 382–390. (a)

Jones, M. C. A laboratory study of fear: The case of Peter. *Journal of Genetic Psychology,* 1924, *31,* 308–315. (b)

Kanfer, F. H., Karoly, P., & Newman, A. Reduction of children's fear of the dark by competence-related and situational threat-related verbal cues. *Journal of Consulting and Clinical Psychology,* 1975, *43* 251–258.

Kazdin, A. E. Assessing the clinical or applied importance of behavior change through social validation. *Behavior Modification,* 1977, *4,* 427–452.

Lick, J. R., & Katkin, E. S. Assessment of anxiety and fear. In M. Hersen & A. S. Bellack (Eds.), *Behavioral assessment.* New York: Pergamon Press, 1976.

Marks, I. M. Behavioral treatment of phobic and obsessive-compulsive disorders: A critical appriasal. In M. Hersen, R. M. Eisler, & P. M. Miller (Eds.), *Progress in behavior modification* (Vol. I). New York: Academic Press, 1975.

Mattison, R., Cantwell, D. P., Russell, A. T., & Will, L. A comparison of *DSM-II* and *DSM-III* in the diagnosis of childhood psychiatric disorders: III. Multiaxial features. *Archives of General Psychiatry,* 1979, *36,* 1217–1222.

Miller, L. C., Barrett, C. L., Hampe, E., & Noble, H. Revised anxiety scales for the Louisville Behavior Checklist, *Psychological Reports*, 1972, *29*, 503–511.

Neisworth, J. T., Madle, R. A., & Goeke, K. E. "Errorless" elimination of separation anxiety: A case study. *Journal of Behavior Therapy and Experimental Psychiatry*, 1975, *6*, 79–82.

Ollendick, T. H. The Fear Survey Schedule for Children—Revised. Unpublished manuscript, Indiana State University, 1978.

Ollendick, T. H. Fear reduction techniques with children. In M. Hersen, R. M. Eisler, & P. M. Miller (Eds.), *Progress in behavior modification* (Vol. 8). New York: Academic Press, 1979.

Ollendick, T. H. Self-monitoring and self-administered overcorrection: The modification of nervous tics in children. *Behavior Modification*, 1981, *5*, 75–84.

Ollendick, T. H. Psychometric properties of the Fear Survey Schedule for Children—Revised. Unpublished manuscript, Virginia Polytechnic Institute and State University, 1982.

Ollendick, T. H., & Cerny, J. A. *Clinical behavior therapy with children.* New York: Plenum Press, 1981.

Ollendick, T. H., & Gruen, G. E. Treatment of a bodily injury phobia with implosive therapy. *Journal of Consulting and Clinical Psychology*, 1972, *38*, 389–393.

Ollendick, T. H., & Hersen, M. An historical introduction to child psychopathology. In T. H. Ollendick & M. Hersen (Eds.), *Handbook of child psychopathology.* New York: Plenum Press, 1983.

Ollendick, T. H., & Mayer, J. A. School phobia. In S. M. Turner (Ed.), *Behavioral treatment of anxiety disorders.* New York: Plenum Press, 1983.

Ollendick, T. H., & Ollendick, D. G. Anxiety disorders in the mentally retarded. In J. L. Matson & R. P. Barrett (Eds.), *Psychopathology of the mentally retarded.* New York: Grune & Stratton, 1982.

Quay, H. C. Classification. In H. C. Quay & J. S. Werry (Eds.), *Psychopathological disorders of childhood* (2nd ed.). New York: Wiley, 1979.

Reynolds, C. R. Concurrent validity of "What I Think and Feel": The Revised Children's Manifest Anxiety Scale. *Journal of Consulting and Clinical Psychology*, 1980, *48*, 774–775.

Reynolds, C. R., & Richmond, B. O. "What I Think and Feel": A revised measure of children's manifest anxiwty. *Journal of Abnormal Child Psychology*, 1978, *6*, 271–280.

Reynolds, C. R., & Richmond, B. O. Factor structure and construct validity of "What I Think and Feel": The Revised Children's Manifest Anxiety Scale. *Journal of Personality Assessment*, 1979, *43*, 281–282.

Ross, D., Ross, S., & Evans, T. A. The modification of extreme social withdrawal by modification with guided practice. *Journal of Behavior Therapy and Experimental Psychiatry*, 1971, *2*, 273–279.

Rutter, M., & Shaffer, D. *DSM-III:* A step forward or backward in terms of the classification of child psychiatric disorders? *Journal of the American Academy of Child Psychiatry*, 1980, *19*, 371–394.

Ryall, M. R., & Deitiker, K. E. Reliability and clinical validity of the Children's Fear Survey Schedule. *Journal of Behavior Therapy and Experimental Psychiatry*, 1979, *10*, 303–309.

Scherer, M. W., & Nakamura, C. Y. A fear survey schedule for children. *Behaviour Research and Therapy*, 1968, *6*, 173–182.

Smith, R. E., & Sharpe, T. M. Treatment of a school phobia with implosive therapy. *Journal of Consulting and Clinical Psychology*, 1970, *35*, 239–243.

Spielberger, C. D. *Manual for the state-trait anxiety inventory for children.* Palo Alto, Calif.: Consulting Psychologists Press, 1973.

Watson, J. B., & Rayner, R. Conditioned emotional reactions. *Journal of Experimental Psychology,* 1920, *3,* 1–14.

Wolpe, J. *Psychotherapy by reciprocal inhibition.* Stanford, Calif.: Stanford University Press, 1958.

11

Conduct Disorders

Alan M. Gross

CONDUCT PROBLEMS are the most commonly cited reason for referral of a child or adolescent to a behavior therapist's office (Patterson, Reid, Jones, & Conger, 1975). Parents of these youngsters often complain that their children display high rates of one or more of the following responses: disobedience with adult authorities, aggressiveness toward others, physical destructiveness, temper tantrums, and high rates of annoying behavior (e.g., yelling). In some instances there also are reports of community rule violations such as stealing (Patterson, 1974; Wells & Forehand, 1981). Typically, these behaviors do not occur in isolation, and most youths considered to be conduct problems by parents and/or teachers display a variety of these responses. Parents of these youngsters often report feeling helpless and unable to control their children's behavior. Although these youths have been referred to as *oppositional* or *socially aggressive* (e.g., Wahler 1969), they are more commonly labeled *conduct-disordered children*.

For many years the most utilized treatment approach with families of conduct-disordered children was traditional insight-oriented psychotherapy. Following publication of reviews in the early 1960s suggesting that this form of treatment did not yield improvements very different from what was observed when these children received no treatment (Levitt, 1963), however, there was a dramatic increase in experimentation in treating this disorder by use of behavioral methods. Recent literature reviews suggest that behavioral therapies are capable of ameliorating conduct disorders in children (Graziano, 1977) and that behavior change produced is most often maintained (Patterson & Fleischman, 1979). The purpose of this chapter is to discuss various behavioral approaches to treating conduct disorders. Rather than present a detailed review of the area, an attempt is made to synthesize this information and present it in a practical "how to" format. Included in this chapter is a brief description of the clinical characteristics of conduct disordered families as well as a discussion of behavioral formulations of this problem. This is followed by a presentation of how to's of conducting a clinical assessment, various treatment techniques, and problems encountered when employing these procedures. Additionally, a case study is included to help illustrate this methodology.

BEHAVIORAL AND FAMILY DESCRIPTION

A number of behavior-analytic studies have been conducted describing the behavioral characteristsics of conduct disordered children and their families. Patterson (1976) observed 27 aggressive and 27 non-problem boys in their home environments. The youth's responses were monitored by using a complex behavioral observation code. In comparing the behavior of the two samples it was noted that the aggressive boys exhibited significantly higher rates of noncompliance, disapproval, negativism, teasing, physically negative responses, yelling, and negative demands. Similar field studies have replicated these findings (e.g., Forehand, King, Peed, & Yoder, 1975; Lobitz & Johnson, 1975).

Studies comparing the families of conduct-disordered and normal children also have revealed significant differences in the behavior of parents toward their youngsters. Lobitz and Johnson (1975) observed parent–child interactions in both normal and conduct-disordered children in home and clinic settings. Parents of the deviant children were significantly more negative toward their children than were the parents of nonproblem youths. Similarly, in a clinic setting, Forehand et al. (1975) observed that mothers of oppositional youngsters emitted a significantly higher rate of commands and criticisms to their children than did nonclinic mothers.

The data presented in the above studies suggest that there are significant behavioral differences between the families of conduct-disordered children and their parents and the families of nonproblem youngsters. In particular, the families of conduct-disordered youngsters are characterized by a high frequency of aversive or negative parent–child interactions. It is important to note, however, that although statistically significant differences have been found between conduct-disordered and normal families, considerable overlap on the behavioral variables measured also exists (Lobitz & Johnson, 1975). For example, in the Lobitz and Johnson (1975) investigation, a number of the children in the clinic sample could not be differentiated from the normal nonclinic youths on the basis of behavioral measures. Examination of the parental perception of deviance questionnaire data, however, revealed more clear-cut differences between referred and nonreferred subjects. This indicates that in some cases parents may consider their child a conduct problem although he or she cannot be differentiated from normal youngsters on the basis of behavior. This latter point highlights the importance of considering parental standards for child behavior when assessing and treating conduct disordered youngsters and their families.

BEHAVIORAL FORMULATIONS OF CONDUCT DISORDERS

Patterson (1976) has developed a theory accounting for the development of conduct disorders. The coercion hypothesis is based on the principle of negative reinforcement. Patterson's observations revealed that in conduct-disordered families the most common form of behavioral control exhibited by family memberts involved aversive control strategies. He suggested that aversive behaviors such as crying may be instinctual in newborns. In fact, these behaviors are adaptive in that they serve to shape skills in the mother (e.g., feeding) that are necessary for the infant's survival. As the child grows older it is assumed that the youngster will learn more socially appropriate behavior to cue parental responding, rather than continue to rely on aversive control methods. In certain instances, however, the child may fail to acquire these new skills. Patterson (1976) speculates that this social skill deficit could possibly occur as a result of a lack of exposure to appropriate models, failure of parents to reinforce prosocial behavior, or parents continuing to respond to the child's coercive behavior, thus failing to set the stage for extinction of these responses.

In the above situation, youngsters will continue to apply aversive control stategies with their parents because these behaviors are frequently negatively reinforced. That is, their aversive behavior (e.g., cyring) results in the elimination of a parental aversive behavior. For example, children often throw tantrums on being told they must turn off the television and go to bed. If the tantrum (aversive child behavior) is followed by removal of the command (parental aversive behavior), the tantrum behavior (as well as use of an aversive control strategy) is negatively reinforced. Moreover, this same paradigm also can account for the development of coercive behavior in parents. In the example cited above, it also is possible that rather than removing the parental command following the occurrence of the tantrum, the youngster's mother might repeat the command and begin to yell or threaten the child. If this coercive parental behavior is followed by compliance from the child, parental aversive behavior would be negatively reinforced by the removal of an aversive (tantrum) event. Hence it can be seen that the potential for the development of a high rate of coercive behavior between parent and child is indeed great. In support of this position, Patterson (1977) has recently presented data indicating that coercive parent–child interactions in conduct-disordered families are generally initiated and accelerated by a family member's negative behavior.

Wahler (1976) suggests that positive reinforcement also plays a large part in the development of conduct disorders. He believes that many of the aversive or inappropriate behaviors displayed by children are positively reinforced through physical and verbal attention from parents. A number of investigators have demonstrated that contingent adult attention can serve as a reinforcer in children's behavior modification programs. It is also the case that following the display of bad behavior by children, significant adults (e.g., parents, teachers) provide them with attention by attempting to reason with them about why they should not emit these responses. Wahler suggests that in instances where parental attention rarely occurs in the presence of appropriate behavior but regularly follows the child's bad behavior and attention is a reinforcer for a child, this parental response serves to reinforce inappropriate responding. In all probability it is most likely that both positive and negative reinforcement contribute to the development and maintenance of conduct disorders.

CLINICAL ASSESSMENT

A necessary component of every treatment intervention is the clinical assessment. Initially, this process helps in defining the problem, identifying the target behavior(s) and controlling variables, and selecting the appropriate treatment strategy. Following implementation of the treatment program, assessment serves to monitor the progress of therapy as well as to provide feedback for making clinically sound adjustments in treatment. The behavioral assessment of conduct disorders in children generally involves one or more of the following procedures: behavioral interviews, behavioral questionnaires, and direct observation.

The interview is the first contact the therapist has with the referred child and his or her parents. The therapist's goal during this meeting is to verbally identify the behaviors to be treated as well as the antecedent and consequent conditions surrounding these responses (Atkinson & Forehand, 1981). The focus of the interview is on both parent and child behaviors. This is consistent with that conduct disorders are a function of parent–child interactions, and as such both parent and child behavior will be targeted for treatment.

The therapist generally begins the first interview by meeting alone with parents. During this time, demographic information about the child and his or her family (e.g., age; grade in school; number of siblings; parents' ages, education and occupation) is gathered. This is followed by an attempt to obtain data concerning typical parent–child interactions that are considered to be problems. This latter issue often is initiated by general questions from the therapist. For example, parents may be asked what brought them to the clinic or to describe the problems they are having with their child. Because emphasis of the interview is to ascertain the antecedents and consequences of the child's behavior, the therapist prompts parents whether various problem situations that are common to conduct-disordered children are also a problem in their family. In particular, they can be asked if the youngster is disruptive in situations such as meals, bedtime, in the car, while shopping, or when given instructions to do a chore. On identifying a problem area the therapist begins to probe in greater depth. Questions asking for a description of the problem situation, the child's behavior ("Tell me what your child does exactly"), the parent's behavior ("What do you do when your child behaves in that manner?"), and the youngster's response to parental actions ("What does your child do after you do that?") are appropriate. This line of questioning continues until the therapist has a clear understanding of parent–child interactions. Additionally, information concerning duration and frequency of problems responses is also collected.

As opposed to simply asking parents open-ended questions about problem situations and behaviors, some therapists structure the initial interview. Patterson et al. (1975) have parents fill out a Symptom Checklist. Each symptom is presented with a clear definition to enable parents to clearly understand the meaning of the term. If parents consider a behavior from the checklist to be a problem, the therapist asks detailed interview procedure has yet to be conducted. However, there appears to be little reason to believe that one would be significantly better than the other at extracting the necessary information.

Some interviewers also seek to obtain from parents developmental history data on the youngster. This information generally is not very useful in treatment development. However, Haynes (1978) suggests that such information may assist parents in understanding how the problem developed and may pinpoint conditions under which the problem is likely to reemerge.

A portion of the initial interview should be reserved for talking alone with the child. With children under 5 years of age, the therapist can expect that this will lead to little content information of utility, although this is not necessarily the case with older youngsters. This interview generally begins with the therapist asking the child why he or she thinks he or she has been brought to the clinic. Following the child's response, the therapist usually shares his or her opinion about this issue with the child. The therapist's reply attempts to convey to the child that the whole family would like to work to make things more pleasant for everyone at home. The therapist may also ask about family and peer interactions as well as personally preferred activities. These questions help the therapist to determine events that may serve as rewards in the treatment program. It is important to note that although some practical information can be obtained in the interview with the child, the major goal is to convey that the family and not the child is going to be the focus of treatment and that his or her thoughts and feelings will be important factors in the formulation of the intervention strategy.

After interviewing the child the therapist generally concludes the assessment interview with a brief summary discussion with the youngster's parents. During this time the therapist presents his or her conceptualization of the problem to the parents. Suggestions as to which problem area should immediately be targeted are also discussed. Finally, the parents are given an overview regarding the therapist's approach to treating this type of disorder.

BEHAVIORAL QUESTIONNAIRES

All assessment devices must meet certain levels of reliability and validity. Unfortunately, there are few empirical data demonstrating that the behavioral interview is a reliable and valid assessment tool. However, it is clear that it is, and will continue to be, one of the most popular assessment tools available to clinicioans. It has been suggested, therfore, that because of its limited empirical underpinnings the interview should be used in conjunction with other assessment devices (Atkinson & Forehand, 1981).

Behavioral questionaires have been used as an extension of the behavioral interview. Haynes (1978) suggests that questionnaires have several advantages over interviews: (1) they are self-administered; (2)

scoring and interpreting are not very time-consuming; (3) and most importantly, they provide quantitative data. It is also possible that as a function of their comprehensive list of problem behaviors they may tap problems that were not identified in the interview (Ciminero & Drabman, 1977).

A variety of questionnaires are available for assessing problem behavior in children. However, none is specifically designed for assessing conduct disordered youths (Atkinson & Forehand, 1981). Currently utilized questionnaires focus on aggressiveness and acting out, as well as on problem behaviors such as hyperactivity, destructiveness, lying, stealing, enuresis, irritability, and crying, to name only a few. In the assessement of conduct disorders, the Bipolar Adjective Checklist (Becker, 1960), the Walker Problem Behavior Identification Checklist (Walker, 1970), the Behavior Problem Checklist (Peterson, 1961), and the Parent Attitude Test (Cowen, Huser, Beach, & Rappaport, 1970) are commonly employed.

The Parent Attitude Test (PAT) is the most popular questionnaire used in the assessment of conduct disorders and therefore will be the only one discussed in detail. The PAT consists of four separate scales that measure parent perceptions and attitudes about child behavior. The individual scales include the (1) Home Attitude Scale, (2) School Attitude Scale, (3) Behavior Rating Scale, and (4) the Adjective Checklist. The Home Attitude Scale contains seven items designed to tap parental perceptions about the child's adjustment at home. Each question is rated on a scale from 1 to 5, with 1 meaning very poorly and 5 meaning very well. Questions like the following are found on this scale: "As far as my child's behavior at home is concerned, he is doing. . . ." Constructed along similar guidelines is the School Attitude Scale. This scale contains four school-related items (e.g., "When my child talks about school, it seems as if. . . .") that are noted on a 1–5 continuum of "dislikes it very much" to "likes it very much." The Behavior Rating Scale of the PAT contains 25 items that refer to overt deviant behavior (e.g., crying, yelling, tantrums). Each item is scored on a scale of 1–5 with 1 meaning does not apply and 5 meaning shows very strongly. Finally, the Adjective Checklist Scale consists of 34 adjectives that are intended to reflect personality characteristics or behaviors. Examples of items from this scale include adjectives such as alert, shy, careless, and tense. The items are noted on a continuum from 1 (does not apply) to 3 (shows very strongly). Cowen et al. (1970) have presented reliability and validity data in support of this instrument. Additionally, Forehand and his associates (Forehand & King, 1977, Forehand, Sturgis, McMahon, Aguar, Green, Wells, & Breiner, 1979) indicate that changes in the PAT often accompany changes in behavioral measures of treatment effectiveness in families of conduct disordered families.

As mentioned earlier, questionnaires are inexpensive and relatively simple methods of collecting assessment data. However, they are not without their limitations. The answers provided by parents on these indices are subject to situational biases. Forehand, Griest, and Wells (1979) found that parental responses to the PAT do not always reflect the observed behavior of children in natural settings. Reliability and validity data for these instruments are not always very strong (Wells, 1981). Additionally, questionnaires do not provide information that will help the clinician identify antecedent and consequent conditions that control problem responses.

The major strength of parent questionnaires is in identifying problem areas that are overlooked during the parent interview. These situations can then be explored in more depth by verbally questioning parents (Patterson et al., 1975). When combined with direct observations of the child, questionnaires may also help the clinician determine whether parent expectations for child behavior are overly high and whether there is a need for educating parents about age-appropriate child behavior. Finally, the use of questionnaires pre- and posttreatment may provide a measure of parent satisfaction with treatment outcome. It is important to emphasize that questionnaires and rating scales are useful as an additional component of a clinical assessment. Used in isolation, however, they are an inadequate measure on which to attempt to develop a comprehensive treatment program.

DIRECT OBSERVATION

Perhaps the best assessment tool for use in treating conduct-disordered children is direct observation. Direct observation avoids many of the limitations of other assessment strategies and can provide a detailed account of parent–child behavior. In particular, this approach allows the therapist to obtain measures of relative frequency and duration of the inappropriate behavior as well as to obtain a better understanding of the antecedent and consequent conditions that influence the occurence of the response.

Unfortunately, direct observation is expensive and time-consuming, and few private practice clinicians have the luxury of graduate assistants or paraprofessionals who can observe the child and his or her parents in the home setting. However, a number of investigators have suggested that useful information regarding parent–child behavior can be gathered by observing their behavior in the clinic (Hughes & Haynes, 1978).

Clinical observations are generally conducted in a playroom setting. The room is equipped with a one-way mirror, table and chairs, and age-appropriate toys. Although observation procedures differ, most provide parents with instructions that are intended to elicit problem behaviors from the child. Eyberg and Johnson (1974) instruct parents to engage in six different interactions with their child during the observation session. Forehand and Peed (1979) use a similar procedure, providing instructions to parents using a parent bug in the ear electronic communications device. In particular, parents are instructed to alternate between child-determined and parent-directed play. It is hoped that by switching from free play to parent-directed play there will be optimum opportunity to observe the youngster display noncompliant behavior as well as to monitor parental responses to such responding.

While viewing through the one-way mirror the therapist codes a number of parent and child behaviors. Child behaviors of compliance and noncompliance to parental requests and inappropriate responses are most often monitored. Additionally, the following parental behaviors are also noted: rewards, commands, questions, attends, and warnings, as well as the use of punishment procedures (e.g., time out). Frequency of behavior over 30-second intervals is a method of recording commonly employed (Peed et al., 1977). This allows data to be summarized in either total number of responses, rate per minute, or percentage of intervals in which the response occurred. Forehand and his colleagues (Forehand & Peed, 1977; Peed et al., 1977) recommend that observations should last 10 minutes. This relatively short monitoring period allows for observations to be made during every clinic visit. The technique thus allows for continuous monitoring of treatment progress, providing information to therapists so they can give feedback to parents regarding their use of procedures taught.

Because clinical observation systems are used as an analog measure of child–parent behavior occurring in the home environment, the validity of this method must be addressed. Although most studies have found that parent–child interactions observed in the clinic reflect those occurring in the home, there are conflicting data (Hughes & Haynes, 1978). This suggests that if both clinic and home observations are not feasible, the therapist must use the interview situation to question parents about the similarity of clinic behavior to behavior exhibited in the home (Atkinson & Forehand, 1981).

Although direct observation of parent–child interactions in the home can be expensive and time consuming, it is the optimum approach to assessment. A number of home observation systems for use with conduct-disordered children have been developed. One of the first technologies invented was the Behavioral Coding System (BCS) (Patterson, Ray, Shaw, & Cobb, 1969). The BCS was designed to monitor family social interactions. Each BCS observation session lasts approximately one hour. During this time each family member's behavior is monitored for a continuous five-minute segment. After every individual in the family is viewed, the observation series is repeated. While the observation is being conducted it is required that every family member be present and remain in two adjoining rooms, with no guests permitted in the home, no outgoing telephone calls made and incoming calls answered only briefly, no television viewing permitted, and no discussion with observers allowed. Each persons social interactions are coded according to 29 behavioral categories. These categories are divided into two groups, responses and consequences. Command, cry, yell, talk, humiliate, and tease are examples of items considered responses. Consequences include ignore, approve, compliance, and attention. [For a complete description of the BCS, see Patterson and Cobb (1971).]

Similar to the clinic observation methods described, a frequency count on the various behaviors is conducted. The data are most often summarized in a rate-per-minute figure. Additionally, the BCS provides information regarding antecedent-response-consequences relationships (Patterson, 1977). Finally, Patterson suggests using the BCS throughout the treatment program. This yields important information about treatment impact. Home observation systems modeled after the BCS have been developed by Wahler, House, and Stanbaugh (1976) and Forehand and Peed (1979). Moreover, validity data on these three observation techniques indicate that the procedures can reliably discriminate problem from nonproblem youngsters (Atkinson & Forehand, 1981).

Direct observation of problem behavior in the natural environment clearly has many advantages over interview and questionnaire assessment techniques. However, there also are various difficulties associated with this approach. In particular, observer error, reliabiltiy of observation, reactivity of subjects to the monitoring process, and the effect of setting instructions can influence data collection. These difficulties can be minimized by utilizing procedures such as numerous hours of observer training, observers being subject to frequent reliability checks, use of observers who are unaware of treatment conditions, and frequent assessments. All these procedures increase the amount of time and personnel that must be devoted to assessment. Few practicing clinicians have the flexibility required to implement such a formal system.

The three major assessment techniques carried out in work with conduct disordered families have been presented. Although direct observation in the natural environment is the best available technique, it is clear that it may be the most difficult for practicing therapists to utilize. As such, the behavioral interview will remain the most common approach to assessment. It is recommended that this procedure be supplemented with clinic observations. When a discrepancy arises between clinic observations and parental reports of behavior, however, home observations are indicated. In such cases it may be helpful for clinicians to keep in mind that the behavioral coding systems described were designed to provide a rigorous measure of treatment impact in clinical research settings. As desirable as it may be to implement such programs in the private practice setting, it also is important to acknowledge the limitations of private practice clinicians. Skilled clinicians who are aware of these systems may be able to adapt them to their needs.

Classroom behavior problems are often seen in conjunction with conduct disorders. As such, it is often necessary to perform an assessment of child–teacher difficulties. Use of the guidelines presented in the assessment procedures described for use with parents will provide the necessary information regarding antecedent–response–consequence stimuli. Chapter 12 provides an excellent examination of assessment and treatment of school problems. As such, this component of treating conduct disorders is not addressed here.

TREATMENT—PARENT TRAINING

The behavioral formulation of the development of conduct disorders suggests that these deviant behaviors are shaped and maintained by positive and negative reinforcers delivered through child–parent interactions. Hence, it comes as no surprise that the emphasis in treatment has been on teaching parents to alter their behavior toward their children.

Early intervention programs involved teaching parents to ignore inappropriate behavior and provide attention for appropriate child responses. Williams (1959) reported eliminating bedtime tantrum behavior in a 21-month-old boy. The boy's parents were instructed to place the child in bed when it was time for him to go to sleep and not to reenter his room regardless of his aversive behavior. Tantrums ceased after the procedure had been in effect for eight days. Similarly, Russo (1964) has reported modifying oppositional and aggressive behavior in two children by instructing the youth's parents to ignore deviant behavior and to attend to their prosocial responses.

Although training parents in the use of differential reinforcement has been reported as an effective procedure, a number of investigators have failed to successfully alter deviant child behavior using this technique. Wahler (1969) found that differential attention resulted in an increase in oppositional behavior in five families in which the target youngster exhibited high rates of deviant behavior. Herbert, Pinkston, Hayden, Sajwaj, Pinkston, Cordua, and Jackson (1973) have reported similar results.

Following the observation that differential attention was not an effective technique with all conduct-disordered children, a number of investigators suggested that its effectiveness might be enhanced if used in conjunction with a punishment procedure. Zeilberger, Sampon, and Sloane (1968) treated a 5-year-old conduct problem boy using a combination of differential attention and time out. The youngster's mother was instructed to place the boy in an isolated place in the house for two minutes following the display of deviant behavior. She was also told to deliver attention to the youth when he exhibited prosocial behavior. It was reported that the procedures rapidly produced the desired behavior change. A number of other investigators have indicated that the combination of differential attention and time out from reinforcement can be an effective treatment with conduct-problem children (Kelley, Embry, & Bahr, 1979; Wahler, 1969).

Initially, the investigation of parent training as a treatment modality primarily involved case studies. The promising success rate evidenced with this approach led to the development and evaluation of more comprehensive training programs. The first such program was created by Patterson (Patterson, 1974; Patterson, Cobb, & Ray, 1973). His treatment program is divided into three stages. Movement from one stage to the next is dependent upon successful completion of the preceding stage. The first phase of training involves teaching parents the language and concepts of behavioral theory. Parents are required to read one of two programmed texts that have been written by Patterson (Patterson, 1971; Patterson & Guillon, 1968). These texts cover concepts such as reinforcement, punishment, and response–consequence relationships. Additionally, the practical aspects of the procedures associated with these concepts also are presented. When the parents pass a written test on this material they may begin the second stage of treatment. Here, parents are taught to define deviant behavior and monitor and record its occurrence. Additionally, they are asked to specify two of their child's deviant responses and two of his or her appropriate responses. Parents then are instructed to record these behaviors in the home for a three-day period. This homework assignment provides parents with the opportunity to experiment with the procedures. Moreover, this initial practical experience stimulates discussion about parental perceptions regarding frequency and intensity of their child's inappropriate behavior. Following successful completion of this assignment, the third stage of treatment is implemented. Parents attempt to modify one or two of their child's problem behaviors. They are told to continue monitoring the occurrence of these responses and to begin delivering specific consequences to the child for these actions. Generally, parents are taught to set up a point system whereby the youngster is awarded points (and social reinforcers) for appropriate behavior and loses points for inappropriate responding. The points are later exchanged for back up reinforcers (a more detailed description of token economy point systems will follow shortly).

Patterson has provided extensive data demonstrating the effectiveness of this treatment program (Patterson, 1974: Patterson et al., 1973); Patterson & Reid, 1973). Additionally, his findings suggest that the procedures result in long term maintenance (Patterson & Fleischman, 1979) and that treatment effects may generalize to untreated siblings (Arnold, Levine, & Patterson, 1975). Although some investigators have reported difficulty replicating Patterson's results (e.g., Ferber, Keeley, & Shemberg, 1974), their findings are very likely a function of their not being as familiar with the application of this program as the Patterson group.

Forehand (1977) has developed a parent training program modeled after Patterson's. Forchand's program, however, differs in a number of ways. Rather than target one deviant behavior, the program attempts to foster a general change in parent–child interactions. As such, training takes place in a controlled learning environment (clinic) in which parent behaviors are directly shaped during in vivo training. Additionally, rather than emphasizing the use of a point system to modify behaviors, Forehand concentrates on teaching parents better verbal commanding skills in conjunction with differential attention and time out procedures. Finally, the children of parents in the Forehand group are usually 2–8 years of age, whereas Patterson's subjects most often are 5–13 years of age (Wells & Forehand, 1981).

The essence of the parent training programs described involves teaching parents to alter the immediate parental antecedents and consequences of deviant and positive child behaviors. In particular, regarding antecedent behaviors, parents are taught to give clear, direct commands to their children ("Pick up your toys right now."), to issue simple warnings about the consequences that will occur if misbehavior occurs a second time, and the use of explicitly stated rules regarding behavior consequence relationships (e.g., "If you fail to go right to bed tonight, you will go to bed ½ hour earlier tomorrow."). Procedures used to alter consequences involve tangible rewards (tokens, treats) and/or attention for appropriate behavior (e.g., "What a good girl you are, picking up your toys!"), and ignoring or delivering time out for inappropriate behavior.

A procedure commonly taught to parents in order to help them reward their child's prosocial behavior is the Premack principle. This involves making the occurrence of a high probability event contingent on the occurrence of a low probability behavior. For example, room cleaning can be rewarded by it earning the youngster an opportunity to go out and play. Similarly, completing the day's homework assignment can earn the youth the privilege of watching television. This procedure is relatively easy to employ, and its use may lead to assisting parents in learning to explicitly state behavior–consequence relationships and rules.

As noted above, time out from reinforcement also is generally used in parent training programs. Recent research suggests that a number of variables may influence the effectiveness of this procedure. For example, White, Nielsen, and Johnson (1972) found that in comparing differing time-out durations, previous experience with this procedure influenced the effectiveness of the various time out periods. Scarboro and Forehand (1975) reported that although there was no difference in overall effectiveness between time-out procedures in which a child's mother either left the youngster alone or merely discontinued contact with the child, within-room time out required significantly more applications of the technique to obtain the desired behavior change. After reviewing the literature, Hobbs and Forehand (1977) suggested that the following conditions enhance the effectiveness of time out: (1) duration of three to five minutes, (2) release from time out contingent on good behavior during time out rather than dependent on time alone, (3) and leaving the child during time out as opposed to merely ignoring him or her. Following the youngster's return from time out he or she should be placed in the original problem situation and given the opportunity to perform the desired response. This allows the parents to reward the youngster for prosocial behavior as well as to facilitate the discrimination of the consequences for prosocial and deviant behavior in that setting.

HOME TOKEN ECONOMIES

The use of token economies in the home setting has also been included in treating conduct-disordered children. As mentioned earlier, Patterson employs a token point system in his parent training program.

Unlike Patterson, however, investigators who advocate this approach place less emphasis on the use of differential attention and time-out techniques and concentrate on training parents to set up a comprehensive program in which the child's good behavior is rewarded with tokens and his or her bad behavior results in a loss of tokens. The tokens, in turn, are used by the youngster to purchase privileges.

Alvord (1971) was the first to enumerate the advantages of using token programs in the home. He suggested that parent–child arguments may be reduced because parental expectations of child behavior and consequences for child behavior are predetermined. He also stated that tokens provide parents with a means of delivering an immediate consequence to the child for desirable and inappropriate behavior. Finally, the salience of behavior–consequence relationships is increased because the tokens provide a consistent and discriminable stimulus in the child's enviornment.

Christophersen (Christophersen, Arnold, Hill, & Quilitch, 1972; Christophersen, Barnard, Ford, & Wolf, 1976) has conducted the most extensive evaluation of this treatment approach. In his program, the majority of training is conducted by the therapist in the patient's home. Parents are asked to list deviant and prosocial behaviors that they want to target. They are also asked to identify rewards for which their child should work. Generally, the rewards chosen are privileges (e.g., television, use of toys) that the youngster enjoys independent of his or her behavior. Once these factors have been delineated, an exchange system is developed. That is, prices are established for each back-up reinforcer, and pay for each behavior performed is determined. Here, the attempt is made to set up an exchange rate such that a minimum level of appropriate responding must occur daily in order for the youngster to enjoy any privileges. Typically, the child's most highly valued reward (e.g., daily television) is priced such that it requires the performance of the major target responses each day. After an exchange rate is established it is frequently suggested that the behaviors and rewards and their point value be written and posted in a public place in the home. Additionally, a medium of exchange is selected. Poker chips are frequently used with younger children whereas note cards and points are employed with older youngsters. Finally, a time is established for the daily exchange of tokens. At this time the following day's privileges are purchased.

Christopherson et al. (1976) believe the program is most effective when the therapist conducts training in the home. This allows for modeling of how to contingently administer and remove points. Alvord (1971), however, has reported successfully using token programs with conduct-disordered children without home training. Additionally, observing parents utilize the procedures allows for immediate feedback. Christophersen's investigations have shown this approach to be effective in altering conduct-problem behaviors and that the home token economy is more effective than traditional outpatient psychotherapy (Christophersen et al., 1976).

The home token economy is a very comprehensive approach to modifying child and parent behavior. Although it has several advantages, there are a number of difficulties associated with it. The use of points and tokens can become very difficult to administer, practically speaking. Children can lose their tokens or forget to carry their point cards. This can lead to parent–child arguments over how many tokens were earned in a given day. Establishing an exchange rate is also difficult. Additionally, the logistics of delivering backup reinforcers can present problems. For example, inclement weather may prevent a child from utilizing a reward, or a day's activities may prevent the opportunity to engage in a rewarding activity (e.g., family trip). In these instances, the youngster's incentive to perform may be greatly decreased. Furthermore, in cases where numerous behaviors are to be targeted for treatment the potential for the token economy becoming extremely complex is great. It appears that the token program may be most useful in situations in which a very limited amount of deviant behavior is targeted. In other cases, parent training programs that teach a set of generalizable child management skills (e.g., Forehand, 1977) may be a better treatment approach. In particular, having generalizable skills may increase parents' ability to adapt a deviant child behavior across a variety of situations (e.g., home, visiting friends, shopping).

NEGOTIATION AND CONTRACTING

The treatment procedures described thus far are most commonly employed with youngsters 13 years and younger. Although the child management skills discussed are appropriate for adolescents, a more common approach to dealing with conduct problem children of this age group involves teaching negotiation and contracting skills to their families. Stuart (1971) has suggested that much deviant behavior is a result of dysfunctional family interaction patterns. These families are characterized by a general lack of reciprocally reinforcing interactions between parent and youth. In these families such interactions revolve mainly around maladaptive behaviors. Contracting and negotiation skills provide an alternative and, hopefully, positive manner for family members to influence each other's behavior on a reciprocal basis (Alexander & Parsons, 1973).

It is the principle of reciprocity that distinguishes contracting from the other interventions described (Wells & Forehand, 1981). In parent training and token economy programs parents serve essentially as administrators. That is, they select target behaviors and manage the newly designed contingencies. In negotiation and contracting interventions, however, the children have a much more active involvement. Their opinions and suggestions regarding the selection of behaviors for themselves and their parents, rewards, and ways of dispensing these rewards are included in the development of the contract.

Stuart (1971) suggests that contracts must contain a number of components. They must detail the target behaviors each party is to perform and the specific privileges each person expects to gain for exhibiting these responses. A system of sanctions for failing to meet responsibilities must also be established. Additionally, a method of monitoring the occurrence of target behaviors is necessary. Finally, a provision for additional rewards for adherence to the contract is a valuable asset to a contracting intervention.

Weathers and Liberman (1975a) have outlined a program for teaching adolescents and their families negotiation and contracting skills. Families are taught that in a conflict situation the youth and his or her parents should first identify each other's behavioral demands. This should be followed by having both parties delineate the rewards he or she desires for performing those behaviors and then set priorities on those rewards. The child and parents are then instructed to stop for a moment and imagine being in the other person's position. After this imagined role-reversal the family members are told to begin suggesting various compromises that would result in both negotiating parties getting close to what they originally requested. Weathers and Liberman (1975a) suggest that these skills be practiced in the clinic with the therapist modeling and role-playing applications of these behaviors to various hypothetical and real conflict situations. When the family can reliably negotiate a conflict, they are then taught to write out their compromise in a specific contract format.

A number of investigators have reported that deviant adolescent behavior can be modified using negotiation and contracting. Stuart (1971) used a contracting intervention to eliminate truancy, drug abuse, and running away in a young girl. Alexander and Parsons (1973) found that contracting was more effective than psychodynamic family therapy in reducing antisocial behaviors in juvenile delinquents. Finally, Kifer, Lewis, Green, and Phillips (1974) decreased parent–child conflict in the home by using negotiation and contracting training.

The above studies suggest that contracting is an effective treatment program for conduct disordered families; however, a number of investigators have failed to replicate these findings. Stuart, Jayartne, and

Tripodi (1976) used contracting in an attempt to modify the deviant behavior of 60 youths. A therapist met with each youth and his or her parents and helped them to negotiate a behavioral contract. Thirteen measures of treatment effectiveness were evaluated including classroom performance, school attendance, and home behavior. It was reported that of these measures only four evidenced significant change following the intervention. Weathers and Liberman (1975b) have found contracting to be ineffective in altering the deviant behavior of predelinquent adolescents. It appears that contracting may be most effective when combined with a larger treatment intervention (Gross & Brigham, 1980).

CASE STUDY

Having described assessment and treatment strategies for use with conduct-disordered children, it seems appropriate to provide a brief case report to illustrate the applications of these procedures in the clinical setting.

Jerome is a 6-year-old Caucasian male brought to the outpatient clinic by his single mother because of his noncompliant behavior. At the inital appointment, while Jerome waited in the reception room, his mother, Mrs. A., explained to the therapist that she felt unable to control the behavior of her son. She reported that he frequently refused to comply with her instructions. Mrs. A. indicated that yelling and spankings seemed to have no effect on his behavior. After Mrs. A. explained what had prompted her to come to the clinic, the therapist told her that he wanted to ask her some very specific questions about her interactions with Jerome. Mrs. A. was asked to describe a recent difficulty with Jerome.

Mrs. A.: Well, we had an argument over picking up his toys just yesterday.

Therapist: What happened?

Mrs. A.: I told him to pick up his toys and he refused.

T: Tell me what you said to him.

Mrs. A.: I simply said "Jerome, you better pick up your toys, they are all over the room."

T: How did Jerome respond?

Mrs. A.: He did not do anything. He kept watching television.

T: What did you do next?

Mrs. A.: I raised my voice and began to yell at him to get moving.

T: What did Jerome do then?

Mrs. A.: He ignored me.

T: Did you continue to scold him?

Mrs. A.: Yes, but I got so mad and tired of yelling that I began to pick up the toys myself just to be finished with the whole thing.

Continuing with this questioning strategy, the therapist asked Mrs. A. about a number of other examples of her son's noncompliant behavior.

After obtaining a fairly clear description of parent–child behavior in these problem areas, the therapist met alone with Jerome. The therapist attempted to assess the youth's knowledge of why he was in the clinic as well as identify potential rewarding stimuli.

T: Do you know why you are here Jerome?

Jerome: No. Maybe cause mom and I fight a lot?

T: Well, your mom wants you and her to learn to get along without yelling and spankings. Would you like that?

J: Yeah.

T: I think we can make that happen if you, your mom, and I work together.

J: OK.

T: Your mom tells me you like football. What is your favorite team?

J: I like the Atlanta Falcons.

T: Do you watch them on TV?

J: Every Sunday if I can.

T: Do you like TV?

J: I love to watch TV.

Following his discussion with Jerome the therapist observed Mrs. A. and Jerome in the playroom. Mrs. A. was given the following instructions:

T: I want to watch you and Jerome interacting in the playroom for a few minutes.

Mrs. A.: That's fine.

T: Please begin by letting Jerome select a game with which the two of you will play. When you hear a knock on the window I want you to direct the play activities to a new toy. Do the same thing when you hear a second knock. I will then tap on the window a third time. On hearing this, please instruct Jerome to put away all the toys.

The therapist then observed Mrs. A. and Jerome through a one-way mirror. He coded parent–child behavior according to the Forehand observation system described earlier. The observations revealed that Mrs. A. often did not wait for her son to perform a task she requested, but rather she completed it for him. Additionally, she criticized Jerome for off-task behavior and did not respond to his appropriate responses. Although Jerome was not extremely disruptive during observation at the clinic, it was evident that he did not attend to his mother's instructions.

At the conclusion of the playroom observation, the therapist met alone with Mrs. A. At this time he presented a brief summary of his assessment observations and an overview of what therapy would probably entail.

T: There are a number of things that we can do that will help to alleviate the problems you are having with Jerome.

Mrs. A.: That would be great.

T: It is very trying to ask your child to do something and get no response. Frequently, when this occurs parents became impatient, scold their children, and then complete the task themselves just to end the difficulty. Unfortunately, in relieving her own stress, mom teaches the youngster that if he ignores mom's request then mom will do the chore after she finishes hollering at him. From your description of what occurs and home and what I saw in the playroom, this type of interaction seems to characterize some of your interactions with Jerome.

Mrs. A.: That's true. Sometimes it is just easier to do it myself and not argue.

T: Another result of child noncompliance is that it results in a great amount of one-to-one parent attention. Some of this attention may appear to be aversive to you and me, such as yelling and scolding, but nevertheless it is attention. For example, it is easy not to say anything to Jerome as he sits quietly watching TV or playing a game. If he becomes disruptive, however, he is immediately spoken to. As such, bad behavior receives all the attention and appropriate behavior is largely ignored.

Mrs. A.: I understand what you're saying but it is hard to ignore him when he is disruptive.

T: I understand that. However, there are a number of strategies we will discuss in order to help you alter these old interaction styles. Between now and when you come next week please keep a record of the frequency of Jerome's deviant behavior as well as your responses to this behavior.

The results of the assessment interview indicated that Jerome's behavior was most likely being supported by parental attention and avoidance of performing unenjoyable tasks. As such, it was decided that in therapy Mrs. A. should be given training in parenting skills. She was taught to use direct commands, state response reinforcer relationships clearly, use time out, and deliver rewards for appropriate behavior. These procedures were described in the therapist's office and were followed by Mrs. A. attempting to apply them in the playroom while being observed by the therapist.

T: You have done a great job collecting data on your interactions with Jerome. As we briefly discussed last week, frequently when Jerome does not do what you request you perform the task. Today we will discuss some methods of changing that behavior pattern.

It is very important that when you issue a command, you give Jerome a chance to display the behavior. You must also convey to him the consequences that are associated with compliance and noncompliance. When you ask him to do something and he doesn't respond, do not yell at him. Rather, repeat the command and add a description of what will occur if he does or does not do what you ask. For example, if he doesn't pick up his toys after being told to do so, you should say, "Pick up your toys and you can continue to watch television. However, if you don't pick your toys up right now the TV will be turned off and you will go to time out for five minutes. After the five minutes are up you will come back and again be asked to pick up your toys." Additionally, when he does do what you ask, he should receive a great deal of verbal praise and affection.

Mrs. A.: That seems easy enough. What is time out?

T: I will explain that in a moment. First, let me add that by stating your command in this manner you begin teaching Jerome response–consequence relationships. Also, by repeating the command a second time you give him the opportunity to make the appropriate response after an initial failure. This provides a chance to be successful and earn a reward for good behavior rather than simply being punished for bad behavior.

Time out is a punishment procedure. After issuing a command in the manner described above and failing to obtain compliance from Jerome, you are sure to have him stand by himself in the corner of a room for a five-minute period. During this time he should be required to face the wall and have no contact with anyone. He is to stand quietly, and it is understood that the time period doesn't start until he is quiet. A kitchen timer can be used to measure the period spent in time out. After completing his time out period, you repeat the command and reward him for task completion. If he still fails to obey, send him back into time out and start again.

The remainder of this and the following therapy sessions involved observing Mrs. A. interact with Jerome in the playroom and providing feedback regarding her application of the procedures. Initially, the therapist remained in the room and modeled the technique when appropriate. Therapist intervention was gradually faded out over the course of eight therapy sessions.

At the conclusion of each session Mrs. A. was instructed to use these techniques in the home. Mrs. A. was required to collect data on Jerome's deviant behavior throughout the treatment intervention. These data allowed the therapist to evaluate treatment effectiveness. Additionally, the information helped delineate practical problems associated with the application of the procedures and identify new problem situations. When problems occurred, time was spent explaining how to best utilize the techniques in these difficult settings. A total of nine weekly therapy sessions was required to effectively alter Jerome and his mother's behavior.

The case described is a relatively straightforward and simple treatment program. A mother brought her child to the clinic complaining about his noncompliant behavior. She reported no academic or school behavior problems. An assessment consisting of interviews and clinic observation was performed and target behaviors identified. A parent training program was implemented. Data collection by the child's mother throughout the intervention period revealed that treatment resulted in a large improvement in the youngster's behavior.

Most conduct-disordered families seen by practicing clinicians are likely to involve difficulties more involved than the case presented. In some instances, the assessment process may need to be expanded (e.g., questionnaires, home observations), whereas in other cases treatment may require additional components (e.g., contingency contract). However, the treatment format outlined in the example provides a framework on which to structure an approach to treatment.

PRACTICAL PROBLEMS

The assessment and treatment procedures described have been relatively successful at modifying the behavior of conduct disordered children (Wells & Forehand, 1981). One factor crucial to their effectiveness is parental cooperation. All the methods described require active parental participation, and this cooperation is necessary during both assessment and treatment stages of intervention. Parents are generally motivated to learn effective methods for controlling the behavior of their children. However, a number of investigators have reported failing to obtain parental cooperation (Alexander & Parsons, 1973) or that levels of parental cooperation declined rapidly over the course of treatment (Gross, in press: Gross, Brigham, Hopper, & Bologna, 1980).

Unfortunately, therapists control very few reinforcers for parent behavior. Although this increases the difficulty involved in maintaining parent motivation, there are still a number of procedures that many enhance cooperation. Eyberg and Johnson (1974) offered treatment for conduct-disordered families in a group format. They reported that parental cooperation was increased when the amount of time parents were given during a session was made contingent on performance of the procedures taught. Other investigators have required deposits at the onset of treatment that were returned contingent of parental performance. A possible variation on this latter idea would be to offer patients price reductions for therapy continGent on completing therapy-related tasks.

Before leaving the discussion of parental cooperation it is important to note that in instances where it is difficult to obtain parent participation, efforts might be made to teach the children to alter their own behavior (Gross & Drabman, 1982). Gross (Gross, in press; Gross, Brigham, Hopper, & Bologna, 1980) has reported that youngsters are capable of learning to use behavior technology to modify their own behavior as well as the behavior of others.

Another problem encountered with training parents in behavioral skills is that they often fail to adequately utilize the reward procedure component of the intervention. They are very effective at learning to issue commands clearly and to apply time out, but they often exhibit a very low rate of praise for appropriate child behavior. In some instances parents report finding it difficult to think of ways to praise their children. In order to facilitate children's learning to discriminate rewarding and aversive consequences associated with their behavior, the praise component of these interventions is crucial. Constant therapist prompting and modeling of these behaviors may help parents improve in this category. Additionally, teach each parent to prompt the other as well as praising him or her when this response is emitted may also help to increase the occurence of this behavior. Moreoever, having parents self-monitor their performance of the treatment program may in some instances lead to an increase in these behaviors.

Finally, parental expectations can also present a problem for therapists. As already noted, parents may hold unreasonably high expectations for child behavior. What they may consider as deviant may in fact be simply normal age-appropriate responding. In such cases it may be decided to increase parenting skills as a goal of therapy. However, it is imperative that a major portion of therapist–parent contact be devoted to educating parents regarding normal child development.

Parents can also be unreasonable regarding their expectations of their responsibility in the treatment process and as to the rapidity with which they should see behavior change in their youngster. For example, after two weeks of using time out for bad behavior and praise and rewards for good behavior, they may anticipate that their child's problem should be corrected and "things can go back to the way they were." This attitude, and the behavior likely to accompany it, would set the stage for reemergence of the target difficulties. Moreover, parents may begin to doubt the effectiveness of the intervention should they fail to see sufficient behavior change within what they consider to be an adequate period of time. In order to circumvent this potential difficulty, therapists must discuss these issues across the course of therapy. In particular, it must be clearly presented that the target behaviors were acquired over a long time period and as such may require a fair amount of time to be altered. Parents also must learn that behavior is a function of its consequences. Procedures taught thus are skills that are appropriate for use throughout the child-raising process, and not simply until their child becomes less of a problem.

SUMMARY

The present chapter described a systematic approach to the treatment of conduct-disordered children. A case study illustrating the use of these procedures was presented. In order to help therapists to be prepared for some of the problems frequently encountered in the treatment of conduct-disordered families, a number of common treatment difficulties were reported and remedies for these difficulties were suggested. It is hoped that by describing both the strengths and weaknesses of the behavioral approach to the treatment of conduct-disordered families, clinicians will be able to utilize these techniques in the most successful manner possible.

REFERENCES

Alexander, J. F., & Parsons, B. V. Short term behavioral intervention with delinquent families. *Journal of Abnormal Psychology*, 1973, *81*, 219–225.

Alvord, J. R. The home token economy: A motivational system for the home. *Corrective Psychiatry and Journal of Social Therapy*, 1971, *17*, 6–13.

Arnold, J. E., Levine, A. G., & Patterson, G. R. Changes in sibling behavior following family intervention. *Journal of Consulting and Clinical Psychology*, 1975, *43*, 683–688.

Atkinson, B. M., & Forehand, R. Conduct disorders. In E. J. Mash & L. G. Terdal (Eds.), *Behavioral assessment of childhood disorders*, New York: Guilford Press, 1981.

Becker, W. C. The relationship of factors in parental ratings of self and each other to the behavior of kindergarten children as rated by mothers, fathers, and teachers. *Journal of Consulting Psychology*, 1960, *24*, 507–527.

Christophersen, E. R., Arnold, C. M., Hill, D. W.. & Quilitch, H. R. The home point system: Token reinforcement procedures for applications by parents of children with behavior problems. *Journal of Applied Behavior Analysis*, 1972, *5*, 485–497.

Christophersen, E. R., Barnard, J. D., Ford, D., & Wolf, M. M. The family training program: Improving parent–child interaction patterns. In E. J. Mash, L. C. Handy, & L. A. Hamerlynck (Eds.) *Behavior modification approaches to parenting*. New York: Brunner/Mazel, 1976.

Ciminero, A. R., & Drabman, R. S. Current developments in the behavioral assessment of children. In B. B. Lahey & A. E. Kazdin (Eds.), *Advances in clinical child psychology (Vol. 1)*. New York: Plenum Press, 1977.

Cower, E. L., Huser, J., Beach, D. R., & Rappaport, J. Parental perceptions of young children and their relation to indexes of adjustment. *Journal of Consulting and Clinical Psychology*, 1970, *32*, 97–103.

Eyberg, S. M., & Johnson, S. M. Multiple assessment of behavior modification with families. Effects of contigency contracting and order of treated problems. *Journal of Consulting and Clinical Psychology*, 1974, *42*, 594–606.

Ferber, H., Kelley, S. M., & Shemberg, K. M. Training parents in behavior modification: Outcome of and problems encountered in a program after Patterson's work. *Behavior Therapy*, 1974, *5*, 415–419.

Forehand, R. Child noncompliance to parental requests: Behavioral analysis and treatment. In M. Hersen, R. M. Eisler, & P. M. Miller (Eds.), *Progress in behavior modification* (Vol. 5). New York: Academic Press, 1977.

Forehand, R., Griest, D., & Wells, K. C. Parent behavioral training: An analysis of the realtionship among multiple outcome measures. *Journal of Abnormal Child Psychology*, 1979, *7*, 229–242.

Forehand, R., & King, H. E. Noncompliant children: Effects of parent training on behavior and attitude change. *Behavior Modification*, 1977, *1*, 93–108.

Forehand, R., King, H. E., Peed, S., & Yoder, P. Mother–child interactions: Comparisions of a concompliant clinic group and a nonclinic group. *Behaviour, Research and Therapy*, 1975, *13*, 79–84.

Forehand, R. & Peed, S. Training parents to modify noncompliant behavior of their children. In A. J. Finch & P. C. Kendall (Eds.), *Treatment and research in child psychopathology*. New York: Spectrum, 1979.

Forehand, R., Sturgis, E. T., McMahon, R., Aguar, D., Green, K., Wells, K. C., & Breiner, J. Parent behavioral training to modify child non-compliance. Treatment generalization across time and from home to school. *Behavior Modification*, 1979, *3*, 3–25.

Graziano, A. M. Parents as behavior therapists. In M. Hersen, R. M. Eisler, & P. M. Miller (Eds.), *Progress in behavior modification* (Vol. 4). New York: Academic Press, 1977.

Gross, A. M. Self-management training and medication compliance in children with diabetes. *Child and Family Behavior Therapy*, in press.

Gross, A. M., & Brigham, T. A. Behavior modification and the treatment of juvenile delinquency: A review and proposal for future research. *Corrective and Social Psychiatry*, 1980, *26*, 98–106.

Gross, A. M., Brigham, T. A., Hopper, C., & Bologna, N. C. Self-management and social skills training: A study with predelinquent and delinquent youth. *Criminal Justice and Behavior*, 1980, *7*, 161–184.

Gross, A. M., & Drabman, R. S. Teaching self-recording, self-evaluation and self-reward to nonclinic children and adolescents. In P. Karoly & F. Kanfer (Eds.), *Self-management and behavior change*. New York: Pergamon Press, 1982.

Haynes, S. N. *Principles of behavioral assessment*. New York: Gardner Press, 1978.

Herbert, E. W., Pinkston, E. M., Hayden, M. L., Sajwaj, T. E., Pinkston, E., Cordua, G., & Jackson, C. Adverse effects of differential parental attention. *Journal of Applied Behavior Analysis*, 1973, *6*, 15–30.

Hobbs, S. A., & Forehand, R. Important parameters in the use of time out with children: A re-examination. *Journal of Behavior Therapy and Experimental Psychiatry*, 1977, *8*, 365–370.

Huges, M. M., & Haynes, S. N. Structured laboratory observation in the behavioral assessment of parent–child interactions: A methodological critique. *Behavior Therapy*, 1978, *9*, 428–447.

Kelley, M. L., Embry, L. H., & Baer, D. M. Skills for child management and family support: Training parents for maintenance. *Behavior Modification*, 1979, *3*, 373–396.

Kifer, R. E., Lewis, M. ., Green, D. A., & Phillips, E. L. Training predelinquent youths and their parents to negotiate conflict situations. *Journal of Applied Behavior Analysis*, 1974, *7*, 357–364.

Levitt, E. E. Psychotherapy with children: A further evaluation. *Behavior Research and Therapy*, 1963, *1*, 45–52.

Lobitz, G. K., & Johnson, S. M. Normal versus deviant children: A multimethod comparison. *Journal of Abnormal Child Psychology*, 1975, *3*, 353–374.

Patterson, G. R. *Families: Application of social learning to family life*. Champaign, Ill: Research Press, 1971.

Patterson, G. R. Interventions for boys with conduct problems: Multiple settings, treatments, and criteria. *Journal of Consulting and Clinical Psychology*, 1974, *45*, 471–481.

Patterson, G. R. The aggressive child: Victim and architect of a coercive system. In E. J. Mash, L. A. Hamerlynck, & L. C. Handy (Eds.), *Behavior modification and families*. New York: Brunner/Mazel, 1976.

Patterson, G. R. Naturalistic Observation in clinical assessment. *Journal of Abnormal Child Psychology*, 1977, *5*, 309–322.

Patterson, G. R., Cobb, J. A., & Ray, R. S. A social engineering technology for retraining the families of aggressive boys. In H. Adams & L. Unikel (Eds.), *Issues and trends in behavior therapy*. Springfield, Ill.: Charles C. Thomas, 1973.

Patterson, G. R., & Fleischman, M. J. Maintenance of treatment effects: Some considerations concerning family systems and follow up data. *Behavior Therapy*, 1979, *10*, 168–185.

Patterson, G. R., & Guillon, M. E. *Living with children*. Champaign, Ill. Research Press, 1968.

Patterson, G. R., & Gullion, M. E. *Living with children: New methods for parents and teachers.* Champaign, Ill.: Research Press, 1968.

Patterson, G. R., Pay, R. S., Shaw, D. A., & Cobb, J. A. *Manual for coding of interactions.* New York: Microfiche, 1969.

Patterson, G. R., & Reid, J. B. Intervention for familis of aggressive boys: A replication study. *Behaviour Research and Therapy*, 1973, *11*, 383–394.

Patterson, G. R., Reid, J. B., Jones, R. R., & Conger, R. E. *A social learning approach to family intervention: Families with aggressive children.* Eugene, Ore.: Castalia Press, 1975.

Peed, S., Roberts, M., & Forehand, R. Evaluation of the effectiveness of a standarized parent training program in altering the interaction of mothers and their noncompliant children. *Behavior Modification*, 1977, *1*, 323–350.

Peterson, D. R. Behavior problems of middle childhood. *Journal of Consulting Psychology*, 1961, *25*, 205–209.

Russo, S. Adaptions in behavioral therapy with children. *Behaviour Research and Therapy*, 1964, *2*, 43–47.

Scarboro, M. E., & Forehand, R. Effects of two types of response-contingent time-out on compliance and oppositional behavior of children. *Journal of Experimental Child Psychology*, 1975, *19*, 252–264.

Stuart, R. B. Behavioral contracting within the families of delinquents. *Journal of Behavior Therapy and Experimental Psychiatry*, 1971, *2*, 1–11.

Stuart, R. B., Jayaratne, S., & Tripodi, T. Changing adolescent deviant behavior through reprogramming the behavior of parents and teachers: An experimental evaluation. *Canadian Journal of Behavioral Science*, 1976, *8*, 133–134.

Wahler, R. G. Oppositional children: A quest for parental reinforcement control. *Journal of Applied Behavior Analysis*, 1969, *2*, 159–170.

Wahler, R. G. Deviant child behavior within the family: Developmental speculations and behavior change strategies. In H. Leitenberg (Ed.), *Handbook of behavior modification and behavior therapy.* Englewood Cliffs, N.J.: Prenctice Hall, 1976.

Wahler, R. G., House, A. E., & Stambaugh, E. E. *Ecological assessment of child problem behavior.* New York: Pergamon Press, 1976.

Walker, H. M. *The Walker Problem Identification Checklist.* Los Angeles: Psychological Services, 1970.

Weathers, L., & Liberman, R. P. The family contracting exercise. *Journal of Behavior Therapy and Experimental Psychiatry*, 1975(a), *6*, 208–214.

Weathers, L., & Liberman, R. P. Contingency contracting with families of delinquent adolescents. *Behavior Therapy*, 1975(b), *6*, 356–366.

Wells, K. C. Assessment of children in outpatient settings. In M. Hersen & A. S. Bellack (Eds.), *Behavioral assessment.* New York: Pergamon Press, 1981.

Wells, K. C., & Forehand, R. Childhood behavior problems in the home. In S. M. Turner, K. S. Calhoun, & H. E. Adams (Eds.) *Handbood of clinical behavior therapy.* New York: Wiley, 1981.

White, G. D., Nielsen, G., & Johnson, S. M. Timeout duration and the suppression of deviant behavior in children. *Journal of Applied Behavior Analysis*, 1972, *4*, 11–120.

Williams, C. D. The elimination of tantrum behaviors by extinction procedures. *Journal of Abnormal and Social Psychology*, 1959, *59*, 260–270.

Zeilberger, J., Sampen, S. E., & Sloane, H. N. Modification of a child's problem behaviors in the home with the mother as therapist. *Journal of Applied Behavior Analysis*, 1968, *1*, 47–53.

12

School Problems

Mary Margaret Kerr and Phillip S. Strain

Teacher: Class, it's time to get out your math books.
First student: I don't have mine.
Second student: So, who needs it?
Teacher: What's all that racket about?
Second student: Oh, we were just discussing higher mathematics.
Teacher: If I've told you once, I've told you a hundred times: *get out your books!*
First student: See? She's into higher math, too. She's counting to a hundred!

WHERAS STUDENTS such as these and their beleaguered teachers argue the finer points of compliance (or higher mathematics), other problems emerge daily in schools across the country. In fact, it has been estimated that nearly 6% of America's school children "manifest persistent and serious school conduct problems that exist with most teachers, for most years, and in most schools" (Safer, 1982). Discussion of the range of possible school problems is a task beyond the scope of a single chapter; therefore, we limit our duscussion to classroom management problems, or disruptive behavior. Our rationale for this focus is based on three factors: (1) disruptive behaviors are the classroom management problem cited most frequently by teachers, (2) dis-

Preparation of this chapter was supported in part by a grant from the Richard King Mellon Foundation. Correspondence regarding this manuscript should be addressed to the senior author at Western Psychiatric Institute and Clinic, 3811 O'Hara Street, Pittsburgh, Pennsylvania 15213.

ruptive behaviors are a major roadblock to school success in elementary and secondary school programs, and (3) disruptive behaviors, often limited to the classroom setting, may not receive attention in other clinical settings.

Within its focus on disruptive behaviors, this discussion emphasizes children in the age range 5–12 years, since the population of concern to readers usually will fall within this group. Furthermore, the assessment practices and interventions take place within the classroom environment—the primary setting for outpatient behavior therapy for school problems.

DEFINITION OF SCHOOL PROBLEMS

Walker (1979, p. 3) describes a disruptive student as "one who defies teacher-imposed rules, structures, and/or procedures . . . a consistent rule breaker . . . spends a great deal of time in nonacademic pursuits [and is therefore] often deficient in key academic skills." Other terms to describe students with disruptive school problems are: "noncompliant," "off-task," "unmotivated," and "defiant." Table 12-1 displays additional descriptions, written in teachers' words. Teachers are concerned about disruptive behaviors like those in Table 12-1. "Failure to complete assignments" is another complaint heard by school consultants and may be a way of saying that a disruptive student engages in nonacademic pursuits, one of the characteristics highlighted by Walker and Buckley (1974).

Teachers sometimes describe problem behaviors vaguely, and their explanations may not be very helpful to a consultant. Accordingly, we have described these noxious behaviors more precisely in the right-hand column of Table 12-1.

Several different disruptive behaviors are classified as school problems. The behavioral therapist must translate global statements (as reflected in the left-handed column of Table 12-1) into operational definitions that can be included in treatment plans. A thorough clinical assessment of the child's school problem is a vital prerequisite to any treatment plan.

ASSESSMENT OF SCHOOL PROBLEMS

Identification of School Problems

The first step in the assessment and treatment of school problems is usually a referral from the teacher. The referral may be informal (e.g., a teacher stopping a consultant in the school hallway to discuss

Table 12-1   Description of School Problems

Teacher-Referred Problem	Operational Definition
Unmotivated; spacy	Looking out the window, looking around the room, looking out in the hall, or sitting with eyes closed (Ferritor, Buckholdt, Hamblin, & Smith, 1972)
Jumpy; hyperactive	Movement from chair when not permitted or requested by the teacher; no part of the child's body is touching the chair (Drabman & Lahey, 1974)
Disruptive; immature; pesky; into everything	Talking out without raising hand; hitting another student; making audible noises such as animal calls; scraping desk on floor or drumming pencil on desk or wall; or throwing pencils, paper, or books (Ferritor et al., 1972)
Minds other kids' business	Using material object as an extension of hand to touch others' property (Ferritor et al., 1972)
Disrepectful; defiant	Failure to initiate appropriate response requested by teacher (Ferritor et al., 1972)

a problem child) or may be formalized throug a referral form. Figure 12-1 displays the initial referral form for Lisa, the student discussed later in our case study.

Several features of this referral form, adapted from Deno and Mirkin (1978), are noteworthy. First, the consultant saves valuable time by asking the teacher to provide demographic information (i.e., student's address, parents' names, date of birth, and classroom location). Second, the teacher describes the student's problem. Next, the teacher offers convenient times for a meeting with the behavior therapist. This information eliminates telephone calls to arrange a suitable date and time. Finally, space at the bottom allows the consultant to reply. Too often, consultants never receive a referral yet are held responsible for failing to act.

In addition to (or in lieu of) a referral for behavior therapy, a teacher may refer a student for a special education evaluation. The passage in 1975 of the Education for All Handicapped Children Act (Public Law 94-142) provided teachers and parents with a legal avenue for obtaining special education services. The PL 94-142 referral process includes these provisions:

1.   The policy shall include a system by which persons who may be in

Directions: Please complete all items on the top part of the form. Leave this form in the school mailbox assigned to Dr. Karen White, or mail it in the attached envelope.

Request for Consultation

To: Dr. Karen White

From: _Alice Johnson_   Date: _October 17_

Re: _Lisa N._

Age: _9 yrs. 10 mo._   Rm. # _207_

Parents: _Mr. Olivia Dinson_

Parents' Address: _6613 Oakmont St. Apt. 2 B_

Home Phone: _463-2198_

Reason for Referral (Describe problem briefly)

Lisa can't take criticism; is desirous of having her own way. Very defiant. Usually gets along well in science. Has trouble socializing or being in large groups. Pugnacious. Behavior attitude very negative.

Figure 12-1 Referral form.

Request for Conference with Referrer

Please list three alternative days and/or hours during the next school week which
would be convenient for you to meet with Dr. White.

	TIME	TIME
Monday	1 - 1:15	
Tuesday	10 - 10:30	
Wednesday	1 - 1:15	
Thursday	any	time
Friday	—	—

Communication with Referrer   To: Ms. Johnson

Your request for assistance for ___Lisa H.___ was received on ___10/20___ .
                                    Name of child   Date

Dr. White will meet with you in ___teacher's lounge___ on ___10/24___ at
                                     room #   Date

___1 pm___ .   Please bring any notes you may have.
  time

337

need of special education are referred by parents, teachers, school nurses, and other professional employees for evaluation.*

2. The policy shall include a provision for . . . any parent who believes that his or her child is exceptional and is not receiving appropriate special education programming . . . to request, in writing, an evaluation of the child.

3. A conference shall be scheduled within ten days of receipt of the written request. The conference shall include, but shall not be limited to, the parent, the teacher of the person, and a supervisor of special education or principal. Any person the parent wishes to invite may attend. Prior to the conference the school district shall prepare written evidence supporting the appropriateness of the present regular education program of the person or a recommendation for an evaluation (Commonwealth of Pennsylvania, undated, p. 15).

Specific regulations regarding the process of referral are not enumerated within Public Law 94-142, so a consultant should check with the local school to ascertain the appropriate steps.

Formal Instruments to Assess School Problems

Following (or occasionally prior to) a teacher or parent's referral of a student for school problems, the referring individual might be asked to complete a formal rating scale or behavior problem checklist. To illustrate the information obtained through such a procedure, Table 12-2 displays sample items from the major rating scales used with teachers.

To complete a rating scale, the evaluator reads a list of descriptive behavioral statements and decides how accurately each statement describes the named student. Rating scales provide a consultant with information about a student's school problem, while requiring very little teacher or parent time. (Most rating scales can be completed within 20 minutes.) A rating scale should not be completed by an individual with limited knowledge about a student, however, and information provided through such a procedure should always be confirmed through the direct observational procedures described later. Readers interested in stardardized rating scales and behavior problem checklists should consult Salvia and Ysseldyke (1981) or Mash and Terdal (1981).

---

*Evaluation standards are described explicitly in the regulations of PL 94-142 and should be studied thoroughly by persons involved in behavior therapy with special education students. The reader is referred to Turnbull, Strickland, and Brantley (1982) for an excellent summary of the regulations.

Table 12-2   Rating Scale Items

Instrument	Items
Devereux Child Behavior (DCB) Rating Scale (Spivack & Spotts, 1966)	Teases or bullies other children? Blames others for his or her actions? Annoys or provokes peers into hitting or in other ways attacking him or her? Disobeys the rules in games or in the house?
AAMD Adaptive Behavior Scale (Nihira et al., 1975)	Disrupts others' activities? Resists following instructions, requests, or others? Ignores regulations or regular routines? Is inconsiderate of others?
Walker Problem Behavior Identification Checklist (Walker, 1976)	Complains about other's unfairness and/ or discrimination toward him or her? Makes distrustful or suspicious remarks about actions of others toward him or her? Argues and must have the last word in verbal exchanges? Does not obey until threatened with punishment?

After a teacher provides the behavior therapist with descriptive statements through a referral form, informal conversation, or a formalized behavior rating scale, the next step is to determine more about the variables contributing to the school problem. In the next section procedures for examining the antecedent and consequent events surrounding problem behaviors are described.

Anecdotal Records

Narrative records may not help a behavior therapist who has already defined a target behavior. Nevertheless, when therapists are faced with nebulous or contradictory descriptions of a student's behaviors, they may enter the classroom and simply take notes. These notes would be called an *anecdotal record*. Most anecdotal records are written in abbreviated narrative form and are completed within a short period of time (e.g., 20 minutes). The behavior therapist then reviews the record to determine whether behaviors warrant further study. For example, does the child exhibit any of the problems referred? The record may indicate different inappropriate behaviors, too, and these should be observed more carefully.

The next phase of assessment is to determine the events immediately preceding and following each disruptive behavior. A simple procedure, known as an *antecedent–response–consequence record* (ARC), will help the behavioral consultant to answer any questions.

Antecedent–Response–Consequence Record

Analyses by the ARC method [sometimes called *antecedent–behavior–consequence* (ABC) records] provide answers to some of the following questions about disruptive behavior:

- What are this child's specific behavior problems?
- Do these behaviors occur predictably or do they occur at random?
- Does the classroom environment contribute to these behaviors?
- Does another person maintain or elicit these problem behaviors?
- How do others react to these behaviors?
- What does the child gain from these behaviors?
- If the student were not being inappropriate, what activities could he pursue?
- Do several students have the same problems?

To answer these questions, the consultant or teacher should conduct ARC analyses throughout a school day. As this is not practical, however, we present alternative ways in which the information can be recorded. First, let us review Figure 12-2, a standard ARC record, on our case study student, Lisa. This record represents one observation conducted by Dr. White, the behavioral consultant. Note that the target behaviors listed in the central column (i.e., the "response" column) are drawn from the referral from displayed in Figure 12-1.

In Figure 12-3 we present an abbreviated ARC record, to be completed by the classroom teacher on each instance of the problem behavior. The teacher simply checks items, reducing the time required to complete the record. Column headings may be modified to suit behaviors of interest.

A third antecedent–response–consequence analysis, displayed later in our case study, is an interview with the classroom teacher and other school personnel.

At this point in the clinical assessment, the consultant should define each of the child's classroom behavior problems. Often, multiple behaviors are identified. The behavior therapist must select which problems will be addressed initially. We recommend the straighforward establishment of intervention priorities at this early phase of behavior therapy for two reasons: (1) the consultant who does not establish priorities at this time may discover later that intervention on every behavior was too ambitious, and that the interventions failed; and (2)

Student: _____ Lisa H. _____   Observer: _____ K.W. _____

Target Behavior(s): 1. defiance (failing to follow teacher's verbal
instruction) 2. talks back to teacher _____

Date: _____ 10/27 _____   Time: _____ 10-10:30 _____
Activity: _____ Math _____   Teacher: Mrs. Johnson _____

Antecedent	Response	Consequence
Mrs. J. asked class to take seats	L.H. refused - stood at door	Mrs. J repeated request to L.H.
Mrs. J: "What are you doing?"	"The art teacher took my book - I hate her."	Mrs. J. "Don't talk back. Sit down!"
	L.H. went to desk, didn't sit.	Mrs. J: "I'm going to take your book, too, if you don't sit down!"
	L.H. started crying - "no one likes me."	Mrs. J: "Come on, now. It will be o.k."

Figure 12-2 Antecedent–response–consequence record.

by asking the school staff to agree on an intervention priority, the consultant united persons to solve the problem. We ask school personnel to state their intervention priorities on a form developed originally by Deno and Mirkin (1978). Figure 12-4 displays the form, within information regarding our case study student, Lisa.

Problem behaviors and target behaviors are listed on this form. These statements may be incorporated into an Individualized Education Program (IEP), if the student has been declared eligible for special education services. The IEP, mandated under Public Law 94-142, is a type of contract between the parents, student, and the school. This powerful document contains long and short-term instructional (and behav-

Directions: Complete this checklist for <u>each</u> aggressive behavior the student has exhibited.

Person Completing Form: __Mrs. Hall__   Student: __Lisa__   Date: __October 16__

Description of the behavior	When did this behavior most recently occur?	Where did this behavior take place?	Who else was in the setting?	Was the aggression directed towards anyone? or towards property? Whom? What?	What was going on immediately (15 min.) before the aggressive behavior?	What happened immediately (15 min.) after the aggressive behavior?	Did you directly observe the behavior?	Comments: (Describe anything that was unusual about the schedule, setting, or student when the event took place, or anything you think would be helpful to consider.)
Came into room; threw book on desk; refused to open it. Threw book on floor. Cursed me. Refused to leave. Resisted, was verbally abusive.	Yesterday.	Regular Reading Class	Other students (entire class)	More towards teacher	was in art and came down the hall to reading class	I told her again to open that book. Told her to pick it up. Told her to leave room. Took her hand to lead her. Bagged the principal's office.	Yes	She seems to often come to class already mad or upset.

Figure 12-3 Antecedent–response–consequence checklist.

Student: _Lisa H._

Age/Grade: _9 / 4th_

Date: _10-25_

Priority Ranking Form

Name of Person Completing This Form: _Mr. Cleveland, recess supervisor_

Below are listed some behaviors to be increased as well as some to be
decreased. Please rank each set of behaviors separately, assigning a "1"
to the most important, then ranking the rest.

Rank	Behaviors to be decreased
2	Back talk to adults
3	Refusing to follow directions
1	Fighting with other kids
4	Talks to others during class

Rank	Behaviors to be increased
3	Carry on pleasant conversation with adult
4	Keep a friend for at least a month
1	Play cooperatively at recess
2	Follow directions from adult

Figure 12-4   Priority ranking form.

ioral management) objectives for the child as well as an explication of
how these objectives are to be met. In selecting behaviors of high priority for behavior therapy intervention, a school team may develop
short-term objectives for the IEP. [For a thorough, yet very readable,
discussion of IEPs, the reader is referred to Turnbull, Strickland, and
Brantley (1982).]

Once a general intervention objective is established by the behavior therapist or multidisciplinary IEP team, it is necessary to measure
the behavior. This important step tells the behavior therapist how to
monitor the progress of an intervention and to decide when, and
whether that intervention should be altered. In the case of disruptive
behaviors, the usual measurement is *direct observational recording*.

Direct Observational Procedures for Assessing School Problems

One of the simplest ways to count a student's disruptive behavior is
with a frequency checklist or tally. This procedure can be summarized
in four sequential steps:

Step 1: Select an operational definition of the behavior to be observed (see Table 12-1 for examples).

Step 2: List these behaviors on the left side of a sheet of paper, allowing space on the right for a simple tally of each time such a behavior occurs.

Step 3: Make a note of the exact minute that the observation was begun and completed, so that frequency tallies may be converted into rate per minute data.

Step 4: In instances in which peer data are to be included, complete a separate tally of targeted behaviors as exhibited by peers.*

The advantage of a frequency record is that it requires very little preparation or time. Frequency records are appropriate only for behaviors that have a clear beginning and ending point. For example, hitting, fighting, swearing, destroying property, or stealing are behaviors monitored appropriately by a frequency checklist. On the other hand, nondiscrete, continuous behaviors are not appropriate for a frequency tally. For these behaviors, the consultant might use an *interval record.*

In an interval record, behaviors are tallied within blocks of time. Use a stopwatch or second hand to count the 10 seconds within each interval. If the designated behavior occurs with the time period, make that box with a symbol. In Figure 12-5 we exhibit an interval record to record the the behaviors of the case study student. Note that target behaviors were established for observation purposes and that each interval was marked as to the presence or absence of the behaviors.†

We suggest that you obtain at least three 20-minute observations on the target student's level of problem behavior (as well as levels of similar behavior represented in his or her peer group) before proceeding with an intervention program.

INTERVENTIONS FOR SCHOOL PROBLEMS

Many intervention programs are effective for the remediation of school problems. Entire textbooks and journal issues have been devoted to the topic, and an in depth discussion of behavior managment is beyond the scope of this chapter. Instead, we highlight an interven-

---

*Peer data are often gathered to determine the discrepancy between the targeted child's classroom behavior and that of his or her "normal" classmates.

†Frequency and interval measures represent only two of the many direct observational measurement procedures available to the behavioral therapist. For an in-depth discussion of these and other procedures, consult Sulzer-Azaroff and Mayer (1977) or Kerr and Nelson (in press).

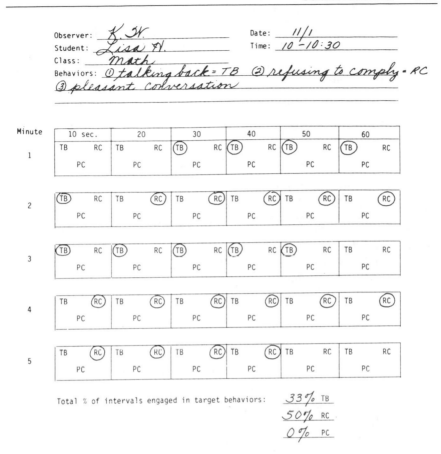

Figure 12-5   Interval record.

tion for disruptive classroom behavior and provide recommended readings for those who wish to pursue the topic further.

This section is organized around a basic treatment strategy for school problems: a contingency contact. We believe that the reader will find this procedure useful in the remediation of many school problems. Furthermore, the contract allows the behavioral therapist to examine not only a student's behaviors, but the influential behaviors of his or her partner in the classroom—the teacher.

A written explanation of contingencies to be used with a student by her parents or teachers is called a *contingency contract* (Homme, 1970). One variation of a basic contingency contract, labeled a *home-based report*, involves parents' provision of reinforcing activities in return for receiving a positive progress note from the students teacher. Both kinds of contract have been documented in the remediation of disruptive behaviors (Colman, 1973; Schumaker, Hovell, & Sherman, 1977; Todd, Scott, Bostow, & Alexander, 1976).

Guidelines for establishing a contingency contract between a teacher and a student may include:

- Explain a contingency contract to the child and teacher. This explanation should be modified to the conversational level of the student and might include examples of contractual agreements.
- Introduce to the child the behaviors targeted by the consultant and other school staff. Explain to the student that work on these behaviors is his part of the contract. Encourage the student to suggest one or two behaviors.
- Ask the teacher and student to agree on one or two behaviors for the first contract. If a third party (e.g., principal or parent) is to be involved, be certain that they have approved the list of tasks.
- Ask the teacher and student to work together to identify reinforcing activities for which the student will reduce on the problem behaviors.
- Determine how many (or how much) of the reinforcer the student will earn for accomplishing his or her part of the contract.
- Ask the teacher to specify how the student's goals will be measured (e.g., completion of homework paper with less than five mistakes, remaining quiet during a silent reading period of 20 minutes, interrupting others no more than twice per day).
- Establish a schedule for the student to receive his or her reinforcers. At the beginning of a contract, provide the student with frequent feedback and reinforcement.
- Select a day for reviewing the contract within two weeks.

In Figure 12-6 we present the contingency contract for Lisa and her teacher. The remainder of this section is devoted to an analysis of the salient feature of this and other contracts.

Student Responsibilities

In the first part of the contingency contract displayed in Figure 12-6, Lisa stated her target behaviors. These behaviors were identified earlier by the school team and the behavior therapist. Behavioral standards should be explained to students throughout the school year, however, in the form of classroom rules. Rules are the mechanism by which children come to understand the standards for social behavior imposed by their teacher and the school. Regrettably, rules are not always written but may be reflected instead in disciplinary decision

Date _10 - 28_

CONTRACT

This is an agreement between _Lisa_ and
Mrs. Johnson . The contract begins on _October 29._
It will be reviewed on _November 10_ .

The terms of the agreement are:

Lisa will ① _not fight at all for five days, before earning a treat._
② _will not talk back to any adult for at least four periods a day._

Mrs. Johnson will _give Lisa the watering can and allow her to water plants each day she meets her ② goals. Each week, Lisa doesn't fight, she can fertilize and repot one plant with fertilizer and soil the teacher gives her._
If Lisa does not make one of her goals, she has to scrub the plant shelf and replace the shelf paper that week with no planting, watering, or fertilizing.

Principal: _The principal will schedule a weekly meeting with Lisa to review her progress sheet._

Child's signature _Lisa_
Teacher's signature _Alice Johnson_
Principal's signature _Ralph Jernigan_

Figure 12-6 Contingency contract.

made on a day-to-day basis. The behavior therapist should check a classroom's rules to see that they meet the criteria established by Worell and Nelson (1974):

1. Select the fewest number of rules. Too many rules are difficult to remember, and frequently are so specific that pupils can easily find exceptions to them.
2. Use different rules for different situations. Obviously rules for classroom activities should be different than for the playground, lunch line, or bus-waiting area.
3. Rules should be stated behaviorally and should be enforceable. Rules which are not enforceable invite tattling as well as testing, both of which can lead to disruptions.
4. Rules should be reasonable. The most common response to an un-

reasonable rules it to challenge it, which may lead to a serious power struggle. Another option is to give up, rather than try to meet the expectation. . . . The best way to ensure that rules are reasonable is to develop them with students.

5. There must be consistent consequences for rule-fulfillment or infraction. Rule consequences should be posted with the rules themselves, or taught until all pupils know them thoroughly. It has been demonstrated that without consequences, rules have little effect on behavior.*

In summary, students may be taught standards for classroom behavior from a carefully delineated set of behaviors outlines in a contingency contract or through rules posted for the entire class. In either case, the standards should conform to the stated quidelines because classroom rules constitute an ongoing contract between a teacher and his or her students.

After Lisa listed her target behaviors on the contingency contract, she informed the teacher and consultant which reinforcers who would like to earn. Note that the contract includes a provision for losing reinforcers, too. Loss of a reinforcer is referred to as "response cost." In planning this feature of a contract, the behavior therapist should be sure that students will not "go into the hole" and lost more privileges than they can possibly earn within a day or week. To prevent this, the therapist should establish gradual steps toward the final goal, allowing the student to make a few unpunished mistakes while working his or her way toward acceptable behavior throughout the entire day. This procedure of reinforcing gradual steps is called *shaping of successive approximations.*

Teacher Responsibilities

Contingent events are articulated in a contingency contract, yet other forms of consequation take place throughout the typical course of a school day. These interactions also warrant the behavior therapist's attention. Let us focus on these student–teacher interactions, as we refer to the teacher's section of the contract.

In our case study contract, Mrs. Johnson agreed to provide a contingent, reinforcing activity to Lisa when the child met her goal. In addition, the teacher planned a response-cost procedure and provided Lisa with appropriate work for her instructional level. The contract became a formal restatement of Mrs. Johnson's responsibilities to her student. Still, a multitude of teacher behaviors remain outside the

---

*From Worell, J., & Nelson, C. M. *Managing instructional problems: A case study workbook.* New York: McGraw-Hill, 1974, pp. 23–24. With permission.

boundaries of this simple document. These behaviors play an influential role in the determining the ultimate outcome of the behavior therapist's work. For example, Lisa's teacher might have followed the letter of the contract, without adhering to its spirit, by making demeaning remarks to the student about her inability to complete work on schedule. The research on naturally occurring rates of teacher verbal feedback does indicate that teachers engage in more reprimands than approvals, and teachers often give positive attention for inappropriate student behaviors (Strain, Kerr, Stagg, Lambert, & Lenkner, 1982). The behavior therapist can assist teachers to become more aware of their verbal interactions with students. A simple self-monitoring activity, such as teachers counting the number of times they catch themselves attending to off-task students, demonstrates the importance of contingent feedback and praise. Or teachers should be asked to set a kitchen timer at random times to remind themselves to praise students behaving appropriately when the timer sounds. Finally, teachers may need assistance in discrimininating between neutral statements (e.g., "Okay," "All right," "Let me see what you've done") and approval statements (e.g., "Good thinking!" "Tremendous work," "I knew you could do it").

In summary, a contingency contract outlines responsibilities for a student and his teacher(s) and assign monitoring or intervention responsibilities to a third party, if appropriate. Although a few duties are described in the agreement, we have presented other factors for the behavior therapist to consider in monitoring student–teacher interactions. To review, the student must understand the standards for behavior in each classroom, because research indicates that these stardards vary from teacher to teacher (Strain et al., 1982). We highlighted the importance of teachers' verbal feedback and cited activities a behavior therapist might implement to help teachers become aware of their attention to students who are on- and off-task. In the following case study, we illustrate the contracting procedure used for Lisa, a chronically disruptive fourth-grader.

CASE STUDY*

Lisa was a 9-year-old fourth-grader in a public inner-city elementary school at the time of this behavior therapy consultation. Lisa's third-grade teacher described her as "extremely antagonistic and aggressive, cannot take any criticism, is desirous of always having her own way. Very defiant." This statement was written in the school record at the end of the third grade. When

---

*This case study is based on material provided by Donna Lenkner and Sylvia Mendelsohn.

Lisa entered the fourth grade, her homeroom teacher also encountered discipline problems and referred her to a behavior therapist. The week after this referral, Dr. White, the behavior therapist, reviewed Lisa's school records and discovered that she had missed several days of school during each of her four years of attendance. Her grades, however (mostly As and Bs), reflected her ability to master grade-level work. In fact, the second-grade science teacher wrote that "Lisa seems particularly interested in our study of plants and leaves." Lisa was suspended twice for "backtalk and defiance of teachers." Before each suspension, the principal had contacted Lisa's single mother and informed her of the problem. On the other hand, Lisa's mother had requested a school transfer for her daughter at the end of each school year. The record documented a breakdown in school–parental communications. The principal and the teachers blamed Lisa, and Lisa's mother blamed the school, stating in her transfer request that "Lisa is a good student, but the rules they make are just unreasonable and they always single her out as a troublemaker."

After studying the school record, Dr. White reviewed the schedule and found that Lisa was instructed by four teachers and that her outdoor activity was supervised by a fifth adult. The principal and these five teachers would need to be involved in any consultation activity, so Dr. White scheduled a joint meeting with them for purposes of clarifying Lisa's school problems. Lisa's mother chose not to attend this meeting, but she requested that Dr. White telephone her after the conference.

At the meeting, the teachers and the principal presented their opinions about Lisa's defiance and disruptive behavior. To elicit this information, Dr. White used the structured ARC interview form displayed in Figure 12-7. To begin the discussion, Dr. White asked participants to recall their most difficult incident with Lisa. Each person described a different event, providing all the details he could remember. In comparing the results of this interview activity later, Dr. White recognized that Lisa and her teachers were engaged in "power struggles." Dr. White then gave the staff a list of problem behaviors and appropriate behaviors and asked them to rate the importance of each one. The Priority Ranking Form completed by one teacher is displayed in Figure 12-4.

Dr. White calculated median rankings assigned to each behavior and proposed that a few behaviors be addressed in a contingency contract developed by the behavior therapist and Lisa's homeroom teacher. Before finalizing the contract, however, she spent three days making interval records of Lisa's targeted behaviors, as a way of validating the concerns expressed by the adults. One completed interval record is displayed in Figure 12-5.

Two weeks after her initial contact with the principal, Dr. White met with Lisa and Mrs. Johnson (the homeroom teacher) to implement the contingency contract according to the guidelines in this chapter. Lisa was initially resistant to the idea of establishing goals for her own behavior, stating, "It won't matter anyway. They all think I'm a bad kid. I don't know why I should bother with this." Convinced by the behavior therapist to give the contingency contract at least one week's effort, Lisa volunteered that she would like to water the school plants as a reinforcing activity. Her continuing skepticism was reflected, however, when she complained, "You watch. They will decide that I'm too dumb and crazy to handle the plants and measure the fertilizer."

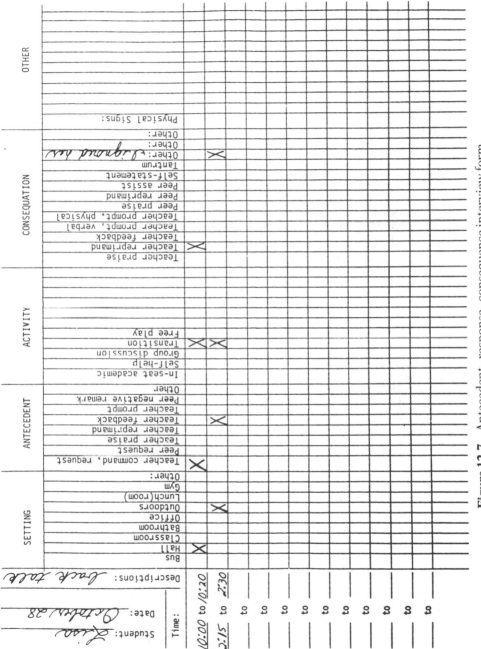

Figure 12-7 Antecedent–response–consequence interview form.

That afternoon, Dr. White and Mrs. Johnson met with the other school personnel to explain their new intervention and to underscore the importance of consistency and fairness in adult interactions with Lisa. Each member of the team received a copy of the contract and was asked to give Lisa positive feedback whenever she attained her goals. To assist in this team effort, the principal offered to post a chart reflecting Lisa's progress in the teacher's lounge. To maintain confidentiality regarding Lisa's problem behaviors, progress was indicated by listing the dates on which Lisa watered, repotted, or fertilized plants, reflecting mastery of one of her behavioral goals. When one of Lisa's teachers complained that the contracting procedure was not appropriate for her to implement in an art class of 40 students, Dr. White suggested that she try the kitchen timer-reminder activity instead.

The behavior therapist monitored Lisa's progress by completing a five-minute interval record three times a week for one month. These records showed that Lisa was learning to manage her behavior, and the slighly improved grades reflected her willingness to pursue academic tasks in lieu of inappropriate activities. At a two-month follow-up conference, Lisa's principal stated, "I would never have believed it. She is like a different kid." Lisa was only one of the persons whose behavior was modified through this intervention. Anecdotal records indicated that Lisa was receiving contingent positive feedback for her accomplishments in the four classrooms. Finally, Lisa's mother requested a meeting with Mrs. Johnson to find out more about the program Lisa enthusiastically described at home.

ISSUES IN REMEDIATING SCHOOL PROBLEMS

In this section, we review a few issues that behavior therapists may encounter as they try to remediate school problems. The topics in this section are presented according to their respective stages of behavior therapy consultation.

Identification and Assessment of the Problem

One of the most common experiences we have as behavior therapists in school settings is what we term "the tip of the iceberg phenomenon." In other words, a single child is referred as having problems, but that child reflects only a small portion of what is essentially a classroom-wide problem. In many instances, this type of referral requires a group intervention, as described in Chapter 4 of Kerr and Nelson (in press).

The second issue one many encounter at the assessment phase is what we call "stemming the tide." The conflict here is about time lines. School staff want a student's behavior remediated immediately, whereas the conscientious behavior therapist insists on a comprehensive clinical assessment of the problem. Needless to say, we support the latter position. To alleviate the problem, involve school personnel as often as possible in assessment activities such as the Priority Rankings and ARC interviews.

Implementing and Monitoring Interventions

In the introduction to this chapter we refer to the wide range of school problems that a behavior therapist may encounter. This diversity must be addressed with an equally broad range of intervention skills rarely possessed by a single consultant. We find it helps to work with another specialist, combining different areas of expertise. What is *not* helpful in this situation (although many consultants try this approach) is to present oneself as a "jack-of-all-trades." Remember that teachers and other school staff members may be good sources of specialized information. For example, a special education supervisor or a mathematics department chairman may have just the expertise needed to complement the skills of the behavior therapist. The reading recommended in this chapter will help school behavior therapists to expand their knowledge base.

Behavior therapists who work in schools *must* understand educational terminology and school system policies, particularly those of Public Law 94-142. Unlike work conducted primarily in clinical settings where the behavior therapist is surrounded by others with similar training, school consultation most often takes place in educational settings, where the behavior therapist may be working exclusively with *educators*.

Finally, the most difficult aspect of behavior therapy in schools is good progress monitoring. The cry, "No more paper work!" is all too common in most schools, and readers faced with this problem will find it useful to consult Deno and Mirkin (1978) for their strategies on how to accomplish data-based consultation.

SUMMARY

In this chapter we have described a few assessment and interventional tools useful to behavior therapists working in schools. The school problem we emphasized is classroom disruption. We are certain that behavior therapists are asked most frequently to correct such disciplinary problems. Also, there is every reason to believe that chronic disruption is associated with poor achievement and future, more serious rule violations.

The effective behavior therapist recognizes that disruptive behavior in the classroom can result from (1) problems in the curriculum, (2) a long history of academic failure (considered by us to be an instructional—not a child-centered problem, (3) dysfunctional teacher attitudes and behaviors toward students, or (4) an absence of clearly understood consequences for appropriate and inappropriate behavior. Given the frequent operation of these "etiological" variables, it is not suprising that the most effective behavior therapists in schools are skilled in assessment, classroom interventions, and basic principles of human behavior. We encourage you to expand your knowledge of these areas by consulting the references cited throughout this chapter.

REFERENCES

Colman, R. G. A procedure for fading from experimenter-school-based to parent-home-based control of classroom behavior. *Journal of School Psychology*, 1973, *11*, 71–79.

Commonwealth of Pennsylvania, Department of Education. *Standards for special education*. Harrisburg, Pa., undated.

Deno, S. L., & Mirkin, P. K. *Data-based program modification*. Reston, Va.: Counsel for Exceptional Children, 1978.

Drabman, R. S., & Lahey, B. B. Feedback in classroom behavior modification: Effects on the target and her classmates. *Journal of Applied Behavior Analysis*, 1974, 7, 591–598.

Ferritor, D. E., Buckholdt, D., Hamblin, R. L., & Smith, L. The non-effects of contingent reinforcement for attending behavior on work accomplished. *Journal of Applied Behavior Analysis*, 1972, 5, 7–17.

Homme, L. *How to use contingency contracting in the classroom*. Champaign, Ill.: Research Press, 1970.

Kerr, M. M., & Nelson, C. M. *Strategies for managing behavior problems*. Columbus, Oh.: Charles E. Merrill, 1983.

Mash, E. J., & Terdal, L. G. (Eds.). *Behavioral assessment of childhood disorders*. New York, NY: Guilford Press, 1981.

Nihira, K., Foster, R., Shellhais, M., & Leland, H. *Adaptive behavior scale*. Washington, D.C.: American Association of Mental Deficiency, 1969.

Safer, D. J. *School programs for disruptive adolescents*. Baltimore, Md.: University Park Press, 1982.

Salvia, J., & Ysseldyke, J. E. *Assessment in special and remedial education*. Bost, Ma.: Houghton-Mifflin, 1981.

Schumaker, J. B., Hoval, M. F., & Sherman, J. A. An analysis of daily report card and parent-managed privileges in the improvement of adolescents' classroom performance. *Journal of Applied Behavior Analysis*, 1977, *10*, 449–464.

Spivack, G., & Spotts, J. *Deveraux child behavior rating scale*. Devon, Pa.: Devereux Foundation Press, 1967.

Strain, P. S., Kerr, M. M., Staff, V., Lambert, D. L., & Lenkner, D. A. *Naturalistic assessment of children's compliance to teachers' requests and consequences for complaince*. Journal of Applied Behavior Analysis, in press.

Sulzer-Azaroff, B., & Mayer, G. R. *Applying behavior-analysis procedures with children and youth*. New York, Ny.: Holt, Rinehart & Winston, 1977.

Todd, D. D., Scott, R. B., Bostow, D. E., & Alexander, S. B. Modifications of the excessive inappropriate classroom behavior of two elementary school students using home-based consequences and daily report-card procedures. *Journal of Applied Behavior Analysis,* 1976, 9, 106.

Turnbull, A. P., Strickland, B. B., & Brantley, J. C. *Developing and implementing individualized education programs.* Columbus, Oh.: Charles E. Merrill, 1982.

Walker, H. M. *Problem behavior identification checklist.* Los Angeles: Western Psychological Services, 1976.

Walker, H. M. *The acting-out child: Coping with classroom disruption.* Boston, Ma.: Allyn and Bacon, 1979.

Walker, H. M, & Buckley, N. K. *Token reinforcement techniques: Classroom applications for the hard-to-teach child.* Eugene, Ore.: E-B Press, 1974.

Worell, J., & Nelson, C. M. *Managing instructional problems: A case study workbook.* New York, Ny.: McGraw Hill, 1974.

13

Problems in Adolescence: Assessment and Treatment of Bulimia Nervosa

Francis C. Harris and L. K. George Hsu

MOST PEOPLE WOULD AGREE that adolescence is the most turbulent period in one's life. Some of the major characteristics of this period are (1) rapid physical maturation, (2) a great deal of concern with physical appearance, (3) increased interest in members of the opposite sex, and (4) establishment of some independence from the family (Conger, 1977). Considering the myriad of problems associated with these issues, it is not surprising that many adolescents experience adjustment problems. Fortunately, the vast majority of adolescents and their families somehow manage to adjust reasonably well to these problems. However, in some cases these problems become so troublesome to the family or the adolescent that professional attention is required. One such adjustment problem that often affects female adolescents is *bulimia nervosa*. There has been a great deal of interest in the etiology and treatment of this problem in recent years. The interested reader is referred to recent reviews by Hsu (in press) and Bemis (1978) for comprehensive discussions of these eating disorders.

Purging by means of self-induced vomiting or the use of laxatives or diuretics as a means of weight control traditionally has been viewed as a variant of anorexia nervosa (Russell, 1979). The primary diagnostic features of anorexia nervosa are (1) weight loss of at least 25 percent of original body weight, taking into account expected weight-gain from normative height–weight charts for patients less than 18 years old, (2) disturbance of body image, (3) intense fear of becoming obese, (4) refusal to maintain a normal body weight for age and height, and (5) no known physical illness that would account for the weight loss (APA 1980).

Recently, however, it has been suggested that purging to control body weight is a primary characteristic of a distinct clinical entity known as *bulimia nervosa*. Its two other primary diagnostic criteria are (1) current episodes of binge eating, prior to the purging, in which there is a sense of loss of control and (2) a "morbid" fear of fatness (APA 1980; Fairburn, 1981; Fairburn & Cooper, 1982). Evidence for the independence of bulimia nervosa from anorexia nervosa has been provided by Fairburn and Cooper (1982). In an epidemiological study of 669 women who admitted to using self-induced vomiting as a means of weight control, they found that 83% met the primary criteria for bulimia nervosa, but not anorexia, at the time of the study. Perhaps even more interesting is the fact that less than half of those who met bulimia—but not anorexia—criteria had ever been of low enough body weight to be diagnosed anorexic. Thus, there appears to be some empirical support for the existence of bulimia nervosa as an independent entity. Such a state of affairs certainly presents a problem for empirically oriented clinicians who work with bulimia nervosa patients and base their assessment and treatment practices on previous research that did not differentiate between the two disorders.

Empirically oriented clinicians who work with adolescent bulimics encounter still another difficulty when they attempt to base their work on the extant literature. This is because the vast majority of the published work does not differentiate adolescent from adult patients in terms of etiology or treatment outcome.

Until the differential diagnosis and developmental issues are sorted out by research, therefore, we must pool what we know from clinical experience and commonly used behavioral procedures with the relatively scant amount of useful information provided in the eating disorders and general adolescent problems literature to develop a strategy for treating adolescent bulimics.

The remainder of this chapter is devoted to presenting the strategy we have developed for assessing and treating adolescents whose behavior problems meet the diagnostic criteria for bulimia nervosa. This strategy, for the most part, is based on our collective experiences in treating more than 50 such patients on an outpatient basis.

ASSESSMENT

In general, our view is that binging and purging is shaped and maintained in the context of a negative reinforcement paradigm. Vomiting after eating is negatively reinforced by removal of the likelihood of weight gain, which produces strong subjective feelings of anxiety due to the fact that the patient has had a history of being overweight (Fairburn & Cooper, 1982). As this negative reinforcement process continues it is likely that the patient experinces similar subjective feelings of anxiety which are not weight-related. But because of her* reinforcement history, she comes to deal with them in the same way that she deals with weight-related feelings of anxiety (i.e., by eating and purging). One of the primary goals of the assessment process, therefore, is to identify those other stimuli that set the occasion for subjective feelings of anxiety in the adolescent patient.

The binge–purge cycle also often is negatively reinforced when the adolescent learns that her parents avoid giving her instructions and otherwise "tiptoe" around her in an effort not to exacerbate her eating problem. Another goal of the clinical assessment, then, is to identify the specific features of such a process, if they exist.

Continued involvement in binging and purging sometimes is strengthened through positive reinforcement. This might occur if family members or peers give the patient special privileges for being "ill," or if she is praised heavily for being able to maintain a "normal" weight while eating an apparently large amount of food. The clinical behavioral assessor should be on the lookout for such a process.

Kanfer and Saslow (1969) provided an excellent outline of topics that should be covered in a comprehensive behavioral assessment of any clinical problem. Our basic assessment plan is based on their outline, with additional topics added and certain areas emphasized rather heavily based on our clinical experiences and relevant research. An outline of the questions we endeavor to answer in the course of our assessment is given in Table 13-1.

ASSEESSMENT METHODS

Interview

The interview certainly is the most widely used assessment procedure in outpatient behavior therapy. In addition to providing information regarding the patient, her environment, and the presenting problem, it provides an excellent opportunity for developing a ther-

---

*Since the vast majority of adolescents who present with bulimia nervosa are female, the pronouns "she" and "her" are used throughout this chapter.

Table 13-1 Topics Covered in Assessment of
Adolescent Problems

Presenting problem

  Binge eating

    Does the patient experience "uncontrollable" urges to eat?

    How often does she experience those urges, and how long do they last?

    What are the antecedents of those urges?

      What does she think of prior to an urge to binge?

      What activities does she engage in prior to experiencing an urge to binge?

      At what time of the day does she binge?

    When she eats in response to those urges:

      What types and quantities of foods does she consume?

      At what rate does she consume?

      What other activities does she engage in while eating?

      Where does she eat?

      Does she eat alone or in the presence of others?

      What does the patient think of while eating?

      How frequently, in terms of episodes per week, does she binge?

    Why does the patient terminate the binge?

    What are the consequences of the binging episodes?

      What are the patient's "self-statements" immediately after binging?

      What is her mood after binging?

      How do other people react to her binging?

      What activities does she engage in after binging?

  Purging

    Does the patient experience urges to purge by vomiting or using laxatives or diuretics?

    What are the antecedents of those urges?

      Does she experience them after "nonbinge" eating as well as after binges?

      Are the urges stronger (or weaker) after consuming certain foods?

      What are her self-statements and subjective feelings immediately prior to purging?

  Vomiting

    How frequently, in terms of episodes per day or week and number of times per episode, does she vomit?

    What procedures does she employ to induce vomiting?

    Is vomiting difficult and/or painful?

    How long after eating does she vomit?

    What were the circumstances of the first episode?

  Laxative and/or diuretic use

    How frequently does she use them?

    What types of laxative or diuretics does she use?

    In what amounts does she ingest laxatives or diuretics?

    What were the circumstances of the first episode?

Other eating information

At what times of the day does the patient eat?

Does she eat regular meals?

Does she plan in advance any of her consumption?

What types and quantities of food does she consume?

What is the nutritional composition of her diet?

Does she have an understanding of basic nutritional requirements?

Does she have opinions/attitudes regarding eating which interfere with her eating a normal diet?

Body weight

What is her present height and weight?

What would she like to weigh?

Does she view herself as being overweight?

Is she extremely frightened at the prospect of gaining weight?

How has her weight varied in conjunction with her binging and purging?

What has been her highest weight?

What has been her lowest weight?

Other behavioral and developmental problems

Has the patient ever been brought to the attention of mental health or special education professionals?

What was the reason for the professional involvement?

What are/were the extent, results, and present status of the involvement?

At what ages did the patient walk, talk, and use the toilet independently?

What does the patient and her family see as having been behavioral problems?

Medical considerations

What is her metabolic status (i.e., her electrolytes—particularly the potassium level? (Low potassium can cause cardiac arrest and sudden death.)

Is her renal function normal? (Vomiting and/or laxative and diuretic abuse can cause renal damage.)

What is her thyroid status? (Sometimes hypothyroidism occurs as a result of the eating disorder.)

Are her menstrual periods regular? (A gynecological consultation may be indicated if she has amenorrhea or irregular menstruation.)

Many bulimic patients have an abnormal dexamethasone suppression test (Carroll, 1982). The significance of this abnormality in bulimic patients is unknown. Nevertheless, it may be worthwhile to perform this test as it may indicate a biological depression that might be treatable with medication.

Family information

Current household

With whom does she reside?

What is her relationship to each person in the household?

Is she or are any of her siblings adopted?

What is the age, educational level, and occupation of each family member?

(continued)

Table 13-1 (continued)

If the patient is living with both of her biological parents:

    Has either biological parent been divorced or had children with another partner?

    When did the divorce(s) occur?

    Does the divorced parent have other children not living in the present household?

    What is the parents' economic and personal involvement with each member of his or her "other" family?

If she is living with only one of her biological parents:

    Are her biological parents divorced or separated?

    What is the prospect of her biological parents getting back together?

    With whom is the absent biological parent living?

    What is the extent of the absent parent's personal and economic involvement with each member of the patient's current household?

    What are the patient's feelings toward the absent parent as a function of the divorce or separation?

    What is the extent of the patient's involvement with each member of the absent parent's "new" family?

If the patient is living with neither biological parent:

    Is she adopted? When did the adoption take place? How much information does she have regarding the circumstances of her adoption and the identity of her biological parents?

    What is the extent of her relationship with her biological parents or their families?

Has the makeup and/or location of the patient's household ever changed (other than as noted above)? If so, what changes have taken place?

Is there any history of eating disorders (including obesity), alcoholism, depression or other psychological problems in the patient's immediate and extended family of origin (or residence)? Did the affected family member receive treatment for any such problems?

Social relationships outside the family

  Peers

    How many people comprise her circle of friends?

    Does she have a best friend?

    What things does she have in common with her friends?

    Does she have a boyfriend?

    To what extent has she been sexually active?

    Are any of her peers aware of her presenting problem? What are their reactions to it?

    What aspect(s) of her peer relationships would she like to see changed?

  Others

    Does she have any significant social relationships with people outside her peer group and family? Who are those people, and what is the extent of the relationship(s)?

Activities

  What is the patient's daily routine on weekdays, weekends, and vacation days?

  In what organized activities (e.g., sports, clubs) does she participate?

Academic achievement and goals
   What is her current grade level?
   Are her grades above or below average?
   What are her best and worst subjects?
   Has her achievement level relative to her peers changed since she entered school?
   What precipitated such changes?
   What are her future academic and career goals?
      Do her goals seem congruent with her achievement level?
      Are her goals in accord with her family's expectations?
Motivational factors
   What benefits does she receive as a function of her bulimic behavior? The most
   frequently seen benefits are:
      Control of other peoples' behavior.
      Satisfaction with her "effective and easy" method of weight control.
      It gives a good excuse for not engaging in social activities.
   What negative consequences would be likely to occur as a result of "giving up" her
   bulimic behavior? The most frequently seen negative consequences are:
      Giving up the use of her bulimic behavior as a means of controlling others and
      having to develop more adaptive communication patterns.
      Giving up the use of her bulimic behavior as a means for controlling her weight
      and having to learn and employ more appropriate, relatively difficult weight-
      control methods.
      "Losing face" by admitting that the problem behavior was under her control
      all along.
      Taking responsibility for her own behavior and not blaming others for it.
   What is the potential reinforcing power of commonly used rewards such as social
   approval from significant others, money, special privileges, and nonessential clothing?

---

apeutic therapist–patient relationship (Goldstein, 1975). In most adolescent cases, the interviewer's task is complicated somewhat in that
the patient's parent(s) also must be interviewed. Indeed, usually the
parent first identifies a behavior problem as being serious enough to
warrant professional attention, makes the first appointment, and
accompanies the patient to the office. In actual outpatient practice
where logistical and economic considerations typically preclude more
"direct" assessment methods such as observations by independent
observers, the added "cost" of interviewing parents is very worthwhile
in terms of providing different points of view on the same set of problems. Obviously, there are numerous possible formats for interviewing the patient and her parents. A thorough assessment interview takes
approximately three hours over two separate meetings.

   We have found the most useful format for conducting the *first* interview, which typically lasts two hours, to be as follows:

• A relatively brief meeting with the adolescent and her parent(s) to solicit each person's general impressions of the development and current status of the presenting problem and the family's reactions to it. This portion of the interview also gives the therapist an opportunity to observe the family's style of interaction as the problem is discussed. During this time the therapist also should inform the family of the cost of the initial meeting if it was not discussed when the meeting was scheduled, describe the four parts of the initial meeting, and come to an agreement with each person regarding the confidentiality of information shared with the therapist when all family members are not present. Our usual agreement with regard to confidentiality is that the therapist shall be free to use his or her clinical judgment to decide when information discussed in the absence of one or more family members should be discussed with the absent member(s). However, this should be presented such that it does not imply that the therapist will make it a point to keep all family members informed regarding the details of all communications. It should be stated specifically that the therapist will not routinely inform the parents of information given privately by the adolescent regarding the frequency of her bulimic episodes, her social relationships, and her day-to-day activities. Given adolescents' general concern regarding privacy, often such a statement is necessary to create an atmosphere in which she feels free to discuss with the therapist such important personal matters.

• A longer interview with the adolescent alone to determine her likely commitment to participating actively in treatment and to ascertain her perspective on each of the assessment questions outlined above.

• A meeting with the parent(s), without the adolescent, to get their perspective on each assessment question except, of course, those dealing with the adolescent's cognitions and subjective feelings.

• A "wrap-up" meeting with the patients and her parent(s) during which the therapist (1) makes a general statement regarding the degree to which the parent and adolescent interviews yielded answers to the outlined assessment questions and how much more time is likely to be required to complete the interview portion of the assessment; (2) briefly reviews the typical treatment options that might be used; (3) indicates that when the initial assessment is completed (usually at the end of the second session) a specific course of treatment, including time lines, will be planned; and (4) answers questions.

The second interview typically is scheduled one week after the first one, but there is no particular reason why it could not be scheduled sooner as long as the therapist has had the opportunity to review and assimilate the information obtained during the first interview. The purpose of the second meeting is to complete the initial assessment, present the therapist's conceptualization of the case, and outline the specific course of treatment. Generally, the following format is followed during the second interview, which usually lasts one hour:

• A meeting with the adolescent to fill in any "gaps" in the assessment outline, review her eating diary, present and discuss the case conceptualization, and present the treatment(s) that would be undertaken. (Since the presentation of the conceptualization is viewed as a major component of treatment, its specific details are presented in the Treatment section of this chapter.)

• A meeting with the parents and adolescent during which the conceptualization and specific treatment procedures are reiterated and questions are answered. At the conclusion of this meeting the family is encouraged to go home and discuss the information that was presented and discussed during the two initial meetings and to decide whether they are willing to participate in the proposed treatment. They are requested to call and schedule an appointment if they wish to continue in treatment.

Diary

The patient is requested to record all food and beverage consumption, including that which occurs during a "binge." She records (1) the type and *amount* of food, (2) the time of day it occurred, (3) the time of day of each instance of vomiting, (4) each urge to vomit (noting her overt behavior prior to, during and after the urge), and (5) an outline of her significant social interactions. The consumption entries are for data collection purposes only during the assessment period, but later also reflect the patient's planned consumption.

TREATMENT

Overview

Perhaps the most perplexing problem in deciding on the course of treatment for the adolescent who presents with bulimia nervosa (or any behavior problem, for that matter) is whether to treat the patient individually by use of a basically "adult" treatment approach or to engage the patient and her family in behavioral family therapy. Unfortunately, there have been no controlled treatment outcome studies comparing individual behavior therapy, behavioral family therapy, and/or some combination of the two in the treatment of adolescent anorexia or bulimia nervosa. The behavioral family treatment procedure for treating adolescent problems that have been investigated most thoroughly is contingency contracting (Alexander & Parsons, 1973; Stuart & Tripodi, 1973; Weathers & Liberman, 1975). At best, these studies have been fraught with methodoligical problems such as inadequate control groups (Stuart & Tripodi, 1973) and random inclusion of different therapeutic techniques, making it impossible to evaluate the impact of the contracting procedure. And at worst, they have suggested that contingency contracting is ineffective (Weathers & Liberman, 1975).

More recently, behavioral family therapists have incorporated the training of contingency contracting skills into more broadly based problem-solving/communication skills treatment programs (Robin, Kent, O'Leary, Foster, & Prinz, 1977; Robin, 1981a, 1981b). Initial results of these programs are quite encouraging. They have not been used as yet, however, with families in which the adolescent meets criteria for *any* psychiatric disorder.

In the absence of evidence suggesting that behavioral family therapy is the treatment of choice for adolescents who present with eating disorders, we must base our treatment choice decision on clinical and pragmatic considerations. The general treatment approach we advocate is to give the adolescent the opportunity to assume responsibility for her own behavior and to engage her in individual behavior therapy for a limited time (usually eight weeks). At the end of that time, if success (i.e., a 75 percent reduction in the frequency of binge–purge episodes) is not achieved and the family situation appears to be playing a major role in the maintenance of the problem, behavioral family treatment, often in the context of structural family therapy (Minuchin, Rossman, & Baker, 1978), is recommended.

Fairburn (1981) presented a two-stage plan for treating bulimic patients. Stage 1 deals with controlling food consumption through methods developed for treating obesity (Mahoney & Mahoney, 1976; Stuart & Davis, 1972) and training problem-solving skills. After the binge–purge cycle frequency is reduced to "once every few days," stage 2 is begun. The purpose of the second stage is to develop the patient's skills in dealing more appropriately with stimuli that formerly led to frequent episodes of binging and purging. Stage 2 thus may be viewed as a means for programming maintenance and generalization. The specific type of coping skills training must be tailored individually according to the needs of each patient. For example, we have engaged in the training of general social skills, assertiveness, study skills, and anxiety management techniques, including progressive muscle relaxation and systematic desensitization.

Both the habit management and coping skills components of treatment are based on the assumptions that the adolescent must take responsibility for her own behavior. It is assumed that she has the capacity for developing the skills necessary to control her problematic behaviors and to cope with stressful events in a more adaptive manner than by binging and purging. Throughout treatment it is emphasized that abstinence from binging and purging will be quite difficult and that she must be willing to "pay the price" if she truly wants to give up her problem behavior. The "price," of course, would be the discomfort she is likely to experience during the course of giving up "old" behavior patterns to which she has become accustomed and learning a new set of behaviors. Cognitive restructuring techniques are used throughout treatment to keep these important points in focus.

Obviously, it would be impossible to explain in great detail each of the numerous techniques we might use to develop coping skills in these patients in stage 2. Instead, we present the stage 1 procedures common to most of our cases. These common procedures are self-management training and problem-solving training.

Self-Management of Eating Related Behavior

The purpose of the first half of each of the first two treatment hours is to instruct the patient in the basics of implementing a comprehensive self-management program designed to control her eating behavior. Since of one of the primary goals of such a program is the maintenance of a healthy body weight, it should not be surprising that many of the strategies we advocate have been used effectively with obese patients. These strategies include: (1) selecting a target weight, (2) selecting a daily calorie intake target, (3) self-recording of all consumption, (4) meal planning, (5) eating only in certain locations, (6) slowing the pace of eating, and (7) programming regular exercise. Specific strategies for training patients to use such procedures have been described repeatedly in the behavioral literature. Two references we rely on are *Slim Chance In a Fat World* (Stuart & Davis, 1972) and *Permanent Weight Control* (Mahoney & Mahoney, 1976). We instruct patients to purchase the volume by Stuart and Davis (1972) and encourage them to read the entire book. During the first two weeks of treatment, we make specific assignments of (1) the section of the book that covers the topics outlined above and (2) the programmed learning section. After the patient completes the programmed learning section at home, she is given the opportunity to discuss with the therapist any parts of the material that are unclear. The patient also is instructed to purchase a dietary scale for weighing all food eaten at home, and to practice estimating the weights and volumes of different foods to facilitate relatively accurate recording in those situations in which it is difficult to make direct measurements.

The basic self-management package also inlcudes self-recording of (1) the frequency and duration of urges to binge; (2) self-statements prior to, during, and after each episode of binging and purging; and (3) the circumstance associated with each episode. The patient keeps all of her self-report data in a diary that is reviewed by the therapist at the start of each subsequent session.

Problem-Solving Training

The second half of each of the first two treatment sessions usually is devoted to presentation and discussion of a general problem-solving model, which later is applied to various aspects of the patient's eating disorder. The basic tenets of this model, which is based on that provided by D'Zurilla and Goldfried (1971), are as follows:

- Problem situations may be described in terms of an individual's goals for that situation. These goals most often are in terms of either thoughts and feelings, or effects on the environment, including reactions from others.
- There are numerous alternative courses of action in almost any problem situation.
- It is possible to predict the likely outcome, in terms of achieving the goals for the situation, of selecting each alternative.
- It is possible to identify the pros and cons of implementing each alternative. These pros and cons include whether the patient has the skills required for implementing a given alternative, (2) the degree of effort required by each alternative, and (3) the presence of physiological arousal or cognitive distress that might make it very difficult to implement a particular problem solution.
- It is possible to select the "best" option and decide on a course of action to enable the patient to implement that option.

After discussing the general model with the patient, the therapist uses information gathered in the initial assessment as the focal point of a dialogue intended to begin laying the groundwork for getting the patient to view her problem behaviors in "problem-solving terms." Extreme care is taken to make sure that the patient understands the concept that, at last, theoretically, there are alternatives to binging and vomiting even though many of those alternatives are not necessarily easy to implement.

After the patient appears to understand the general problem-solving model as it applies to the retention or giving up of her eating disorder, the therapist identifies the major stressors that set the occasion for bouts of binging and vomiting. For each of these stressors, the patient is engaged in a Socratic dialogue intended to provide a description of that stressful situation in terms of the problem-solving mode. Table 13-2 shows a completed outline for a typical stressor. We have found that a completed analysis of this sort enables the therapist to set the stage for presenting specific behavioral intervention strategies that might be used. For example, in the situation outlined in Table 13-2 it is clear that (1) cognitive restructuring procedures might need to be implemented in the second phase of treatment to modify the patient's maladaptive attitudes regarding perfection in all areas, and (2) the therapist should meet with the patient's parents to discuss their expectation for her and what they might do to assist in the intervention effort. In other cases, specific strategies such as systematic desensitization or social skills training might be indicated. In addition to providing a context for selecting and discussing specific behavioral strategies that might be used later, problem-solving analysis makes clear the "motivational" factors associated with "giving up" binging and vomiting as a way of reacting to stressful events and provides the foundation for the development of self-talk that can be used when the patient experiences an urge to binge.

We instruct each patient to engage in problem-solving self-talk whenever she experiences an urge to binge. This self-talk typically takes the following form:

1. I'm feeling an urge to overeat.
2. This urge probably is in response to my *earning only a 95 percent on my algebra exam.*
3. My options in this situation are:
   a. Binge and vomit.
   b. Engage myself in some other activity like calling a friend or going for a walk.
   c. Suffer through the urge until it goes away.
4. If I:
   a. Binge and vomit, it will *take my mind off of my 95 percent grade temporarily but I will be very mad at myself later for being so weak.*
   b. Call a friend or take a walk, I still will have the urge to binge for awhile and that will be very uncomfortable for awhile, but if I can avoid binging and vomiting by doing one of those things I probably will feel a lot better off about myself later on then if I would binge.
   c. Try to suffer through the urge. I will feel completely miserable and it probably won't work anyway and I will probably feel worse than if I had binged in the first place.

Problem situation: The patient binges and vomits when she does not get *perfect* grades. For example, she binged and vomited after getting *only* a 95% on an algebra exam.

Goals: 1. Eliminate anxious feelings.
2. Feel good about ability to cope with problems without binging and vomiting.
3. Attain parents' approval for academic achievement.
4. Remain near the top of her class academically.   .

Table 13-2 Problem-Solving Outline for a Typical Stressor

Likely Outcomes

Alternatives	Positive	Negative
1. Binge and vomit	1. Will take mind off anxiety. 2. Feels good to eat without gaining weight. 3. Parents might stop putting pressure on her to do well because she is sick.	1. Will lead to feeling bad about being able to handle problems. 2. Vomiting is painful.
2. Put more time in studying.	1. Will learn material better. 2. Might lead to better grades. 3. Will be able to avoid social activities with peers.	1. Will make even more anxious. 2. No time for other things she likes to do.
3. Learn to accept 95% as OK without studying more.	1. Will reduce anxiety in the long run. 2. Will feel better about ability to handle problems appropriately.	1. Parents might not approve of *imperfect* grades. 2. Will have to work very hard to implement.

5. I guess I'll give myself a chance to feel better by calling a couple of my
    friends and trying to "fight off" the urge.

There are two purposes to having the patient engage in such self-talk:
it gives the patient a chance to review her options and assume some
responsibility for her actions, and it simply delays her from acting
impulsively.

The remaining six weeks in the first phase of treatment are devoted
to monitoring the patient's adherence to the self-management program
and use of the problem-solving self-talk each time she experiences an
urge to binge. Whenever, during the course of treatment, it is clear
that the patient is not complying with the basic treatment strategies,
the therapist reviews with her the problem-solving model as it related
to her noncompliance, placing particular emphasis on the likelihood
that the patient probably is being noncomplaint because the rewards
for continuing to binge and vomit are greater than those that she would
receive if she would eliminate her current behavior patterns.

During the final (eighth) week of the first phase of treatment the
patient's progress is evaluated and plans for future treatments are
made. We see in many of our adolescent patients approximately a 75%
decrease in the frequency of binging and vomiting during the first 10
weeks (two weeks of assessment and eight weeks of treatment) of
contact. When the frequency is reduced to such a degree the discrimi-
native stimuli for engaging in the program behavior become even more
clear, especially to the patient. At this time the therapist recommends
and describes the other individual behavior therapy procedures such
as social skills training, systematic desensitization, or continuing cognitive restructuring or problem-solving training. When a significant
decrease in binging and vomiting is not achieved during the first treatment phase, one likely reason is that the adolescent is not committed
to change within the context of individual behavior therapy. As alluded to earlier, this phenomenon usually is explicable in terms of the
desirability, from the adolescent's point of view, of continuing with
binging and vomiting as opposed to "giving it up." When commitment
is not demonstrated, the therapist must choose from among several
options for the future management of the case. These include (1) increased involvement of the patient's parents in behavioral family therapy (Robin, 1981a, 1981b, Robin et al., 1977) if it appears that family
factors are playing an important role in the problem's maintenance;
(2) continuing individual work adding other behavior therapy strategies to the ongoing self-management and problem-solving procedures;
(3) short-term (usually four weeks') hospitalization where a response
prevention program can be implemented if it appears that, in spite of

an apparent commitment on the patient's part, the intensity of the problem is such that continued attempts to manage it on an outpatient basis would be likely to be ineffective; or (4) a treatment hiatus if none of the other options is feasible. After discussing the likely further course of treatment with the adolescent, we typically meet with the patient and her parents to finalize the decision.

CASE STUDY

Anne C. was a 15-year-old, 5-ft, 7-in. 135-lb white female residing with her mother and father (48 and 52 years old, respectively) and a 13-year-old sister. She was in the appropriate grade for her age and always had been an average to below-average student. She had one or two close friends and was unhappy with her social life.

She had been overweight since early childhood, and approximately one year before presenting for treatment she weighted 170 lb and began a "diet" that consisted of approximately 1200 cal/day. After three weeks of dieting during which she lost 4 lb, she became frustrated because the weight loss was not rapid enough to suit her. At that time she began to vomit after eating and, naturally, her weight loss accelerated. Within four weeks her weight had dropped to approximately 135 lb. The rapid weight loss became a matter of major concern to both parents, who encouraged her repeatedly to eat. During this period her parents became very concerned and suspected that their daughter was vomiting to control her weight. When they confronted her with this, she admitted to vomiting and told them she would try to stop it. After approximately six months of "trying to stop," her parents insisted that she seek professional help. In addition to the information presented above, the initial assessment interview indicated that (1) her usual diet consisted of a great deal of "junk foods," such as candy, potato chips, cookies, and soft drinks; (2) she rarely ate meats, fruits, or vegetables; (3) she was binging and vomiting three to five times per day; and (4) she was able to exercise a great deal of control over her parents as a result of her "eating disorder." Following is an edited segment from the first treatment session during which the problem-solving strategy was introduced. It makes clear the patient's reasons for wanting to give up her problem and her reasons for wanting to hold onto it.

Therapist: Let's take a look at your binging and vomiting and try to figure out the benefits and problems it brings your way. I'll fill in this chart as we talk, OK?

Patient: OK.

T: Like you said before, it seems that you react to a lot of stressful situations by binging and vomiting. What would be good about not reacting that way?

P: I probaly wouldn't always feel as weak as I do now, I'm only about half as strong as I used to be.

T: OK. You would be stronger. What else?

P: I wouldn't feel so shitty everyday, and I wouldn't spend all day trying to figure out, or plan, what I can pig out on.

T: OK. So you wouldn't feel disgusted with yourself and you wouldn't spend all your time thinking about food. What would you do with all that free time that you would otherwise have spent thinking about food?

P: I don't know.

T: You don't know.

P: No.

T: Maybe you'd be thinking about some of those things you told me you don't like about yourself?

P: Maybe. I guess.

T: I see. So there's one good reason not to give up binging and vomiting, isn't there?

P: I guess so.

T: Any other reasons for keeping it?

P: I don't know. I'd probably gain weight, I guess.

T: That's a good reason to keep it, isn't it? It's a very simple, quick, and easy method for keeping your weight down without having to go on a diet and eat all that food like fruits and vegetables that you can't stand.

P: Right.

T: Any other things you're worried about happening if you stop? Sometimes people I talk to are scared to give it up because everybody would say they could control it all along and they just did it to be obnoxious.

P: Maybe. Sometimes they say I just do it for attention. I've had that dropped on me about a million times. My friend's mother says that. She's somebody with a big mouth who has to tell everything. She makes me feel stupid.

T: That's another good reason for wanting to keep it. Any others?

P: No.

T: How about things at home?

P: What do you mean?

T: You've probably got your parents pretty scared. Scared to death, I bet.

P: Oh. [Giggles.]

T: Do they stay out of your way and try not to aggravate you?

P: Sometimes they bother me, but yeah, they pretty much don't hassle me.

T: So you've got a lot of control over them, don't you?

P: I guess.

T: That's a terrific reason for wanting to keep this problem, huh?

P: Sometimes.

During treatment the patient made, at best, only a token effort at complying with the instructions to complete her food diary and implement our suggestions. At the end of eight weeks the patient's self-reports indicated she was binging and vomiting approximately three times daily; she repeatedly stated that she wished to withdraw from treatment. Expecting this course of events, the therapist met or talked on the telephone with Anne's mother to begin laying the groundwork for involvement in family therapy. Unfortunatly, Anne and her father repeatedly refused to participate in family treatment, and at the end of the first stage of treatment an agreement was made to suspend treatment until a later date. The therapist has kept in touch with the family for the past six weeks, and according to Mrs. C.'s report, there has been no noticeable change in Anne's eating and vomiting behavior.

Space limitations make it impossible to go into further specifics of the case, but it should be clear that this has been one that has been extremely resistant to treatment. We chose to present this case in the present chapter to illustrate the point that very often it is all but impossible to implement a behavioral management program, family or individual, when there is no good reason from the patient's point of view to make a commitment to change.

PROCEDURAL ISSUES

The major procedural issues specific to the outpatient treatment of adolescents are (1) confidentiality of information provided in the absence of parents or the adolescent, (2) to what degree parents should be involved in treatment, and (3) what to do when the adolescent refuses to participate actively in treatment. Each of these issues has been addressed in earlier sections of this chapter.

Another less frequently occurring, but nonetheless important, procedural issue relates to financial responsibility for therapy. We have found it useful to strongly suggest that adolescents who have the means to do so (e.g., those who hold part-time jobs) pay for at least a portion of the cost of treatment. This sometimes serves to strengthen the commitment to therapy and makes clear, in a tangible way, the patient's responsibility for controlling her own behavior.

SUMMARY

This chapter presents a strategy for the behavioral clinical assessment and treatment of bulimia nervosa in adolescents. Although it focuses on bulimia nervosa, many of the topics covered are directly applicable to the assessment and treatment of adolescent problems in general. For example, we present a relatively comprehensive set of assessment questions to be answered prior to developing and implementing an intervention program with an adolescent patient, and we discuss the procedural issues such as those related to deciding on an individual behavior therapy plan or a family-oriented treatment regimen. In addition, we illustrate a problem-solving context for therapy that we have found to be useful for a variety of clinical problems. A description of the first stage of treatment of one case is presented. The case currently must be classified as a treatment failure, unfortunately, but we feel it is instructive in that it highlights some of the difficulties typically encountered when working with adolescents.

REFERENCES

Alexander, J. F., & Parsons, B. V. Short-term behavioral intervention with delinquent families: Impact on family process and recidivism. *Journal of Abnormal Psychology*, 1973, *81*, 219–225.

American Psychiatric Association. *Diagnostic and statistical manual of mental disorders (DSM-III)* (3rd ed.). Washington, D.C.: Author, 1980.

Bemis, K. M. Current approaches to the etiology and treatment of anorexia nervosa. *Psychological Bulletin*, 1978, *85*, 593–617.

Carroll, B. J. The desamethasone suppression test for melancholia. *British Journal of Psychiatry*, 1982, *146*, 292–304.

Conger, J. J. *Adolescence and youth: Psychological development in a changing world* (2nd ed.). New York: Harper and Row, 1977.

D'Zurilla, T. J., & Goldfried, M. R. Problem solving and behavior modification. *Journal of Abnormal Psychology*, 1971, *78*, 107–126.

Fairburn, C. A cognitive behavioral approach to the treatment of bulimia. *Psychological Medicine*, 1981, *11*, 707–711.

Fairburn, C. G., & Cooper, P. J. Self-induced vomiting and bulimia nervosa: An undetected problem. *British Medical Journal*, 1982, *284*, 1153–1155.

Goldstein, A. P. Relationship-enhancement methods. In F. H. Kanfer & Press A. P. Goldstein (Eds.), *Helping people change*. New York: Pergamon Press, 1975.

Hsu, L. K. G. The etiology of anorexia nervosa: A review of the literature. *Psychological Medicine*, 1983, in press.

Kanfer, F., & Saslow, G. Behavioral diagnosis. In C. M. Franks (Ed.), *Behavior therapy: Appraisal and Status*. New York: McGraw-Hill, 1969.

Mahoney, M. J., & Mahoney, K. *Permanent weight control: A total solution to the dieter's dilemma*. New York: Norton, 1976.

Minuchin, S., Rosman, B. L., & Baker, L. *Psychosomatic families: Anorexia nervosa in context*. Cambridge, Mass.: Harvard University Press, 1978.

Robin, A. L. A controlled evaluation of problem-solving communication training with parent-adolescent conflict. *Behavior Therapy*, 1981, *12*.(a)

Robin, A. L. Parent-adolescent conflict: A skill training approach. In D. P. Rathjen & J. P. Foreyt (Eds.), *Social competence: Interventions for children and adults*. New York: Pergamon Press, 1981. (b)

Robin, A. L., Kent, R., O'Leary, K. D., Foster, S., & Prinz, R. An approach to teaching parents and adolescents problem-solving communication skills: A preliminary report. *Behavior Therapy*, 1977, *8*, 639–643.

Russell, G. Bulimia nervosa: An ominous variant of anorexia nervosa. *Psychological Medicine*, 1979, 9, 429–448.

Stuart, R. B., & Davis, B. *Slim chance in a fat world: Behavioral control of obesity.* Champaign, Ill.: Research Press, 1972.

Stuart, R. B., & Tripodi, T. Experimental evaluation of three time-constrained behavioral treatments for predelinquents and delinquents. In R. D. Rubin, J. P. Brady, & J. D. Henderson (Eds.) *Advances in behavior therapy (Vol. 4).* New York: Academic Press, 1973.

Weathers, L. & Liberman, R. P. Contingency contracting with families of delinquent adolescents. *Behavior Therapy*, 1975, 6, 356–366.

14

Somatic Disorders in Children

Majorie A. Pelcovits, Bernard V. Silver,
and Dennis C. Russo

RECENT YEARS HAVE WITNESSED significant changes in the role of clinical psychologists in the treatment of children with physical illnesses and somatic disorders. Previously, the primary function of psychologists treating children with somatic disorders had been to ameliorate the emotional pathology seen as contributing to and/or resulting from their physical difficulties (Wright, 1975). With the accelerating development of behavioral approaches, however, there has been an expansion of this role to include the use of behavioral procedures not only to palliate difficulties secondary to children's somatic disorders, but also to alter the somatic problems themselves. This specialty area has been termed *behavioral pediatrics*. As a burgeoning field, behavioral pediatrics is beyond the scope of this chapter; for a comprehensive treatment of this area, we refer readers to other sources (Christophersen, 1982; Russo & Varni, 1982).

Behavioral pediatrics can be distinguished from therapeutic approaches aimed at alleviating the psychopathology assumed to underlie physical problems and subsumed under the label "pediatric psychology" by its emphasis on the development of skills to facilitate symptom reduction. Behavioral pediatrics also differs from the larger field of behavioral medicine by its focus on children, child development, and parent–child interactions. Finally, behavioral pediatrics can be distinguished from child behavior therapy in its exclusive focus on medical problems and medical settings. Although these distinctions may, at first, seem artificial, they point out the collaborative and interdisciplinary arrangement necessary between psychologists and physicians when dealing with somatic problems in children.

In this chapter we focus on those disorders that have been most frequently treated by behavior therapists on an outpatient basis. Outpatient treatment of somatic disorders clearly represents a subspecialty of behavioral pediatrics, which involves both inpatient and outpatient care. We further limit our discussion to that part of behavioral pediatrics addressed to the amelioration of physical symptoms and do not attempt to describe treatment for illness-related concerns in children whose somatic symptoms are under control. Again, readers are directed to other sources (e.g., Melamed & Siegel, 1980; Russo & Varni, 1982) for additional information on these topics.

The purpose of this chapter, therefore, is to acquaint readers with the behavioral treatment approaches that have been used with somatic disorders in children and to delineate considerations that can be used to guide a clinician's choice of treatment methods. Limitations of space and the doubtful relevance of a discussion of many of the less frequently seen disorders to most clinicians engaged in outpatient behavior therapy further prohibit us from providing an exhaustive review of the numerous applications of behavioral procedures in treating children's somatic disorders. Rather, it is our intent to describe a model of treatment that can accommodate any of the range of somatic problems that may be seen in children presenting for treatment in an outpatient setting.

Unfortunately, no catalog or list of somatic disorders seen by outpatient behavior therapists currently exists. Guidelines for selecting disorders to illustrate applications of the model we describe are provided by several sources of information. First, surveys conducted in pediatric practices suggest that the problems for which parents most often seek help from pediatricians include problems of elimination, particularly enuresis and encopresis (Schroeder, 1979; Toister & Worley, 1976). Another source of information emanates from a survey of outpatient visits to the medical services of the Children's Hospital Medical Center, which indicated that asthma and seizures were the most commonly seen disorders in children. Finally, an examination of referrals to the outpatient Behavioral Medicine Clinic at Children's Hospital reveals that, in order of referral frequency, the following somatic disorders were most commonly seen: headaches, dermatitis, encopresis, and enuresis. Although such samples are admittedly biased, the disorders noted above are used in this chapter to illustrate some of the ways in which the clinical methods and techniques of behavioral pediatrics can be applied in outpatient practice.

A MODEL FOR ASSESSMENT AND TREATMENT OF SOMATIC DISORDERS IN CHILDREN

Conceptually, the model we propose is predicated on the assumption that, as in any other area of behavior therapy, treatment plans for children's somatic disorders should be dictated by the findings of a thorough functional analysis of the presenting problem and not by the nature of the presenting problem per se. In the case of somatic disorders, such an analysis should include careful examination of the medical history, a sound understanding of the nature of the disorder, and ongoing medical liaison in addition to assessment of those factors more routinely addressed when working with children. On the basis of the results of such assessment, treatment procedures should be prescriptively selected from the large armamentarium of techniques available to the behavioral clinician.

ASSESSMENT

In each case, the clinician must obtain an adequate description of the problem behavior, the child, and potential contributing factors; collect data that will aid in the selection of appropriate treatment procedures; and establish guidelines relevant to the implementation of treatment. Several steps are necessary to attain these goals: (1) medical screening, (2) clinical interview, (3) baseline recording of the problem, and (4) ongoing assessment.

Medical Screening

All children presenting with somatic problems should receive a medical examination as a prerequisite for behavioral treatment. When a child with a somatic disorder is referred for treatment, the immediate priority is to determine the appropriateness of behavioral intervention for his or her particular presenting problems. Medical evaluation is invaluable in this regard because of the information it can provide about the presence or absence of organic pathology.

In those instances in which physiological or structural impairment is indicated by the medical examination, knowledge about the dis-

order's physiological mechanisms and course will have several implications for the implementation of behavioral treatment. First, in some
cases this information will suggest that the child's somatic disorder
can be treated effectively and safely through medical and/or surgical
means alone and that behavioral intervention is either inappropriate
or unnecessary. Second, in those cases in which behavioral treatment
is warranted, knowledge of organic pathology is necessary to determine whether behavioral procedures should be used alone or in combination with other forms of treatment and whether, in the latter
instance, behavioral treatment should be instituted simultaneously
or sequentially with the other procedures. Information about physiological processes can be quite important in fostering the success of
behavioral programs in two additional ways: (1) by ensuring that the
goals of the treatment program are within the physical capabilities of
the child, and (2) by making it possible to predict at the beginning of
treatment the rate of improvement that might realistically be expected
and thus prevent later disappointment if progress is slow.

A physical examination is also imperative from ethical and legal
perspectives. Ethically, the behavioral practitioner is obligated to refer the child to rule out or affirm the possibility that the child's physical symptoms are indicative of organic pathology. Legally, a behavior
therapist providing an explicit opinion regarding the nature of a particular ailment or implementing a specific treatment program could
be construed as diagnosing and treating a disease. In such a case,
statutes governing the practice of medicine may be applicable and individuals may be placed at risk for malpractice action (Knapp &
Vandercreek, 1981).

Clinical Interview

After the results of the medical screening have been obtained, the
next step in assessment is the clinical interview. The clinical interview is divided into four areas: (1) description and history of the
problem; (2) developmental, family, and medical history; (3) family
functioning; and (4) previous and ongoing treatments.

The interview should be conducted with the child and the parents
both together and alone to obtain their understanding of the problem.
It is especially important that the parents and child be observed
together, in order to determine how much control the parents are able
to exercise over the behavior of the child.

The child and parents should be placed at ease early in the interview.
It is essential to establish rapport since this will be beneficial in developing parental cooperation and can result in the therapist becoming

a significant source of motivation and positive reinforcer for gains made by the child. Although the interview should be structured to some degree, the interviewer must be flexible enough to allow the parents and child latitude for elaboration in the interest of building a therapeutic relationship and acquiring maximum information.

Information regarding the history of the somatic disorder should include data relating to the onset, frequency, severity, and duration of the problem. As with other target behaviors, the relationships between environmental stimuli and disordered somatic behaviors should be explored by inquiring about antecedents, consequences, and organismic variables related to both the initial manifestation and subsequent occurences of the problem.

The second area of assessment focuses on the developmental history, family background, and medical history. In planning treatment for somatic disorders, it is useful to know about the child's general health, level of cognitive functioning, emotional stability, behavior problems, school performance, and general motor and social development. A child's age and maturity should be regarded as major factors in making decisions about treatment plans. For example, a program for treatment of obesity in a bright, independent 12-year-old might focus on teaching self-management strategies such as self-monitoring, self-reinforcement, and stimulus control techniques, whereas the treatment plan for a less mature child of the same age might instead emphasize parental training in contingency contracting for weight loss.

The use of parent questionnaires and observations of parent–child interactions can also yield an estimate of the child's compliance. Certain treatment procedures with younger children require considerable child–parent cooperation and may be contraindicated when a child is noncompliant with parental requests. In such cases, noncompliance should be treated prior to interventions aimed at somatic problems. Children with emotional problems and lower-than-average intelligence also may require closer supervision than other children. School attendance and performance should be assessed since it is sometimes manifest in somatic problems. Conversely, avoidance of academic or interpersonal activities in school may be a factor in maintaining the child's somatic symptoms. Teacher reports may confirm or disconfirm parental reports of a child's social and emotional functioning and provide additional information on a child's peer interactions. Discrepancies between teachers' and parents' reports should be carefully evaluated to determine what person, events, or settings are influencing the child's symptoms.

Another area of questioning focuses on the general functioning of the family. Information should be obtained about siblings with similar problems and any history of somatic difficulties in the paternal and maternal families. Parents who themselves had similar problems may have unrealistic expectations on the bisis of their own experiences. Parents' competence and mental status—as well as their ability to understand directions, tolerate the frustrations of treatment, and maintain complaince subsequent to treatment—should also be assessed to determine the type and amount of supervision that will be needed from the therapist. Child-rearing attitudes, parenting skills, and interest in the child's welfare should be considered, since these factors will also influence the likelihood of treatment success.

A frequently ignored area of assessment is the stability and quality of the parents' marital relationship. The presence of marital discord can be an important determinant of changes in the pattern of the child's somatic problems. Such conflict may also be an obstacle to the effective execution of any parent-admininstered treatment program and may need to be reduced before treatment for the child's presenting problem is undertaken.

Recent, ongoing, and future life changes, such as family vacations or the end of school, are important in assessing somatic problems and in developing treatment plans. Although such changes do not necessarily preclude treatment, they can clearly influence the implementation of treatment. At times, treatment is best deferred pending completion of changes in the child's life. For example, we have found that children's headaches occur with much less frequency during the summer vacation months. Therefore, we sometimes find it desirable to postpone treatment until the academic year resumes.

A final area of inquiry to be addressed during the interview is that of current and previous involvement in other forms of treatment. For children participating on an ongoing basis in alternative types of therapy, it is important to ascertain that involvement in behavioral treatment is compatible with involvement in the other treatment. Specifically, information should be gathered about why parents feel that multiple treatment programs are necessary for determination of the demands that participation in other interventions makes on the child's and parents' time and effort. In some cases, it may be advisable to suggest to the parents that behavioral treatment be deferred until the other treatment is completed.

In instances in which parents have previously sought other forms of treatment for their children, it is important to obtain complete information regarding any systematic or unsystematic treatment attempts in order to prevent them from rejecting or criticizing the proposed treatment on the basis of previous unsuccessful efforts. Information about prior treatments and how they were executed, the outcome of these efforts, attitudes toward treatment of the somatic problem, and knowledge and expectations of the parents and the child regarding the disorder should be evaluated. In this regard, discussion of the speculated mechanisms of therapeutic action will increase the parents' confidence in the therapist's skill and may enhance their willingness to cooperate.

Knowledge of the prognosis of the disorder when left untreated should also be weighed against the degree to which behavioral intervention is expected to facilitate improvement. Similarly, knowledge of developmental norms for certain somatic disorders may prove invaluable in determining whether intervention should consist of parent education regarding child development rather than, or in addition to, symptom reduction procedures. For example, nocturnal enuresis has been reported to have an incidence rate of 15%–20% in five-year-olds (Holeys, Schwartz, & Ciminero, 1981). However, a recent survey revealed that parents thought their children should be dry, on the average, by 2¾ years of age (Shelov, Gundy, Weiss, McIntire, Olness, Staub, Jones, Haque, Ellerstein, Hcagarty, & Starfield, 1981). Knowledge that the problem is relatively "normal" may persuade both the parents and the therapist to postpone treatment.

Baseline Recording

The assessment of any somatic problem requires collection of baseline data to detect any patterns in the occurrence of the disorder. This information should be obtained during a pretreatment period of one to four weeks, depending on the parameters of the problem. For instance, high-frequency, highly aversive symptoms will necessitate of shorter baseline period than will lower-frequency, less aversive somatic problems. The procedure for recording the data should be carefully reviewed with the parents and the child. Cooperation with data collection will be enhanced if recording sheets have been prepared in advance and parents do not have to design their own.

Pretreatment data collection serves several purposes: (1) it establishes a baseline against which to compare the effects of treatment; (2) it serves as a means of assessing parents' compliance with instructions and their willingness to keep records; and (3) and most importantly, it should provide information to aid in the selection of treatment procedures.

Ongoing Assessment

Data collection and assessment should continue throughout treatment to monitor the effects of intervention. A multitude of management problems can arise during treatment, and the collection of behavioral data should serve as the vehicle by which to alter the treatment program. Although many problems can be anticipated by a thorough assessment, some cannot; the therapist must remain flexible and informed in his efforts to adjust the treatment program.

TREATMENT

Numerous treatment procedures can be used singly or in combination in working with children with somatic disorders. Since no formal relationships between specific disorders and techniques designed to ameliorate them should be assumed on a a priori basis, we briefly discuss broad classes of treatment techniques rather than particular methods of intervention. These techniques can be grouped into three categories: operant and social learning procedures, cognitive and behavioral self-management procedures, and biofeedback and physiological self-regulation procedures (Russo & Varni, 1982). These categories are indicative of the three primary means by which somatic disorders can be ameliorated: (1) by altering environments that are thought to elicit and/or reinforce dysfunctional behaviors, (2) by teaching skills to cope with and reduce the impact of environmental stressors, and (3) by modifying autonomic responses directly. Some of the more commonly used techniques in each category are listed in Table 14-1. Although this schema of representing possible interventions is not the only one possible and clear overlap exists between the categories, it does indicate that the goal of these therapies is to improve functioning both behaviorally and physiologically.

To illustrate the treatment process, our discussion of therapeutic techniques for children's somatic disorders focuses on three frequent areas for intervention: (1) medical fears, (2) compliance problems, and (3) symptom management. These categories are not mutually exclusive, and only an adequate assessment will reveal at which level a clinician's intervention should be aimed. For example, a child's fear of self-inoculation may lead to noncompliance with his or her diabetic regimen. Although the child might have been referred for noncompliance, intervention might best be targeted to reduce the child's fears. We first address the treatment of medical fears, next discuss approaches aimed at improving compliance, and then address the treatment of several of the more commonly seen somatic disorders. Rather than attempt a comprehensive review of every procedure that has been used to treat a given disorder, we focus on describing comprehensive approaches that incorporate several techniques. Throughout our discussion, we provide case examples to illustrate various points regarding assessment and treatment.

Table 14-1   Behavioral Techniques for Treating Children's
Somatic Disorders

Operant and social learning procedures
Contingency management procedures
Direct reinforcement (social, material, or primary)
Prompting and shaping
Behavioral contracting
Token economy
Extinction
Response cost
Time out
Punishment
Modeling
Behavior rehearsal and feedback
Stimulus control
Overcorrection
Positive and negative practice
Cognitive and self-management procedures
Relaxation training
Assertiveness training
Social skills training
Problem-solving training
Communication training
Cognitive restructuring
Systematic desentization
Biofeedback and physiological regulation procedures
Relaxation training
Biofeedback
Direct specific training
Nonspecific training

Before proceeding with a discussion of treatment procedures, several points germane to introducing treatment and making the transition from assessment and baseline to treatment and ongoing evaluation should be noted. The therapist should attempt to integrate the medical, interview, and observational information into a parsimonious explanation of the referral problem. The relationship between this information and the selection of a treatment approach should be outlined for the parents and child. The therapist should further describe the program, its known efficacy if available, and the therapist's, child's, and parents' roles in treatment. It is important to provide accurate information rather than give unreasonable expectations for treatment success. At this point, some parents may decide that treatment represents "too much work"; if so, it is better to learn this prior to the implementation of treatment than to experience a low degree of motivation and noncompliance once intervention has begun. Under these circumstances, goals often can be reformulated with the possibility that early improvement as a result of treatment will pave the way for continued family involvement. Compliance with the treatment protocol and maintenance of motivation are critical to treatment success, particularly when results of the intervention are slow to appear.

Medical Fears

Many fears are experienced by children in their normal course of development. In some children, their fears become debilitating and interfere with their daily functioning. When such fears disrupt a child's health, they are termed *medical phobias*. These phobias can both maintain and exacerbate the symptoms of a variety of somatic disorders in children whose health depends on what are often painful diagnostic and treatment procedures. In some cases, medical phobias can be life-threatening. For example, injection phobias in children with juvenile diabetes who require regular administration of insulin pose potentially serious consequences.

The two approaches that have been used most often to alleviate such phobias are systematic desensitization and modeling. Both techniques are well suited for use in an outpatient setting. Although many of the applications of these techniques to reduce children's fears about medical procedures have been carried out in inpatient setting (Melamed & Siegel, 1980), this seems attributable more to reasons of convenience than necessity. However, two constraints appear applicable when choosing treatment methods to use in outpatient settings. First, because of limitations in resources, some treatment modalities that have been found extremely effective in inpatient settings may not be appropriate for use in outpatient settings. For instance, modeling films showing peers using coping strategies, such as behavioral rehearsal, relaxation, pleasant imagery, and distracting tasks have been found to be successrul in allaying children's fears and inappropriate avoidance behaviors (Melamed & Siegel, 1980). Unfortunately, the cost of developing such films may limit their use to inpatient settings in which the numbers of children viewing the films can justify their expense. Second, treatment strategies that involve actual performance of feared procedures, such as participant modeling and in vivo desensitization, should at least initially be limited to settings where supervision by behavioral and medical personnel is available. The following case illustrates the use of behavioral rehearsal, relaxation, modeling, and imaginal and in vivo desensitization in the treatment of a 14-year-old adolescent with a potentially life-threatening medical phobia.

CASE STUDY 1

Mara, a 14-year old female of Mediterranean descent, was referred to the Bahavioral Medicine Clinic by her hematologist for assessment and management of fears of self-inoculation. Mara was diagnosed as having thalassemia, a hereditary blood disorder. This disorder involves a defect in red blood cells causing severe anemia and excessive retention of iron in the body. Therapy aimed at managing the disorder involves both periodic transfusions and pharmacological treatment. It is common for patients to be required to wear an autosyringe apparatus that provides a metered does of medication throughout much of the day. This device is worn on the belt. To use it, the patient must place a small gauge needle attached to the device in the tissue of the abdomen each morning and then remove it after several hours. Because of her fears of self-inoculation, Mara had refused to use this apparatus despite warnings from her physicians, her own awareness of the issues, and frequent joint pain.

The initial evaluation revealed a small, frail, dark-complexioned girl who had some difficulties in ambulation due to pain. She resided at home with her family, infrequently attended a local middle school where she received average grades, and engaged in few extra-curricular activities. Mara and her parents reported a history of excessive fears throughout childhood and current difficulties with joint pain and sleep-onset insomnia. She willingly discussed her fears of needles, whether self- or other-administered, and her previous attempts to overcome her problems in this area. As a result of the initial evaluation, Mara was asked to monitor her average daily pain, distance walked each day, time to sleep onset, and general anxiety level in a diary.

Evaluation of baseline data collected over several weeks indicated that, in addition to complaints of joint pain, sleep-onset insomnia was a major problem. Given the patient's history of fears, her concerns over her abilities to self-inoculate, and her passive, withdrawn personality, the insomnia was made the first target for intervention. This decision was based on the observations that insomnia was less significant to the patient and required similar relaxation and coping skills training approaches to those that would be used in management of the referral problem.

A training program in progressive muscle relaxation combined with continuing self-monitoring and an alteration of presleep activities resulted in a dramatic decrease in time to sleep onset. On the basis of this success and her increased self-confidence and motivation, Mara and the therapist agreed after five weeks of treatment to being a program of fear reduction aimed at assisting her to self-inoculate.

The program consisted of both imaginal and in vivo desensitization and modeling. An eight item hierarchy of feared scenes regarding self-injection was developed. The scenes ranged from approaching the clinic building where the first self-inoculation session would take place through actual placement of the needles. Presentation of these scenes was paired with relaxation over the next four sessions. Additionally, Mara began to structure her day at home such that, at a prearranged time each morning, she would spend ½ hour engaged in relaxation exercises and handling materials related to self-injection. During these times, she had no actual medicine and did not self-inject.

Mara was then brought to the clinic where, with the assistance of a pediatric nurse practitioner and the behavior therapist, an education session regarding the medications, their preparation, and the self-injection routine was conducted. At each stage, Mara would stop, relax, and continue only when calm and relaxed. The session culminated with Mara preparing all materials, preparing her site, and self-injecting with little reported anxiety. A maintenance program was then established involving gradual fading from weekly meetings to biweekly and then monthly sessions. Sessions focused on establishing a carefully defined daily self-injection and needle removal routine and continued practice of her relaxation skills. Self-report data confirmed by Mara's parents indicated increased distance in walking, reductions in joint pain, and decreased anxiety in addition to continued reduction in time to sleep onset as a result of treatment. Despite several setbacks that required brief booster sessions, at one year follow-up Mara was self-injecting daily. Consistent use of the pump over this period had resulted in improved disease status as well as a more positive emotional state.

Medical Compliance

When a child is referred for treatment of a somatic disorder that has failed to respond to standard medical treatment that usually is effective with other children, one of the first questions a clinician must ask is whether the child has been compliant with that treatment. Often, assessment reveals that the child has not benefited from treatment because he or she has failed to comply with the prescribed medical regimen and not because he or she has been a nonresponder to an otherwise effective therapy.

A number of factors are known to influence compliance, including the complexity of the therapeutic regimen, duration of the treatment program, beliefs in the efficacy of therapy, the speed with which the regimen alleviates discomfort, presence of aversive side effects, saliency of cues for implmenting the treatment program, and the ease with which the regimen fits into the daily life pattern (Melamed, 1980; Melamed & Siegel, 1980). Conversely, such variables as the patient's knowledge about his or her illness, socioeconomic status, personality, and motivation have consistently failed to be predictive of adherence to medical advice (Melamed, 1980; Melamed & Siegel, 1980). Like other classes of behaviors, therefore, health-related behaviors appear to demonstrate a clear-cut relationship to the events that precede their occurrence and to the consequences that follow.

Several strategies have been suggested to improve compliance in children with various somatic disorders. Rapoff and Christophersen

(1982) have outlined a multidimensional approach that includes (1) facilitation of the child's and his or her parents' understanding of the regimen through written handouts and the practitioner's modeling of required behaviors, (2) gradual implementation of the regimen in a step-by-step fashion, (3) tailoring of the regimen to fit in with the personal habits and routines of the child and his or her family (e.g., by suggesting that prescribed exercises be done while watching late-afternoon cartoons), (4) frequent telephone contacts and/or clinic visits to monitor patient progress, (5) capitalizing on the reactive effects of self-monitoring by asking the child and/or his or her parents to monitor compliance and physical symptoms using standard recording forms, and (6) teaching parents behavior management techniques, such as providing positive reinforcement when their children comply with their treatment and using a response cost or a time-out procedure when their children refuse to take medications.

Failure to adhere to medical regimens is often the primary factor maintaining a number of the more commonly seen somatic disorders in children, such as encopresis. While a more complete description of the treatment of encopresis is presented later in this chapter, the follow case example illustrates the importance of assessing the functional aspects of noncompliance in an encopretic adolescent.

CASE STUDY 2

Wendy, aged 15, was referred to the Behavioral Medicine Clinic because of her difficulties with chronic constipation and encopresis. In addition to numerous outpatient visits. Wendy's problems with pain due to constipation had resulted in several emergency room visits and five hospitalizations. Previous treatment efforts had involved vigorous cleanouts using enemas and a regular maintenance regimen including various cathartics. During her most recent hospitalization prior to referral for behavioral treatment, her constipation was so severe that surgical disimpaction, although never implemented, was considered.

Wendy was accompanied to the intake interview by her mother. They presented as a noncommunicative, lower-middle-class family, composed of Wendy, an older borther and sister not living at home, two younger stepbrothers, her mother, and her stepfather. Wendy's mother reported that Wendy refused to take her medication unless closely supervised. She added that she "just couldn't understand" why Wendy continued to become constipated when she knew the medication would alleviate the problem. When interviewed with her mother present, Wendy appeared sullen and offered only terse answers to questions addressed to her. Regarding her noncompliance, she offered no explanation other than that she "didn't feel like" taking her medication.

When interviewed alone, Wendy's mother expressed her extreme frustration with Wendy's situation. She said that she had tried everything she could think of to get Wendy to be compliant with her medication and that she no longer had the patience to supervise Wendy's adherence to her regimen.

When Wendy was interviewed alone, she stated her belief that failure to comply with her medical regimen and becoming constipated were the only ways in which she could get any attention in her family. According to her, all the attention was directed to her stepbrothers except when she was sick. Wendy added that she hated her stepfather and living at home, and that she looked forward to leaving as soon as she was old enough to do so. She stated her intention of remaining noncompliant with her medical regimen until that time arrived.

Wendy's compliance difficulties were conceptualized as being due to problems with negative communication and ineffective problem-solving in the family. If these problems were to continue unchanged, it appeared likely that Wendy's problems with constipation and encopresis would continue also. Altering the family's maladaptive patterns of communication thus, was chosen as the means of achieving the goal of increasing Wendy's compliance with her medical regimen.

Wendy and her mother attended two 1-hour treatment sessions, during which they were taught problem-solving communication skills. Wendy's stepfather was unable to attend because he was a long-distance truckdriver with an irregular schedule. Wendy and her mother were taught to center discussions of specific disagreements around a problem-solving model that included the following steps: defining the problem, listing solutions, evaluating the consequences of these solutions, and planning to implement the solutions. Two major issues were discussed during the sessions: taking medication and helping with household chores.

Through these discussions, Wendy agreed to take her medication and perform regular household chores in exchange for obtaining privileges like choosing her own clothes and staying out with friends. After the first two treatment sessions, Wendy and her mother were referred to a therapist closer to their home. At this point, Wendy's mother felt enough progress had been made to no longer warrant the 1½ hour drive to the hospital on a regular basis. Both Wendy and her mother agreed that some tensions had been alleviated at home. They both reported that Wendy was fairly compliant with her medical regimen and was having regular bowel movements.

Symptom Management in Somatic Disorders

In our discussion of somatic disorders, we focus on three groups of problems: (1) disorders that represent deviations from developmental norms, (2) disorders in which stress or other psychological factors are presumed to play a central causal or precipitating role, and (3) problems related to a chronic disease state. Although these categories are by no means mutually exclusive, they are useful in alerting the clinician to issues of particular relevance to different classes of disorders.

The disorders in each category whose treatment we describe in some detail to demonstrate the application of behavioral assessment and treatment procedures are as follows: the developmental problems of enuresis and encopresis, the psychophysiological problems of migraine headache and atopic dermatitis, and the chronic illnesses of asthma and seizures.

Developmental Problems

Somatic disorders classified as developmental problems are those whose occurrence can be considered "normal" in very young children. By definition, these disorders are usually thought to warrant treatment only if they perist beyond the age by which they have resolved or improved in most children. Nocturnal enuresis and encopresis are the most common problems in this group of disorders. Our earlier discussion of the need to be aware of the course of normal development is particularly relevant to intervention with children presenting with these disorders.

Nocturnal Enuresis

Nocturnal enuresis is defined as the involuntary passage of urine during sleep beyond the age of five years, when children usually gain bladder control (Doleys & Dolce, 1982; Doleys, Schwartz, & Ciminero, 1981). Some investigators have also suggested that a distinction between primary enuresis (the child has never achieved consistent control) and secondary enuresis (bedwetting has recurred after a period of sustained control) is useful in the selection of appropriate treatment (Doleys et al, 1981; Melamed, 1980). Primary enuresis usually requires more complex treatment because toileting skills have never been acquired, whereas secondary enuresis, which is often due to illness or, more frequently, periods of stress, implies less need for elaborate skills training.

Additional information that should be considered in determining the most appropriate treatment procedures can be provided by assessing patterns of nocturnal and diurnal wetting and functional bladder capacity (Doleys et al, 1981). For example, knowledge about the child's sleep behavior and arousability will help to determine the child's sensitivity to bladder distention and the feasibility of using a urine alarm in treatment. Finally, although it is important to assess family functioning in treating all somatic disorders in children, assessment of these factors is particularly critical in designing treatment programs for enuretic children. Certain treatment procedures, such as the dry-bed training approach of Azrin, Sneed, and Foxx (1974), require a considerable amount of parent–child interaction and parental involvement in executing treatment. In families in which parental motivation is low or where the child's compliance with parental requests is problematic, such procedures whould probably not be considered until these conditions have been modified.

Many behavioral methods have been used for treating enuresis, including urine detection (bell-and-pad) alarms, bladder retention control training, contingency management (rewards provided for dry nights), and combination of these procedures (Christophersen & Rapoff, 1979; Doleys & Dolce, 1982; Doleys et al, 1981). Based solely on its success rate, the dry-bed training procedure of Azrin and his colleagues (Azrin et al, 1974), which combines the urine alarm, contingency management, and retention control training procedures, would appear to be the treatment of choice. In addition to the use of a urine alarm, this procedure involves training in inhibiting urination by means of hourly awakenings, positive reinforcement for correct use of the toilet, training in toileting behaviors through positive practice, training in rapid awakening, increased fluid intake, self-correction of accidents through cleanliness training, and increased praise from parents and other relatives following each dry night. This program typically requires one night of intensive training followed by a period of posttraining supervision. During the posttraining period, the child is routinely awakened and taken to the bathroom once during the late or midevening after each dry night. Each night after the occurrence of bedwetting, cleanliness training and postive practice in toileting are also instituted. After seven consecutive dry nights, the posttraining supervision phase is discontinued. At this time, the urine alarm is no longer used and the nighttime awakenings are stopped. If bedwetting occurs again, cleanliness training is reinstituted in the morning after the accident and positive practice trials in correct toileting are provided before bedtime the following night. These conditions remain in effect unless two or more wet nights occur within a week, in which case the posttraining supervision phase is reintroduced.

As noted earlier, dry-bed training requires a significant commitment from parents because it demands more active participation than do other procedures. Depending on the age and/or developmental level of the child and the involvement of the family, assessment frequently indicates that procedures that are less time-consuming, less complicated, and less expensive (e.g., regular awakenings, restricted fluids, retention control training, positive reinforcement for toileting, or urine alarms) may be attempted either individually or in combination with a higher probability of success.

Encopresis

Encopresis is defined as the involuntary passage of feces into a child's clothing beyond the age of 3 years (Doleys et al., 1981). The disorder is usually accompanied by chronic constipation. The prolonged periods of stool retention present in encopresis often result in relaxation of the sphincter muscles and distention of the colon, so that a thorough physical evaluation must be carried out prior to the use of any behavioral procedures.

Medical managment of encopresis generally involves disimpaction of the bowel with enemas and suppositories followed by the use of stool softeners, laxatives, and mineral oil to stimulate daily bowel movement. This regimen allows the colon to regain its normal muscle tone and thus avoid further fecal impaction and constipation (Christophersen & Rapoff, 1979). Dietary recommendations also are made to reduce the consumption of milk and increase the amount of roughage and fresh and dried fruit. Finally, patients are encouraged to sit on the toilet and attempt a bowel movement once or twice each day, usually about one hour after meals to take advantage of the gastroileal reflex. Such regimens have a high success rate in restoring regular bowel movements, but, since muscle tonus often takes several months to return to normal, problems with compliance often occur.

Behavioral treatment programs for encopresis are concerned largely with teaching necessary toileting skills and arranging environmental contingencies to facilitate adherence to medical regimens. Selection of specific treatment techniques will depend on the results of the functional analysis. As in the case of enuresis, evaluation of whether a child is a primary or secondary encopretic suggests a differential emphasis on toileting skills training versus stress management or contingency management. For primary encopretics, who have never displayed control over defecation, instruction in toileting skills (e.g., removing clothing and exerting necessary muscular pressure while sitting on the toilet) is more likely to be necessary. In secondary encopresis, where bowel control was previously evident, modification of the stimulus conditions that accompany soiling behavior and of the consequences that follow soiling will usually be necessary. For children whose previous experience with painful defecation has led to the development of "toilet phobia," or excessive fear of sitting on or being near the toilet, a program of in vivo and/or systematic desensitization may be required. However, the most frequently used behavioral treatment approaches for encopresis have focused on operant techniques providing reinforcement (in the form of parental praise, tokens for access to favorite activities and toys, and material rewards) contingent on defecation and appropriate toileting behaviors, discontinuing parental attention for soiling, and providing punishment (in the form of response cost, loss of privileges, and/or requirements that the child change and clean his or her soiled underwear) contingent on accidents. The following case illustrates the assessment and subsequent treatment of an encopretic child. The case also shows the necessity of modifying the treatment program on the basis of information from ongoing assessment.

CASE STUDY 3

Larry, a 6-year-old child, was referred to the Behavioral Medicine Clinic because of recurrent problems with soiling. His parents had brought him for treatment since their previous unguided efforts had failed. The family had tried a number of methods to deal with the problem, including sending Larry to his room following an accident, taking away a favorite toy, and rewarding him for his successes. None of these strategies had produced positive results.

Larry had been successfully bladder trained by three years of age. Bowel training had been inconsistent but was achieved for a period of several months when he was 4½ years old. During prior visits to the pediatrician, mineral oil had been prescribed without effect. While Larry had occasional bowel movements in the toilet, most voiding occurred in his underwear. His mother explained that it often appeared that accidents took place only a few minutes after Larry had been on the toilet. He also had additional soiling accidents during the day.

Accidents usually occurred at home. In fact, Larry's mother said that during the past year he had never had an accident at school. Larry didn't seem to be uncomfortable when he soiled his pants and rarely told his mother that he had had an accident. Following accidents, Larry's mother usually changed him herself, although she said that Larry was able to undress himself. While she changed Larry, he often engaged her in conversation, asking if she was angry, expressing concern that she might not love him, and requesting that she not tell his father.

Larry demonstrated awareness of his problem and said during the interview that he couldn't go to the toilet. According to his mother's report, Larry had progressed well in other areas of his development and had had no problems in school. However, he was begining to have problems with peers and was frequently left out of activities with other children. Larry's problem with soiling had also begun to interfere with family activities since they were unable to plan trips away from home.

At the end of the interview, the parents were asked to keep a record of Larry's soiling and bowel movements for one week. They were to check his pants one hour after each meal and also once prior to bedtime to determine if he had soiled. They were also instructed to confirm the occurrence of bowel movement in the toilet and note the size and consistency of each stool. Larry was also referred for medical evaluation which revealed no physical abnormalities to account for his toileting problems.

Baseline data gathered by the parents revealed that there were eight instances of soiling and one appropriate defecation in the toilet. On the basis of these baseline data and interview information, the follow plan was formulated. Larry's mother was told to stop cleaning him when he had an accident. Initially, she was to supervise his changing himself but was not to engage in any extended conversation with him. Any questions were to be addressed by saying one time, "I'm not going to talk about that now" and then ignoring any further attempts to engage her in conversation. Larry was asked to sit on the toilet for five minutes approximately one hour after each meal when he was at home. In addition, a token reward system was instituted in which stickers were earned for clean pants at the two clean pants checks and for each bowel movement in the toilet. Two stickers earned Larry an ice cream treat, with three stickers earning him a prize of an opportunity at a grab bag containing toys of his choosing.

During the first two days of this program, Larry had three bowel movements in the toilet. However, he hadn't earned any bonus prizes because he had continued to soil his underwear. The following week, the program was altered so that Larry earned a sticker for nonsoiling, and any toileting success earned an opportunity at the grab bag. Larry's mother reported the following week that there was some improvement, with one day free of any soiling accidents. However, Larry's mother still felt he was making little progress. At this point, the reinforcement contingencies were changed to provide for more immediate exchange for prizes so that Larry could earn small prizes for being clean at each cleanliness check and a larger prize for each toileting success. This program, too, produce a few toileting successes, with Larry still soiling frequently. However, a phone contact during the week after this program was instituted revealed that Larry's mother had failed to follow through on the contingencies for clean pants and had also changed his diet without seeking medical advice. This resulted in increased instances of soiling.

During the fifth session, a new program was implemented that reinforced approximations to toileting. Larry was required to sit on the toilet for five minutes to earn TV time, going outside, or ice cream. If he had a toileting success during these or any other times, he would earn a trip to the neighborhood playground or would be allowed to stay up late. If he had an accident, he was required to clean himself up and stay in the house for 30 minutes without access to the TV or toys. The next appointment was canceled; however, Larry's mother reported in a phone call that, although Larry had been resistant at first, the program changes had been successful. Larry had had only three soiling accidents during the week. During the following week, Larry had only once accident. A follow-up visit two weeks later indicated that Larry had had no soiling accidents during this period. At the six-month follow-up, the parents reported that they were able to go on vacations without difficulty and Larry's interactions with peers had improved. Only isolated occurrences of soiling were noted.

Psychophysiological Disorders

Psychophysiological disorders include those somatic disorders that are thought to result from a combination of emotional arousal and physiological predisposition. Because of the central role accorded ineffective coping with stress and other psychological factors in precipitating and maintaining physical symptoms, stress management training is usually a particularly important feature of intervention programs for children with these disorders.

Migraine Headache

Headaches are among the most common physical complaints in children and adolescents (Shinnar & D'Souza, 1981). Migraine headaches are paroxysmal headaches characterized by unilateral pain, nausea and vomiting, and a positive family history of similar headaches. Several considerations specific to migraine headaches must be addressed in treating children with this disorder. First, treatment should occur only following referral to a neurologist to rule out any organic basis for the headaches. Second, the child should be instructed to monitor the occurrence of headache activity to identify precipitating factors and consequent events. We have found that children as young as seven years of age are capable of accomplishing this self-monitoring. Monitoring forms that are returned neatly filled in by the child's mother or father also have diagnostic implications and may indicate the need for a partial "parentectomy" as part of treatment. The stimulus conditions associated with the onset of headaches should be analyzed to determine what skills the child might need to learn to make his or her environment less stressful. For example, cognitive restructuring and self-instructional training may be helpful in reducing headache-related anxiety associated with academic performance. In addition, the reactions of family members, peers, and others to the child's headaches should be examined to determine to what extent positive and/or negative reinforcement may be maintaining headache activity and whether contingency management procedures are required.

Biofeedback, relaxation training, and contingency management have all been found effective in reducing headache activity in children. Clinically, we have found that additional procedures such as cognitive coping skills and assertion training have enhanced treatment effectiveness with older children and adolescents. Results of a research program recently completed at Children's Hospital indicate the success of a multifaceted treatment package for treating pediatric migraine. In this program, children with migraine headaches were instructed in biofeedback-assisted meditative relaxation and were given behavioral counseling to modify maladaptive lifestyle factors (e.g., eating irregularly, lack of sleep) and to increase skills for coping with head-ache-exacerbating or -precipitation situations. Parents also were instructed in the use of contingency management techniques to increase adherence with relaxation practice and to decrease pain-related complaints and school avoidance. This program resulted in significant reductions in headaches activity that were maintained at a one-year follow-up.

The following case describes the treatment of a boy with migraines. This case also is instructive in providing a reminder of the value of individually tailored treatment programs and of the dangers of over-reliance on standardized treatment packages.

CASE STUDY 4

Jerry, aged 8½, was referred for behavioral treatment of his migraine head-aches by his neurologist. He lived alone with his mother, since his father had been killed in an automobile accident two months before his birth. Jerry had been diagnosed as having petit mal epilepsy when he was three years old. He was successfully treated with anticonvulsant medications, which were discontinued one year prior to his referral for behavioral treatment. Jerry remained entirely seizure-free throughout the year. At approximately the same time his medications were discontinued, however, Jerry began complaining of headaches on a regular basis. His mother said that his headaches had gradually increased in frequency, duration, and intensity during the past year to the point where he had been reporting very severe headaches as often as 10 times a day during the week immediately preceding the interview. Extensive testing done by Jerry's neurologist had revealed no physiological basis for this increase in headache activity. Medication was prescribed, but Jerry's mother feared its side effects and give it to Jerry only sporadically.

Jerry described his headaches as occurring both frontally and laterally and as being accompanied by nausea and heightened sensitivity to lights and sounds. He said that he had recently begun experiencing pain in his legs, eyes, and stomach in between headaches. According to Jerry and his mother, approximately half of Jerry's headaches lasted less than a minute and half lasted 15 minutes to one hour. Jerry's mother noted that she could always tell how severe Jerry's headaches were by the amount of grimacing accompanying them.

On the average, Jerry missed one day of school each week because of his headaches. At these times, he would stay at home and either watch television or play with his toys all day. Whenever a headache occurred, he would tell his mother about it and then resume playing. Jerry said that he liked the academic side of school and most of his classmates, but that he hated having to take the school bus because several of the class bullies rode the bus with him. These bullies also lived in his apartment complex and frequently beat him up, so Jerry disliked playing outside at home as well.

Jerry was asked to monitor his headaches for two weeks. The monitoring sheets were returned filled out by his mother. They showed that Jerry had headaches "off and on" throughout the late afternoon and evening after his return from school, each so brief in duration that no sooner had his mother written down that a headache had started than Jerry told her the headache had stopped. Two or three times each week he had a headache of 20–45 minutes' duration; each of these occurred following the few occasions he played outside.

Given this information, it was hypothesized that both operant factors and physiological reactions to the stress of interacting with the neighborhood rough-necks were maintaining Jerry's headaches. During the first treatment session, it was emphasized that Jerry should fill out the self-monitoring sheets and that his mother should respond to his complaints of headaches as calmly and straightforwardly as possible. Biofeedback-assisted meditative relaxation was implemented to help Jerry manage stress in encounters with the bullies, and he was instructed to practice daily during the coming week. Social skills training was not considered necessary because, as confirmed by his teacher, Jerry had a number of friends in school. Furthermore, since the bullies picked fights with almost all the children in the class, it seemed that there was little Jerry did to provoke their hostilities.

Despite the previous week's instructions, the monitoring sheets were returned for the second treatment session still filled out my Jerry's mother. Jerry reported that he had only practiced relaxation once. Furthermore, biofeedback conducted during this session indicated that Jerry was unsuccessful in controlling his autonomic functioning using mediatative relaxation. He reported that instead of concentrating on the word "relax," his attention wandered during relaxation practice to inventing stories about "being on a space warp." To help Jerry concentrate only on relaxing, an audiotape was made of the "letting go" form of relaxation. To increase his practicing frequence and redirect his mother's attention away from his pain complaints and toward his coping efforts, the following contingencies were instituted: Jerry was told to record every time he practiced relaxation, and to have this verified by his mother. She was then to praise him and give him a baseball card to add to the collection he kept. Each time he told her of a headache or other pain, she was to respond by not permitting him to resume playing and by instead sending him to lie down for 10 minutes in a darkened room by himself.

With these contingencies in place, Jerry began to practice relaxing twice daily. His mother reported finding it easier to respond calmly to his pain reports when she had something to do besides ignore them. With his mother's encouragement, Jerry began practicing relaxation on the bus and before going outside to play as well as during quiet times. By the seventh treatment session, Jerry's reports of brief, "on and off" headaches and assorted aches had ceased completely. He had had only one severe headache during the last three weeks, and he was able to reduce it to mild intensity and then abort it after ten minutes. Moreover, Jerry had had a perfect attendance record at school during the last four weeks of treatment. A phone call to his mother one month later found that these improvements had been maintained.

Atopic Dermatitis

Atopic dermatitis is on inflammatory skin disorder characterized by redness, swelling, crusting, scaling, and intense itching. Although the precipitating factors in the initial appearance of the disorder are unknown, the disorder is maintained and exacerbated by scratching. Topical medications are the mainstay of the management of atopic dermatitis. However, effective treatment requires control of the itch–scratch–itch cycle that perpetuates the disease. The goal of the behavioral clinician in treating children with atopic dermatitis is to increase compliance with the recommendation to stop scratching so that the prescribed medications can be effective.

Whereas scratching a pruritic area provides its own reward in the form of temporary relief of itchiness, assessment often reveals that scratching by children with dermatitis is also maintained by a variety of antecedent and consequent events. Factors that often increase the frequency of scratching include stressful events that provoke its occurrence, a limited repertoire of skills for combating the urge to scratch, and inadvertent reinforcement of scratching by parents and peers following its occurrence. The treatment strategy usually followed with children with dermatitis thus involves teaching the children to identify situation that elicit scratching and to execute alternative behaviors incompatible with scratching in these situations and/or teaching parents to differentially reinforce their children by providing attention contingent on periods of nonscratching and ignoring all episodes of scratching.

Considerations regarding a child's age and maturity are important in determining which procedures to focus on in treatment. For younger children, operant procedures have been found to be very effective. The use of these procedures with a 3-year-old girl is illustrated by the following case.

CASE STUDY 5

Three-year-old Ellen's parents sought behavioral treatment for her because of her scratching of her atopic dermatitis. The dermatitis had been well controlled until six weeks before the initial interview, when Ellen began scratching behind her knees. The frequency of scratching gradually increased so that her thighs, belly, face, elbows, and wrists as well as her knees were red and scaly at the intake interview.

Observations of Ellen's interactions with her parents showed that they generally had excellent control over her behavior. However, they said that the one area of behavior they were unable to influence was scratching. They reported that the scratching occurred most often before Ellen fell asleep at night, when she awoke from daytime naps, and at other times when she seemed especially bored, tired, or anxious.

Ellen's mother stated that the scratching first became problematic around the same time she began applying medicated cream to Ellen's skin on a regular basis. She remarked that the cream may have had a paradoxical effect because of all the attention it brought to the scratching. Ellen's father expressed his concern that her scratching was aggravated by his behavior, since he also had atopic dermatitis and sometimes scratched in front of her. Ellen's parents also said they thought their behavior was somehow responsible for Ellen's scratching because, to the best of their knowledge, she has never scratched when playing with friends or at nursery school.

Ellen's parents had tried two methods of attempting to reduce her scratching on their own. When they saw her scratching, they would either try to distract her or point out what she was doing and ask her to stop. This tactic only rarely worked. In addition, two weeks before the interview they had implemented a "star" system, in which Ellen could earn stars for not scratching, which, in turn, earned her a reward at the end of the week. While they felt the stars had helped Ellen to decrease the scratching somewhat, they acknowledged the system's impact may have been reduced by their waiting too long to follow through on giving her a reward.

In view of Ellen's father's guilt about being responsible for Ellen's aggravation of her dermatitis, the first step in treatment was to emphasize to both parents that Ellen's scratching was maintained by being its own reward as well as by their actions and that, although they could create conditions to help her control the scratching, they could not control it for her. Additionally, after a week of baseline data recording that confirmed the parents' reports during the interview, several recommendations were made. First, Ellen's parents were told to keep their attempts to distract her from scratching very brief; if they were unsuccessful in immediately distracting her, they were to ignore any further scratching. Second, they were instructed to make their attention contingent on gradually increasing periods of not scratching. Using naps as a rehearsal for bedtime, they were to make reading her a story or playing with her when she woke up contingent on her staying in bed for a specified period without scratching. Third, alterations were made in Ellen's bedtime routine so that, instead of reading her stories immediately after she climbed into bed, her parents would delay the stories until she had been in bed a few minutes without scratching. Finally, the star system was modified to include immediate as well as long-term rewards for periods without scratching. The immediate reinforcer took the form of being allowed to play a game in which Ellen was given opportunities to earn a reward by choosing a flap on a board. Each flap covered a different surprise (e.g., a sticker, chewing gum, a balloon, a trip to the playground, new crayons, candy, etc.) to prevent satiation on any one type of reward.

Two weeks after this program was implemented, Ellen's parents reported a dramatic decrease in Ellen's scratching. Because of their high level of motivation and comfort in executing the treatment plan, no further sessions were scheduled. Follow-up phone calls one and two months later both indicated that

Ellen was scratching very infrequently, that her parents were able to quickly terminate all scratching she began, and that the pruritic areas on Ellen's skin had healed.

Older children and adolescents are often embarassed by their parents' and peers' comments about their scratching, and may restrict their scratching to situations in which no one else is present. Therefore, treatment strategies appropriate for this age group typically involve greater emphasis on training in self-control and stress management skills. By monitoring the types of situation that most often produce the urge to scratch, it is possible to determine the most appropriate skills to be taught.

CASE STUDY 6

Gina, a 16-year-old black female, was referred by her dermatologist for behavioral treatment to help her control her scratching secondary to dermatitis. She was interviewed and seen for treatment without her parents, since they were not willing to take time off from work to accompany her. Gina's self-report and baseline data indicated that she was scratching about two hours each day in association with events that produced strong emotions, such as anger (after arguments with her mother), frustration (when doing difficult homework), and anxiety (when thinking about reciting at church). Gina's scratching occurred only when she was by herself. She said she never scratched when with friends or at school and would either go into her room or wait until her parents were out of sight to scratch at home.

Gina's dermatitis was visible on her wrists, forearms, heels, and calves. It only mildly detracted from her attractive, well-groomed appearance. Gina's primary source of motivation for learning to control her scratching was her desire to become a model after graduating from high school. Otherwise, Gina's skin problems interfered with her functioning in only very limited ways. The appearance of her skin caused her few problems with friends, although she was occasionally teased by acquaintances. Gina reported having a large number of friends and a steady boyfriend and staying out too late with her friends.

During the first treatment session, Gina was taught meditative relaxation and was instructed to sit on her hands and practice relaxing whenever she had the urge to scratch. She was also taught how to self-reinforce and was told to give herself a special reward (e.g., go to a movie, use perfume, buy a bottle of nail polish) each day she scratched for less than two hours. Self-monitoring during the following weeks indicated only a slight reduction in scratching frequency. Gina was then told to imagine herself as a model being admired for her flawless skin as she walked down a runway as an additional step in the sequence of behaviors she was to perform in response to urges to scratch. This modification resulted in further decreases in Gina's scratching frequency, and her dermatitis began to heal. However, total healing was prevented by the scratching Gina engaged in following arguments with her parents.

Communication training and instruction in behavioral contracting were undertaken to help Gina interact with her parents with less friction. Without Gina's parents present, however, these unilateral interventions were only partially successful. Gina's scratching in response to arguments was reduced slightly but was not eliminated.

After ten treatment sessions, Gina was scratching for 10–20 minutes a day. Because Gina agreed that it was unlikely that her scratching frequency would decrease any further unless treatment included her parents and because her parents insisted they were unable to attend sessions, treatment was discontinued at this point. At follow-up one month later, Gina reported her situation was unchanged. Her dermatitis was much less evident than at the beginning of treatment and continuing to improve but was still perpetuated to some degree by low levels of scratching.

Chronic Illnesses

Effective intervention with children with chronic illnesses requires understanding of the special problems that often accompany this group of disorders. These problems can make the lives of chronically ill children extremely stressful, with the stress, in turn, exacerbating and perpetuating their physical symptoms.

Besides the painful medical procedures that must be endured in managing many chronic disorders, growing up with a chronic illness may entail being subjected to lenghty hospitalizations, frequent separations from family members, high rates of school absence, and parental overprotectiveness. In addition, depending on the nature of the specific disorder, children with chronic illnesses may suffer from self- and/or peer-imposed social isolation due to such factors as symptoms that cause embarrassment, inability to participate in sports and other strenuous activities, unusual appearance related to the disease process itself or to medical or surgical interventions, and treatment regimens that mark the child as "different" and that interfere with social activities. Thus, many of the characteristics associated with chronic illness not only engender stress, but also restrict children's opportunities to acquire the age-appropriate social and academic skills needed to deal effectively with environmental demands. These considerations suggest that, more often than not, behavioral treatment for children with chronic illnesses will require teaching multiple coping skills rather than using single techniques in isolation.

Asthma

Asthma is a respiratory disorder characterized by intermittent, variable, and reversible constriction of the bronchial passages. Symptoms include labored breathing, especially when exhaling, wheezing, coughing, shortness of breath, and anxiety accompanying a feeling of suffocation (King, 1980; Melamed, 1980; Melamed & Johnson, 1981). The disorder affects 2%–4% of the pediatric population and accounts for 25% of all school absences due to chronic illness (Melamed, 1980; Melamed & Johnson, 1981).

Asthmatic children are not a homogeneous group with regard to either etiology or severity. Hereditary predisposition, allergy, respiratory infection, environmental factors, and emotional variables all have been identified as being involved in the development of asthma and/or precipitation of attacks (Christophersen & Rapoff, 1979; King, 1980; Melamed, 1980; Melamed & Johnson, 1981). Behavioral interventions for asthmatic children have addressed the last two factors by using contingency management procedures to alter the child's social environment and biofeedback, relaxation training, systematic desensitization, and assertion training to improve the child's ability to cope with emotional arousal. Although behavioral treatments have been successful to varying degrees in decreasing many of the symptoms of asthma and the frequency of attacks, it should be emphazised that they have not been found to alter lung function significantly in asthmatic children (Alexander, Cropp, & Chai, 1979). It is, therefore, of critical importance that outpatient behavioral treatment of asthma be considered adjunctive to medical management (Christophersen & Rapoff, 1979; King, 1980; Melamed, 1980), and not be carried out in settings where adequate medical coverage is unavailable.

With asthma, as with other chronic diseases, the behavioral clinician must carefully manage the treatment program to avoid untoward reactions to the implementation of contingencies. In some children, the initial response to a behavioral program may be an escalation in the severity of attacks that could lead to hospitalization. Under such circumstances, the clinician must consider whether intervention poses more risk than benefit. With some children, targeting behaviors unrelated to the asthma itself may be a necessary first step toward the goal of more directly influencing symptoms of the disorder.

Given the many ways in which asthma attacks can be elicited and in which asthma can be disruptive to a child's functioning, multifaceted programs developed in response to thorough analyses of the events that precede, occur concurrently with, and follow attacks usually are required to significantly affect asthmatic behavior (King, 1980). In most cases, self-monitoring for identification of high-risk situations for asthma attacks and of those symptoms that mark the early stages of an asthma attack will be a mainstay of treatment. Information about high-risk situations is helpful both in identifying skill deficits and reinforcement conditions that may contribute to the maintenance of symptoms and in facilitating anxiety management training in which the children can rehearse coping with emotional events. Information about symptoms at the onset of attacks is helpful in teaching the child to seek treatment when it is likely to be optimally effective.

The case of the 14-year-old girl whose treatment illustrates the application of multiple treatment techniques has been described by King (1980). Self-monitoring revealed a chain of events in which being asked to perform several tasks at school requiring academic and social skills produced anxiety. The anxiety, in turn, led to having asthma attacks. The asthma attacks were followed by removal from the classroom to allow her to rest and use a bronchodilator. Her return to the classroom was typically followed by expressions of concern about her health from her teachers and her early release from school to be taken home by her parents. This case required that the child be taught relaxation and cognitive coping techniques to help her deal more effectively with the anxiety associated with her attacks as well as a variety of academic and social skills to enable her to cope more adequately with the antecedent stressors and thus attempt to prevent attacks. In addition, consultation with the child's teachers and parents was necessary to reduce the amount of attention given the girl contingent on her attacks. This prevented her from avoiding schoolwork by having attacks and increased her adaptive behavior by redirecting attention to her efforts to circumvent severe attacks.

Seizures

Seizures are defined as abrupt, involuntary alterations in or loss of control of the motor, sensory, and/or automonic functions of the body. Seizures can vary in intensity from brief lapses in consciousness (petit mal) to prolonged interruptions of consciousness accompanied by severe convulsions (grand mal). Management of seizure disorders requires regular medical care, which almost invariably includes the use of medications. Anticonvulsant medications produce significant decreases in seizure activity in the majority of cases. However, it has been estimated that as many as 50% of the children who take these medications continue to have occasional seizures, whereas an additional 20% are completely refractory to pharmacological treatment (Melamed, 1980; Melamed & Siegel, 1980).

Behavioral procedures have been used efficaciously to decrease the frequency and severity of several types of seizure disorders (Mostofsky & Balaschak, 1977). Four observations regarding the occurence of seizures have figured prominently in formulating individually tailored intervention programs. First, it has been noted that seizure activity of any etiology can be conceived of as being induced and/or maintained by its operant properties (Balaschak & Mostofsky, 1981; Christophersen & Rapoff, 1979). Seizures can serve as a source of both negative and positive reinforcement in that they can remove the child from unpleasant situation (e.g., tests at school) and provide him or her with considerable attention from adults and peers. These circumstances suggest that seizure activity be reduced by using contingency management procedures and by ensuring that the child has alternative, more appropriate means for obtaining reinforcement (Balaschak & Mostofsky, 1981).

Second, preseizure behaviors have been identified in many children with seizures. Children may report an aura, or parents may notice such behaviors as vacant staring or stereotyped motor activities reliably preceding the occurrence of seizures. Observations of preseizure behaviors suggest that intervention involve interrupting the chain of behaviors that lead up to the occurrence of the seizure itself (Melamed, 1980; Melamed & Siegel, 1980). This can be achieved through the use of contingent punishment or preseizure behaviors and reinforcment of behaviors incompatible with continuation of the chain.

Third, behavioral analyses of seizure activity have shown that some seizures are elicited as a reaction to stress. In such cases, the use of procedures such as relaxation training, systematic desensitization, nonspecific biofeedback, and coping self-statements training is indicated to reduce seizure activity by facilitating stress management.

Finally, the observation that many children with seizure disorders demonstrate abnormal brain waves on electroencephalography (EEG) has resulted in the development of psychophysiological methods attempting to directly alter the electrical activity of the brain. In particular, biofeedback protocols in which feedback is given to help patients produce EEG patterns inconsistent with those that produce seizure activity have been found highly effective in reducing seizure frequency. However, the use of specific biofeedback procedures may have limited applicability to outpatient practice because of the technical expertise and sophisticated equipment required and because a minimum of five or six months of treatment appear necessary to achieve significant results (Mostofsky & Balaschak, 1977).

In addition to thorough analyses of the internal and external events controlling the occurrence of seizures, successful management of seizure disorders requires knowledge and understanding of the physical aspects of these disorders. When working with those children experiencing more serious seizure variants, in particular, the behavioral clinician must be prepared to physically assist a child having a seizure. It thus bears repeating that outpatient care should be provided only in the context of adequate protection for patients through ongoing medical consultation.

The following case of an 11-year-old boy with seizures illustrates several concerns typical of chronic illness and how these concerns can be addressed through the use of the multifaceted intervention program.

CASE STUDY 7

Gene was the youngest of six children in a middle-class family. Gene had been born with a congenital heart defect as well as epilepsy. Surgery at the age of six had fully corrected Gene's heart defect, and Gene's cardiologist had told his parents that no further intervention or activity restrictions were required. Until approximately two months prior to referral for behavioral intervention, Gene's epilepsy has also been well controlled. During the two-month period preceding referral, however, the frequency of Gene's petit mal seizures had changed from a previous level of two or three a year to two or three a day. Gene's neurologist altered the dosage of drugs given Gene to reduce his seizure activity, but the dosage alteration produced no effect on Gene's seizures. The neurologist suspected a psychological component to Gene's seizures and referred him for behavioral treatment.

During the initial interview with Gene and his parents, his mother attempted to answer all questions directed to him. When interviewed by themselves, Gene's parents described him as well-behaved and quiet, but as having no friends. They said he was five years younger than his closest sibling and interacted little with any of them. Gene's mother admitted that she, in particular, was very overprotective towards him because she had always seen him as physically frail and mentally "slow." Following Gene's heart surgery, she had kept him out of school for two months more than his cardiologist had recommended because she had feared "it would just be too much for him." Since that time, Gene had continued to miss quite a lot of school each year because of minor illnesses. In addition, on the few occasions when he had seizures, his mother would keep him out of school for a full week "just to be sure."

Gene's parents said that he had been in regular classrooms aided by one hour of tutoring per week, but had always been at or near the bottom of his class before this year. They agreed that the increase in his seizure activity appeared to have coincided with his placement in a special education classroom at the beginning of this school year.

When Gene was interviewed alone, he unexpectedly stated that he felt under increased pressure in his new classroom. Whereas he though his parents and teachers had always expected him to do poorly in previous years, he though that, with the extra help he was now receiving, they would suddenly expect him to do well. Also, he reported that his former classmates, whom he continued to see on the school bus, spoke to him only to tease him about being in a class for "dummies." As a result, he found school even more aversive than he always had.

Gene's parents and teacher were asked to keep a diary of seizure frequency and events surrounding the occurrence of seizures. This diary showed that seizures most often occurred early in the school day, right before leaving for school, or immediately after dinner when Gene was supposed to do his homework. Their occurrence was always followed by his mother's allowing him to stay home from school and stop working on his homework.

Treatment involved instructing Gene's parents to ignore his seizures, which lasted less than a minute and consisted of ocular twitching, a glazed look to the eyes, and failure to resond to his name. They were also told not to remove Gene from school contingent on seizures. Instead, they were told to praise him for going to and remaining in school and for doing his homework. A token economy was established in which Gene could earn points for staying in school and doing his homework; bonus points were earned for each day on which no seizures occurred. In consultation with Gene's teacher, a daily report-card system was established in which Gene could also earn points for achieving a certain level of accuracy in his work at school. As back-up reinforcers, points could be exchanged at home for participation in activities of Gene's choice with his parents and brothers and sisters.

To help Gene reduce his performance anxiety about school, he was taught meditative relaxation to use at school and home. Both his parents and teacher were instructed to praise him for practicing relaxation before starting any school work. Gene also was instructed to repeat to himself, "The only thing that is important is that I do the best I can. To do this I have to stay relaxed and concentrate on my work. As long as I keep trying, I'll do fine and my parents will understand." Assertiveness training was undertaken to help Gene deal with his former classmates' teasing. Finally, Gene was encouraged to make friends with his new classmates. Skills for initiating and maintaining conversations were rehearsed during treatment sessions, and Gene was given extra allowance money by his parents each time he invited a classmate home to play.

By the end of three months of treatment, Gene reported he was finding school an "okay" place to be. His parents said they were finding themselves pleasantly surprised by his improved academic performance and were beginning to change their attributions of his previously poor performance from his being slow to his frequent school absences. Most important, his seizure activity had gradually decreased to the point where none had occurred during the last week of treatment. Moreover, only one seizure was reported in the two-month-follow-up period.

CONCLUSIONS

Throughout this chapter, we have outlined a number of considerations relating to the outpatient management of somatic disorders in children. We have described a model of assessment and treatment with applicability to a broad range of somatic disorders. This model has emphasized the need for thorough assessment, prescriptive selection of treatment methods, and implementation of treatment in the context of a collaborative liaison between the behavioral practitioner and the physician. Examples of applications of the model were presented for several of the somatic disorders most frequently seen on an outpatient basis at present. However, behavioral pediatrics as a field still in its infancy. It is our expectation that, as medical treatment for various somatic disorders continues to improve so that disorders now seen primarily on an impatient basis can be managed equally efficaciously on an outpatient basis, the role of the outpatient behavioral clinician will also expand. We believe that the behavioral clinician following the guidelines we have discussed will have much to offer in this enterprise.

REFERENCES

Alexander, A. B., Cropp, G. J. A., & Chai, H. Effects of relaxation training on pulmonary mechanics in children with asthma. *Journal of Applied Behavior Analysis,* 1979, *12,* 27–35.

Azrin, N. H., Sneed, T. J., & Foxx, R. M. Dry-bed training: Rapid elimination of childhood enuresis. *Behavior Research and Therapy,* 1974, *12,* 147–156.

Balaschak, B. A., & Mostofsky, D. I., Seizure disorder. In E. J. Mash & L. J. Terdal (Eds.), *Behavioral assessment of childhood disorder.* New York: Guilford Press, 1981.

Christophersen, E. R. (Ed.). Behavioral pediatrics. *Pediatric Clinics of North America,* 1982, *29,* 235–423.

Christophersen, E. R., & Rapoff, M. A. Behavioral pediatrics. In O. F. Pomerleau and J. P. Brady (Eds.), *Behavioral medicine: Theory and practice.* Baltimore: Williams & Wilkins, 1979.

Doleys, D. M., & Dolce, J. J. Toilet training and enuresis. *Pediatric Clinics of North America,* 1982, *29,* 297–313.

Doleys, D. M., Schwartz, M. S., & Ciminero, A. R. Elimination problems: Enuresis and encopresis. In E. J. Mash & L. G. Terdal (Eds.), *Behavioral assessment of childhood disorders.* New York: Guilford Press, 1981.

King, N. J. The behavioral management of asthma and asthma-related problems in children: A critical review of the literature. *Journal of Behavioral Medicine,* 1980, *3,* 169–189.

Knapp, S., & Vandecreek, L. Behavioral medicine: Its malpractice risks for psychologists. *Professional Psychology,* 1981, *12,* 677–683.

Melamed, B. G. Behavioral psychology in pediatrics. In S. Rachman (Ed.), *Contributions to medical psychology* (Vol. 2). Oxford: Pergamon Press, 1980.

Melamed, B. G., & Siegel, L. J. *Behavioral medicine: Practical applications in health care.* New York: Springer, 1980.

Melamed, B. G., & Johnson, S. B. Chronic illness: Asthma and juvenile diabetes.In E. J. Mash & L. G. Terdal (Eds.), *Behavioral assessment of childhood disorders.* New York: Guilford Press, 1981.

Mostofsky, D. I., & Balaschak, B. A. Psychobiological control of seizures. *Psychological Buttetin,* 1977, *84,* 723–750.

Rapoff, M. A., & Christophersen, E. R. Improving complaince in pediatric practice. *Pediatric Clinics of North America,* 1982, *29,* 339–357.

Russo, D. C., & Varni, J. W. (Eds.). *Behavioral pediatrics: Research and practice.* New York: Plenum Press, 1982.

Schroeder, C. S. Psychologists in private pediatric practice. *Journal of Pediatric Psychology*, 1979, *4*, 5–18.

Shelov, S. P., Gundy, J., Weiss, J. C., McIntire, M. S., Olness, K., Staub, H. P., Jones, D. J., Haque, M. Ellerstein, N. S., Heagarty, M. C., & Starfield, B. Enuresis: A contrast of attitudes of parents and physicians. *Pediatrics*, 1981, *67*, 707–710.

Shinnar, S., & D'Souza, B. J. The diagnosis and management of headaches in childhood. *Pediatric Clinics of North America*, 1981, *29*, 79–94.

Toister, R. P., & Worley, L. M. Behavioral aspects of pediatric practice: A survey of practitioners. *Journal of Medical Education*, 1976, *51*, 1019–1020.

Wright, L. Pediatric psychology and problems of physical health. *Journal of Clinical Child Psychology*, 1975, *4*, 13–15.

Index